# ORGANIZATION and MANAGEMENT of a COMPUTER CENTER

# ORGANIZATION and MANAGEMENT of a COMPUTER CENTER

MARTIN GRAEF
REINALD GREILLER

**Macmillan Publishing Company**
New York

Collier Macmillan Publishers
London

Macmillan Publishing Company
866 Third Avenue, New York, NY 10022

Collier Macmillan Canada, Inc.

Printed in the United States of Amerca

printing number
1 2 3 4 5 6 7 8 9 10

**Library of Congress Cataloging in Publication Data**

Graef, Martin.
Organization and management of a computer center.

Translation of: Organisation und Betrieb eines Rechenzentrums.
Includes index.
1. Electronic data processing departments.
I. Greiller, Reinald. II. Title.
HF5548.2.G635513 1985 658'.054 84-17190
ISBN 0-02-949990-9

# CONTENTS

# PREFACE TO THE ENGLISH LANGUAGE EDITION

The organization of automated data processing has in the past ten years undergone profound changes and developments. From the original rigid and monolithic computer center organization a variety of forms have developed that combine improved cost efficiency with a flexible adaptation to the particular needs of the user. Decentralization and distributed data processing once were catchwords that seemed to forecast the imminent demise of the computer center. However, computer centers not only did not die out like dinosaurs but became the indispensable focal points of our modern information systems, networks, and telecommunication systems.

Data processing as a composite of computer linkage, of centralization or decentralization, according to the demands of the task, has emerged as the optimal organizational form. This book is an attempt at presenting an integrated framework of these concepts. For this purpose it was revised for its second edition and has been further adapted for its English language publication. It is intended to offer detailed and practice-oriented support to managers, administrators, students, and others interested in this specialized field. Considerations of specifically German situations, especially in the area of data security legislation, have been omitted in this translation. The references have been updated and adapted to the English-speaking world.

This translation was prepared by Brigitte Schaeffer. With considerable effort and personal engagement she achieved a version faithful throughout to the original except for intended adaptations. The collaboration between the translator and the authors was exemplary, for which the authors express their sincere thanks.

Furthermore, the authors are grateful to the Macmillan Publishing Company and the Forkel Verlag for the publication of this English language edition. Particular thanks are due to Dr. Abram F. Goldman, on the United States side, and Dr. Wolfgang Heilmann, on the German side, for their organization of this collaboration. Without Dr. Goldman's tireless initiative and without Ms. Schaeffer's superb translation the present edition of this German standard work would not have been possible.

Finally, we would like to express our appreciation to Dr. Dennis Ojakangas, Director of Computing at the University of California, Davis, for the application of his expertise to the task of reviewing the text for this edition.

MARTIN GRAEF AND REINALD GREILLER
Tübingen and München

# PREFACE TO THE GERMAN LANGUAGE SECOND EDITION

In a preface to a second edition readers expect the answer to two questions: "Why a second edition?" and "What is new in it?" There is a simple answer to the first question: the book was extremely well received in professional circles and is now considered a standard work in its field. Even the English-speaking world has not produced a work that is able to compete with it. The rapidly progressing evolution of data processing and its applications leads to an answer to the second question: this edition contains additional, current information. The authors have retained the basic structure of the first edition, but each chapter has either been thoroughly reworked or in some cases completely rewritten.

An additional fundamental question to be asked is existential in nature: Can the computer center in its old form still do justice to its tasks in view of the evolution of data processing from central storage and processing to the varied forms of decentralization? The computer center in its traditional sense no longer exists in organizations with completely decentralized data processing. Each department stores and processes its own data, and thus one "computer center" has divided into many "computer locations." A comparison of the advantages and disadvantages of distributed data processing is not the topic of this preface, but the authors contend that the future lies neither in total centralization nor total decentralization. Depending on individual requirements, distributed data processing will maintain itself in the sense that data will no longer be stored exclusively in a central computer center but will also be stored in decentralized locations. In this manner data processing will have partially overcome its unwieldy aspects and adjust to the requirements of the user with much greater flexibility than before.

Whatever the decentralized nature of the system, however, there will have to be some kind of organization to manage the hardware and some kind of organization to manage the total system. Thus it is to be noted that the co-existence of batch and online processing has determined the revision in the content of this edition. Every specialist knows that in this context the concept of punched cards (and their processing) has had to be set aside. In this sense the second edition can actually exist independently of the first edition.

In the past few years the relationship of the computer center to its environment has changed, even within a business organization. Along with the change in the relationship of the computer center to its environment there have been drastic changes in the concept and function of computer center management to the degree that the computer center has become a world of highly qualified specialists who need an understanding of the applications and economic aspects of EDP. As a result, the chapters on operations organization, planning, and personnel were thoroughly revised and updated.

In recent years another topic which received little attention in the pioneer days of data processing has gained importance. That topic is data protection and security. The new chapter on this subject attempts to provide advice and assistance to computer center managers and accountants.

In the revision of each chapter, special emphasis was added to practical experience. Even though some examples of technically older systems were retained, the accuracy of each case was verified. References have been updated to mid-1981. Although some longer references have been deleted, the amount of professional literature cited was almost doubled in size.

The first edition was typed on an OCR typewriter and the text stored on magnetic tape. The second edition was produced from this tape via display terminal by the data processing center of the University of Tübingen with the text system of the Department of Literary and Documentary Data Processing. The authors wish to thank the University of Tübingen for this service, which has rendered the textual arrangement more attractive and readable. In addition, phototypographical methods allowed for a high degree of accuracy. The authors with to express their appreciation to IBM, Siemens, and Univac for making the latest professional literature available to them.

The authors with to thank all those who collaborated on this new edition, especially Mr. Dirk Kottke for his careful and thorough reading of the manuscript and the publisher for permitting the numerous changes. We also wish to thank Dr. Ott, Director of the Department of Literary and Documentary Data Processing, for many valuable discussions and suggestions. Since the book profited directly from the practical operations of the Data Processing Center, we also wish to thank Mr. Edgar Maier, Manager of the Department for Systems and Operations, for his suggestions. Finally a word of special thanks to Pagina Co. for their understanding and cooperation in designing the external form of the book.

MARTIN GRAEF AND REINALD GREILLER
Tübingen and München

*Note:* This is a translation from the German of *Organisation und Betrieb eines Rechenzentrums*, authored by Martin Graef and Reinald Greiller, 2nd Edition, 1982, Forkel-Verlag, Stuttgart-Wiesbaden.

# ORGANIZATION and MANAGEMENT of a COMPUTER CENTER

# ONE

# TYPES OF COMPUTER CENTERS AND THEIR TASKS

The term "computer center" contains two concepts: computing and center. The concept of computing refers to the manner of internal processing in which data undergo binary encoding and are interpreted as binary integers. Depending on the type of task and the encoded data, these numbers are used to execute computing functions. This means that the principle of internal processing operates independently of the task itself. The spectrum of such tasks is diverse and comprehensive and may include static calculations for the construction of a bridge, payroll accounting, sorting and printing of telephone directories, data retrieval from a file, or the preparation of a text ready for printing. These examples briefly point out the very general character of the term "computing."

On account of their versatility and speed but also the considerable cost involved, these computers—commonly refered to as electronic data processing systems—are even today primarily centrally operated in order to make the available performance options accessible to as many users as possible. While this defines the parameters of the term "computer center" on the one hand, it also raises the problem of how to operate a resource that is to respond to such varied interests and expectations.

Before introducing the different types of computer centers, it is important to answer the question of which criteria are used to classify the variety of already existing computer centers.

From the computer center manager's point of view it is of secondary importance for the organization and operation of the EDP system whether it operates on tubes or monolithic circuitry. Much more significant, however, is what types of organizational support technology can provide in the form of standard programs (operating systems, systems software, compilers, databank software, etc.). Thus the functional efficiency of the standard programs plays a decisive role in such classifications. On the other hand, should one desire a classification according to computer generations, the following breakdown applies:

| | |
|---|---|
| First generation: | Exclusive blocktime scheduling. No support of operations scheduling via standard programs. Open operation handled exclusively by programmers. |
| Second generation: | A transition to a closed operation is feasible because a simple, continuous operation is possible and standard programs are available which, however, do not yet constitute integrated components of the total systems software complex. |
| Third generation: | Consistent closed operation because of a continuous multiprogramming mode. Distinct support via standard programs in operations, scheduling, and long-term data storage. |
| Fourth generation: | Incorporation of diversified remote peripheral devices such as remote batch terminals, teleprinters, and VDUs. Jobs are now entered into the system both within the computer center and by remote stations. |
| Fifth generation: | Actual processing occurs in more than one location. Computer networks and distributed storage and processing generate new technical and organizational challenges. |

In order to delimit the term "computer center" within the total complex of electronic data processing we offer the following definition of a computer center:

***A computer center is an organizational unit that provides storage and processing capacity and implements automated storage and processing functions, including all necessary auxiliary services.***

The concept of implementation with the aid of data processing (DP) systems is to be considered a significant characteristic and may be compared with an abstract manufacturing process roughly divided into development and manufacturing. In an industrial manufacturing process, development consists of engineering design and detail construction that correspond to systems analysis and programming in automated data processing. Production juxtaposes

Raw materials and data

Manufacturing facilities and EDP systems

Production of goods and program flow

Two points of view are possible with respect to the computer center's disposition towards job orders:

- The computer center furnishes partial services for the various job originators; i.e., block times (use of the entire system) or use of individual resources in multiprogram operations. This corresponds to the concept of a service order in which the computer enters into an agreement to turn over certain resources to a user for the purpose of executing jobs which are to be further specified.
- The computer center may also enter into an agreement to execute a task fully described in the job order. This corresponds to a work order and predominates in commercial computer centers. The necessity of controlling and testing the quality of various products demands operations scheduling similar to industrial manufacturing processes.

The location of program development is not yet specified in this context. These two order categories, of which the latter is becoming more and more prevalent, do not yet fully describe the demands made on the computer center. It will have to assume responsibility for data and program storage as well.

Thus the computer center fulfills the following responsibilities:

Precise regulation of production

Schedule accuracy

Security and confidentiality

Competent and cost effective implementation

Coordination of tasks

This generally applies to all computer centers. The combination of manufacturing concepts together with the broad spectrum of applications makes the computer center a service organization, whether it is internal to an enterprise or operates independently as a service center. A comparison of features found in various computer center types as outlined below shows that these types should not be considered in and of themselves. Instead, it is best to derive specific features from general guidelines. Since most of the features are either held in common or are interrelated, it is possible to choose between a task-oriented or a size-oriented point of view.

## 1.1 Tasks of a Computer Center

The tasks of a computer center vary from case to case. Nevertheless we shall attempt to present a general overview which will provide individual computer centers with suggestions for rethinking the scope of their tasks. In addition to operational and technical factors, time plays an important part. In general, the tasks of a computer center 20 years ago were similar to those of today; in particular, however, certain essential differences are recognizable, above all in the form of new tasks as well as the number of tasks.

Tasks are generally categorized into three groups:

1. Tasks that directly determine the performance of the data processing function
2. Tasks that do not necessarily belong to data processing activities
3. Tasks that do not absolutely need to be executed by the computer center, such as benefits, personnel, and supplies

Only the first two categories will be considered here. Those tasks are essentially:

Central data collection, for example on diskettes, magnetic tape, or online within the computer center. Since there is a large number of technical options for cost-efficient decentralized data collection, centralized data collection is no longer as popular today as it was 10 to 20 years ago. Many computer centers no longer even have centralized storage.

Automated storage and processing of data in EDP systems, among them the following processes in particular:

- Program translation
- Test runs
- Production runs (single runs in which the program is handed over to the computer center with the job originator responsible for the run)
- Routine runs in which the computer center is responsible for programs and data. This includes the planning and preparation of tasks necessary for optimal operation of the EDP system

Conversion of data to another data medium. Such tasks should only be worked on during transition periods.

Use of EDP systems via user stations. This includes the operation of terminals in shared operations such as real-time processing as well as participating operations, for example interactive terminal operations. Also included is the operation of remote batch stations.

Access to other computer systems via networks. A number of different reasons may underlie this option. It is at any rate one of the responsibilities of a computer center to establish and maintain such connections.

Consultation concerning use of the system.

Management of mass storage.

It is not always easy to determine which of the tasks belonging to the second group should actually be assigned to the third. Generally, however, the following tasks should be considered as part of the second group:

Securing the availability and storage of storage media, such as

- Punched cards with different imprints
- Magnetic tape
- Magnetic disks
- Diskettes

Maintaining a stock of continuous forms columnar paper, plotter paper, and the like (This includes inventory control. Continuous forms such as check forms are rarely managed by individual departments.)

Maintenance of storage media, such as cutting, separating, sorting, and binding

Notification of task completion

Execution of control functions (completion control, schedule control, security control)

Shipping and messenger service

Maintenance of a program library for general applications programs, such as linear programming, mathematical statistics, inventory processing, or simulation programs (The maintenance of program libraries consisting of main and subprograms are of special importance to college and research computer centers.)

Maintenance of a program library for general user application programs, especially routine programs in a company computer center

Systems software support (usually group one)

Maintenance of archives

Development of user instructions

Training of personnel for task planning and machine operation (usually group one)

Technical information via a library; this is only relevant if such a library is not maintained elsewhere (section 6.2)

Space planning, capacity planning, bookkeeping, and accounting (usually group one)

## 1.2 Characteristics of a Commercial Computer Center

Most EDP systems are operated in computer centers that are organizational units of a variety of business enterprises. Therefore the features of these computer centers will be discussed first, and other portions of this book will primarily refer to this type.

The commercial computer center is primarily characterized by a variety of administrative tasks (billing, payroll, general accounting) which can be accomplished more rapidly and competently with the help of EDP systems. Thus routine jobs predominate in which large amounts of data must be processed against deadlines. This in turn requires efficient task planning. Occasionally technical and scientific jobs from research and development are added but in general they do not affect the rhythm of operations.

Test runs take up a sizeable portion of the system's total capacity during the period of introduction of EDP to an enterprise or a new task. Testing operations will subsequently diminish to a fixed measure which depends on the type of tasks, the size of the programming team, and the alteration procedures. A test proportion of 20% is normal, less than 5% is the exception.

From a practical organizational point of view it is advantageous to have a regular circle of users, because clearly defined task and volume areas facilitate capacity estimates. It is also more expedient, in this context, to have EDP production and application in the technical departments under the same management.

Since peak capacity requirements in a firm must be provided for, it is especially difficult in smaller enterprises to achieve a balance and to run an economical yet efficient operation. This is an important point because in small and medium-sized firms EDP costs make up a substantial proportion of total expenses and demand especially economical operational procedures. There are also correspondingly higher demands on planning and supervision (Chapter 7). Teleprocessing tasks present the possibility of optimal inclusion of private rather than public links.

## 1.3 Characteristics of a Shared Computer Center

The problems mentioned above that arise when small businesses operate EDP systems have led to the notion that several small enterprises could maintain shared computer center facilities. This involves consideration of two factors: maintenance of one's own computer center on the one hand and use of an independent service center on the other. Even though some general views have been published on the subject, each enterprise must decide whether the advantages in favor of participation in a shared computer center outweigh those of a service center or possibly even having one's own facility.

Shared computer centers develop when several small enterprises combine to operate a joint facility. Examples are partnerships and cooperatives, banks with branch operations, or community governments. It has been found that consolidated EDP activities are especially advantageous if the enterprises involved are not in the same type of business and thus not in competition in the manufacture and sale of their products. Moreover, problems of security and confidentiality are more easily resolved, and peak capacity requirements can be more easily balanced. Thus firms with varied peak loads are especially suitable for such partnerships.

As in commercial computer centers, recurring routine jobs are most prevalent. Testing operations determine work flow only at the beginning and will take up no more than a nominal proportion later on.

Machine capacity requirements are easily determined because the participating firms generally plan for EDP use on a long-term basis. Cost sharing can be handled with an accounting system or with a fixed percentage rate based on total cost. Shared computer centers are always advisable when the participating partners require large total capacities for short periods of time, for example, special peripheral devices or large disc storage for certain processing sequences that are not fully utilized otherwise. If this situation does not exist, a medium-sized data system might be considered.

The size of the user circle is an important organizational consideration, since the larger and more heterogeneous the user group, the more exactly organizational guidelines must be described. A shared computer center has the additional obligation of safeguarding the interests of its partners, possibly through a joint computer center committee (section 2.3.4).

## 1.4 Characteristics of Service Centers

Manufacturers of EDP systems have for some time maintained free service center facilities. In addition to the business advantages, this service provides switch-over possibilities for customers in cases of bottlenecking, breakdowns, or transition periods. Moreover, manufacturers should not underestimate experiences accumulated during the use of their equipment on the market rather than in their laboratories and computer centers. After all, manufacturers must have an interest in offering their customers more than theoretical and technical solutions; the decisive factor is a system's practicality and economy. The expansion in this particular area is an indication that service centers offer numerous positive aspects.

The idea of a "profit center" is basically responsible for the creation of independent service centers. If a computer center is to operate along strictly economic guidelines, the question of utilizing possible further advantages (e.g. tax advantages) arises; this may necessitate removing the computer center from the enterprise and setting it up as an independent business. Related to this is the consideration that it would then no longer have to fit structurally into the parent firm, and that the system would be better utilized. Generally speaking, the productiveness of an EDP system increases upon separation from the parent firm, with the reasons determining such separations varying from case to case.

However, separation has certain disadvantages: the parent firm becomes the computer center's customer and as such has to adjust itself to time and capacity planning. Cost is another factor, inasmuch as another service center may offer lower rates. Overall costs may increase with the requirement of an additional administrative structure.

An essential advantage of independent service centers is the necessity for a cost-effective operation. Each individual task, from conversion to testing to production, is subject to efficiency controls. All jobs are considered equal, as preferential treatment affects cost effectiveness and results in higher operating expenses. This point of view is prevalent in many computer centers.

A further advantage is the necessity for a clear delineation of responsibility between the technical departments, systems analysis/programming, and the computer center. Systematic analysis of these interfaces has often resulted in suggestions for commercial or shared computer centers. The service center especially is forced into this delineation because it deals with a large and heterogeneous user circle. The economic interests of the computer center are, however, not the primary factor, since every user is free to change over to the competition.

One additional feature of service centers remains to be mentioned: job acquisition, not only in terms of procuring jobs but also in maintaining a well-balanced job profile. A large number of jobs brought in for processing are of little use if schedules overlap or resource demands are in conflict with one another. It goes without saying that test jobs, unique production runs, and routine jobs are all given the same importance, but program management occasionally regrets no longer being able to set priorities.

There are several points of view concerning the preparation of routine tasks through operations scheduling. This is not to be considered a self-understood additional service often lacking in American service centers. The possibility of a teleprocessing hookup suggests that work preparation should be handled by the customer, thereby ensuring data security as well.

Basic considerations for choosing a suitable service center from the user's point of view will not be discussed here. Such considerations are, however, of interest to the management of service centers inasmuch as they provide suggestions for the formation of an optimal service operation.

A second basic consideration concerns the question of operating one's own facility or using a service center. The decisive factor is usually whether or not a time-sharing service is offered. By and large, today's market demands this type of EDP service.

## 1.5 Characteristics of Computer Centers in Public Health

The characteristics of computer centers in public health are determined by their specific applications and the resulting spectrum of tasks. Examples are:

Medical research facilities such as institutes for radiation research, the Max Planck Institute, the German Cancer Research Center, and numerous theoretical and clinical facilities within colleges and universities

Hospitals of all sizes and service levels with different tasks and managerial systems

Public and private medical insurance companies

Health plan associations

The special role of computer centers in public health is best recognized by their tasks in hospitals of over 1000 beds. There is a fundamental difference in EDP application between theoretical institutes (biomathematics, statistics, surgical research) and EDP support in hospital operations.

Each in- or outpatient treatment consists of diagnostic and therapeutic measures interconnected with numerous administrative processes. While there is a close link between medical and administrative services, these services are rendered by different personnel categories.

An EDP system designed to provide cost-efficient clinical support must serve both medical and administrative functions. Thus computer centers in hospitals have specific tasks and features:

- The computer center is a central facility supporting all medical services as well as research and administration; this mixture of tasks is typical for computer centers of this type.
- The computer center is the focus of an EDP system with both distributed storage and medical and administrative data processing.
- The computer center manages and operates, if necessary, all data processing systems in the hospital.
- The computer center coordinates, advises, and supports the hospital and its departments in the planning, acquisition, and initiating operation of data processing systems, specifically in the areas of hardware and software.

- The computer center ensures the protection and storage of personal data in automated storage and processing system.

A hospital computer center thus has essentially the characteristics of a service; its main tasks are the storage and processing of medical and administrative data, and the support of a wide spectrum of users through knowledgeability and experience. Reliability and continuity of service represent the operational philosophy of such a computer center.

## 1.6 Characteristics of Computer Centers in Research and Education

There was a time when EDP systems were called almost exclusively "electronic calculators" and were only operated in educational and research facilities. Today it is taken for granted that every college and university maintains its own computer center and every research institute has its own EDP system. Yet computer centers at universities play a special role. Their scope of tasks is extremely diverse, and they must keep pace with increasing numbers of highly motivated students. This means a higher level of services than in most commercial computer centers, but on the other hand the security factor and the need to handle large volumes of data and recurring operations are less pronounced.

EDP tasks at educational institutions consist of research, teaching, and administration. Their basic functions are as follows:

Execution of programs and programming systems for students and scientific personnel in various operational modes such as batch processing, remote batch processing, and conversational mode operations

Computer supported instruction

EDP application in library work and health services

EDP application in management and administration

Operation of information systems

Control and simulation with analog and hybrid computers in research, development, and application

Instruction in the user of EDP facilities

Dissemination of knowledge and experience.

These tasks cover the demands made on the computer center as well as occasional work performed for outside clients.

Test functions are usually in the foreground while recurring routine jobs take up a negligible portion of time. As a result, there is less emphasis on operations scheduling and data collection. The large and—in colleges—constantly changing circle of users requires a tightly organized interface between user and computer center, and the broad range of academic disciplines contributes to a variety of requests for special projects. Consultation takes on greater importance than in commercial or service computer centers. Computer center services concentrate on the predominantly decentralized use of terminal and scientific-technical applications. References to the "loneliness of the user" are often heard in this context. Operators must be able to use a substantially larger standard software package, but the consequences of operating errors do not tend to be as serious as in commercial computer centers.

The opportunities offered by the capabilities of computer networks require certain organizational adjustments on the part of college computer centers, although organizational innovations are often stifled by a multitude of clauses, conditions, and legal regulations.

A characteristic feature of this type of computer center is that capacity estimates necessary for long-range planning (section 7.3.1) are difficult and uncertain. In contrast to commercial computer centers, the consequences of inaccurate capacity estimates in these centers are not felt immediately but rather midway towards a deadline with correspondingly serious implications, especially in view of the fact that budgetary restrictions and specific technical requirements make it impossible to use outside facilities. Economic considerations and funding play a major role in this context.

Examples of this type include computer centers at universities, colleges, and technical schools as well as research departments in industry. In addition, the computer centers of a variety of other facilities show characteristics of this type, such as less emphasis on scheduled work and a greater percentage of test jobs for short-range projects.

## 1.7 Operation of Special Systems

A great many EDP systems do not fall into the categories described above, and the organizational units operating such systems are usually not designated as computer centers. Prime examples of this type are real-time systems and process computers. No one can possibly refer to the location of a process computer controlling a power station or assembly line as a computer center in the conventional sense. Since the programs in this type of system are loaded permanently or transitionally and operated only in exceptional situations, a discussion of such systems is excluded from consideration in this book. However, if real-time and batch processing jobs are run in the same system, the real-time operation is organizationally embedded in the computer center.

A further category of EDP systems which does not fit into the formats described above are the systems in the manufacturer's development laboratories. They can be excluded from consideration if they are subject to further hardware modifications. Software development, on the other hand, has much in common with the work done at research institutes (section 1.6). Since an economical operation of these systems requires a tight organizational structure, some manufacturers now apply the organizational standards of computer centers to these operations. Since the specifics of such centers are not of general interest they will not be discussed here.

Medium-sized data processing equipment operates technically on the same principle as a large system, but is not really considered a computer center. Such devices are used in technical departments for specific work processes, unlike the variety of applications characteristic of a computer center. Even though many computer center managers viewed the development of minicomputers as endangering the computer center as a species, recent trends have caused them to be considered as auxiliary devices in the sense of providing distributed data processing functions.

## 1.8 Influence of Applications

It used to be much simpler to associate the characteristic features of the task with the organization of the computer center. There were technical-scientific tasks with intensive calculating programs and commercial tasks with nominal internal processing and large input/output demands. The two areas were rarely mixed, because machine configurations were adapted to specific tasks.

The development of general purpose machines has increased the importance of understanding the characteristics of tasks for optimal EDP operations. However, these characteristics are not as easily determined as they once were.

The following sections are an attempt to categorize areas of application by building on older concepts. It should be kept in mind that in view of the complexity of modern applications these categories are not mutually exclusive.

### 1.8.1 Commercial Applications

Included here are economic-industrial as well as automated management tasks characterized by high input/output demands, the size of peripheral storage devices, and scheduled deadlines. Centralized data files predominate in connection with integrated data processing. Tasks of this type demand well organized task planning and control teams. Organizational measures are necessary to ensure data security. Large data sets often create problems in networking transmissions and in response times in inquiry systems.

### 1.8.2 Mathematical-Technical Applications

Scientific applications are excluded here because of their essentially unique features. The entire range of engineering and the natural sciences provides examples for mathematical-technical applications with a high demand for internal processing and a diminished need for input/output functions. Programs are decentrally developed and do not usually run at periodic intervals. Centralized data files are rarely used as the various areas of application are not usually integrated. The deadline structure for program runs is not subject to the same demands for regularity as in commercial tasks. Operations scheduling is substantially different in view of the fact that computer center personnel are unable to handle the control functions for complex mathematical computations. Both data security and program security measures are necessary for the protection of processes developed at great expense. The tasks of mathematical-technical applications are not suitable for computer networks because many different programming languages and standard program packets must be stored while few data are transmitted.

### 1.8.3 Planning and Research Applications

Not only colleges but also large business enterprises have developed tasks that do not fit into any of the categories mentioned. On the one hand these tasks may make demands on input/output and storage as in text preparation; on the other hand they require intensive computational functions as in operations research. They are all characterized by a certain experimental program character; testing and production are not easily differentiated and completion deadlines are less than firm.

At first glance this group appears ideally suited for supplying stand-by volume, except that its experimental character occasionally imposes major operational and advisory demands on the computer center. Operations scheduling, however, is reduced to a minimum.

### 1.8.4 Training and Program Conversion

As program conversion is to a certain extent a part of every computer center, it can develop into a major task in conjunction with programming and data processing instruction. This type of situation then determines the organization of the computer center which is characterized by a large and growing circle of users. Since conversions require major input/output activities, the demands on internal processing diminish. There is practically no long-term data storage; instead there are users delivering a great many small programs and demanding immediate results. Instruction in programming and EDP applications is increasingly handled through conversational mode systems.

Every computer center must be able to handle a certain number of conversion tasks, but they do not always result in increased utilization. In this context it is worth mentioning that long-term capacity estimates are difficult. For short-term estimates conducted for concurrently running program conversions constant resource demands (e.g., main storage capacity) are characteristic.

## 1.8.5 Online Operations

Examples are dialog operations for program development and testing, online data collection, or a partnership operation for an information system. Characteristic are the operation of peripheral equipment, the demand for constant operational readiness, and a predetermined response time within certain time spans. Processing programs run over large periods of time are resident and are run without direct control through operations scheduling.

Since online tasks, as already shown, may deviate from tasks of the classical computer center they are considered here only insofar as they do not exceed 50-60% of the total load of the system because of the response time factor involved. A further characteristic is that capacity planning may be influenced in an unforseeable manner (section 7.3), since jobs are brought to the EDP system from sources other than the computer center. Pure online processing is conducted today on smaller specialized equipment.

TWO

# ORGANIZATIONAL STRUCTURE

An investigation of organizational structure precedes the detailed examination of a computer center. The first part of this chapter therefore deals somewhat more generally with the theoretical aspects in order to indicate for the more practical minded the causal relationship between the components within the concrete organization of different computer centers. Our considerations are based on the commonly accepted view that a computer center needs to be organized along the strictly economic lines of a business operation. The technical viewpoint is of less importance in this context.

In theory, the term "organizational structure" is understood as the integral and interconnected structure of the component functions that are to comprise a social unit. Organizational structure implies a meaningful and fair setup of a working organization as a prerequisite for orderly work processes. One needs to differentiate between a computer center as a functional part of the organizational structure of an enterprise and the organizational structure of the computer center itself. In the former (section 2.2) the computer center represents a functional part of the total complex; in the latter (section 2.3) the individual functions of the computer center itself are listed separately.

Since organizational structure describes the relationships of the various functional units, the question arises regarding the number of these relationships. According to organizational theory it is possible to differentiate five types:

- *Distributional relationships*: Characteristic here are the relationships that emerge in regarding the total structure as a distributed system. Examples are questions of centralization or decentralization in the transaction of partial tasks—problems which can assume major importance in data processing.
- *Managerial relationships*: Here the internal interrelationships of an enterprise are described, as illustrated, for example, by an organizational chart.
- *Staff relationships*: This concerns the connection between management functions and those technical support functions that can be identified as belonging to staff.
- *Work relationships*: This term comprises the informational and cooperational relationships during the work process.
- *Committee relationships*: Here the cooperative advisory function of employees of equal rank—as on boards and panels—is emphasized.

## 2.1 Organizational Structures

### 2.1.1 Objectives of Organizational Planning

As the problems of organizational structure cannot be solved by the mathematical methods of operations research, we are largely dependent on practical experience. The insufficient predictability is due to the strong influence of psychological and sociological factors. These factors are also the cause of the diversity in the realization of organizational structures. The objective of all these variations is the achievement of maximum economy within the organizational structure through proper technical and personnel planning. The objectives of the organization are therefore in the foreground as the decisive factors in organizational planning.

Regardless of whether the formation of functional units into departments is envisioned as a combination model (i.e., the integration of different functions under one heading) or as a delegative model (i.e., the delegation of tasks to subordinate levels), a scalar chain such as the following may result:

Manager or director

Managerial department

Departments

Groups

Subgroups or teams

Individual workers

Each element on each level can be assigned an objective that represents a partial goal of the total organizational task. This is essential for the organizational integration of a computer center as well as for its own subdivisions.

On the other hand, a hierarchical arrangement poses the question of how many jobs can be subordinated to a higher ranking position. In simple terms, how many subordinates should a superior have? This does not take into account the indirect subordinates whose superior is at an intermediate step.

Practical experience has shown that the span of control must be limited, that is, the number of subordinates must be restricted in such a way as to guarantee meaningful leadership. Older theories might have specified no more than six subordinates, for instance, but more recent practices allow for the fact that not every worker requires an equal amount of time on the part of his superior. It would be more appropriate to use defined capacity of each manager as a starting point; this capacity can then be exceeded in one of two ways:

- The performance tasks required may be technically so complex and differentiated that the manager in charge is unable to fulfill them adequately. When this capacity is exceeded we speak of "qualitative overload." Since this can be the case in large computer centers with wide-ranging functional spectrums (see the job description of a computer center manager in section 5.1.1), the manager must be relieved through delegation of certain technical tasks to a staff position. In this manner the unity of the computer center as a whole remains intact, a fact that has a number of advantages.
- The span of control in a superior-subordinate type of structure may be too large to cope with the volume of work to the point where there is insufficient time to fulfill all managerial functions. This is a case of "quantitative overload" and is usually resolved by a division of management tasks.

A third possibility is to delegate portions of management tasks to subordinates. This is called the leadership principle of delegation of authority.

In determining the maximum span of control the following must be considered: the greater the number of subordinates per manager, the shorter the necessary official channels and the more efficient the total organization. Bleicher describes a practical if not quantifiable method embracing the following factors:

Nature of tasks subdivided into

- Similarity
- Difficulty
- Scope of decision
- Division of management tasks

Type of leadership

Personality

Auxiliary resources

The type of organizational structure to be chosen depends on the objectives, the spectrum of tasks, and the prerequisites attendant on each individual. These are described in terms of:

Responsibility and accountability

Division of labor

Ways and means of communication

From the point of view of its communications system the organization of a computer center appears in a particular perspective which can merge directly with its organizational system.

### 2.1.2 Line Organization

Organizations characterized by a hierarchical structure are referred to as management systems. Essential characteristics of such systems are decisions based on the development of objectives and directives aimed at the achievement of objectives. A management system consists of its managerial echelons. In graphic representations such as organization charts these echelons are typically depicted by rectangles containing information on the persons or subject matter in question. Straight lines connect the rectangles in such a way that the chart resembles a tree's root system.

Management theory distinguishes between two forms of a "pure management system":

- Single line systems
- Multiple line systems

A single line system, generally known as a line system or line organization (also known as a front system or military system), is a clear hierarchical allocation system. Each subordinate level receives directives only from one superior level. This is the realization of Fayol's principles of unity of command and unity of direction, in which responsibilities extend vertically. There are no horizontal connections (Figure 2.1)

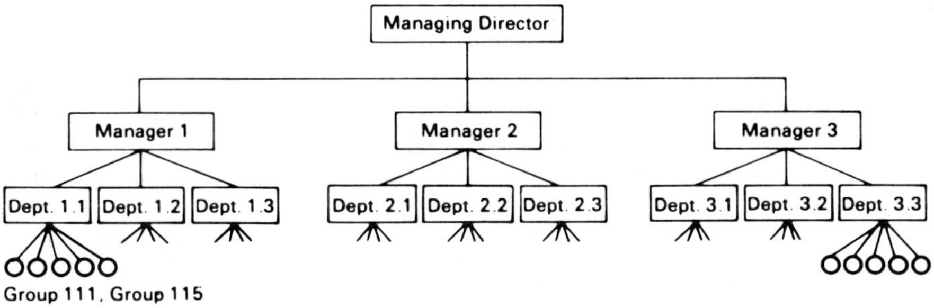


**Figure 2.1** Line Organization

A line organization has the following advantages:

A clearly delineated scope of responsibility, since each worker has only one superior

A clearly defined organizational structure, since there is only one unmistakable authority

Ease of control, because the authority of the superior covers that of the subordinate

Ease of communication from the top down

The disadvantages are as follows:

Superiors are not always able to comprehend special cases

Superiors tend to be overloaded with responsibility, as some specialized fields may get too large

The absence of a superior may lead to difficulties because the chain of command is gauged to one person

The hierarchical system results in poor upward communication

The above-mentioned advantages show that the single-line system is a suitable organizational form for the internal structure of a computer center. The disadvantages are of lesser importance because of the high professional qualifications expected of management.

However, the disadvantages take on greater importance when the computer center itself is integrated into a line organization.

### 2.1.3 Functional Organization

The functional organization, also called a multiple-line system, is a purely functional authority system. Depending on the diversity of functions, each level may be subordinate to a number of higher levels (Figure 2.2). The principle of the shortest distance replaces unity of command. Individuals have varied tasks and may have a different supervisor for each.

The functional organization is derived from Taylor's functional system of shop management (1880), in which specialized foremen take the place of general foremen. Frederick Winslow Taylor (1856-1915) is commonly regarded as the father of scientific management. With the goal of increased productivity he instituted a series of new organizational models. In the context of the organization of a computer center a study of his functional organization provides valuable ideas.

The following advantages characterize the functional organization:

Lack of autocratic control

Development of specialization, whereby specialized knowledge benefits all

Use of the shortest distance between levels within the framework of managerial relationships

Achievement of maximum productivity through training of specialized services

In comparison, the disadvantages are:

Unclear scope of responsibility, allowing for slackness in working habits in individual cases

Difficulty in maintaining shop discipline

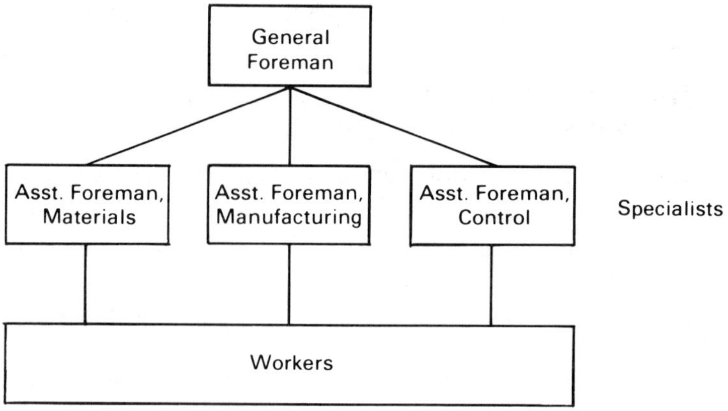


**Figure 2.2** Functional Organization

Possible problems of coordination among managers (i.e. functional foremen)

Increased bureaucracy resulting from efforts to resolve problems of authority

A degree of instability within the organization because the specialists work independently of each other

The loss of overall responsibility, which may reduce initiative among some managers

The functional system of organization is often used in the development of EDP projects in the form of mixed project groups. The disadvantages mentioned above characterize the often occurring weaknesses of EDP projects. However, in limited-time project groups these disadvantages are less pronounced and are outweighed by high efficiency.

### 2.1.4 Staff/Line Organization

The discussion of the two pure management systems should have made it apparent that in practice, mixed forms are more suitable. A mixture of line and functional organization does not warrant special mention here, as no new aspects are added; it simply opens up a wide field of intermediate steps and therefore the possibility of better adjustment to actual conditions.

The situation changes when staff levels are added to the mixed forms of an organization. Line functions are responsible for production, thus also for decision making and execution. The staff functions are:

Advisory

Planning

Research

Development of criteria for control, evaluation, and decision making

The staff thus carries the preparatory and advisory function for the line decisions. This does not mean that no decisions are made at the staff levels, but rather that they are made within the framework of the staff's advisory and planning functions, as they must decide methodological alternatives. However, staff levels have no influence over the acceptance or execution of their proposals. The lack of authority of staff vis-à-vis line shows that the function of staff can only be explained from the point of view of line. One should not be deceived by the fact that staff levels are integrated very high on the organizational chart. Each staff level is parallel to a line management level and is always parallel to the one which it is to advise and support (Figure 2.3).

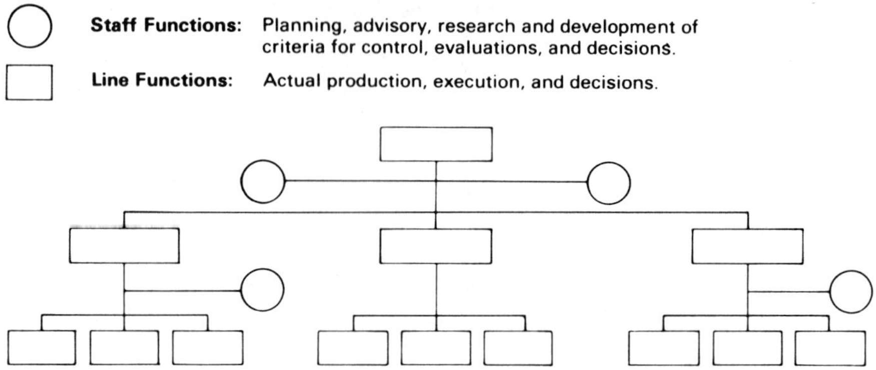


**Figure 2.3** Staff/Line Organization

The staff principle is very old but it came into full use with the military—for example, the general staff organization of von Scharnhorst and with it the creation of the Prussian general staff. In the business world it did not get a foothold until the turn of the century, particularly in the United States in connection with scientific business management. In Germany the introduction of staff in business organizations coincided with the gradual decline of absolutism.

The functional cooperation of staff and line is important if staff functions are to be given optimal use in a line organization. Twelve guidelines are to be considered here:

Staff cannot issue commands nor give directives to line.

Staff has the right to receive information from other levels.

Each member of management and each line position has the right and duty to receive pertinent information from staff and to take advantage of its advisory capacity.

In cases where line decisions deviate from staff advice, staff is obliged to inform the next higher level.

Staff proposals concerning line functions are submitted to line management only after a vote taken by the line in question.

In cases where a staff department feels it necessary to modify an existing line situation for being contrary to company interests, the staff manager is required to inform the line manager.

Each staff position is required to inform other staff positions on all matters concerning them, unless management considers this undesirable in individual cases.

Staffs are to be apprised as early as possible of basic proposals, reports, or plans concerning them.

In cases where staff positions working on a project differ as to procedure, the person in charge is to obtain instructions from management.

In submitting final proposals, reports, or plans, the signatures of all staff members involved are required.

Each staff position is required to advise and inform all other staff.

Staff members are not empowered to issue directives to each other unless one is technically subordinate to the other (official staff channels).

The interplay between staff and line described here is of importance to a computer center insofar as it may have a staff position at its disposal or depend on the collaboration of other staffs (e.g., systems analysis/programming) and has to assume staff functions with the introduction of shared data processing.

A staff/line organization has the following advantages:

The scope of responsibility is clearly defined.

Organized work methods are possible, as staffs are to interface only in exceptional cases.

Line has easier access to specialized information without the need for multiple-level subordination.

Similar promotional opportunities for staff and line are possible.

It is easier to create horizontal interrelationships between staffs, because there is not the same psychological barrier between staff and line as between line levels.

These advantages contrast with the following disadvantages:

Longer lines of authority slow down communication.

The tendency towards coordination with the staffs slows down decision making.

Clashes on questions of authority may occur between staff and line.

Staffs increase administrative and personnel costs.

Because of the importance of specialists in EDP there will be further references to the staff functions detailed here.

### 2.1.5 Committees

Committees are organizational structures that

- are formed to perform special tasks
- function temporarily for set periods of time
- consist of individuals from different levels and technical fields who meet only at certain times and who otherwise perform tasks pertinent to their positions

Because such committees assume functions in EDP in general and the computer center in particular they warrant a brief general discussion at this point.

A committee represents a special form of collaboration that differs from the usual cooperation among members of a department, because the focal point is not division of labor but rather commonality. The work of a committee is characterized by total commonality of interests in a task that is not further subdivided. This does not preclude the possibility that certain tasks can be divided, for example by the formation of subcommittees.

Even though the gathering of information and its relationship to decision making are at the nucleus of a committee, different objectives determine a variety of types:

- *Informational*: serving to exchange information
- *Advisory*: making use of gathered information to prepare for decision making (for example, planning committees to evaluate bids for increases in EDP capacity are customary in university computer centers)
- *Deliberative*: formed for the purpose of solving specific managerial problems
- *Executive*: formed for the purpose of acting on decisions (this type is not common in EDP)
- Mixed forms of the above

Committees are common in EDP because of the short time limits imposed on them and since they are created because of the lack of existing bodies capable of resolving certain technical or coordinational tasks.

Even though standing committees theoretically do not strictly speaking belong to this category, they should be mentioned here. They differ in that they have decision-making and commanding authority within their given spheres, that is, they assume line functions while committees in the narrow sense of the word exercise staff functions. This plurality of power sometimes occurs in the form of a multipersonal management committee that assumes the functions of a computer center director in some colleges in an attempt to accommodate a broader range of interests. As a permanent institution the standing committee restricts itself to supervisory and advisory functions. A case in point is §31 of the university statutes of Baden-Ẅurttemberg, according to which the EDP committee no longer has a line function and the computer center is managed by one director.

The advantages of a committee in combining a multiplicity of technical backgrounds and abilities are not offset by the following disadvantages:

A prolonged decision making process

Overlapping spheres of responsibility causing confusion

A necessity for long-range and time-consuming communication

Possible problems in coordination

Committees within the range of EDP activities are not only useful but recommended. In the following sections they will be listed and detailed appropriately according to their functional significance. Because of their awkwardness and because responsibility must be vested in an individual and cannot be assumed by groups, authority remains limited to certain positions, and committees function increasingly in an advisory rather than a decision-making capacity.

## 2.2 Organizational Classification of a Computer Center

In the preceding section a number of organizational theories were presented. These will now be applied to the computer center. In practice organizational classification and subdivision do not exist independently of each other. Since they must be discussed in sequence, we will begin with a definition of the computer center's position.

### 2.2.1 Position of the Computer Center in the Data Processing Division Structure

Each organizational structure is subject to constant change, and must therefore adapt itself to the exigencies of the moment. This applies especially to enterprises affected by the continuing development of EDP technology. Practice shows that hardware and software developments continue the concept of centralization because decentralized data processing application to distributed data processing is only possible with centralized coordination in view of today's demands on the capabilities of EDP systems.

The rapid development of hardware is not the only decisive factor—the introduction of EDP into an enterprise generally means some uncertainty in its organizational development. Independently of when this first step takes place a period follows that is essentially characterized by changes in planning and revision. During this time there is correspondingly little, if any, production in the EDP system and the computer center.

After this phase the computer center works productively and fulfills the function of a service division in the enterprise.

The general characteristics of a service division were not touched in the preceding discussion because they must be seen as concrete relationships. Every business enterprise has a number of service departments: clerical, switchboard, shipping, receiving, and transportation. In a college or university the main library might be added. Generally speaking, these are not primary but secondary functions of an enterprise or institution.

A service division cannot make independent decisions and evaluations within the framework of its responsibilities, but instead fulfills its job-related duties within its technical feasibilities. This is characteristic for a productively operating computer center that receives jobs in the form of programs and their documentation. A test run must then be viewed as a job process and a type of production, namely the staff function of planning and program development.

The scope of such tasks generally depends on organizational structure—specifically the structure and function of the data processing department—and it increases with technological progress and technological possiblities. If the scope becomes very large—a frequent occurrence with computer centers—the service area requires a hierarchical structure corresponding to a line organization. This applies not only to computer centers, but also the case in general.

When examining the organizational integration of a computer center in specific cases, its service character must be kept in mind without excluding the service function of the entire EDP department. What remains is the special role played by the computer center relative to the status of EDP in an organization. This may serve to explain why in the following considerations the computer center is not necessarily tied organizationally to systems analysis and programming. Tables 2.1 and 2.2 provide an overview of the position of EDP with respect to other departments.

| Department / Status of EDP | Buildings and grounds 1 | Inventory 2 | Sales 3 | Service 4 | Government 5 | Trade 6 | Other 7 | $\overline{X}$ Weighted |
|---|---|---|---|---|---|---|---|---|
| EDP represented in management | 4 | 5 | 11 | 15 | 11 | 9 | 29 | 0 |
| EDP reports to management | 68 | 64 | 60 | 61 | 43 | 79 | 49 | 61 |
| EDP reports to directorial level | 28 | 28 | 22 | 15 | 41 | 9 | 19 | 24 |
| EDP is independent service division | — | 3 | 7 | 9 | 5 | 3 | 3 | 5 |
| Total | 100 | 100 | 100 | 100 | 100 | 100 | 100 | 100 |

**Table 2.1** The Status of EDP in the Organization

**TABLE 2.2 Users per trade group and industry (West Germany)**

| *No.* | *Trade Group* | *Industries* | *% Share* | *Total Share* |
|---|---|---|---|---|
| 1. | Raw Materials & Capital Goods | Coal & oil | 19 | |
| | | Stone, earth | 21 | |
| | | Iron | 3 | |
| | | Mineral oil | 9 | |
| | | Chemical | 45 | |
| | | Rubber | 3 | |
| | | Total | 100 | 12.8 |
| 2. | Investment Goods | Steel, metals | 3 | |
| | | Machines & vehicles | 53 | |
| | | Electrical | 22 | |
| | | Optics | 6 | |
| | | Metal Products | 16 | |
| | | Total | 100 | 19.7 |
| 3. | Consumer Goods | Glass, ceramics | 6 | |
| | | Wood products | 8 | |
| | | Toys, jewelry, sporting goods | 2 | |
| | | Paper, plastics, leather | 16 | |
| | | Textiles & clothing | 28 | |
| | | Food, luxury goods | 40 | |
| | | Total | 100 | 21.0 |
| 4. | Services | Transportation | 6 | |
| | | Press & publishing | 16 | |
| | | Banks, savings inst. | 32 | |
| | | S&Ls | 4 | |
| | | Insurance | 20 | |
| | | EDP services | 22 | |
| | | Total | 100 | 20.6 |
| 5. | Public Agencies Administrative | Federal & state | 18 | |
| | | Community agencies | 24 | |
| | | Judicial agencies | 28 | |
| | | Education, research | 30 | |
| | | Total | 100 | 11.1 |
| 6. | Trade | Trade | 100 | |
| | | Total | 100 | 8.4 |
| 7. | Other | Other | 100 | |
| | | Total | 100 | 6.4 |
| | | Total | | 100.00 |

## 2.2.2 The Computer Center as Part of a Line Division

The computer center may be a part of a line division such as accounting, bookkeeping, or statistics when it has developed from a punched card department or where several EDP plants exist (Figure 2.4). In older installations this was often the result of technical considerations such as data transport and data collection. The computer center remained in this division for historical reasons and because data processing managers made efforts to promote conventional and later electronic data processing equipment even though other departments (such as sales or production) could have made use of it. Today this is considered the first step in the process of development.

This applies largely to other computer centers as well. College computer centers were originally part of specific institutes such as mathematics or science, and as a result the use of data processing equipment failed to be appropriately deployed.

It is generally assumed that the subordination of a computer center to a line is appropriate only insofar as the EDP system works for that line. Today this is economically justifiable only in special cases such as process or production control. The use of minicomputers or microdata terminal (MDT) equipment and intelligent terminals does not justify the term "computer center" because such equipment is not used for central processing of a *variety* of tasks.

Technical and economic factors thus underline the service character of an EDP installation. The computer center is less strictly structured in decentralized programming and the increasing purchase of standard application software no longer needs to be assigned to a technical department. This avoids conflicts of

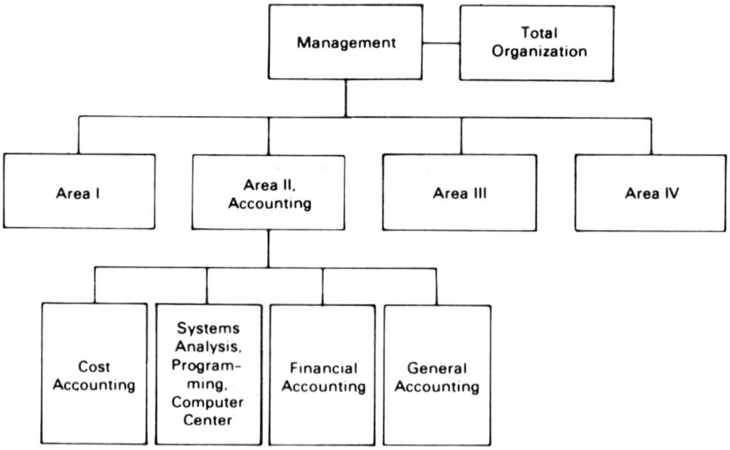


**Figure 2.4** The Computer Center in a Line Division

interest. The specialized use of individual EDP installations and minicomputers remains untouched. Nowadays such computers are integrated into special tasks; these structures no longer fit the term "computer center" because the central character no longer exists.

The advantage that optimum data processing solutions offer can often be realized for individual tasks in such special departments and stands in contrast to the following possible disadvantages:

The manager of a decentralized computer center may give preference to tasks of his own department.

Integration of technically related fields via EDP is impeded on account of possible rivalry.

Lack of contact or one-sided contact between EDP and management can result because management has little interest in such EDP systems

EDP systems may not be put to optimum use because of one-sided job profiles.

EDP is organizationally placed too low with this type of integration.

## 2.2.3 The Computer Center as Part of the Central Data Processing Organization

In the process of decentralizing systems analysis and programming (such as in colleges and research institutions) the computer center can be detached from a special institute and made independent. Businesses, on the other hand, typically maintain centralized systems analysis and programming. In the process of detaching a computer center from a technical department, a center for data processing and organization is often formed on a staff level because of its planning and advisory function. The computer center then becomes a part of this staff (Figure 2.5).

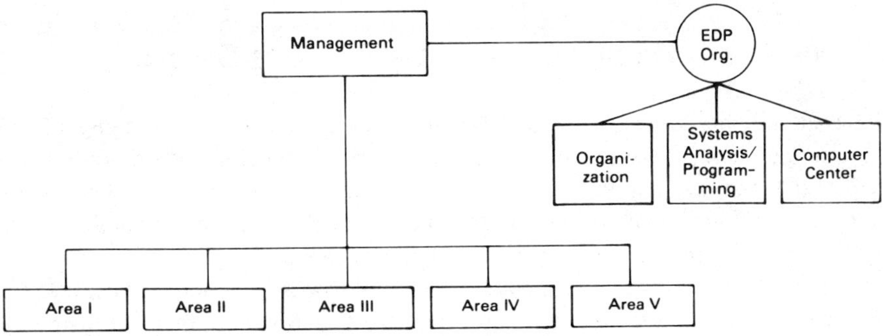


**Figure 2.5** The Computer Center as Part of a Staff Division

The question of whether or not all EDP operations should be subordinated to a higher management level is not under discussion here, only the operation of data processing equipment itself on these staff levels. The computer center does not exercise a staff function, and staff is unnecessarily expanded in its takeover. Nevertheless, the close integration of EDP systems within the organization is an advantage in cases where task assignment is still in a state of flux:

The computer center remains objective towards different areas of application because it operates independently of specialized technical fields.

Unified management and close contact with the organization lead to more effective coordination between planning and execution.

Short-term personnel shifts can be used more effectively, provided the possibility exists at all.

High administrative rank within the organization means better contact between EDP and management.

The computer center is better able to handle growth.

The disadvantages are:

Increased staff functions and personnel requirements

The risk of economically unfeasible expansion both in terms of personnel and equipment

Less effective computer center supervision

The risk of overevaluating the computer center

Difficulty in estimating development costs of individual projects when the computer center and programming have the same cost allocation

## 2.2.4 The Computer Center as a Separate Division

It has already been mentioned that EDP functions are not necessarily consolidated in an organization. The simultaneous occurrence of standing and one-time jobs, and of development and production can lead to serious disadvantages. One of the dangers of unified management is that in a personnel shortage planning loses workers to EDP production, i.e., the computer center.

Figure 2.6 shows an organizational structure with the computer center as a separate entity. In the example it is located as a department in the administrative

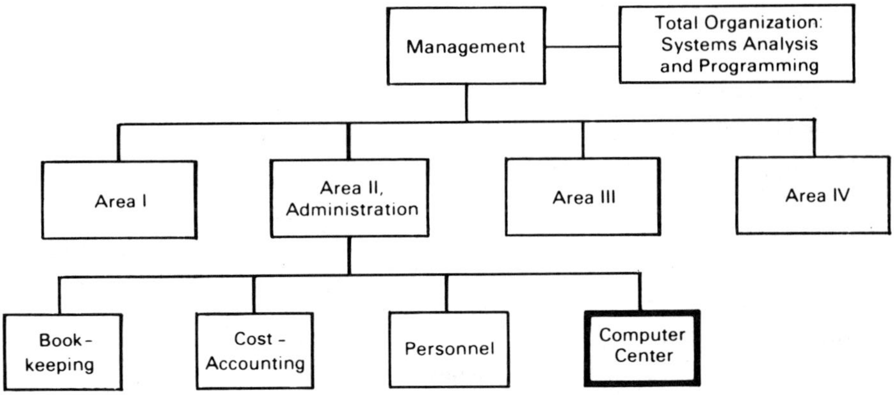


**Figure 2.6** The Computer Center as a Separate Division

division. Other service departments such as clerical also belong on that level. The trend seems to point toward separating the computer center from EDP. The use of standard application software justifies this separation because in that way the purchase of software is a tangible alternative.

In smaller EDP departments the separation of the computer center from systems analysis/programming is less easy to accomplish because one individual performs a variety of functions and a strict closed shop system is difficult to maintain. A separation is therefore not recommended. But even with larger EDP departments with substantial equipment the separation need not be done in the prescribed manner. This is especially the case when *decentralized* data processing at different computer centers is combined with a *centralized* EDP organization with systems analysis and programming.

The computer center as a separate division has the following advantages:

Control of economic efficiency is improved.

The separation suits a closed-shop establishment.

Specialized training in programming or systems operation results in highly qualified technicians.

The computer center as a separate department allows for decentralized programming in technical departments, since higher programming languages are preferred where it improves documentation and avoids tricky programming.

A centralized organizational structure furthers the use of application software.

It facilitates management by exception.

The disadvantages are:

The separation weakens the position of the computer center because staff employees have characteristically strong personalities.

The cost of program transfer is higher; however, it also requires better documentation and results in greater accuracy.

Program changes are more complicated.

Two additional points need to be mentioned separately. One concerns systems programming which must functionally remain with the computer center—a special position within the organizational structure is not recommended. The second point concerns promotional opportunities in the data processing department. The changeover from programming to systems operation in the career of an individual is no longer simple, because the job requirements for these functions have become considerably divergent, especially in large data processing operations.

The organizational integration of the computer center may take any of the forms described above. The determining factors are as follows:

The historic development of data processing in the organization

The state of conversion

The size of the organization

The type and scope of tasks

Personnel requirements

Table 2.1 provides an overview of the position of data processing and the computer center in an enterprise.

### 2.2.5 Organizational Position of the Computer Center in a Computer Network

A computer network is the interconnection of several autonomous data processing systems by means of telecommunication. The problems of locally interconnected multistation systems are not addressed here because these are usually part of a uniform computer center organization and are therefore less complex. Also excluded is the exchange of machine-readable media between computer systems, which will be discussed elsewhere.

The goals of a computer network can be roughly classified into four types:

Load network (use of computer services from a remote facility)

Function network (use of special computer functions from a remote facility)

Data network (use of data files on other systems at a remote facility)

Safety network (use of a backup system in case of equipment failure)

Generally there is a variety of reasons for a network. The increased efficiency of small computers has also caused some differentiation in the use of the term, depending on equipment size:

A network of small computers for distributed data processing

A heterogeneous network of large and small computers representing a computer hierarchy with corresponding hierarchical task distribution

A homogeneous network of large computers combining systems of equal capability

Mixtures of the three forms are commonly found. The technical aspects of networks no longer pose basic problems, as numerous positive experiences are reported. The organizational aspect is a different problem, and is more easily resolved within an organizational unit (e.g. a business with branch location) than in a network of organizationally independent units because it deviates from the hierarchical principle.

It is important to keep in mind that network participation is an appeal to the service character of the computer center. The procurement and use of a service is basically a bilateral agreement which in a homogeneous association works in both directions. Correspondingly, the organizational structure of a network must consist of a number of bilateral relationships. Essential points are:

Discussion about the use of outside services; it is possible that the user's own computer center can provide the service needed.

The accounting system of the network computer centers must not appear punitive toward its users.

Agreements on management responsibility are to be made by the network system.

Data security measures must fit the requirements of all users.

A further consideration is important. In a network the computer center is given a staff function in planning, advice, and development of network controls in addition to the line function based on production. The computer center maintains these staff functions even in cases of total distribution of services through distributed data processing. Moreover, it must combine a number of service functions without which a data processing system can no longer be considered acceptable.

This is essentially true of minicomputer networks which require an operating system and technical support. Only occasional separatists dream of operating a computer center without software support. The latest prognosis points toward the development of centralized functions.

## 2.3 Organizational Structure of a Computer Center

During the integration of a computer center into an organization a broad spectrum of possibilities exist which are influenced by many factors. But the structure of the computer center itself must be subject to functional considerations. The size, number, and applications of EDP systems determine organizational structure. Small centers will have to consider systems analysis and programming as well. Large centers have the option of introducing a variety of shifts.

### 2.3.1 Size-Dependent Structure

Until now the size of an enterprise has not been considered an organizational criterion. Section 2.2 includes systematic considerations relative to integration. These discussions provide suggestions for the structure of a computer center relative to the size of an enterprise, and assume that computer center size is approximately proportionate to the size and EDP requirements of the enterprise.

The production character of the computer center suggests a single line organizational structure independently of whether it is integrated as staff or line (see section 2.1.2). Generally speaking, the number of management levels in the computer center depends on its size and number of personnel. Larger computer centers by their very nature require more subdivisions to avoid the excessive spans of control and workloads already mentioned. The computer center in smaller EDP departments hardly requires a separate organizational structure, as programming and operating functions are combined. Empirical studies have indicated the following size-dependent divisions:

Small departments: up to 14 employees

Medium-sized departments: 15-59 employees

Large departments: 60 or more employees

#### 2.3.1.1 Small Data Processing Departments

A small data processing department employs up to 14 individuals. According to Figure 2.7 there are two management levels. The transition between systems

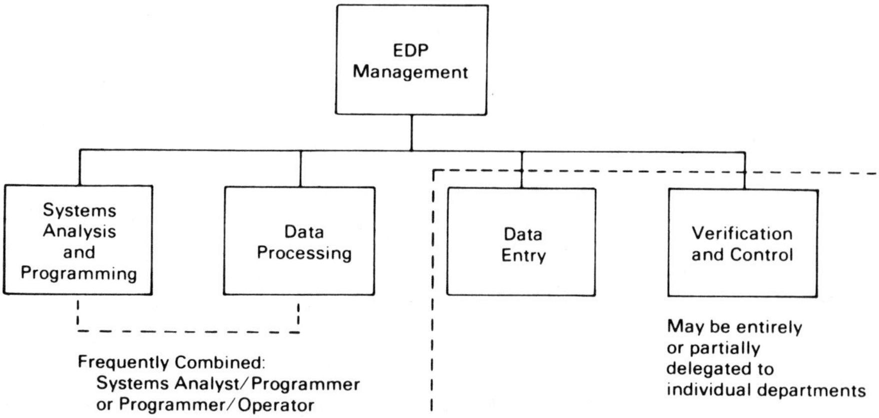


**Figure 2.7** Small Data Processing Department

analysis, programming, and machine operation is not clearly defined. In the past the union of these functions frequently resulted in planning stagnation. Individuals who daily perform routine jobs and planning tasks are more or less forced to take care of the accumulated routine jobs first. As a result, planning tasks are postponed due to lack of time and energy. The manager of a small department is responsible for sufficient personnel and adequate division of work to allow for planning. A functional unit under the heading "task planning" may serve to fulfill this requirement.

The coordinating function in data collection and processing is usually assumed by a technically qualified individual with seniority, often an older employee with a background in punched card technology. Experience has shown that this principle of selection is not always fortuitous because such employees often reject new electronic and automated processes. The functions of coordination and control are frequently assigned to corresponding technical departments instead of EDP.

### 2.3.1.2 Medium-Sized Data Processing Departments

The employment of 20 to 50 workers represents a medium-sized operation. Systems analysis and programming are included (Figure 2.8). A pure computer center with more than 50 employees would be categorized as a large center.

The most significant difference compared with the hierarchical structure of a small EDP operation is the addition of an intermediate management level. This allows top management to delegate tasks required by the next lower level to the intermediates.

In this manner the operation of the EDP department has a delineated character. Actually one should speak of a computer center only when these functions are

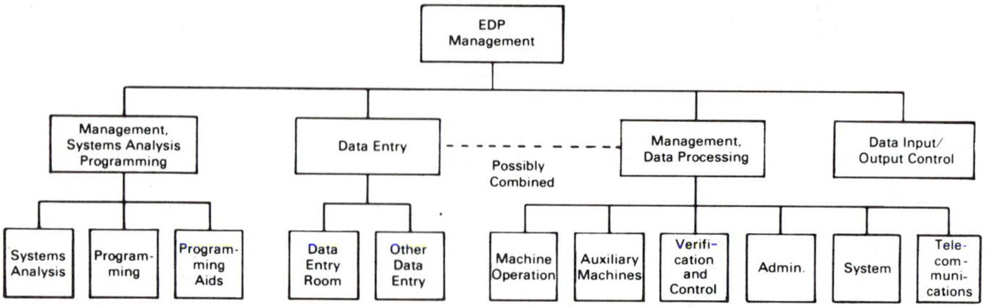


**Figure 2.8** Medium-Sized Data Processing Department

separated. This way the standing and one-time tasks of data processing are clearly distinguished from one another. This is especially recommended in view of the increasing complexity of partial tasks. Data collection and processing are occasionally under one manager, because decentralization has lessened the importance of data collection in the computer center. Machine operation may be further subdivided. Administration includes stockroom, archives, and messenger services. Machine maintenance is usually performed by factory personnel. In cases where the organization requires a maintenance service of its own for reasons of economy, time, and personnel, the maintenance technicians are integrated with data processing as a special group on the same level as machine operators. In an organization of this size systems software maintenance must be handled by the computer center employees.

The organizational treatment of control tasks has a special feature. As was already mentioned in reference to small departments, this function justifies a separate manager in the computer center unless it has been assumed by the technical departments. Since in a medium-sized department the individual functions exist independently of each other, a separate control function was once considered unnecessary, especially insofar as machine controls are in standard usage in larger EDP systems. Later developments have shown, however, that even in medium-sized departments a fourth column of data processing has developed —data processing control—with its own hierarchical slot that includes data preparation.

### 2.3.1.3 Large Data Processing Departments

The three-tiered organizational form of the medium-sized department is inadequate for large enterprises with a large variety of data processing tasks. A further organizational level will probably need to be added in key areas rather than across the board. Figure 2.9 shows a large data processing department with functional sublevels within a total system of subordination.

This type of arrangement is particularly suitable in cases where the computer center is to be integrated as a separate department or separated entirely, because in

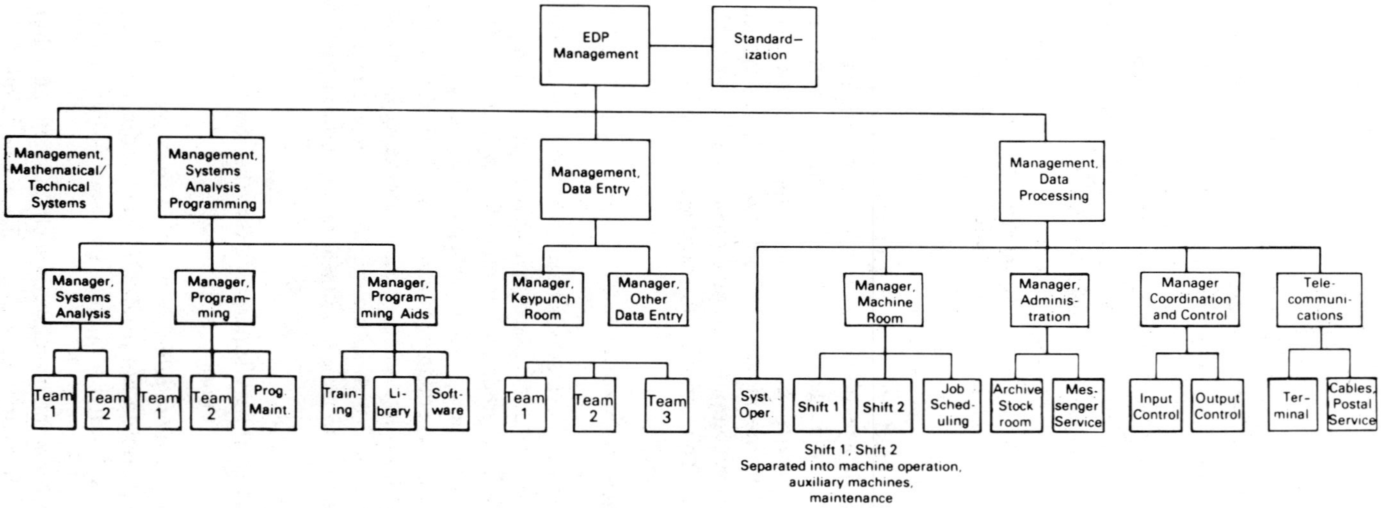


**Figure 2.9** Large Data Processing Department

large departments hardly any further interconnected functions exist whose separation would require additional personnel.

When the computer center is separated out of a large EDP department, the line of demarcation is more or less in the middle of Figure 2.9. In individual cases it must be decided which functions are to be assigned to programming assistance. In general it is useful to assign systems programming to data processing management, because operating systems today have many of the organizational functions of computer operation. Program consultation can, however, remain with systems analysis/programming. From time to time decisions need to be made about training, which can be made an EDP staff function in the sense that training sessons must be coordinated and offered to the technical departments. Training sessions are led by the resident specialists (programmers, systems programmers, chief operators, etc.) or outside instructors. Data collection does not usually require a separate slot, even though Figure 2.9 contains one. In large enterprises this function is increasingly decentralized.

As in medium-sized departments, control takes a special position. It can be subordinated to the data processing manager or can exist independently under EDP management, the advantage of the latter being independent control of work produced by the computer center. A current trend is to leave coordination up to the technical departments insofar as it cannot be handled through the program, and to restrict controls in the computer center to those concerning only EDP, such as task completion control. The transition to teleprocessing supports this concept.

## 2.3.2 Functional Subdivision

In most cases a computer center is subdivided with respect to its partial functions; depending on its size, different managerial levels are required. Since the computer center is considered the production center of EDP, our model is the functionally subdivided one-line system. Whether task planning and control are combined into one group depends on several factors such as size and tasks of the computer center. These factors also determine whether task planning requires one or more shifts. A size-dependent structure such as the one described in the preceding section has several advantages due to a clear delineation of partial tasks. Two major advantages are:

*Continuity*: Disciplinary superiors are at the same time technical superiors and responsible for uniform work process.

*Asynchronous task planning*: In multiple shift operations task planning and machine operation do not need to change shifts simultaneously. The work process suffers through shift changes, especially in small jobs.

Figure 2.10 shows the principle of such a functional subdivision. This form contrasts with the shift-oriented structure described below.

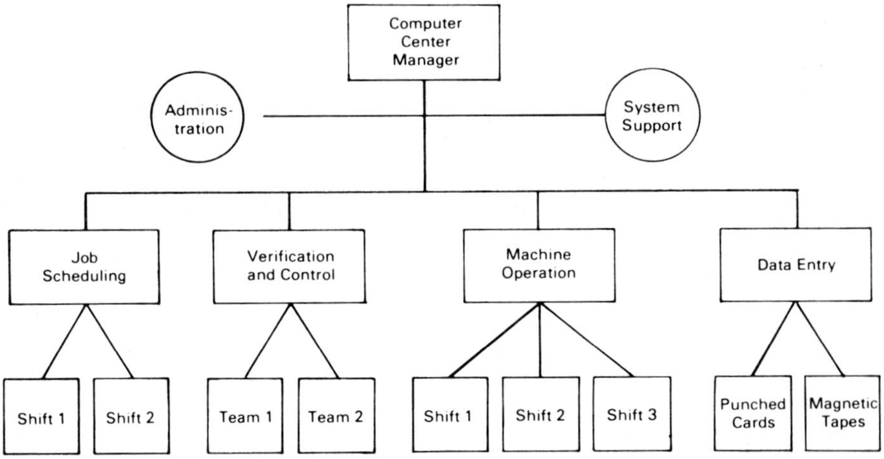


**Figure 2.10** Internal Organization of a Computer Center According to Function

## 2.3.3 Shift-Oriented Subdivision

Within the context of the multiple-line system of section 2.1.3, occasional attempts have been made to subdivide the computer center according to shifts rather than functions. This structure works best when at least three shifts are in operation.

In the shift-oriented structure shown in Figure 2.11, technical and discipli-

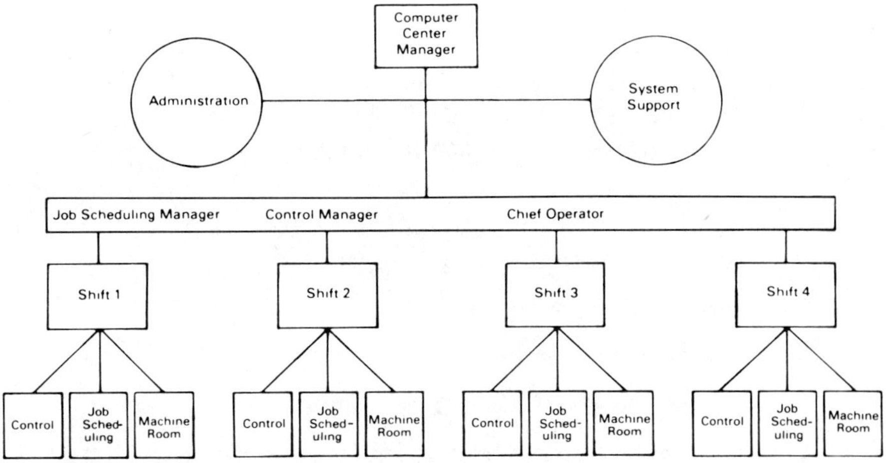


**Figure 2.11** Shift-Oriented or Chronological Structure

nary subordination are separated. In terms of discipline each shift is divided into task planning, control, and machine operation under a shift supervisor. On the technical side the machine room has a chief operator, task planning has a task planning manager, and so on. This form has the advantage of optimum communication between shifts and has proven itself with complex special projects requiring close contacts between task planning and operation. Since this type of situation occurs infrequently, the shift-oriented or chronological structure is rare. It has the following disadvantages:

Communication problems between shifts may cause discontinuity in jobs extending over more than one shift.

The combination of functions is possible only with equal work volume for task planning and machine operation.

It is questionable whether coordination and control should be included in the shifts, as effect control suffers when contact is too close.

A chronological organization is necessarily linked to shift-oriented task planning. However, experience shows that the presence of task planning during shift changes in machine operation can be advantageous.

## 2.3.4 Computer Centers and Steering Committees

The first section of this chapter mentioned the importance of committees in the organizational development of EDP. Because data processing within an organization at times makes effective control difficult, it is advisable to form a data processing steering committee to coordinate planning and control functions for the computer center.

It is commonly accepted that committees with 6-8 members function best. But because the number of members is relative to the task—all interest groups should be represented—this figure is a rule of thumb.

The following representation is generally suggested:

A member of management

The systems analysis/programming manager

The manager of the organization

The computer center manager

Managers of the technical departments involved

A factory representative and external consultant (in exceptional cases)

The internal auditor might also be a member. This has the advantage of achieving close contact between planning/control and auditing. The auditors should be trained in EDP.

The above representation is an example of a horizontal data processing structure. Its drawback is that EDP representatives may assume dictatorial functions over the users. For that reason vertical committees have been given increasing preference. Such committees can be formed by appointing members with EDP and technical backgrounds who represent the interests of the technical areas in meetings. In large managerial departments extensive internal discussions will be necessary to decide which interest groups should be represented. The committee members exercise a staff function and report directly to their respective directors.

The question has been raised whether a member of the employee organization should be included on the grounds that committees may discuss matters pertaining to employees' jobs. However, since these committees discuss predominantly technical matters and all essential decisions are made by management, the prevailing opinion is that matters concerning employee organizations should be discussed elsewhere.

The responsibilities of a data processing steering committee include:

Designing a total EDP concept

Carrying out preliminary expansion studies for more effective decision making

Advising management on questions concerning EDP

Checking on essential EDP activities within the organization (a supervisory auditing and control function), which necessitates the inclusion of the auditing department

Controlling work progress and receiving intermediate reports

Coordinating technical and data processing departments

This clearly shows that data processing committees are appropriate and that the collaboration of the computer center is necessary. One additional point deserves mention. The formation of a data processing committee causes requests and demands on the computer center to be precise. This in turn provides a realistic basis for cooperation between the technical departments requiring EDP assistance, systems analysis, and programming support in changeovers and the computer center which is responsible for the execution of tasks.

For example, the EDP executive board of Schleswig-Holstein consists of 8 members of the state government and 8 members of local governments appointed to 4-year terms. Its responsibilities are:

Regulation of wage and salary scales

Establishment of guidelines for the governing body

Economic planning

Performance bonuses

Preparation of final reports

Modification of statutes (if required)

Independent computer centers have a more general range of responsibilities. Data processing committees within a company have more clearly defined concrete and pragmatic functions, such as establishing priorities in changeovers and outlining the purpose of data processing in the organization. The committee has the right to appoint additional temporary or permanent members for special tasks.

Minutes of each session are to be taken and signed by the chairman for review by the members. Special votes are possible in exceptional cases. Minutes keep management informed of the status of data processing.

## 2.4 Definitions of Responsibility

The organizational development of a computer center is based on a functional division of its total tasks. Groups or departments are formed relative to the scope of individual tasks whereby each computer center determines its own emphasis and individual characteristics. Only very large computer centers will need to form teams for the following functions, while small computer centers are able to combine several functions in one individual. A table of partial functions can be found in Chapter 5.

### 2.4.1 Data Flow in a Computer Center

Figure 2.12 is an attempt at a graphic representation of data flow and demarcation of internal functions. The increase in functions through offline data collection is clearly visible as well as the various paths data can follow from quality control. The following sections summarize the tasks of different areas of responsibility.

### 2.4.2 Task Planning and Scheduling

Receive work instructions from programming

Improve or supplement work instructions according to the requisites of EDP operations

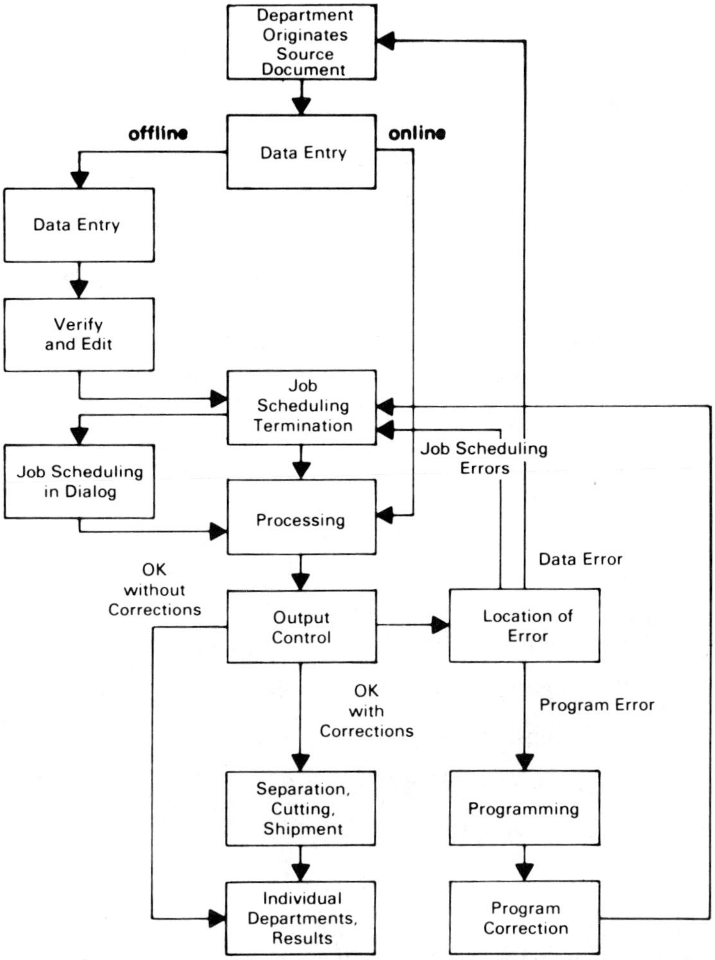


**Figure 2.12** Data Flow Resulting from Improved Technology or Error Recognition

Design or change control statements

Determine program sequences for job input

Prepare job for systems input

Prepare materials (continuous-form printouts)

Plan job schedules and long-term schedule changes

Maintain a machine capacity plan unless done by a separate control group

Schedule waiting periods

Prepare instructions for routine jobs

Prepare labels for data media and dispatch

Collaborate in long-term systems planning

Plan administration of job documentation and mass storage files

Computer centers that administer only isolated routine programs (for example, in colleges) will require only a dispatcher for these tasks. Since program-controlled systems are used in administering magnetic tape and disc files, these jobs are listed under task planning or dispatch.

### 2.4.3 Surveillance

Tasks brought to the computer center must be properly executed. Tasks and data entered through telecommunications present special problems

Data flow must proceed error free and meet deadlines

Online processing must check answering times

Submitted programs must be documented error free and complete

Contact with users must be maintained

Machine capacity and scheduling must be determined

Schedules and deadlines must be established

Economic controls must be established, including use of EDP installations, components, and transmission lines as well as accumulated systems and user software

Deadlines must be met (or information provided about delays), and reminders issued about missing data shipments

Quality controls must be devised (useful only in stacked job processing):

- Input must correspond to guidelines
- Additional resources should be prepared
- Incorrect input data must be eliminated
- Complaints and returns must be recorded
- Output (completion deadline, completeness, planning, and plausibility check) must be controlled
- Output errors must be returned

- Error log and logs on delays in data shipping and receiving must be maintained
- Planning control must be maintained (except in technical departments)
- Stockroom control (availability of sufficient data processing materials) should be maintained
- Data security (for all computer center functions) is necessary
- The computer center is responsible for all security requirements

The control tasks of the computer center were often integrated in the early days of electronic data processing. Control functions in German computer centers have received more attention since U.S. centers enlarged security measures. These functions have increasingly become the responsibility of efficiency control, for which several organizational models exist.

## 2.4.4 Machine Room

There has been a recent shift in tasks in this area because the mechanical tasks of machine operation are decreasing and more demanding systems-related tasks are being added. In general we have the following spectrum of tasks:

Operation of the data processing system from the console; depending on the operating system this could mean many or few tasks

Intervention in case of error, especially with hardware malfunctions or breakdowns (Program errors generally require only program shutdown; in connection with security it is of the greatest importance to determine who has the authority to intervene in program runs.)

Operation of peripherals: tape and disk devices, card readers, card punch, printers, plotters, etc.

Maintenance of a shift log

Preparation of alternatives in case of partial systems breakdown

Trainee education

Performance of simple maintenance jobs not requiring technicians, e.g. cleaning quick printers or tape devices

Maintenance of order and cleanliness in the machine room

Conversion, such as optical character recognition (OCR) documents.

In the interests of delimiting functions it should be emphasized that answers to the following questions addressed to the computer center do *not* constitute machine room tasks:

When will my job be ready?

Which job will run late today?

Which jobs are running today and what are the priorities?

Which job is next?

Where are my lists and/or cards?

Answers to these questions are the responsibility of a user service operated by task planners or the dispatcher. Operators would only be distracted from their essential tasks by such questions. The connection between machine operations and task setting by the technical departments is to be established through documentation provided by task planning. This is an important point because of its connection with improved motivation in machine operations.

## 2.4.5 Responsibilities of Archives

An important, though not always exciting function, is that of maintaining the archives. Tasks here include:

Administration of documentation, data files, and data media

Accurate and timely dispatch of data files

Administration of programs and other documentation in an organized manner for quick and accurate access

Quality control and maintenance of tapes and discs

Provision of information on location of administered materials

Observation of prescribed security measures

These responsibilities are usually combined with those of task planning, especially with automated systems.

## 2.4.6 Data Transmission and Teleprocessing

This is a fairly recent field for computer centers; thus no uniform task description has been developed. However, the following generalized listing is possible:

Development and maintenance of teleprocessing networks

Establishment of control points for teleprocessing errors

Maintenance of teleperipherals

Contact for maintenance technicians

Contact for postal services

Contact for in-house telephone service

Performance of simple equipment repair

Management of workload assignments

### 2.4.7 Systems Support and Systems Programming

This is yet another function of the computer center, and includes:

Generating operating systems

Reporting errors to the manufacturer

System tuning

Program changes for operating systems and service programs

Systems testing support

Coordinating the operating system with computer center requirements

Keeping up to date on recent technical literature

Programmer support

Training and support of machine operators

Support systems expansion

Cooperation in the evaluation and selection of standard application software

Development of processing standards

These tasks should not be entirely delegated to the manufacturer's systems specialists because they contain essential organizational components, and specialists must always be available in case of emergencies. It may also be advisable to combine several computer centers under one systems support group. In any case a shared systems support group is important for purposes of consultation on a common backup system. On the other hand there may be far-reaching consequences when the support group is outside the competency of the computer center.

### 2.4.8 User Services

This includes everything beyond the scope of data processing tasks; for example:

Consultation in program development, especially program testing

Supplying required forms

Telephone consultation on teleprocessing

Notification on completed jobs (some systems automatically notify the user upon completion of large orders)

Shipment of finished jobs

Maintenance of a systems library, such as compiler, service programs, and test programs

Maintenance of a library of general application programs, such as linear programs, batch processors, and information transfer

Maintenance of a library of user-owned programs

Availability of hardware and software user manuals

Terminal access (for time-sharing and real-time tasks)

Support of intermediary personnel in technical departments

The computer center on the one hand is obliged to provide its users with as much unrestricted access as possible; on the other hand this is possible only through close contact with users. The optimum design of service functions is important not only for the users of the computer center but because it can serve to increase employee motivation. An all too strict closed shop operation can easily cause employees to become isolated in their work, but these service functions allow them to maintain contact with data processing applications. By definition, programming tasks are not considered the responsibility of the computer center. The concept of a user service has undergone some decisive changes in the past several years due to changes in the processing technology and mass storage.

### 2.4.9 Data Entry Tasks

As already mentioned, decentralized data entry is on the increase, and a number of computer centers no longer have their data entry systems. But insofar as entry remains a computer center task it includes the following:

Data entry on machine-readable devices or directly into the system (online)

Verification of entered data

Computation of time and output for accounting purposes

Aid in designing forms

Aid in mask design for data entry via cathode ray tube (CRT)

### 2.4.10 Administration

There must be an administrative component where tasks include:

Making cost estimates, cost analysis, and distribution

Maintaining supplies

Maintaining clerical records

Maintaining personnel (partial if the computer center is part of a larger organization)

Arranging for guided tours

Preparing negotiations

Taking minutes of discussions and negotiations

Maintaining files

Supporting management through tables, statistics, and other documents

## 2.5 External Interfaces to a Computer Center

The flowchart depicted in Figure 2.12 essentially shows three external interfaces. The detailed design of these interfaces is among the responsibilities of the operations organization discussed in Chapter 3, but will be examined here insofar as the interfaces constitute the connection between the functions determining organizational structure and the activities determining operations. These interfaces depend on the choice of organizational structure, and agreements governing them must be in writing. Relevant guidelines for the computer center and its users and strict adherence to them are prerequisites for a smooth operation.

### 2.5.1 Interface to User Departments

If the computer center of an enterprise is responsible for centralized data entry, a clear interface occurs between the user departments and the computer center. Agreements are necessary on the following points:

Data delivery deadlines (whole or partial)

Minimum and maximum quotas for data to be entered

Data quality and forms to be used

Complete controls for verifying data

Type, form, and dimensions of data media

Use of data waybills

Completion deadlines

Notification of completion

Activities following completion

Refusal to allow changes after data delivery

Persons responsible for cables, modems, and online collection devices

Storage deadline and/or return of forms

Scheduling hours for online data entry

In the absence of centralized data entry, agreements are necessary for determining the delivery of entered data or the completion mode of online data entry files.

Arrangements must be made between the computer center and the user departments on the processing of data regardless of centralized or decentralized entry, because the user departments have certain time-related and qualitative expectations and the computer center has only a limited capacity to realize these expectations. A smooth and satisfactory work process requires the following agreements at the computer-center–user-department interface for batch processing:

Delivery deadlines, how long before processing data must arrive

Completion deadlines for data entered online

Minimum and maximum quotas for data to be entered

Type and tolerance of data media

Complete controls to verify data at time of delivery

Processing programs

- Provided for each processing job
- Kept in the archives
- Kept on-site in a program library

Criteria for optimum design of systems and jobs

Deadlines for special requests or changes

Availability of program documentation and operating instructions

Emergency procedures

Agreement on possible reruns

Completion deadlines

Notification of completion (in special cases)

Activities following completion

- Initiate further programs
- Shipping instructions
- Controls to verify data are complete

Agreement on safety precautions

These points will be discussed in greater detail in section 3.3, where they constitute the basis for an operations organization. At the present they merely sketch the interface between the computer center and the user department. A number of the points summarized here will be referred to again in section 7.3.

### 2.5.2 Interface to Systems Analysis and Systems Planning

Systems analysis deals with the development of processes to solve the operational tasks of a given EDP system. Systems analysis is often referred to as problem analysis. The differences will not be discussed here, but rather the developmental process in the context of a computer center.

In undertaking new projects, systems analysis essentially depends on the type of computer center installation, and agreement on the following points is therefore of paramount importance:

Operational EDP requirements

- Central storage requirements at each stage
- Peripheral storage requirements, especially drums, disks, and disk packs
- Magnetic devices and tapes, possibly divided into test phase and run phase
- I/O devices and data media
- Standard software components

Equipment capacity
- CPU capacity
- I/O channel and control unit capacity
- Capacity of I/O bottlenecks, such as printers and plotters
- Teleprocessing capacities

Data entry expenditures; including the possibility of online entry.

Agreement on run deadlines

Agreement on forms used in data entry

Technical demands on the computer center (as already mentioned, additional tasks such as separating, checking, cutting, and shipping can be taken over; in planning new tasks these activities should be kept under consideration because they may play a part in taking on new jobs.

Safety precautions may take the form of the following restrictions in agreement with systems analysis:

Maximum number of tape units permissible

No unit record devices during operation (SPOOL is preferred)

Maximum permissible central storage per job

Utilization of checkpoint at certain run times

Determination of a uniform blocking factor

Agreement on start and finish symbols on printers

Use of passwords for programs and files

Automatic terminal shutdown when not in use

Coupling specific job numbers to specific terminals

Systems planning has not developed as uniform a procedure as systems analysis. It is essentially used as the planning component of a total EDP system regardless of where and how it is integrated into an organization. Since both planning and systems analysis are of concern to the computer center, close cooperation in all questions of resource requirements is essential.

In special cases such as EDP equipment changes or operational changes it is a good idea to form teams consisting of the computer center, systems analysis and programming staffs, as well as manufacturer's representatives. The certificate of inspection is of special importance and needs to be agreed upon in advance. This will be discussed in more detail in section 7.6 on hardware planning.

### 2.5.3 Interface to Programming

There is a direct link between programming and operating. Areas such as testing, implementation, and documentation are essentially affected by programs. Program changes will be discussed here together with testing and implementation.

#### 2.5.3.1 Program Testing

Program testing consists of assembly, test preparation, and test runs. Test planning and preparation go hand in hand. Special test instructions may be used in order to make the testing process intelligible for machine operations and programming. These instructions must be coordinated with hardware and operations. Single-program equipment is provided with special testing schedules during the form planning procedure. With multiple-program equipment parallel testing is more practical. Console printouts may be included in testing agreements.

#### 2.5.3.2 Implementation

An inspection system ascertains that the computer center receives tested programs to run (including testing dates, test results, and signature of project leader). Implementation may proceed according to the following formula:

Program number

Program change number

Project number

Control entry on revision of completed tests

Completion of job documentation

Implementation date

Blocking notes

Program media

Takeover confirmation by the computer center

Working instructions

Acceptance of operating instructions

Upon confirmation the computer center has taken over the program and adds it to its library and calendar, or accepts previously blocked programs after revision, as the case may be.

When taking over a tested program for routine jobs the computer center should check it for ease of handling. Essential considerations are:

How can the program be integrated in terms of equipment use?

Do the forms have adjustment markers?

For which instructions and controls is the control desk prepared?

Are operating steps machine checked?

Are data media complete?

Does the program fulfill all guidelines?

Are checkpoints necessary?

### 2.5.3.3 Job Documentation

Job documentation should contain all instructions necessary for the operation of the program and is to be distinguished from a complete program documentation in the following respects:

Run manual

Equipment requirements, e.g., central or peripheral storage

Characteristic run numbers, depending on the number of data sets

Explanation of input, e.g., tape labels, sorting sequences

Organization of job control cards and data cards (without JCL)

Control statement listing (with JCL)

Explanation of output, such as labels and blocking

Control desk and corresponding activities

Printing instructions, header tape

SPOOL instructions

Name and availability of programmer

Information on program changes

Long-term data storage (remote storage)

This point will be discussed in more detail in section 3.5.

# THREE

# OPERATIONS ORGANIZATION

At the beginning of Chapter 2 reference was made to the role of the operations organization in the context of the total organizational structure of the computer center. The organization of the operating process as part of the general operational framework is an essential factor of in-house functions. With respect to the computer center, the term "operations organization" raises these questions:

> How does the computer center handle the operational tasks of data processing, and how do data flow through the computer center?

This refers essentially to the operation itself but also to the handling of job orders and the maintenance of archives and stockrooms. The collections of data media containing programs and data represent the archives in this context, and the stockrooms are exclusively for the storage of blank data processing materials. For reasons of clarity, personnel and finance are separated from operations, although strictly speaking all come under the heading of operations organization. In addition, those aspects of data processing operations belonging to systems analysis and programming are excluded here, even though this separation cannot always be accomplished in a clear-cut manner.

The following are key prerequisites for smooth, faultless, and economical data processing operations in a computer center:

Careful planning of tasks to be executed

Careful review of tasks to be executed

Comprehensive and clear instructions to personnel

Painstaking orderly arrangement of materials such as programs, data files, data media, forms, and other supporting materials

Standardized instructions and records coordinated with systems planning, programming, and technical departments are used for this purpose. When installing EDP equipment in a computer center, the major portion of these supporting documents should be on hand in advance.

In order to achieve this goal a rank-independent allocation of the various task areas must form the basis of an operations organization, including space and time allocations. Among the numerous influences on the design of an operations organization the extensive technical demands of electronic data processing deserve special mention.

## 3.1 Coding as a Prerequisite for Organized Activity Flow

The variety of data media, data files, programs, and forms in use in most cases requires a numbering system that clearly identifies all media, files, programs, etc. Even though the numbers or codes cannot always be assigned under the sole auspices of the computer center, this point needs mentioning because the proper functioning of the operations organization depends on the choice of a suitable numbering or coding system.

A number or code is defined as a piece of information that is clear-cut, well organized, brief, easy to read and memorize, and which can be machine processed.

There is abundant literature on the subject of organization and utilization of coding systems in connection with systems analysis and general data processing organization. These coding systems also play an important part in determining the work flow in the computer center.

Numbers or codes thus are agreed-upon symbols for the individual parts of a mass. For example, each account number represents a specific account belonging to a specific individual, and each employee number a specific individual in the firm, including perhaps the master record in the personnel file.

The individual numbers in the corresponding numerical systems should be differentiated in such a way that the coded object is immediately recognizable. In developing coding systems the characteristics of specific manufacturers' software (operating systems, service programs, etc.) should be kept in mind because they often represent decisive marginal conditions for computer center coding systems.

Aside from specific numerical systems, three code categories can be identified.

Because information codes in their pure form are only conditionally applicable in a computer center, only the system-free and articulative numerical systems will be discussed. Information codes should not, however, be totally excluded from computer centers, since they serve to inform the user about the specific characteristics of the coded object. Thus they are often useful in combination with other codes. The examples given for combined numerical systems will, for example, refer to the fact that the file number contains a symbol for the data medium containing that particular file. This component is an example of an information code.

## 3.1.1 Identification Codes

Identification codes generally are system-free numbers that identify pieces or groups of information without, however, making a statement about the content of such information. Each control number exists only once within its area, thus clearly identifying the item in question. The numbers are assigned sequentially without regard to area of application. It does not matter whether this involves a purely alphabetical, purely numerical, or combination alpha-numerical coding system. The number of digits should be kept to a minimum for ease of handling, but with a view towards possible expansion. On the other hand, the expansion of a numerical code by one digit represents a tenfold increase, and an expansion by one digit of an alpha code a 26-fold increase in code volume.

The identification code does not make a statement. Encoding and decoding is accomplished by means of a table. Codes should be assigned centrally to avoid duplication. Released numbers may be reused after a waiting period and depending on the area of application.

Such codes can be used for the following items in a computer center:

Forms (bills of lading, machine requisitions, operating instructions, test instructions, punched time sheets, etc.)

Punched cards (if there are varied imprints)

Magnetic tape reels (as physical units)

Magnetic disk packs

Data files and programs in predominantly integrated systems, since they can no longer be assigned to a specific area

Data files and programs when classification by area of application is handled via additional codes

System-free numbering by means of identification codes can be summarized as being:

Nonarticulative

Clear-cut

Very brief

Uninterrupted

This provides them with a number of advantages which render them useful at various points in the computer center, especially in combination with other codes.

## 3.1.2 Classification Codes

Classification codes use an articulative numbering system. For that reason they have the widest use in data processing, especially in the computer center. Classification codes identify the most important characteristics of an item categorized by group or class and are thus considerably systematized. Similar to the information code, they provide information about the item in question, not necessarily in abbreviated form but, if necessary, by means of a different code. The meaning of the symbols must therefore be derived from a code listing.

While the information code identifies individual items or groups of items by categories, the classification code begins by collecting the characteristics of all items to be numbered, then classifies them, and finally assigns them systematically to each item.

A good classification code presupposes that the assignment of an item to a group is clearly recognizable. There should be no overlaps between groups or subgroups; instead they must be mutually exclusive. Thus activity codes for repeat runs represent a certain type of production run. All terms for individual characteristics must be defined and delineated accordingly.

Numbering systems categorized by area of application are frequently used for data files and programs. This is especially the case in small and medium-sized computer centers in which integrated data processing has not been fully implemented. Coding depending on the data media used is also widely employed.

The following are a few examples of the use of classification codes in the computer center:

Card codes

Record codes

Document codes for optical character readers or magnetic character readers

Data files or record codes in external random access storage

Programs for data acquisition

Programs for the data processing system, possibly depending on change level

Activity codes for operating sequences in data processing systems

Borderline cases deserve special attention. Problems can develop instances where such cases were not yet clearly recognized during the design phase of the code. Such cases are likely to occur in the rapidly expanding field of data processing in which media and machines come on the market which no one would have dreamed of a few years earlier. User circles are subject to abrupt changes as well, especially when the computer center is separated from the parent firm.

While the information code designates an item clearly, the identification code rarely, if ever, has that capability; it can only identify categories or groups. A narrower identification is possible through expansion of the code, but absolute clarity is difficult to achieve. An expanded code also may become hard to handle and may even exceed the capabilities of a particulr system. It thus loses its articulative ability and results in additional costs both in design and manual or automated application.

Figure 3.1 represents a sample classification code of the type used by Lufthansa Airlines for an output listing. This sample no longer represents a pure classification code inasmuch as a portion of the code, i.e., the job creation number, could be an independent classification code. Such combinations are common.

When designing a classification code it is possible to list the individual components in subordinate and independent order. Dependent coding of subclasses such as day of the week and date is recommended only if a reversal of the group designations is not expected at any time in the future. Since this is rarely the case, classification codes as a rule are formed from a series of independent coordinate components. The generally larger number of digits in such an arrangement facilitates not only coding but later regroupings.

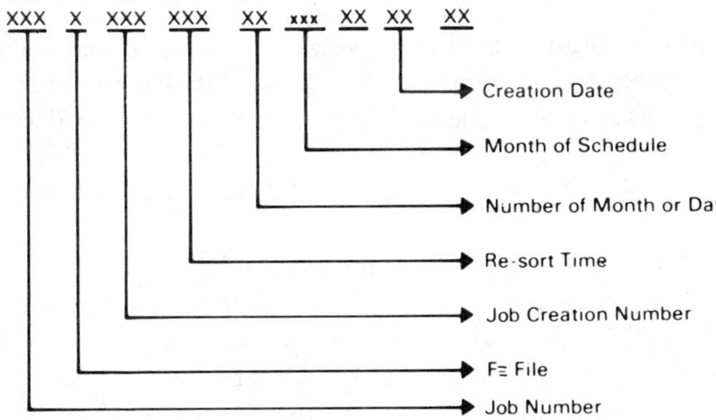


**Figure 3.1** Output Listing as Sample Classification Code

Classification codes can be used to characterize numberings as follows:

Communicative (even in coded form)

Not clear

Usually long

Uniform within the system

Not all variations are meaningful and possible

## 3.1.3 Special Codes

In addition to the two coding systems already mentioned there are a great many codes that are designed for specific purposes. Since they are used primarily by systems analysis and systems planning they will not be discussed in detail.

Control codes and documentation codes deserve brief mention in this context. Control codes automatically monitor the key symbols by means of check characters. In data acquisition the key symbols are expanded by check characters that allow for programmed validity checks in automation processing; such control codes are used, for example, in numbering data files to avoid misfiling. This will be discussed in more detail in section 4.2.

Another special code is the documentation code, which can serve as a cross reference character, pointing to a specific term in the literature, for example, or to a specific part in industrial manufacturing. In the computer center a reference to a specific data file in various areas of application is found in the file coding system. A changeover to integrated data processing tends to create rather large numbers.

## 3.1.4 Parallel Codes

No specific coding system can be considered best suited for all cases. A choice must be made for each particular situation, but even then a pure form of the coding systems described here may not be sufficient. As already mentioned with respect to classification codes, parallel systems are often used within one code. This is an attempt to compensate for the advantages and disadvantages of different coding systems.

Parallel coding refers to the combination of different coding systems into one single code. This method has a number of advantages derived from the combined advantages of different systems. The identification code used for finding and identifying a specific item remains valid and unchanged as long as the item in question exists. It represents the static element in the numbering system of a computer center. It is also short, clear-cut, complete, and can be incorporated into a storage address.

Classification codes are more easily assembled by means of parallel coding, because they consist of a series of coordinate group characteristics which can be changed or expanded at any time without difficulty. This is possible because not all task areas, key indexes, forms, and employees of a computer center are affected.

A combination of system-free and articulative numbers can be accomplished by making the numbers of a file dependent on those of the program that creates it. This solution is recommended only if the file is sequentially processed or when it is created only seldom via special processing.

## 3.1.5 Examples of Coding Systems in the Computer Center

Since most of the coding systems described thus far do not directly concern the computer center, two examples are given below which directly bear upon computer center organization.

### 3.1.5.1 Account Numbers

Program runs in every computer center are allocated to the job originators by means of job numbers, account numbers, or user identification numbers. These numbers are assigned in the computer center in conjunction with systems analysis and programming. The terminology for these types of identification varies with each manufacturer and with each operating system according to the restrictions it imposes. In addition, the computer center type with its internal structure and specific relationships with its users affects the formulation of account numbers. A clear-cut allocation of job numbers to the cost centers of the users is highly recommended. In order to meet these varied requirements parallel codes are generally used with account numbers.

The importance of choosing a suitable code for account numbers needs to be reemphasized, because each job order serves as a control for job execution. The choice of code thus influences the operations organization at various points in the computer center.

Figure 3.2 gives an example of job coding in a commercial computer center. A version number can be advantageous for alterations. The departmental cost center number may be added for performance accounting purposes.

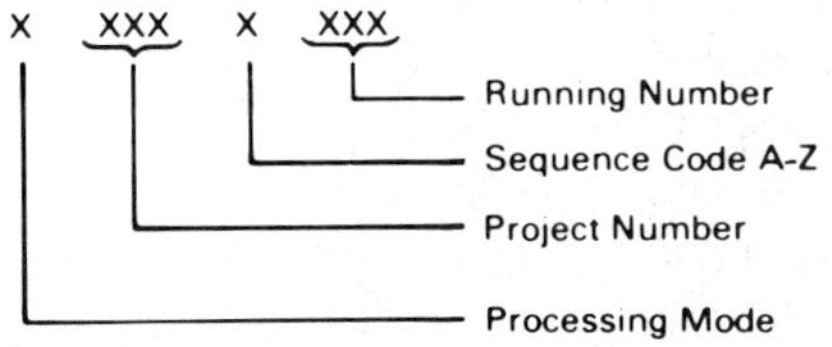


**Figure 3.2** Example of Job Coding in a Commercial Computer Center

The following single-digit abbreviations are used for processing modes:

P—parallel run
R—routine
S—special job
T—test
U—utility

Since these job codes are used for allocations documentation as well, somewhat more detailed information on processing modes is provided. Siemans, for example, used the following activity codes:

| *Code No.* | *Job Type* |
|---|---|
| 0n | productive automatic jobs |
| 01 | productive jobs, chargeable |
| 02 | productive jobs, not chargeable |
| 1n | test/trial run |
| 10 | remote test |
| 11 | erase tape, read/write test |
| 12 | programming test |
| 13 | trial run |
| 14 | operator training |
| 15 | demonstration |
| 16 | tabulate instructions |
| 2n | administrative jobs, coordination |
| 3n | repeat run |
| 31 | repeat for data check |
| 32 | repeat because of hardware malfunction |
| 33 | repeat for program check |
| 34 | repeat for handling check |
| 35 | repeat because of power malfunction |
| 36 | repeat for other reasons (paper jam, card jam) |
| 4n | stall because of malfunction |
| 41 | maintenance |
| 42 | wait for technician |
| 43 | repairs |
| 44 | power failure |
| 45 | equipment modification |
| 46 | maintenance by operator |
| 5n | idle (lack of work) |

| | |
|---|---|
| 51 | idle (lack of work) |
| 52 | idle (work delivery delayed) |

When using an alpha code three digits are not absolutely necessary, since the clarity of a code does not necessarily increase with length. Longer than necessary codes are often used because the operating systems expects a certain number of digits. The following two-digit task identification codes are possible:

PG—purchasing
RD—research and development
FN—finance
PL—personnel
SL—sales
TT—test
SS-standard systems
TA—telephone accounting, etc.

A system-free numbering system would not be useful in this case.

### Job Coding in a University Computer Center

Although the operations organization of a university computer center differs only slightly from that of commercial computer centers, its specific coding systems reflect differences in the scope of tasks. Since university computer centers use predominantly articulative numbers, the principle underlying the account numbers at the Center for Data Processing at Tübingen University provides an illustrative example: the account number consists of 8 digits as expected by operating systems (Figure 3.3).

The first two digits—department and institute—clearly identify the cost center of the originating institute, which facilitates automatic job accounting. The 17 departments and nonuniversity users were allocated the following abbreviations:

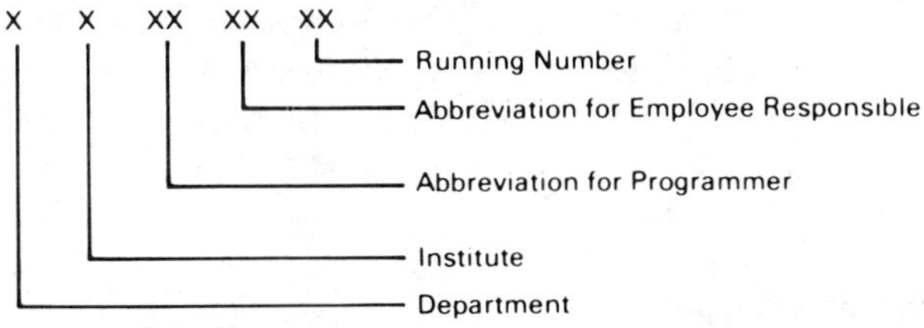


**Figure 3.3** Job Number Composition at a University Computer Center

A —Archaeology and Classics
B —Biology
C —Chemistry
E —Earth Sciences
F —Philosophy
G —Geography and History
H —School of Pharmacy
J —Law School
K —Clinical Medicine
M—Mathematics
N —Linguistics
P —Physics
S —Sociology and Psychology
T —Theoretical Medicine
U —Theology (Catholic)
V —Theology (Protestant)
W—Economics
Y —External Users
Z —Center for Data Processing

The addition of a second symbol designating the institute produces articulative numbers which have proven extremely useful for computer center services, for example in the Department for Clinical Medicine:

KE —eye clinic
KS —surgery clinic
KG —gynecology/obstetrics clinic
KN —ear-nose-throat clinic
KP —pediatrics clinic
KM—general medicine clinic
KO —orthopedic clinic, etc.

### 3.1.5.2 File Identifiers

A data file is defined as a set of like or unlike records assembled under a common denominator. Record size and syntax can be determined by the data medium that stores the file. It is therefore useful to add a code identifying the storage medium to the file identifier (see Figure 3.4). Lufthansa Airlines, for example, uses a two-digit file identifier.

MT —magnetic tape
PT —perforated tape
PC —punched card
VO —voucher
LI —list

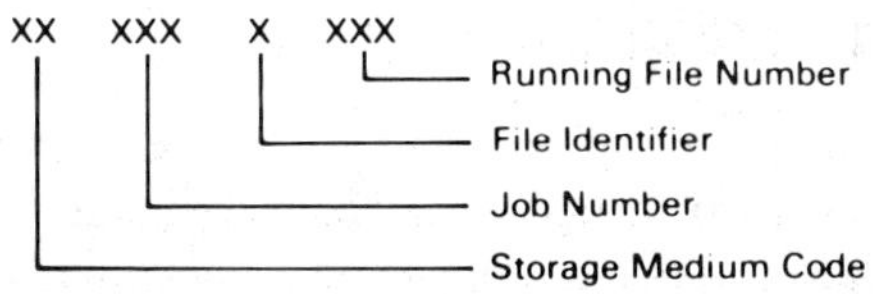


**Figure 3.4** Composition of a File Identifier

FO —form
MD—magnetic drum
MS —magnetic strip
DS —disk storage
RS —random storage
RD —recording disk
MC—magnetic card
DI —direct input
DO —direct output
QS —quick access storage (extended core storage)

### 3.1.5.3 Time-Period Abbreviations

Since parallel coding often includes time references, for example in magnetic tape identification or log books, a sample of abbreviations used by Lufthansa Airlines is represented as follows:

RNG —running
MIN —minute
HOU —hour
DAY —day
CIN —5-day segment
WEK—week
DEC —decade
SMO —semi-month
MON—month
PMO —prior month
CMO—current month
FMO —following month
MAN—month after next
RPE —report period
PRP —prior to report period
FRP —following report period
APP —aperiodic partial period
QUA —quarter
YEA —year
JAN —January, etc., through December
SUN —Sunday, etc., through Saturday

### 3.1.6 Updating Coding Systems

Under some circumstances a totally new coding system may become necessary; all coding systems are subject to changes over a period of time—some terms become obsolete and are replaced so that a reorganization becomes necessary.

If in the development of a new work process a prior numbering system needs to be changed or completely replaced, the documentation and work instructions developing the new code as well as instructions for its use should be worked out as early as possible. Parallel codes are most useful with new coding systems because the identification codes can be retained even though the classification segments undergo substantial alterations.

Such revisions usually become necessary when a new system is installed or when data processing is first introduced. Since revisions generally occur from time to time in data processing, a new organizational specialty has developed known as "change management," which can be called into use for such tasks.

Encoding processes are time consuming and must be carried out with a high degree of accuracy and thoroughness. It is therefore important to begin work on them as early as possible. It has been found that the additional workload also causes delays through allocation problems that necessitate considerable extra work during the changeover phase.

Checklists of the various coding systems facilitate the changeover. The codes needed in assembling data files, such as account numbers for user files, are usually entered on coding sheets, then transferred to punched cards or tapes. A checklist with subsequent coding controls completes this phase.

With respect to ongoing changes the advantages of parallel codes have already been mentioned as only occasional digits are affected. Expansions of classification codes are relatively simple as well. Changes should never involve all task areas, code directories, forms, or employees at any one time, nor should identification codes in current use be changed.

These continuous code changes and updatings will be mentioned at various points in the operations organization. If a new code must be introduced it should be checked against existing codes to avoid duplication or confusion. A central code directory eliminates this problem. All changes should be recorded in it, and each code should be listed on a separate sheet.

Code changes should at any rate be kept to a minimum, not only because they cause extra work and generally disturb operations, but also because in addition to defining group characteristics they are used as search words for storage and processing functions. Since changes cannot be avoided entirely, however, provisions for updating services must be made in the operations organization.

## 3.2 Organization of Data Entry

Punched cards were for many years the predominant data medium. Entry devices such as card data recorders and verifiers could not be used with maximum efficiency in a decentralized operation; thus data entry was centrally handled by the computer center. Technological advances in data entry devices now allow for cost-efficient decentralized entry, especially with the advent of machine readable documents and direct entry without intermediate data media.

The computer center organization needs to take these developments into account. Methods of centralized data entry must be adapted to them, and the service spectrum of the computer center must adjust to the technical possibilities of decentralized data entry. This development has progressed to the point where some computer centers no longer have the capability of centralized data entry, but this is not the rule. In the future both methods will probably exist side by side.

Data entry is and will probably remain a decisive factor in computer center organization. Data acquisition is an integral component in the total processing organization. The following detailed evaluations are offered.

*Advantages of centralized data entry*

Efficient use of data entry devices

Operation of devices by trained personnel, ensuring relatively high accuracy and correspondingly high operator efficiency

Simplified maintenance because of centralized location of devices

Minimization of problems resulting from machine breakdowns

Clear delineation of functions between organization and computer center; economic unity inasmuch as devices and operators can be under organizational and computer center management.

*Disadvantages of centralized data entry*

There is a relatively large separation of operations and processing in terms of space and time

The spatial separation of the economic processes and data entry complicates corrections or classification of disagreements or errors on the primary data media.

Since keyboard entry operators have no contct with processes underlying the data, any kind of verification check is out of the question; the resolution of special problems can be time consuming.

The devices are subject to frequent resetting because processing is done in relatively small batches to avoid load surges; this increases idle time and error sources.

In cases where the necessary primary data media (such as card files) are also needed by other departments, a prolonged absence of these media may be troublesome.

Since primary data media must be returned to the individual departments after transfer to machine readable media, transportation costs and errors increase.

The determination of responsibility for errors requires double security precautions for all data.

The majority of these disadvantages increase in proportion to the distance between the computer center and individual departments, and decrease with online data entry only insofar as the isolation of the operator is eliminated and continuous technical support can be provided.

### 3.2.1 Data Entry Methods

The field of data entry has grown to the extent that entire volumes have been written on the subject. In order to provide the general overview of data entry methods necessary for an organizational analysis, it will be helpful to proceed from the following classification (see Figure 3.5):

- *Data Origination.* Data originate through identification of situations or changes (dynamic description) or the representation of objects or facts (static description). From an organizational point of view it is important to know where, how, and when data originate. Examples can be a bank deposit at a cashier's window or the computation of power consumption by means of a meter.
- *Data Definition.* This includes filling out a deposit form at the bank, reading an electric meter, and recording power consumption on a punchable list.

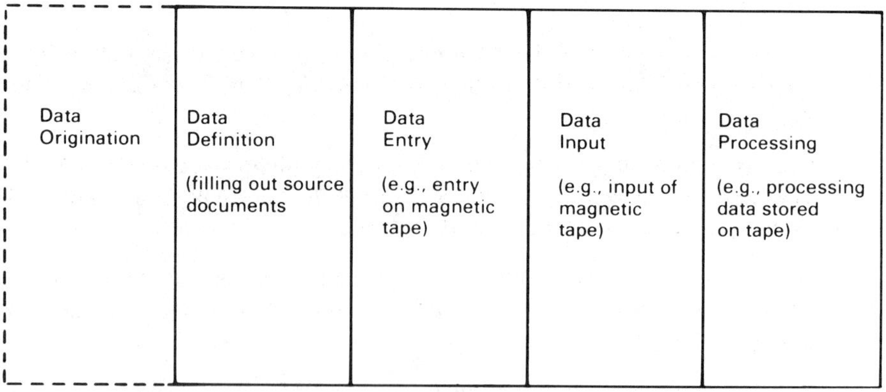


**Figure 3.5** Classification of Data Entry in the Total DP Process

- *Data Entry*. Until now the data to be processed need not exist in machine readable form. But once the bank deposit forms are transferred to punched cards or the meter reader's list to magnetic tape we have typical examples of data entry processes, also known as data transformation because the data themselves are changed only in form.
- *Data Input*. This process admits the data to be processed into the EDP system. Traditionally it meant that the data on punched cards went into the system by means of a card reader.
- *Data Processing*. The inputted data are now processed according to programmed instructions. In one previous example this could mean the bank's account statements or a utility bill. Processing is the first step in the sequence which is no longer a component of data entry.
- *Data Output and Postprocessing*. These steps are mentioned to complete the picture.

This classification of data entry has deliberately proceeded from a conventional point of view because it permits a clear description of each step. The following organizational considerations are in keeping with this point of view. The integration of individual steps made possible by certain technological characteristics and their organizational consequences is an important consideration.

The integration of data definiation and entry should be mentioned first. A direct hookup between data definition and an entry device records data in machine readable form—for example, a perforated tape as by-product of a bookkeeping machine or the punched card of a depth scale. This integration affects organization when data entry is decentralized, i.e., from individual departments, and the computer center receives machine readable data. The guidelines for transferring data to be processed will have to make reference to this possibility.

The second possibility of integrating two previously separate steps concerns online entry which combines data entry and input. Data media need not be involved because the entry station is hooked up to the EDP system. This is of primary organizational importance because it requires computer center operations to allow for such stations. The delineation of authority and the security aspect of day-to-day operations are affected as well. Although in batch processing a critical situation can be resolved by resetting the machine and restarting it, a remote peripheral operation poses a different problem. Another point is that the devices for online data entry need not be located in individual departments but can be in the computer center itself, so that instead of a keypunch room there is an area with online stations for which an analogical organizational design has to be found.

The third possibility of integration is online processing, where data definition, entry, and input are combined in one operation. A typical example is process control. The necessity of taking all possible organizational steps so as not to impede process control operations through technical or operator errors is even more obvious here than in online entry. This is one of the reasons why process control is usually restricted to separate process control computers rather than a large batch processing operation.

Such systematic advance considerations with respect to data entry show the organizational relevance of working with or without data media. The following section will briefly discuss the technological side of data entry in order to lay the groundwork for an analysis of entry procedures.

### 3.2.1.1 Data Entry with Recording Media

The separation of data entry and input requires the use of devices as media and for temporary storage. The punched card has proven itself in its more than 80-year history on account of its many advantages, but since it has been almost totally replaced by other data media it will not be further discussed here.

Data entry on magnetic media is a very different matter; direct entry on tape is common in many computer centers. The advantages of this method are not only that the medium can be reused but that it is fast, easy to use, and almost noiseless. Since these systems require a considerable investment, especially with data collection systems, computer centers usually prefer centralized data entry. This is also the reason why this method receives more attention within the organizational framework of the computer center. The spectrum of data entry systems ranges from single entry devices to intelligent data collection systems (Figure 3.6). Such collection systems often allow for a simple but convenient data entry organization with corresponding checks and controls. This will be further discussed in conjunction with data entry performance in section 3.2.4.

Tape entry devices essentially allow for three steps:

The source document data are keyed in at the entry location one record at a time; characters and block parity are calculated and fixed for compatible tapes.

The records are transferred to a storage device, compared and verified by an additional key-in operation.

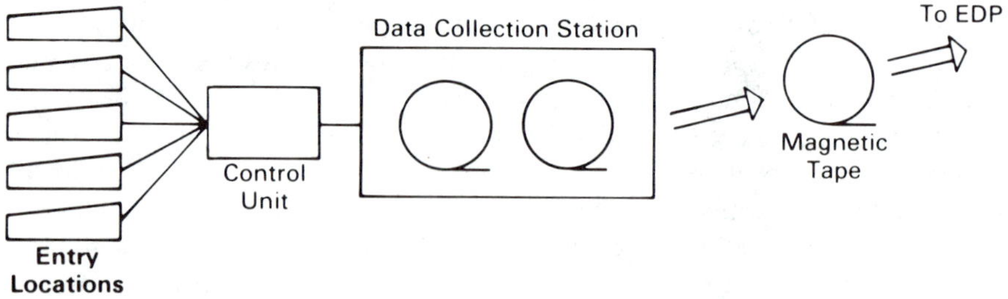


**Figure 3.6** Schematic Representation of a Data Collection System with 5 Entry Locations

A control number stored in the buffer is used to conduct a search; the tape stops when a match has been found.

There are additional possibilities which may be useful in organizing data entry via magnetic tape:

Inputted or read-in data display on the CRT

Data input on corresponding devices

Establishing check digits

Establishing data entry log, possibly by means of an accumulator

Pooling of several magnetic tape stations

Expansion into a data collection system

A number of coding methods have developed from the desire to use data by visual display as well as machine-readable form. The following forms in current use make special demands on the operations organization:

Mark-read form

Magnetic character forms

Optical character forms

Handwritten forms

Special online/offline readers must be made available for processing written codes. In online operations the reader is directly hooked up to the EDP system. In offline operations special work processes are inserted which must be treated as conventional offline jobs in planning and operations. These jobs are usually performed by the rework staffs. The computer center is responsible for furnishing appropriate operating instructions which are an integral part of computer center documentation.

### 3.2.1.2 Data Entry Without Recording Media

It is also possible to hook up entry devices to small EDP systems. The convenience and luxury of direct reasonableness controls and current data files has to be purchased at additional cost for data transfer (lines and modems) and hookup to the EDP system (channels, line control units). Figure 3.7 demonstrates the principle of data entry without media. The various possibilities of delineating authority between the computer center and individual departments can easily be recognized in decentralized online data entry. The technical areas need not be directly subordinate to the computer center. Other interfaces are possible, for example,

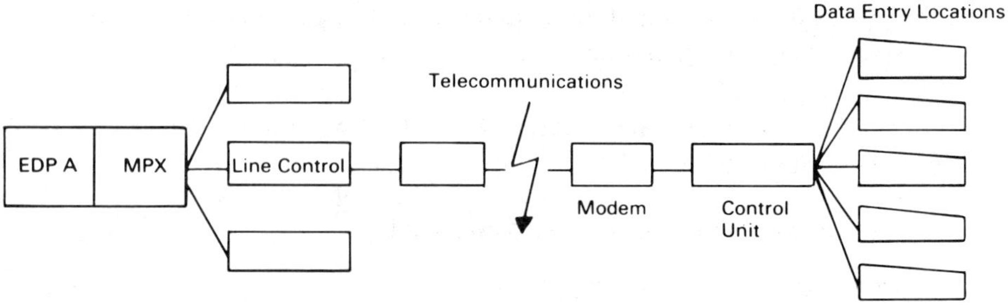


**Figure 3.7** Schematic Representation of an Online Entry System with 5 Entry Locations

between line control and modem in the computer center or between line control and modem in data entry of an individual department.

The two areas of *direct data input* (with hookups), and *direct data entry* (for example CRTs) do not represent a significant difference where the computer center is concerned. In each case, however, it is important for the computer center that in addition to the requirements imposed by hardware and software no unsupervised coldstarts may be permitted in machine operations.

## 3.2.2 Data Entry Procedures

There are essentially four divisions:

General procedures for data definition

Procedures for special data

General procedures for the data entry room

Technical operating instructions for data entry devices

Manufacturers of data entry devices publish their own operating manuals. It goes without saying that these technical operating instructions are known to all entry operators and are readily accessible.

### 3.2.2.1 General Procedures for Data Definition

Since data definition rarely occurs in the computer center, these procedures apply only insofar as centralized data entry in the computer center is made to suffer if they are ignored. There should be an agreement between the computer center and individual departments pertaining to the following rules:

- Data to be entered should be so identified in the source documents.

- Handwritten source documents must be legible; easily confused symbols (numeral 0 versus letter O, numeral 2 versus letter Z, etc.) must be properly identified in the source document. Standard usage such as the symbols on programming sheets should be followed.
- Source documents must be complete; repetition of data or number columns must be identified by appopriate symbols. This area is especially prone to careless writing.
- Data entry fields are to follow the same order as the source documents.
- Documents are to be properly sorted before transfer to data entry.
- A minimum of operator intervention or machine interruption should be necessary
- There should be an agreement between the departments and data entry that only important, manually entered data are subject to verification.

#### 3.2.2.2 Procedures for Data Collection

Instructions must be made available for each entry activity, whether centralized or decentralized, and are usually on printed forms. In designing such instructions the following items should be included.

*At the Top*

Record code

Record description

Program number (this number is to be recorded in the data flowchart and allows data flow to be traced back to the document)

Document identification

Specifications for documents which under certain conditions will yield different record codes; not required in integrated data processing

Name and current date

*In the Main Part by Data Field*

Identification of data field

Box number

Positions per record

Number of digits

Identification of activity

It is important to identify the entered documents, usually by stamping or perforation, if necessary using a rubber finger, and including the date and operator's name. This avoids duplication or misses and facilitates answers to possible questions.

#### 3.2.2.3 Data Entry Management

Personnel problems are nowhere as critical as in data entry. Often young and untrained operators are placed in positions of responsibility where they remain only an average of 3–5 years because they are more interested in a temporary job than a lifetime career.

This situation imposes particular demands on the leadership ability of data entry management. A competent manager should therefore have a good background in bookkeeping, organizational ability, and above all personal leadership qualities in addition to a general background in data processing. In a small work force the manager also takes over the tasks of document reception and job preparation. He is responsible for maintenance of deadlines in conjunction with the job coordination team. He must supervise the receipt of documents and *rapid* data entry. An increase in documents just prior to a deadline often creates extra problems, and experience shows that such documents contain a higher error rate on the part of those submitting them, reflecting greater carelessness in preparation. Last but not least, the manager is responsible for maintaining a continuous flow of documents for entry.

In larger data entry operations it is advisable to appoint selected individuals in job preparation to control functions. These employees must naturally be familiar with the specific area of application as well as having a general overview of the tasks in coordination and machine operations.

### 3.2.3 Scheduling and Control

All work produced by a computer center is tied to specific schedules. As a rule, all functions and thus all teams participate in the total output. Final deadlines can only be maintained if schedules for partial tasks have been planned in advance. In most computer centers concentrating on commercial data processing, data entry as the first processing step determines the total scheduling situation. Therefore scheduling and control must begin here. Strictly speaking, control begins when documents are received, because this is the departure point for centralized data entry. Scheduling control ends only when the results are delivered to the originating department. This means that the departments provide essential preparation activities for the computer center which must be on schedule. Among them are:

Document delivery

Delivery of control numbers

Determination of parameters

Clarification of questionable data

Figure 3.8 represents a delivery control form which can also be used to monitor scheduling. Data entry schedules should provide the following basic information:

Delivery schedule

Delivery operation

Delivery amount

Document type

Time scheduled

Operating schedule of data

Department responsible

Telephone number

Computer center employee responsible

**Data Processing**
**EDP Operations**
**Control Group**

Punch Instructions: HB D 007

Row: 1

**Data Transmittal Form**

**Document Type**: Materials Tickets — **Report Period**: May 1984

**From Department**: — **Building No.**: C106

**Employee**: Mayer — **Telephone**: 2511

| Document in | | Batch No. | Con-tainer No. | Total Tickets | Control Balance | Document Out | | Remarks |
|---|---|---|---|---|---|---|---|---|
| Date | Time | | | | | Date | Time | |
| 5/17 | 11:30 A.M. | 1 | 17 | 452 | 43107 | 5/18 | 8:15 A.M. | only 452 tickets |
| 5/18 | 1:41 P.M. | 2 | 9 | 397 | 29205 | 5/21 | 9:10 A.M. | |
| 5/23 | 11:07 A.M. | 3 | 13 | 612 | 51512 | 5/25 | 8:55 A.M. | |
| 5/28 | 2:30 P.M. | 4 | 8 | 719 | 62491 | 5/31 | 8:35 AM. | end of tickets |
| | | | | | | | | |
| | | | | | | | | Form 2 |

**Figure 3.8** Sample Data Transmittal Control Form

Document delivery to . . .

Documents handed over on . . .

Data entry location and personnel

Special attention should be paid to periodic and aperiodic peak periods which should be balanced to provide for regular and constant work flow. There are essentially three alternatives:

- *Subcontracting*. Many computer centers have established satisfactory routine relations with data entry services.
- *Overtime*. Certain reservations are in order here. The monotony of data entry work tends to cause fatigue and loss of efficiency. The desire to earn extra money may also lead to artificially induced overtime situations.
- *Part-time employees*. The opportunity often exists to hire housewives with data entry experience for peak periods. This has not proven successful because additional entry devices must be kept available and allowances have to be made for adjustment periods.

A fourth alternative—that of keeping data entry capacity available for extreme periods—is not practical, because there is nothing worse for morale in the data entry room than idle operators.

If schedules are to result in maximum efficiency for the operations organization they should be developed by a specialist in the computer center. The person in charge of schedule planning needs to have a good overview of application processes and operations in the computer center and must adjust planning to changing circumstances. Schedules must be coordinated with the departments in question, preferably in scheduling conferences. This has been found to be the most practical and acceptable method of reaching agreements for each application process involved.

In the interest of reducing administrative costs it has often proven useful to develop a master schedule instead of individual schedules for each operation. In this manner schedules are not fixed for a specific calendar day but formulated so as to be generally valid. This is referred to as relative scheduling. Absolute schedules may be sent to individual departments at regular intervals, for example semiannually.

Since scheduling in data entry is closely associated with the total scheduling structure of the computer center, reference will be made to it again from another perspective in section 7.3.

### 3.2.4 Data Entry Performance

Performance evaluation in data entry has two purposes: it serves as an accounting tool for computer center production on behalf of the job originators or departments (section 9.4.2), and it evaluates the performance of individual operators. Performance should be evaluated daily in terms of document type and employee. This allows for an evaluation of data volume per area of specialization for cost accounting purposes as well as control of individual performance. Data entry performance is often evaluated by program at the type of entry into the EDP system.

Formerly performance evaluation data were used as the basis for piecework systems, but this method proved unsuccessful. Sometimes performance data are used as the basis of a bonus system. Special attention in such a system should be given to self-correction of entry errors. Bonus systems exist in which operators correct their own errors outside of the performance evaluation system.

The following information should be included in a good evaluation:

Date, possibly time of day at the beginning and end

Entry period specification (normal working hours, overtime, weekend hours)

Accounting/payroll period

Document identification

Coefficient of degree of difficulty: standards are difficulty here, but in simple cases it involves purely numerical figures. The highest degree of difficulty is usually in punching programs. Any further breakdown is generally not advisable.

Data entry procedure number

Number of records entered

Number of characters per document

Operator's employee number

Operator's working hours

Checker's employee number

Checker's working hours

Remarks, such as errors, interruptions, idle periods

One must keep in mind that a number of factors are beyond the operator's control. In addition to equipment-related factors there are working conditions and conditions related to work stations, so that in the final analysis a performance evaluation is possible only in a general sense because it is impossible to isolate extraneous factors.

At the beginning of this section reference was made to the added technical possibilities of intelligent data collection systems in supporting data entry performance evaluation. In the inforex system the job control register automatically provides performance evaluation as well as time, personnel, and job scheduling.

The job control register contains the number of entered blocks and the number of errors in a continuous write operation. This information can be requested and displayed for each entry location. At the end of each work process a final count is automatically calculated. The Nixdorf System 820 has a master terminal that performs control functions and compiles work statistics and performance evaluations.

## 3.3 Organization of Job Preparation and Scheduling

The reduction of set-up time for EDP systems for maximum systems utilization is of primary importance for the operations organization. Standardized data flow and documentation are contributing factors, and data flowcharts are reliable aids. It is not only a question of national standardizations but above all of unity within an EDP organization. Data and job editing are an important part of job preparation.

Data editing refers to the entire complex of activities prior to actual data processing. Although data entry functionally belongs to this complex it was discussed separately because it represents a rather self-contained and independent area. Decentralized data entry is therefore not only possible but widely used. All other activities leading to input into the system will be discussed here.

Job preparation in its present form in computer centers is a typical batch processing function. Conversational mode processing represents the boundary for job preparation uses. Job preparation tasks are assigned to individual departments relative to the degree of online entry and direct processing via terminals. For purposes of functional unity job preparation is discussed here in the narrower sense; the planning components will be discussed in Chapter 7.

Figure 3.9 provides a total overview of the many functions of job preparation by percentage distribution, based on an investigation of experiential values. The special characteristics of tasks naturally impose themselves on job preparation. The type and extent of instructions and notations developed by job preparation depend on the diversity of tasks.

### 3.3.1 Data Delivery

In data delivery the documents to be processed are handed over to the data receiving station (a function of job preparation) by the departments. These can be data still to be entered or data already on machine readable media. In online entry the data to be processed are made available in mass storage files. Orderly termination of files by data entry is essential for security reasons.

Individual departments collect and check documents to be entered outside of the computer center. It is advisable to use check sums which, depending on the

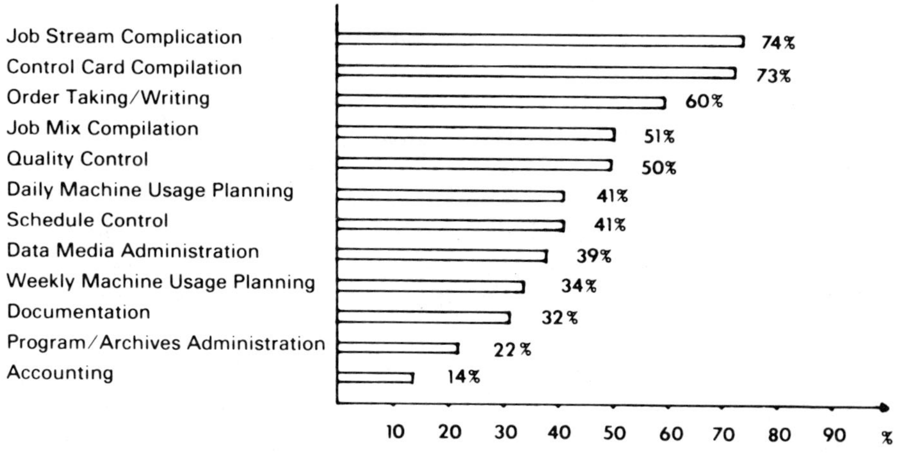


**Figure 3.9** Allocation of Functions in Job Preparation

importance of the data, allow for coordination of either the number of documents or document batches. Such early controls may be time consuming but are highly recommended, especially in periodically repeated jobs, because they facilitate the delivery process in the computer center. Otherwise, if documents are lost in transit erroneous results are produced which necessitate postprocessing and substantial delays. Each document batch, whether it contains coded sheets, perforated tapes, punched cards, or optical character documents, would be sent to the computer center in a container. All containers should be numbered individually. Damaged containers are replaced by new ones with the same number. However, the number of a lost container should be retained to avoid duplication in case the lost container turns up. When replacing lost containers new numbers should be used.

When data are delivered to the computer center it is the responsibility of receiving to accept and unpack them. Even though the data deliverer has already conducted a document check, the computer center repeats the procedure by means of a document control ticket (Figure 3.8). New tickets are used for each report period—for example monthly—and are designed to be used by both departments. The document control tickets should be uniformly made available to all data deliverers who are also responsible for numbering their batches. The computer center uses the control list to determine whether all batches were delivered and whether the data files are complete.

As mentioned in section 3.2, data entry proceeds according to specific instructions for each document type, and these instructions are assigned to specific data flowcharts. It is important for the coordination team and the data entry room to have all containers and routing slips properly identified and numbered.

It is advisable to use routing slips for transporting data from departments to the computer center, especially where longer distances are involved. They should contain information on the amount, original purpose, and date of data. These slips are sometimes used for delivery purposes within the computer center. Routing slips are inserted in the document batch. The slips used by BASF are characterized by fields containing the punch number, document batch number, and report period (Figure 3.10). They also indicate how routing slips may be used within the computer center.

The data receiving station also maintains a receiving schedule as an aid in checking delivery deadlines. Schedules for task completion are usually maintained on scheduling tickets (Figure 3.11). A ticket file is developed for task areas that require time supervision, and if it is arranged according to expected deliveries it

**Data Processing**
**EDP Operation**
**Control group**

**Data Transmittal Form**

**Document Type**: Materials Tickets — **Punch Instructions**: HBD007
**Form Department**: Accounting — **Container**: 17
**Employee** Mayer — **Batch No.**: 1
**Total Documents**: 453 — **Report Period**: May 1984
**Control Balance**: 43107

| Routing | | In | | | Out | | |
|---|---|---|---|---|---|---|---|
| | | Date | Time | Employee | Date | Time | Employee |
| **Delivered by** | X | / | / | / | 5/17/84 | 11:00 A.M. | Mayer |
| **Control group** | X | 5/17/84 | 11:20 | Hauck | 5/17/84 | 11:25 A.M. | Hauck |
| **Keypunch Rm** | X | 5/17/84 | 11:30 | Leitschuh | 5/18/84 | 8:15 A.M. | Krall |
| **Machine Rm** | | / | / | / | / | / | / |
| **Control group** | X | 5/18/84 | 8:20 | Fetigue | 5/18/84 | 8:50 A.M. | Fetigue |
| **Delivered by** | X | 5/18/84 | 9:05 | Mayer | / | / | / |
| | | | | | | | |
| | | | | | | | |

**Remarks** Control balance correct
Document total incorrect
Only 452 tickets Fetigue

**Form 1**

**Figure 3.10** Data Transmittal Form (BASF Co.)

provides an overview of work to be done as well as control of delivery deadlines. In program controlled job preparation systems these schedules may be called up on the CRT.

If the scheduling tickets are filed in order of task completion deadlines a similar control as for delivery is possible. The data receiving station thus supervises delivery of all scheduled external files and if necessary reminds individual departments in case of delay. Occasionally a backlog file may be needed. In addition, all consultations with departments, data collection stations, and delivery contacts must be recorded.

Figure 3.12 illustrates the flow of tasks in data acceptance.

## 3.3.2 Job Preparation and Scheduling Procedure

The term "job preparation" defines an operational function that occurs in practically every production process. Job preparation in a computer center is dependent on the type of production. Even computer centers with a relatively less developed focus on job preparation such as university computer centers recognize the job preparation function.

> Job preparation includes the timely preparation of the production process to ensure economical operations completed when due.

**Period:** Weekly

**Schedule Ticket**

Department: Sales

| In | | Out | |
|---|---|---|---|
| Due | Actual | Due | Actual |
| Wednesday | | Thursday | |
| | | | |
| | | | |
| | | | |
| | | | |
| | | | |
| | | | |

**Figure 3.11** Sample Schedule Ticket Used at a Siemens Computer Center

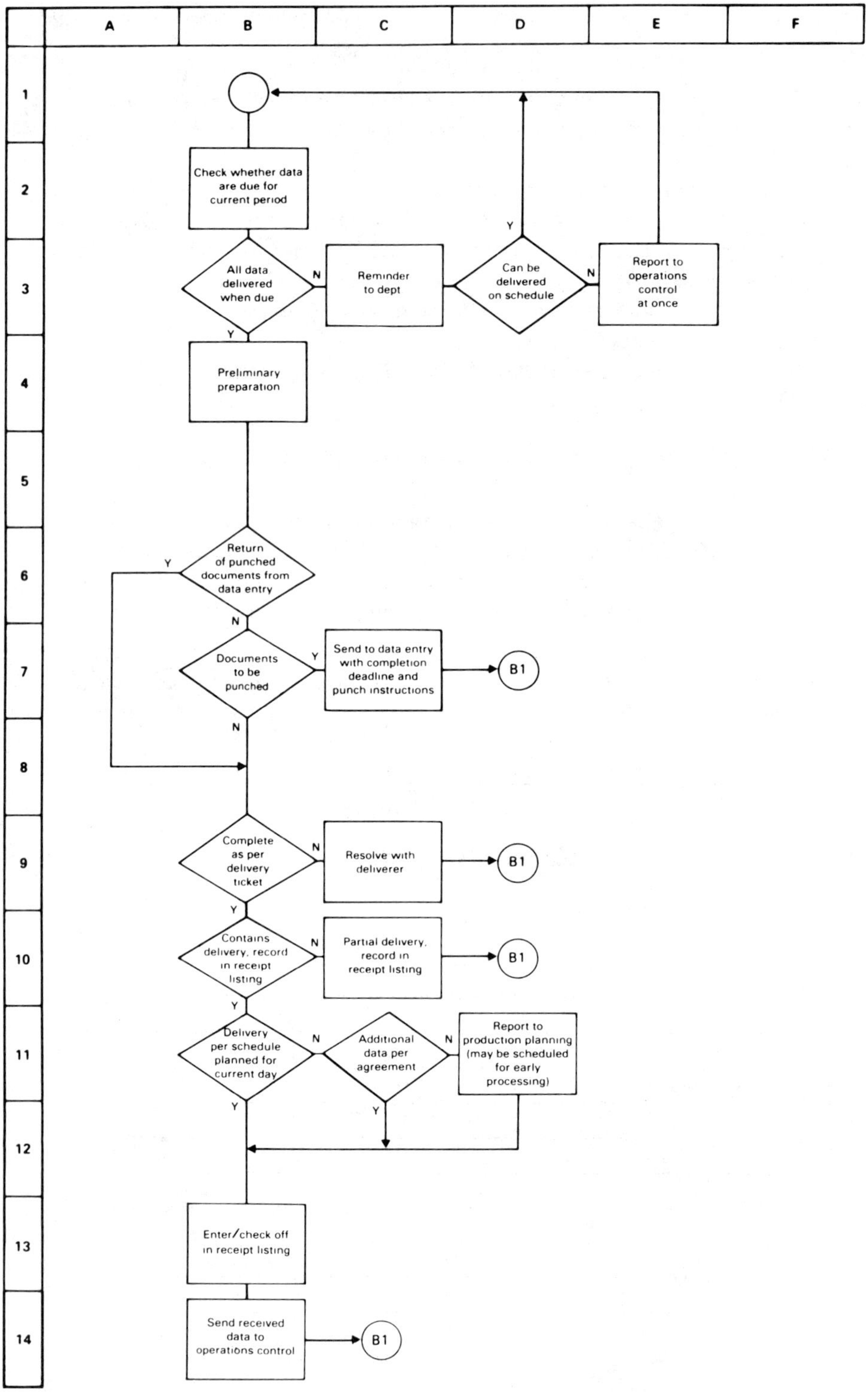


**Figure 3.12** Schematic Overview of Data Reception of Lufthansa Airlines

It has already been mentioned that the computer center here is considered the production center of electronic data processing. Systems analysis and programming, on the other hand, represent the development phase. Therefore the computer center, which in the above sense is a manufacturing operation, should have job preparation even though it may involve differing work processes depending on the area of EDP application.

In online operations job preparation functions may belong to the individual departments. Modern software makes it possible to link job preparation more closely with the departments even in closed shop operations. Control over error situations raises problems even with advanced data storage methods.

Improper planning and coordination can seriously impair or destroy the results anticipated by the EDP system. The importance of job preparation therefore arises both from its position in the computer center and from applicable requirements.

Since job preparation plays a central part in the computer center, it controls the entire work flow. Within the organizational framework of data preparation only the area of job administration can be discussed here. Its tasks can be divided into three basic parts:

Procedure transfer from programming

Preparation of procedures for each program run and maintenance of documents for each job

Scheduling by consultation, and data delivery

Only the preparation of procedures will be discussed at this point. Its integration into the organizational structure of the computer center is illustrated in Figure 3.13. Procedure transfer will be discussed in conjunction with program archives in section 3.5. There are broad-based attempts to integrate and automate the various tasks and job processes.

Scheduling includes systems usage planning and the entire complex of dynamic integration of all computer center equipment. It will be discussed separately in Chapter 7 in conjunction with reports, since appropriate reports constitute the basis of scheduling activities. Usage planning methods are a function of systems planning; in actual practice the methods that are used are more heuristic than analytic-economic.

Such a separation is easily imaginable in the context of data preparation and the appropriation of materials and programs for EDP production, especially when schedules are assumed to be provided. This sometimes leads to an organizational separation of job preparation and job planning. The integration of the job prepara-

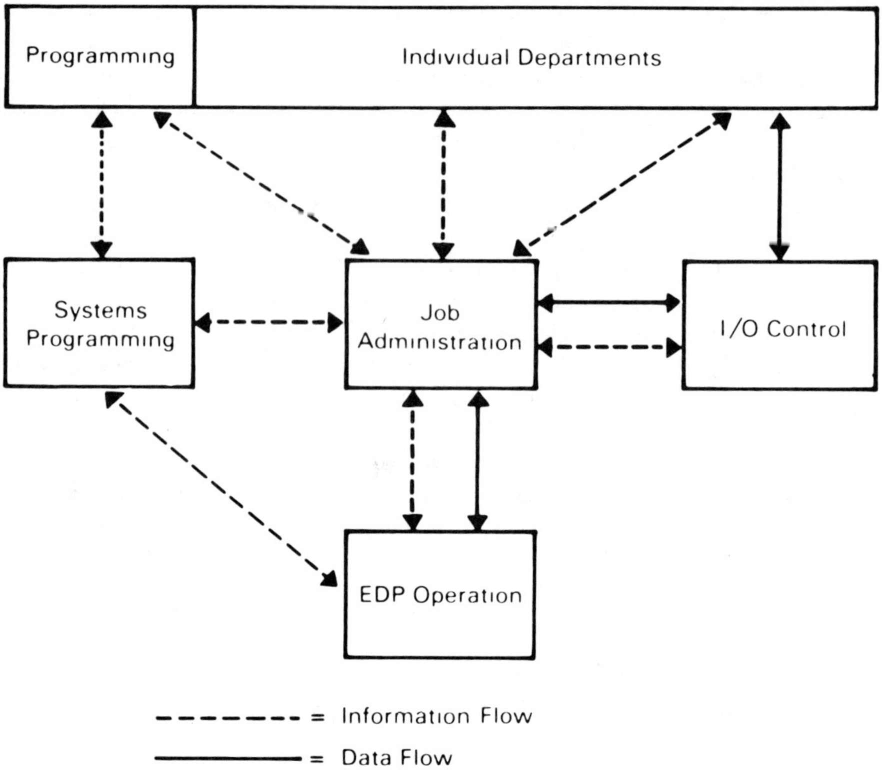


**Figure 3.13** Job Administration as a Component of Job Preparation in a Computer Center

tion complex can then be carried out in the context of work station descriptions in personnel organization.

The preparation of procedures within job preparation, described in a conventional manner before, roughly follow this time sequence:

- Systems usage planning in cooperation with the individual department develops a time schedule which triggers the preparation procedures for each task at the appropriate time.
- A job folder is assembled which in addition to the customary job documentation (operating instructions, console messages, checkpoint/restart information, data flowchart, run specification sheet, file register etc.) also contains work plans and job preparation instructions for each task.
- The work flowchart and job preparation instructions are removed from the

folder and copied; the copy is then modified according to the specifications of a particular task. This includes filling out the variable portion of the control statements, giving the date, number, and quantity of data to be processed. Since the quantity is often subject to considerable fluctuation, the storage area and machine run time need to be adjusted. A work flowchart contains a graphic representation of the job and a textual explanation in the form of work instructions with references to additionally available information. The work flowchart can be used without a schedule indicator for control instructions or with the schedule indicator for control and supervision. In the latter case copies must be made.

- Tapes and disks for a scheduled run are to be requested from the archive. In preparing runs that require a number of tapes or stations it is advisable to monitor the tapes by means of a run specification sheet which is a separate data flowchart for tape usage. The serial numbers of the tapes must be recorded. Figure 3.14 is an example of a run specification sheet. Read tapes are checked out by copying their serial numbers from the previous run's specification sheet. For write tapes the serial numbers are determined from the archive card file where the tapes are then recorded as in use. In automated archive systems job preparation makes tapes available logically (by giving the corresponding instructions), and operators have direct access to the tapes.
- Serial numbers and file numbers must be determined and verified by means of tape files and run specification sheets. A similar procedure is used for drums and disks. The assignment of volume names and file names is important for proper processing and must be entered into the control statement portion of the work preparation sheet.
- Materials are requested from the stockroom—for example, continuous forms with various imprints. The amount of materials needed must be determined by the number of input data and must be inventoried.
- In accordance with the instructions in the work preparation sheet control cards and header cards are now prepared. Control statements have become increasingly important in modern operating systems.

This concerns not only the maximum utilization of possibilities which will be discussed in section 3.5.2, but the likelihood of additional errors. Job preparation therefore needs a separate and independent work process to check control statements prior to use.

- Input data must be checked for completeness. Data transmittal forms have proven very useful here. When data are input on tape a completeness control

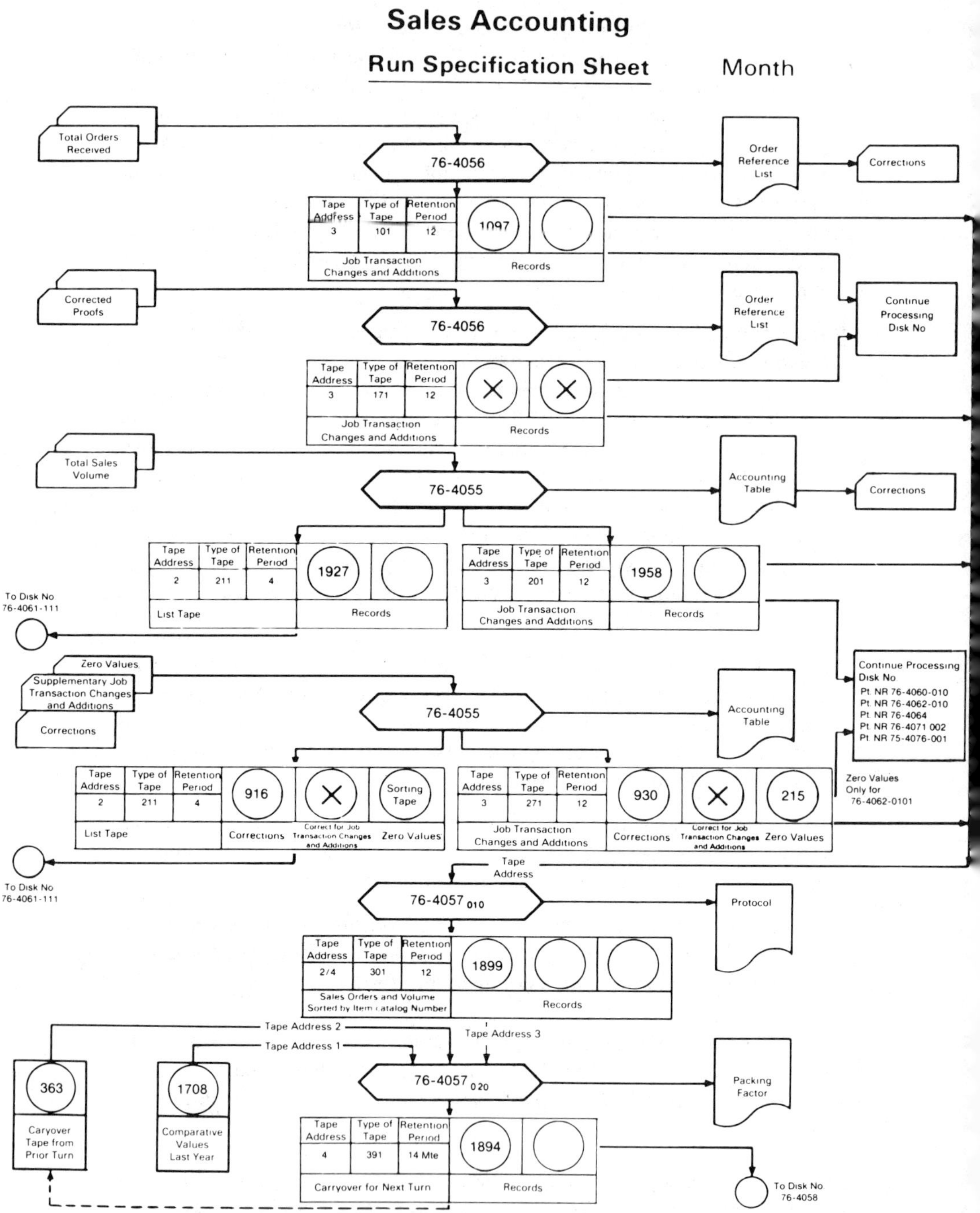


**Figure 3.14** Sample Run Specification Sheet

is virtually impossible; in this case data entry reports must be used. Orderly closure of entry files is important in online entry on disks.

- Audit documentation, which is part of the work folder, should be made available, and labels for all data media must be prepared.
- Finally, the tasks in the form of prepared documents are handed over to machine operations. All materials must be made available to machine operations at least one hour before the actual run in accordance with scheduling and machine usage planning, better still would be at the beginning of the work day or during shift changes. At any rate, it is important to have a sufficient number of tasks planned for the EDP systems a day ahead. It has been proven statistically that improper planning results in underutilization during the first two hours of early shifts. Stand-by tasks (i.e. tasks without a firm schedule) can contribute to better utilization.

As already pointed out, the work schedule developed by systems usage planning is the basis for job preparation. However, the job preparation team is allowed certain liberties with regard to sequencing as long as schedule requirements are observed. It is worth mentioning here that the planning component, which is oriented towards the future, is rarely supported by the operating systems. The job control language (JCL) can be very useful in this context, and interdependencies can be summarized on a job linkage diagram. Some of the criteria for developing job flow in a multiprogram device are:

- *Urgency*: When delays occur the time deficit can be absorbed by less critical tasks. This is generally possible only by individual intervention with the system or operating plan.
- *Effective machine utilization*: This factor should always be kept in mind. Emphasis on machine utilization is a goal characteristic of batch processing operations, since in online systems the operating system usually takes care of short response times.
- *Earning power*: This is important for every cost-effective computer center. Priorities can be recorded in the control statement and should be charged for additionally.
- *Assurance of short response times*: Response times should be less than 3 seconds in simultaneous dialog processing and online entry.
- *Consideration of tolerance possibilities*: In many cases a task can be rescheduled or subdivided.
- *Minimizing delays*: Operating systems provide little support in reaching this goal; software support is usually insufficient.

The following guidelines can be applied when planning priorities in batch processing operations.

First in/first out (FIFO)

The longest tasks have first priority

The most important tasks have first priority

The job planner is responsible for meaningful utilization of these guidelines. Dialog systems are more easily managed from the job preparation point of view (section 3.3.3), but it is more difficult to change established strategies.

Retries generally only repeat a portion of the procedures described. Preparation for a retry is not initialed by the time schedule but by backlog planning and can be automatic as well as deliberate. Section 7.3 will discuss this in more detail. It is sufficient to mention here that specific teams in systems usage planning are responsible for retries. Control cards and header cards must be appropriately identified in this case, usually by means of a special job number index. Automated accounting systems must under no circumstances charge customers for retries caused by the computer center. The job preparation form is an especially valuable tool. It contains:

Textual and numerical identification of task area (section 3.1.5)

Validity periods

Relative schedules (absolute schedules belong under concrete planning)

Processing frequencies

Processing times

All control statements, whereby the variable portions must be identified; reference must be made to which portions are administered via catalog procedures and in what manner

Header cards; the same applies here as in control statements

Fields for identification of process completion (abbreviated)

Name and identification of data files needed

Name and identification of material required

If the job preparation form is used as an accompanying document in the machine room it must contain remarks and instructions for machine operations (sequencing of tapes and disks). This is important in terms of maintaining contact between machine operators and the individual departments whose jobs they run. Concrete and job-related remarks are valuable.

Thus the job preparation form represents a textual description of program preparation. Its tabulated form greatly facilitates the job. Work procedures do not differ significantly in terms of content, but data flow inside the computer center as it relates to specific tasks or programs is represented graphically as a block diagram. It can be designed to function as a work preparation form as well.

The two most important planning aids in operations preparation—the job procedure plan and the job preparation form—are developed in the computer center at the time a program is handed in; there will be a more detailed discussion at a later point. Job preparation staffs should participate in developing these documents because of their importance in their work, especially when standard applications software is used.

A further job preparation aid needs to be further examined: the support of job preparation by an operating system and standard applications software.

The extended functions of operating systems have significantly altered the organization of job preparation. The introduction of job control language (JCL) represents additional organizational support for the description of operations preparations. It has been found, however, that the standard resources of today's operating systems do not suffice; they lack, among other things, the capability of strategic analysis of future tasks, so that a number of computer centers have resorted to developments of their own.

In order to grasp the magnitude of an operating language, it must be conceived as a programming language on a higher level whose instructions are the individual programs or program portions to be developed. It is understood in this context that an EDP task nowadays consists of a series of programs which are utilized according to different operating conditions; the control language of operating systems facilitate such tasks.

The parameters of an operating language depend on the specific operating system. Therefore only a few examples will be listed which, however, need not all be present in any given operating language.

- *Sequencing of interdependent tasks*. Situations of this type are common, and job preparation is responsible for keeping machine operations informed. Instructions must be carefully observed. Otherwise the operating system takes care of following the instructions formulated by job preparation in the operating language.

- *Scheduling instructions*. This concerns above all the usual runtime instructions. This is important not only for testing but for machine usage planning as well (together with other materials requirements). Daily schedules for beginning and ending job processes can be determined by the operating languages of some systems. Finally, most operating systems register the date for purely description reasons, but the date as a controlling influence is little utilized today because there are too many problems associated with it.

- *Program libraries*. Different types of program libraries may or may not be part of the operating system. They are administered by an operating system or systems software and can have a decided influence on job preparation. Some program administration tasks can be transferred to the archives by job preparation. At any rate the technical aspect of job preparation is altered insofar as programs are no longer available on cards or separate magnetic tapes.
- *Exceptional situations*. Job preparation is in a far better position to manage unexpected exceptional situations with the planning instruments provided by the operating system. The activation of alternative solutions in partial systems failures is one example. Through simple alterations in the instructions of the operating language, alternate solutions can be achieved that otherwise would be costly and time consuming. On the other hand there are cases where unplanned programs must be inserted on extremely short notice. With intelligent use of the operating system's capabilities—within the limitations of a particular system—such situations can be resolved without significant loss of machine time. Unfortunately the possibilities of an operating system are rarely utilized in such cases because the systems software group is organizationally not part of the computer center or computer center staffs are insufficiently trained.

## 3.3.3 Automated Job Preparation and Scheduling

The daily volume of work in job preparation along with the readily accessible support through EDP systems have in recent years led to the development of programmed job preparation systems. After a series of individualized solutions, program packages are now available (NAMIC, Infosoft) which are generally suitable. Before such packages were available only the card files and lists were replaced, and job preparation was conducted every morning—as a batch run in some instances. Others changed directly to utilization of video display terminals for documentation and disposition files. Today automated job preparation systems with or without terminals are widely used.

With this in mind the tasks of job preparation are listed in such a way that the use of dialog terminals is clearly demonstrated. There are essentially three areas:

a. Planning and management of computer center tasks

- The computer center collaborates in planning new tasks before conversions are initiated. This is important in regard to later JCL utilization at the terminals.

- Planning of test and takeover tasks during conversions.
- Assumption of documentation after conversion tasks are completed and redesign of the converted task areas. Job documentation should be available on magnetic data media (such as disk packs) at that time.

b. Operations preparation

- Completion of control statements which were developed by means of cataloged procedures.
- Job assembly with the aid of JCL.
- Transfer of materials and documents to the EDP system. With automated systems this is to be understood in the logical sense of the word. Operating receives a list of jobs to be processed.

c. Administrative work

- Cataloging of tapes and disks. Archive administration can possibly be carried out with a separate (programmed) system.
- Inventory accounting and management. These functions run in direct conjunction with the accounting system.
- Administration of the documentation archives by means of editor systems.

The data files containing the information on all upcoming jobs are the core of an automated job preparation system, of which Figure 3.15 provides a concrete representation. In looking at the total volume of data necessary for planning and job preparation which can be expanded into a planning data base, the following general overview is possible:

- An EDP system today breaks down into individual resources which can be planned and assigned separately (main storage, secondary storage, peripheral devices etc.), and which must be at the disposal of the entire job preparation system for all individual tasks.
- The performance record of hardware components is to be kept in a separate file.
- The entire user circle is to be informed of planning and job preparation details. Job numbers, cost center numbers, rates and special conditions are to be considered in practically all job preparation tasks.
- The performance record of this user information is also kept in a separate file.
- The performance record of individual jobs is also kept on file. This includes not only turnaround time but time usage of each resource. Influences on specific performance such as quantity framework and paging rate are often recorded as well, because they provide essential information for an

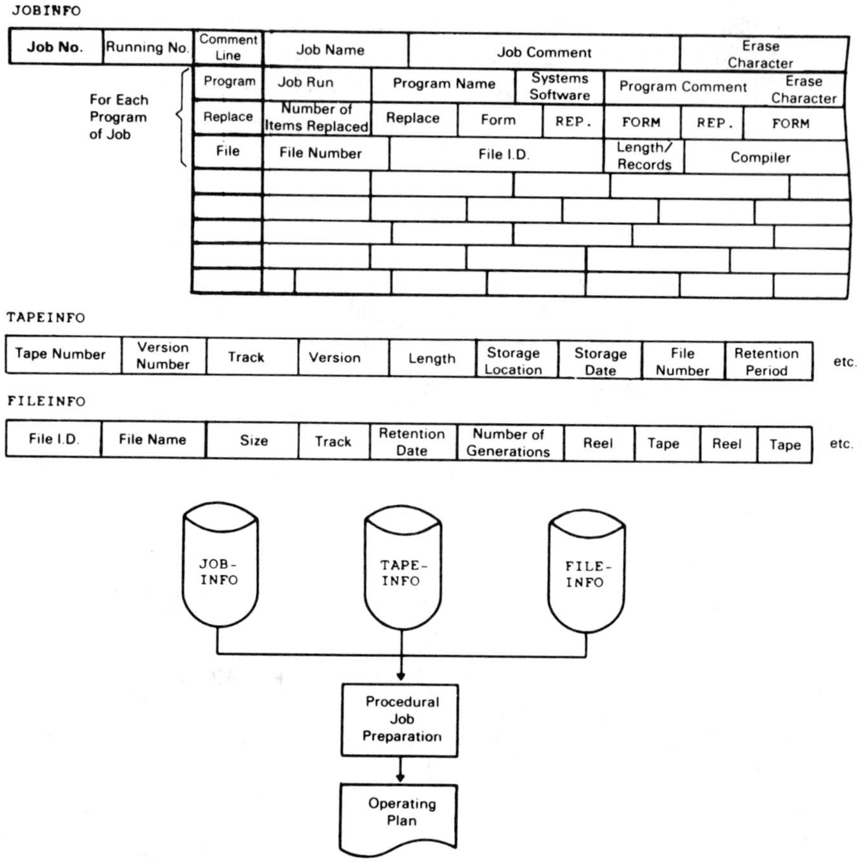


**Figure 3.15** File Design with Automated Job Preparation

"intelligently automated" job preparation. It is important to have evaluation programs available that can recognize and utilize these causal relationships.

- Information on time requirements of already completed job runs is used for scheduling planned jobs and kept in a separate file.
- A further file contains job interdependencies and the formation of job chains. If necessary, jobs scheduled earlier or later are included.
- Schedules and priorities for jobs to be done are to be stored.
- A separate file contains the total system of interdependencies between files and programs, possibly in conjunction with an automated data administration system.
- The calendar with all schedules and attendant responsibilities constitutes a separate file.

All of these files may be involved in diverse job preparation processes, and the static components for scheduling and disposition are derived from them.

Figure 3.16 represents an overview of a concrete job preparation process. In a time-sharing system the production runs (for example, in program run GEN) are generated. Parameter cards, tape allocations, cycle numbers, and start statements for continuation runs are automatically produced. A generation protocol is issued before each job run and checked by job preparation. A second list contains the daily work processes and serves as work instructions for operating. Rerun points for system stops and dump tapes for data bank runs are indicated. During the job run the rerun points are displayed on screen so that the operator can continue processing in case of systems failure. Parallel processing is possible with differently numbered processing chains. Special jobs can easily be fitted into the job flow.

If one considers the possibilities of the most advanced automated job preparation systems, the question arises why these programmed aids continue to run as separate program packages instead of being part of the operating system. The answer lies in the task structure of a dynamic job administration which is character-

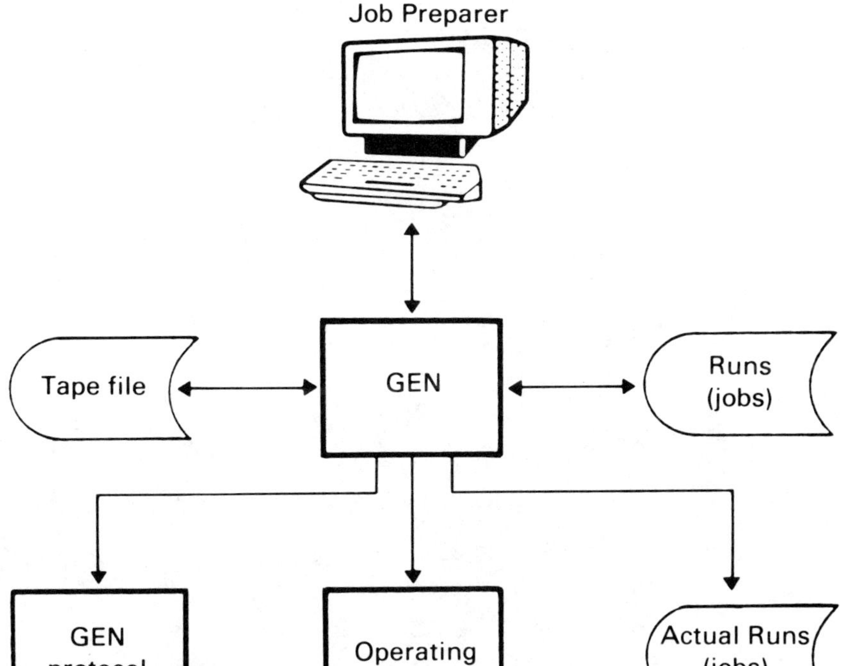


**Figure 3.16** Schematic Representation of an Automated Job Preparation System (Kiessling, H, *Datascope* 29 (1979) pp. 9 – 22).

ized by the fact that a large proportion of tasks are not administered by job preparation but by individual departments. This mixture of task forms existing side by side is typical of many teleprocessing systems in which individual departments operate their own data terminals. Figure 3.17 shows an overview of dispositions that can be called up by individual departments.

It is now the responsibility of job preparation to administer the totality of processing tasks and to provide event-oriented management of operating procedures in accordance with established schedules and priorities. It has been proven that not all jobs can simply be read into the EDP system. Current operating systems often cannot handle tasks submitted in that manner because they do not contain enough future-oriented control algorithms. Event-oriented control of computer center production sets up separate requirements for job preparation. When the main burden on EDP systems increasingly comes by way of communication lines (RJE stations or dialog terminals), automated job preparation systems with event-oriented control are all the more necessary.

The immediate results of event-oriented control are the following:

A stable operations structure is guaranteed.

Schedules are maintained.

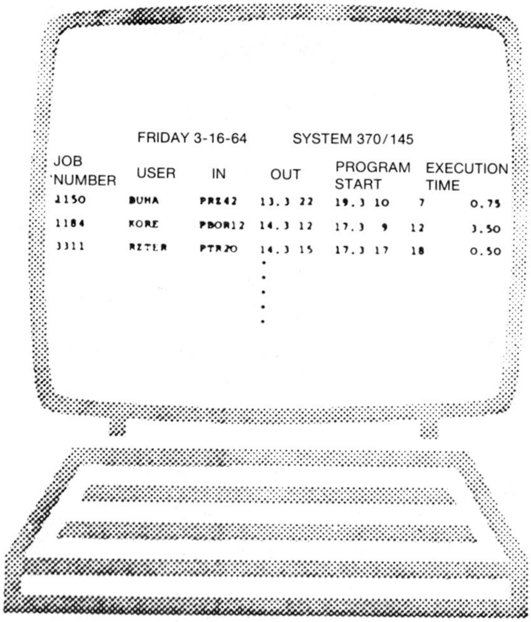


**Figure 3.17** Schematic Representation of Dialog-Oriented Job Preparation (6th EDP Yearbook, 1977)

Responsibility for events is allocated.

Other long-term consequences may be predicted:

Computer center operations will be facilitated.

Usage-oriented operational processes will be favored.

Event-induced variants of operational processes may be either favored or impaired.

It is obvious here that organizational and program-related gaps in teleprocessing and network systems need to be closed, although these may not be readily apparent in purely technical considerations.

Job preparation takes on a new form with these new technical aids. Some obvious advantages are:

Increased security of computer center operations (including documentation)

Increased dynamics in scheduled jobs

Increased dynamics in special jobs

Increased and better-managed EDP production

More easily accommodated future computer linkage

Reduced personnel requirements in job preparation

When introducing automated job preparation systems it is essential to check on the following prerequisites:

Are dialog operations already in use?

Do organizational prerequisites exist?

Have CRT work stations been designed?

Do technical prerequisites exist?

Are software products available? (Individual and costly designs are hardly worthwhile any longer.)

Finally, the economic parameters of automated job preparation systems must be estimated. Concrete individual considerations cannot be avoided here. A good criterion lies at approximately 80–120 jobs per day, above which such a system is profitable. However, the definition of a job is open to interpretation.

### 3.3.4 Verification and Control

Figure 2.12 illustrated the relationship between job preparation and machine operations on the one hand, and machine operations and output control on the other. Because of this close relationship many computer centers combine the functions of job preparation and postprocessing into one organizational unit, even though they are executed by different individuals. For this reason the control functions of postprocessing are discussed with job preparation, although separate teams are responsible for these functions in large computer centers. Security considerations make this a requirement.

When results come out of the machine room together with other programming materials and data media, they by no means leave the computer center unseen. The materials remaining in the computer center must be returned to their proper places if the operating results are in accordance with the stipulations of verification control. This evaluation and verification calls for close cooperation with input/output control and is often carried out by this group. Therefore this point is discussed in conjunction with data preparation rather than subsequent to data processing, although it does follow the latter.

The verification documents and procedures established by the individual departments and procedures development groups form the basis of the review. Controls should concentrate more on completeness than actual correctness; the latter should be carried out by each department unless provided for in the program, because the computer center lacks the specific background for each area of application.

The tracing and correction of errors takes up a considerable part of time for this group. Close cooperation with programming and individual departments is essential.

Verified results are released for distribution or shipping. Therefore the final verification should end with a notification of completion. The originating departments are to be notified in case of error as well.

Run controls for completeness and correctness can be handled using the following guidelines:

Incorrect program release?

Error in JCL statement?

Data errors?

Incorrect or incomplete documentation?

Use of incorrect file labels?

Incorrect or insufficient materials?

Should clues be derived from completion codes?

Reason for program termination?

Operating errors?

Program run results are usually checked by means of verification forms. Figure 3.18 is a sample verification form for a closing balance at a Siemans computer center. Errors must be corrected as quickly as possible and followed by a repeat run.

The various verification procedures for reaching the desired goal are of special interest. In general, verification procedures are increasingly handled by the EDP system in proportion to the refinements of processing procedures. This means that expertise in verification procedures leans more and more towards organization and programming. nevertheless, manual checking procedures should not be eliminated. The possibility of having the values supplied by the EDP system can only be welcomed.

The following questions should be asked in determining the appropriate verification procedure for a problem:

Which checks are necessary?

Which of these checks can be programmed?

How can verification groups be formed?

How many events should a group contain in order to limit an error search to a manageable minimum?

Thus far there is no standardized verification procedure. Each individual case determines the appropriate method. The following procedures are frequently used:

- *Zero method*. The sums of two verification groups amount to zero in addition and subtraction. The resulting value can also differ from zero, but it must equal to the value derived from a third verification process.
- *Parallel method*. Analogous horizontal and vertical sums are calculated. In addition these sums can be calculated in other programs and must balance each other.
- *Longitudinal method with record selection*. For each processed record of a file, sums are stored according to certain criteria, such as record type, article type, account type. The sums of these groups must correspond to the final sums of the program.

The complex of verification and control can be summarized in a flowchart (Figure 3.19). The security problem in the context of verification and control will be discussed separately in Chapter 4. Nevertheless, its importance in this work

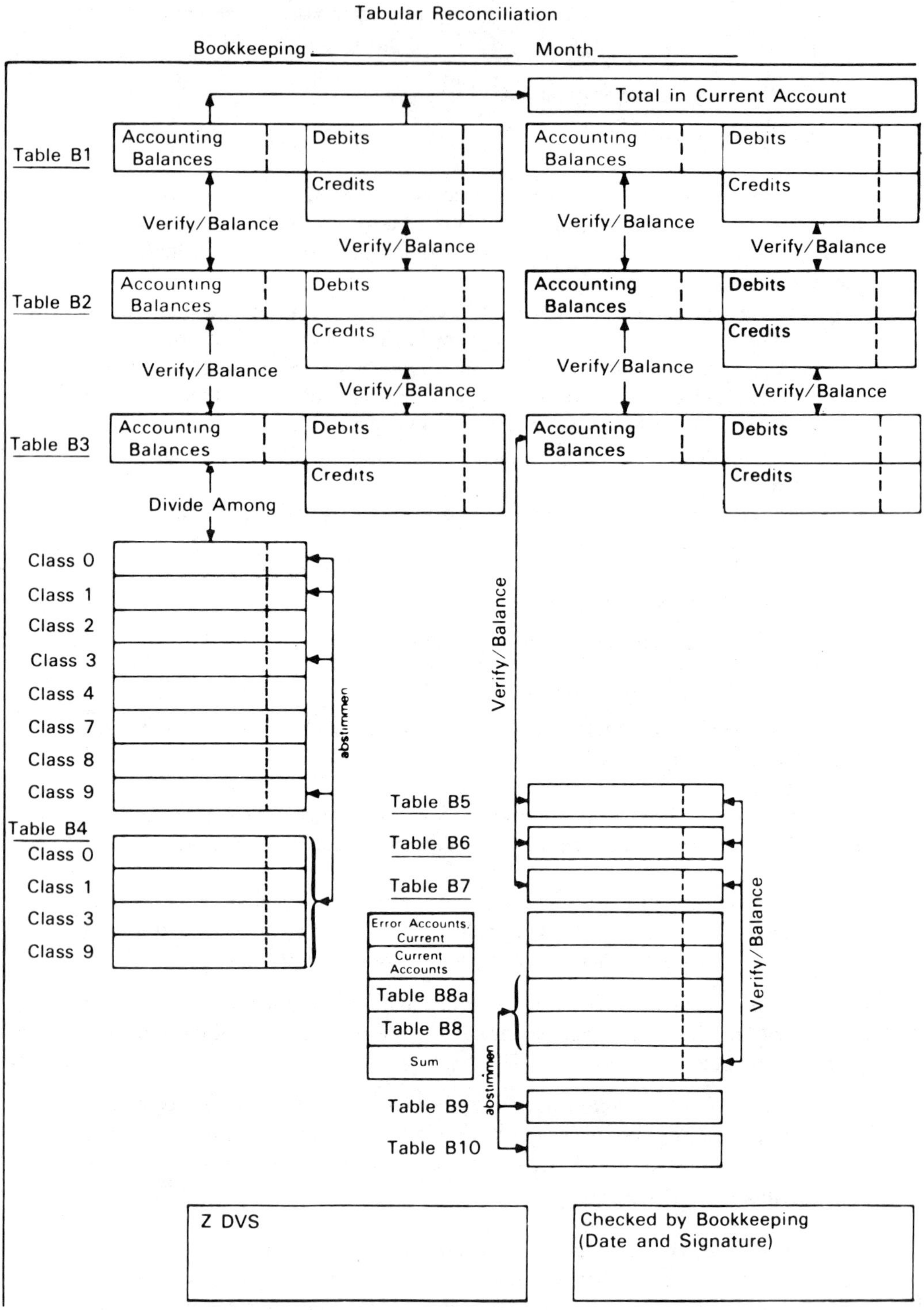


**Figure 3.18** Sample Reconciliation Form (Closing Statement)

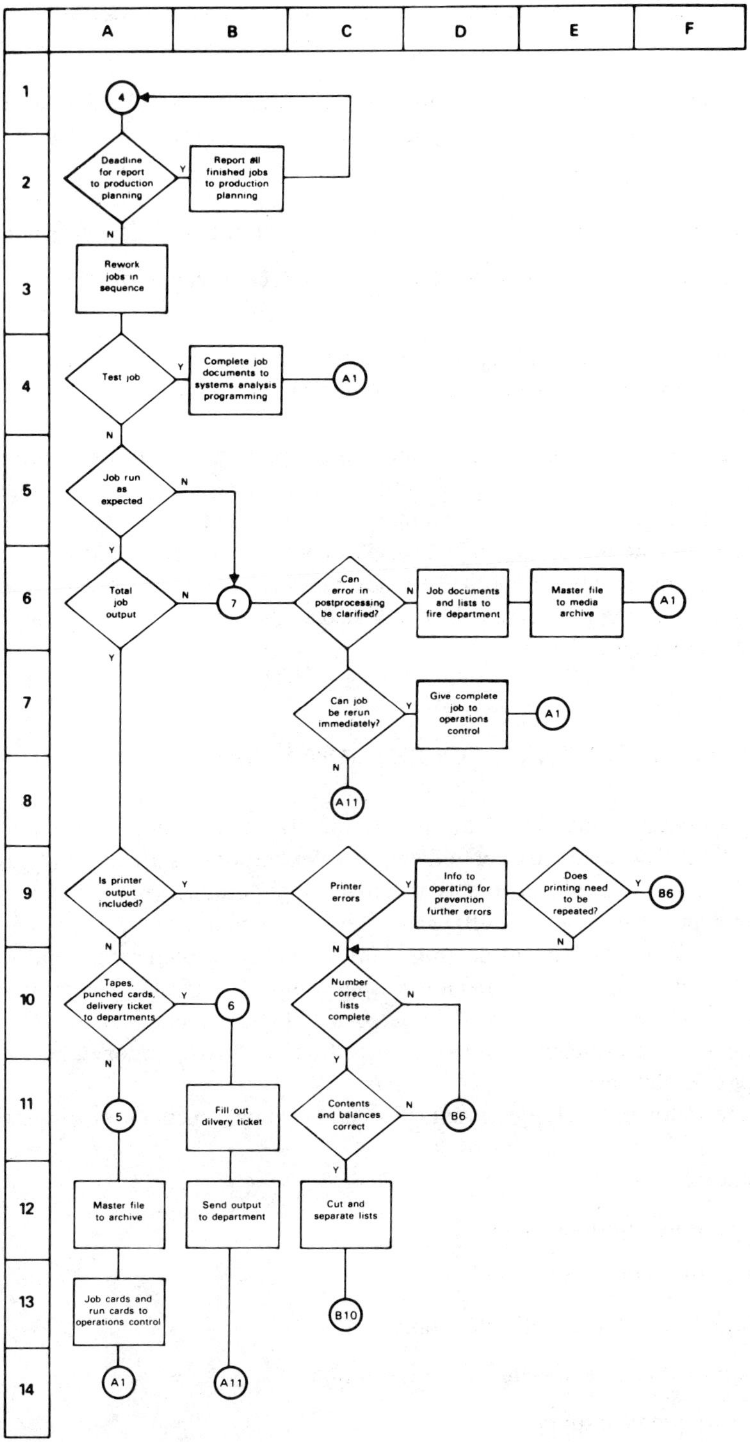


**Figure 3.19** Schematic Representation of Verification and Control

process should be pointed out here, because even in tested and long-running routine programs errors may occur for a variety of reasons.

These may include:

A condition that actually should not occur and that therefore was not tested

Input data containing errors that were not recognized in the reasonableness check

Data records in data files containing errors made in preprogramming, systems errors, or faulty input data (perhaps due to translation errors)

These errors can only be recognized if the program results are examined by diverse criteria. Since the computer center as a service organization has to guarantee error-free results, it is in its own interests to utilize all the possibilities of error detection. It is advisable to conclude each run with a separate verification in order to minimize the number of jobs to be repeated in case of error. For security reasons verification activities should not be conducted by the same employees who prepare jobs or receive data.

## 3.3.5 Data Media Completion and Delivery

Many computer centers send the results directly to the departments following verification. But since the often rather extensive output lists are unwieldy to work with in the respective departments and since single products can often be mailed directly (such as reminders, bills, and other postal shipments), postprocessing of correct results is best handled centrally. This is in keeping with the general concept of the computer center as the manufacturing component of EDP. It adds an area of responsibility that is not directly related to the fulfillment of data processing functions but nevertheless follows organizationally. It is mentioned here for the sake of completeness.

The following activities essentially belong to data media postprocessing:

Interpreting

Collating multiple copies

Bursting output lists

Bursting and automatic stamping

Automatic envelope stuffing and stamping

Packing and shipping

The type and extent of these activities should be part of job documentation. In sorting, cutting, and separating it is more important than ever to be well organized and to observe data security regulations. All documents received from verification and control must be sorted by subject and placed on designated shelves. Large shipments remain on the transporting vehicle and are taken to the cutting room. Empty vehicles should be returned to job preparation immediately. Waste paper must continuously be placed in appropriate containers and regularly taken to the trash room. Since postprocessing devices produce a large amount of dust, they should be kept in separate rooms and away from the tape archives.

Priorities for same-day work must be clearly established. Standardized rules may in part apply, but special cases are to be decided by job preparation management. Finished jobs should be returned to the originator as quickly as possible in order to reduce the amount of materials unnecessarily on hand. This can be done through internal delivery or a messenger service provided by the originating department. Receipts are to be acknowledged on preprinted forms and handed over to usage planning.

Not much can be said about the shipping of data media, i.e., by mail or other delivery systems. Since not only lists but also punched cards and magnetic tapes are shipped, appropriate packing materials must be available, such as special cartons for tapes and disks. A shipping log must be maintained for the purpose of ascertaining when certain shipments were made and by whom to whom. Address labels can be printed by the processing device during the program run.

## 3.3.6 Computer-Output Microfilm—COM

The microfilming of results occupies a special position within the framework of job preparation and postprocessing. It is a question not only of filming EDP lists for originating departments but also of the utilization of economic opportunities by the computer center. Video display terminals have diminished the importance of microfilming job documentations and job preparation materials, but for long-term documentation of console printouts and usage reports COM presents an interesting alternative. The technical possibilities will not be discussed here in detail.

COM devices are sometimes owned and operated by the computerd center if the job volume justifies the expense, but more frequently such jobs are subcontracted. In the former case the device is operated by postprocessing like other offline devices such as plotters, and in the latter the jobs are shipped on magnetic tape.

The shipping of magnetic tapes is very common (e.g., to financial institutions and insurance companies) and requires certain input/output controls in the form of shipping logs and automated tape archive systems. Many computer centers have made it a custom to release only specially marked tapes for shipment to microfilming studios. The finished microfilms need to be checked as part of the standard work routine of computer center control.

### 3.3.7 Update Services

In recent years EDP update services or program enhancements have assumed increasing importance. Such services may involve up to 40% of personnel capacity. Since updates concern primarily job preparation, the management methods developed in the past several years deserve mention here. Major manufacturers have taken on this problem and moved it into the foreground under the term "change management."

***Change management is a procedure-oriented and organizationally balanced methodology whose goal is the systematic direction, planning, and execution of required changes. Problems are to be recognized at an early stage, evaluated, and resolved at minimum cost.***

The development of data processing, characterized by decentralization, far-reaching teleprocessing networks, data banks, and increased online operations, leads to the expectation that the complexity of tasks will direct attention to the techniques and methods of change management. Each system is "alive" and needs to adjust and prove itself continuously.

A decisive factor for change management is a systematic analysis of influences on computer center efficiency as represented in Figure 3.20. The resulting reasons for changes are as follows:

Program corrections

Functional changes and additions in programs

Changes in archive regulations (possibly due to new legislation)

New operating system releases

Operating system corrections

Expansion of hardware configuration

Equipment exchange with or without change of manufacturer

Technical hardware changes (FCO—field change orders)

Expansion and changes of the telecommunication network

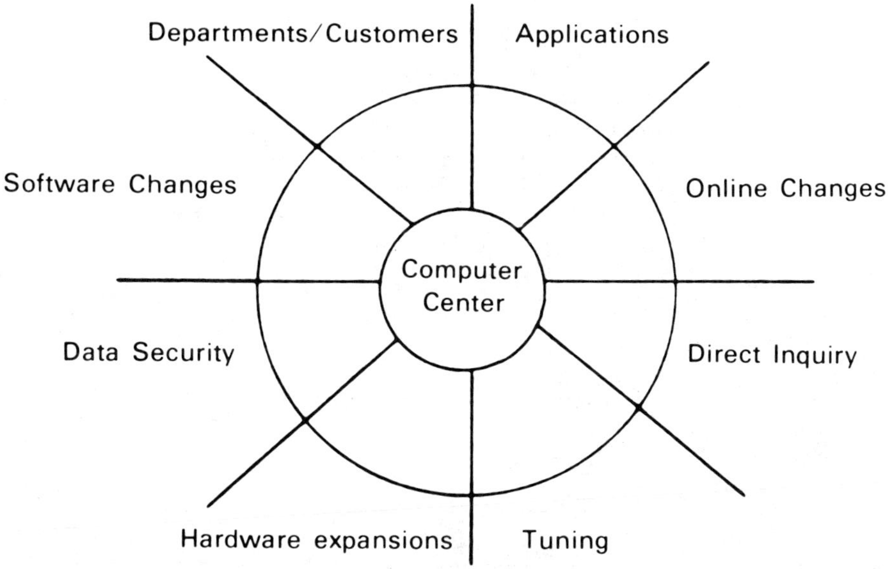


**Figure 3.20** Factors Influencing Computer Center Efficiency

Corrections and changes in air conditioning

Changes in the testing organization

Changes in computer center services (for example, takeover of additional performance)

This list could be continued at some length. At any rate systematic procedures are more important than overhasty trouble shooting when an error is discovered. Figure 3.21 represents the organizational framework for systematic change management which distinguishes between two coordination tasks:

- *Problem coordination*. Problem analysis, problem evaluation, and solution proposal.
- *Coordination of change requirements*. Collection and evaluation of requirements based on available reports.

The systematic coordination of structural and operations organizational methods supported by corresponding software is essential for cost-efficient changes. The consequences of changes can be rather diverse with today's complex systems, but each change in the computer center affects operations, especially in the following:

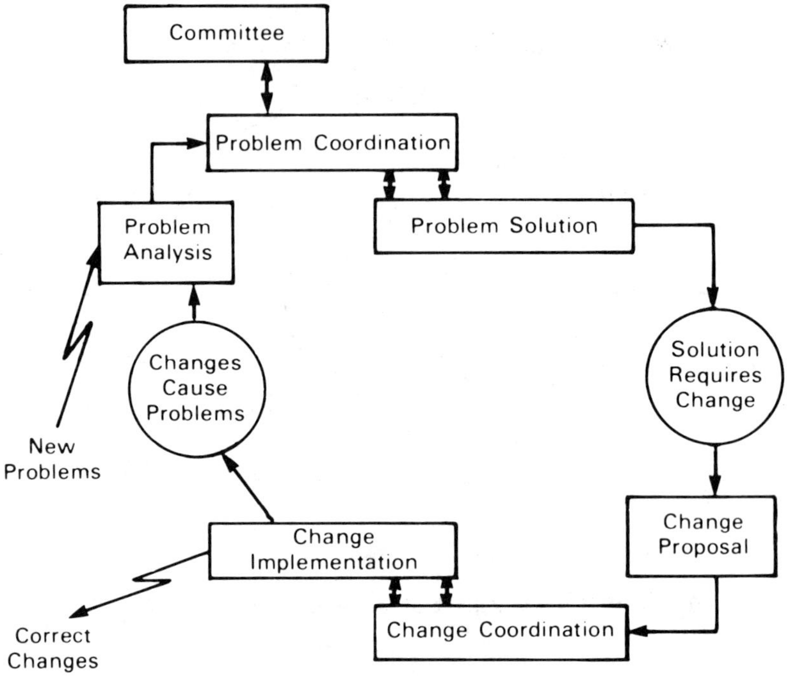


**Figure 3.21** Organizational Framework of Change Management

Time necessary to complete a project

Financial resources required

Personnel requirements to effect changes

Integration with current production

It is possible to accomplish rather substantial changes as long as they are accompanied by controls on the part of the updating services.

## 3.4 Data Processing Organization

The extensive spectrum of technical possibilities today presents a wide field of goals in data processing management. The following requirements are in the foreground of a mixed online/batch system:

User accommodation

Economy

Availability

Ease of maintenance

Security and reliability

The computer center manager must therefore establish an operational philosophy that affects all areas of the computer center as well as allowing for the possibilities of distributed data processing. This means that the established goals are occasionally in a contradictory relationship.

The electronic data processing system is at the core of all data processing operations. The primary responsibility of a computer center is to operate this system with the highest possible efficiency. It is not always possible to list generally valid directions and guidelines—the organization, extent, and content of these guidelines is affected to a large degree by the most diverse factors, of which the following exercise the greatest influence:

- *Size of installation*. Different standards are needed for a relatively small system with 256K storage capacity than for a large computer with several million operations per second and a storage capacity of several megabytes.
- *Equipment features*. This pertains not only to the differences between a purely disk-operated installation and one with a number of tape stations but also to the extent of peripheral paper devices. Equipment features are largely determined by type of application which in turn indirectly affects the organization of machine operations.
- *Job characteristics*. These influence the operating instructions of applications programs and thus determine machine room operations.
- *Teleperiphery*. This must take into account type and extent, as well as percentage participation in total telecommunications load.
- *Installation utilization*. A data processing installation with an average workload and one shift is more easily organized into a problem-free and smooth operation than one running full tilt around the clock.
- *Operating system*. This is generally determined by type and method (e.g., batch or real time), and affects machine operating instructions. Today's EDP systems are exclusively run by means of operating systems which support the entire communication with machine operations. Machine operators thus receive instruction in their specific operation system and need retraining with changeovers to new systems. At this juncture the positive advantages offered by the possibilities of virtual machines are evident; they can also reshape computer center organization.

Since the effectiveness of an EDP system rises and falls with the abilities, qualifications, and dedication of its operating personnel, it is extremely important to support the systems operators by means of organizational measures and operating instructions. Materials must therefore be available that allow them to utilize all types of program-run supports and to recognize and remedy interruptions on their own. Some of these materials concern systems programs and are discussed separately in section 3.4.5. Applications programs in this context will be discussed more fully in connection with program documentaion in section 3.5.2.

The growth of teleprocessing tasks also increases the demand for a failure-proof operation; this can be achieved only through systematic cooperation of hardware, software, and organizational measures. One point needs to be emphasized here: the old concept of maximum hardware utilization has been supplanted by system-oriented and applications-oriented goals.

### 3.4.1 General Operational Procedures

This includes a number of rules that are generally valid for an enterprise and belong among the house rules of a computer center. They are briefly summarized here for the sake of completeness. Brevity and precision are basic prerequisites for the formulation of rules in order to make information available as quickly as possible.

A complete enumeration is impossible here because many rules are contingent on the particularities of an enterprise, but the following rules are considered generally valid:

The machine room is to be kept free of everything that is not involved in currently running programs or program flow, such as old lists, cards, packing materials, and the like.

All incoming jobs are to be clearly marked at once.

All finished jobs or partial tasks are to be clearly labeled immediately and transferred to the control group.

Personal property has no place in the machine room but is to be kept in lockers in the operators' lounge.

Machine operations is responsible for cleaning the machines, especially card feeders, stackers, magnetic tape units, printers, and card punch devices according to a revolving schedule.

Quality and precision are a determining factor in data processing. As soon as any deficiencies are observed, such as poor printing or inaccurate punching, the shift supervisor or chief operator must be informed at once.

Hardware malfunctions must be reported at once and entered into the error protocol of the log. This entry should be as precise and complete as possible in order to facilitate the tracing and repair of defects.

Defects must be remedied as soon as possible even if they do not directly influence the work at hand. In many instances only immediate action can effectively remedy errors and their causes.

Operators should not work alone in the machine room. For reasons of safety and security a second person should always be nearby. Monitoring installations have not proven to be useful in this context.

Special caution is in order when working with or near moving parts. Clothing and hair styles should be geared to safety precautions.

Smoking is not permitted in the machine room, first because of highly sensitive fire alarm systems, and second because smoking itself is a fire hazard and creates extra dust around magnetic tape units.

All operators should be informed of the location of first aid stations.

Accidents must be reported at once and entered in the log. In the case of leased equipment the lessor should be notified as well.

Operators must know what to do in case of fire. Fire drills should be held at least once a year that include practice in the use of fire extinguishers.

Operators of data processing equipment must understand the function of the emergency switch.

Operators must know which data, if at all possible, can be recovered and in what way.

Safety precautions and accident prevention will be further discussed later in this chapter. The present summary of rules is merely intended to provide some suggestions for use in the computer center. Rules should be discussed with each operator in conjunction with operating instructions and should be acknowledged by signature.

Occasionally the question of shutting down EDP equipment in case of thunderstorms has been discussed. Experience to date has shown that no danger exists because a transformer between the power supply lines and the machinery reduces the tension. A certain danger does exist when the power supply comes in on an open-wire line, but this is rarely the case today. Power failures can cause significant disturbances with dialog systems, less on account of lost terminal time than because of interference with schedules in programming and originating departments.

### 3.4.2 Types of Operations

As already mentioned, the characteristics of applications indirectly affect EDP operations. The organizational integration of the computer center into the enterprise and the goal of cost-efficient EDP operations has resulted in the development of different operating methods which need support through organizational measures.

#### 3.4.2.1 Open Shop

In this type of operation the EDP equipment is not operated exclusively by specific operating personnel but also by the programmers. Each programmer has the option of running his or her program, whether routine or testing, on the equipment. Machine operators may provide assistance if available.

Open shops are found predominantly in small, occasionally in medium-sized installations or special applications systems. They are not appropriate for large installations with multiprogram operating systems because the original advantages of this type—following printer output and possible intervention with the program run—are no longer possible. In a multiprogram operation printer output occurs only at the end of a run. Program runs can also no longer be patched from the console. Data security and confidentiality make open shops unfeasible today.

ADVANTAGES OF OPEN-SHOP OPERATIONS

- Communication between the EDP system and programming is facilitated because programmers have direct access to the equipment. Problems occurring during a run can immediately be analyzed and remedied, and misunderstandings due to complicated problem analyses are avoided.
- Programs can be tested more easily and quickly if the appropriate prerequisites are present. This presupposes that the programmer has the technical qualifications, is trained in machine operations, and has a certain amount of experience.
- Because programmers gather experience in and understanding of machine operations, they are better able to prevent possible untenable operating difficulties when developing programs.
- Hardware characteristics can be better utilized by the applications program, and applications, particularly in special operations (such as real time) can be more easily tested. This is especially important when not all equipment is supported by the operating system.

DISADVANTAGES OF AN OPEN SHOP

- The work experience of systems operators is not fully utilized in daily routine operations.
- Since intervention with a program run is possible, corrections and changes from one program to another cause idle time. This diminishes machine

utilization and increases the cost of testing. Before a computer center manager changes to open shop for testing in special cases, the costs of this should be calculated to determine whether they justify the time gained.

- Programmers should be trained in machine operation. This is expensive but necessary both for the programmer's work and the entire operational process.
- Program runs in open shops often lead to tricky programming which is difficult to test and service in routine jobs, especially when the programmer has changed employers. EDP installations today are less limited in their resources than they were 8–10 years ago when programming tricks were occasionally necessary for reasons of capacity. Today such programming is more costly in terms of time than perhaps an expansion of storage facilities.
- With today's often rather extensive accumulation of data the danger of data corruption or destruction is not to be underestimated. The damages caused by inexperienced or insufficiently trained operators can be significant. Much greater care needs to be taken in controlling the time periods during which no personnel is allowed to be present in the machine room.
- The possibility of program correction from the console often leads to incomplete documentation. Occasionally, in order to save time, program changes are improperly recorded with the result that the programmer himself cannot remember why the program works or does not work.
- Machine utilization decreases in open shops. This makes test runs more costly, as already mentioned. But it also necessitates earlier expansion of capacity if idle time cannot be utilized for production.
- The use of higher programming languages (ALGOL, COBOL, FORTRAN, PL/1) and more complex operating systems results in additional problems for open shops because, due to the relocatability of programs, absolute addresses are no longer known.

The advantages of open shops are simply no longer justifiable for EDP systems except for small installations and in special cases such as software testing in the manufacturer's computer center or testing of real-time programs. The increasing opportunities offered by dialog operations have diminished the number of open shop proponents.

### 3.4.2.2 Closed Shop

In closed shops, operation of the EDP system is carried out exclusively by specialized personnel. In a closed operations process the job originator can no longer influence the job process following job submission. The concept of batch processing is increasingly identified with closed-shop operations because it is especially suited for that purpose. The necessity for a means of communication between job originator and operator becomes more pronounced.

The operating system provides an essential support structure by means of its control language (JCL). Communication between programming and the EDP system proceeds for the most part, sometimes exclusively, via the operating system. All instructions necessary for a program run, which in installations with or without insufficient operating systems needs to be in the form of an instruction booklet for machine operations, can now be accomplished by means of parameters in control statements. They include, among others:

Name of programmer and project

Password to protect against unauthorized use

Program name

Materials requirements, such as disks, tapes, main storage, I/O devices

Requests for data files and specifications about their characteristics, such as 7-track tapes of a file extending over 5 spools

Specifications on translators or utility programs to be used

Specifications on a termination program to be originated in case of error (storage contents, register contents, etc.)

This by no means exhaustive listing shows that the advantages of a closed shop are scarcely utilized without an operating system, and that program testing is occasionally simpler and safer than in an open shop operation.

A conversion from open to closed shop requires not only organizational changes in the computer center but a considerable amount of reeducation on the part of programmers; it presupposes possible additional technical resources. One should at any rate guard against allowing the computer center to isolate the users and frustrate the employees. Mutual understanding for the work to be done can easily be destroyed permanently. Only an appropriate extension of service functions (section 2.4.8) can succeed in satisfying the users on the one hand and motivating employees on the other. This will lead to a better understanding of what they are doing.

A summary of the advantages of a closed shop produces the following picture.

#### Advantages of a Closed Shop

- Routine jobs are done easily and with fewer errors, because the work process can be better planned in advance and the job run is carried out by experienced operators rather than specialized outsiders. This is an important point because today, many years after the introduction of electronic devices, when the emphasis is no longer on future realization of EDP projects but rather on efficient and cost-efficient production.

- An operating system, together with efficient job preparation, can achieve a high degree of productivity and service capability. These qualities are especially important today because after the many years of costly EDP introduction the computer center is expected to justify the investment.

- A closed shop requires complete program documentation to be developed and maintained. This is an essential safety factor. Operating and sequence errors decrease along with a decrease in costs for corrections and reruns.

- Programmers need not be trained in machine operation. This is a minor advantage, because even in programming modern systems some knowledge of machine operation is helpful, and in dialog operations a subset of operator commands is permitted at the terminal.

- Program tests must be prepared at the programmer's desk. This may lengthen test periods because of waiting periods, but it significantly reduces machine usage. The question may well be asked whether a reduction of turnaround time during testing could not be achieved by other means. In this sense large installations no longer have specific testing periods, such as mornings from 11 to 12 o'clock or afternoons from 4 to 5 o'clock, and program tests can be run concurrently. Other measures are the installation of a remote batch station as an express station for test runs in the programming department (section 7.4), or the use of dialog terminals and with it the removal of testing from batch operations.

Disadvantages of a Closed Shop

- A lack of direct communication between the EDP system and the programmer may cause delays in testing. This disadvantage can be remedied by organizational measures.

- Misunderstandings between machine operation and programming are possible. This could be advantageous under certain circumstances because it can uncover gaps in documentation.

- Systems operation is further and further removed from applications and identifies itself less and less with actual job runs. There is occasional lack of motivation which repeatedly needs to be stimulated.

Since despite all the advantages testing in a closed shop cannot be carried out consistently, for example in testing special systems characteristics or in especially tight scheduling situations, occasional intermediate solutions cannot be avoided.

Among these, the introduction of a dialog system for programming is recommended. This will be discussed in more detail in section 3.4.2.6.

### 3.4.2.3 Mixed Operation

When an EDP system is not consistently operated as a closed shop it is referred to as a mixed operation. This means that some part of the programs are run by the machine operators while the rest, usually tests, are the responsibility of programmers or employees of specific departments.

When an EDP system is not fully utilized, open shop testing is permissible during the night or on weekends. However, it is important to avoid situations in which programmers with access to the equipment preempt machinery to the exclusion of the operating team or use operators as their assistants. This will rapidly frustrate the operators who are entrusted with the machinery by virtue of their job description. Experience shows that active intervention on the part of programmers causes tension at the machine which must and can be avoided. A further danger of a mixed operation is that it tends to result in overtime for programming, and that additional night work is traditionally prone to producing errors. This in turn cancels out the advantage of shorter test periods. Another factor to be considered is that when a machine is released to a programmer, errors are likely to occur—for example, when documents are no longer at their accustomed place after the programmer has used a machine. Finally, in a mixed operation there is always the possibility that controls can be circumvented and illegal systems use is thus facilitated.

In summary it can be stated that mixed operation is suitable in the following cases and with appropriate controls:

- When programmers and machine operators form part of the same personnel team, as is the case in many small EDP systems.
- If the equipment is not fully utilized during time periods when no machine operation is planned.
- During changeovers from open to closed shop operations. This time period should be kept to a minimum, even though some of the programmers —usually the older and more experienced among them—have difficulty adjusting to a consistent closed shop.
- In exceptional cases when special systems characteristics are being tested. If properly planned, however, such periods can be used simultaneously for machine operator training.

### 3.4.2.4 Unattended Operation

An examination of computer center personnel shows that the number of employees involved in systems operation is steadily decreasing, especially in auxiliary functions. Work today is frequently planned in such a way that the systems are operated on only two shifts, while on nights and weekends the operation runs unattended. This term is deceptive insofar as a system cannot be allowed to run completely without personal supervision. One can only perform precautionary activities for certain unattended periods. Therefore it would be more appropriate to speak in terms of a "limited attendance" operation. However, this word has not come into current usage although it correctly describes many pure dialog systems.

If it is necessary to examine the possibility of introducing unattended operation for certain periods of time it becomes evident that there is a variety of individual components, and that one must distinguish between batch and dialog operations. Thus there is no exhaustive list of prerequisites. However, the following points provide some concrete suggestions:

Systems operation can be achieved through computer linkage. Many activities involved in systems control can be transmitted by another (operated) station. The use of so-called line computers that do not require an operator is another possibility.

Mass storage systems are a basic prerequisite for unattended operation, which is facilitated by the development of disk storage with constantly rising capacities and nonremovable disk packs.

Magnetic tape jobs are limited to the most important activities such as archive and shipping purposes.

Job cycles are checked for unattended load. Occasionally unattended partial periods can be run separately.

COM can be subcontracted.

Job runs should be automated through program controlled execution of processes.

Job preparation should be accomplished via video data terminal (VDT) inside of the shift.

Individual departments could possibly be organizationally adapted to the rhythm of attended shifts.

With online entry an end-of-day run can be moved up and handled by individual departments. Data entered after this artificial cut-off point count towards the next day.

It needs to be emphasized that unattended shifts do not achieve the same degree of systems utilizations as attended shifts, but the elimination of night and weekend shifts more than compensates for that. The use of special systems utility programs for planning control is equally noteworthy, for example, by means of the IBM OPC system (Operation Planning and Control).

In addition to these rather general guidelines it should be noted that an unattended operation must be supported by the operating system in at least the following points:

Automatic recovery of hardware errors must be achieved.

Deadlocks must be avoided if at all possible.

Jobs requiring attended devices (such as printers) must be preempted.

The systems parameters required for this type of operation must be easily adjustable.

Periodic jobs for systems administration must be started automatically.

Priority control must be adaptable to unattended operations.

Beyond that a number of general prerequisites are in order, such as automatic shutdown in case of air-conditioning failure and general safety and security precautions. An astonishingly large number of programs can be adapted to this type of operation. Jobs requiring operators can be separated and shifted to attended time periods (for example, data backup on magnetic tapes).

### 3.4.2.5 Remote Job Entry

The technical possibility of setting up input/output devices outside of the machine room and even operating them at some distance from the EDP system offers new processing opportunities, which in the case of special requirements minimize the disadvantages of open and closed shops.

Such separate input/output stations, usually consisting of card readers and quick printers, are known as remote job entry stations. Usually these stations are hooked up to the EDP system by telecommunications devices, among them data link controls at the output of a multiplex channel or telecommunications computer; a modem can be installed at the other end of the line (which can be a simple telephone line) if a second modem for modulation or demodulation is required. In addition to that, other realizations are possible, some more sophisticated, some less costly.

The organizational advantages of remote job entry stations should be pointed out first. In large computer centers testing processes called express stations have been particularly successful.

In one particular case a simulation program was developed before introducing the express station, which experimentally compared conventional program testing procedures (at times using transport vehicles) with a remote job entry operation. The comparison test clearly demonstrated the superiority of the procedures described here. It should be mentioned, however, that in the above mentioned case a separate air-conditioning system was developed. This is no longer a requirement for all such devices available on the market today.

Another variation in operating an express station is that it does not necessarily have to be operated by in-house personnel. If the choice of equipment is determined by the need for a simple and therefore safe operation, there is no need to hire an extra employee; at the same time the technical desires of the programmers can be satisfied. However, it is impossible to do without regular controls on the part of computer center staff, so that a completely open-shop operation of an express station is feasible only in the immediate proximity of the computer center. This has been confirmed by the experiences of several computer centers. The practice of directly connecting an express station (without telecommunications devices) to the data processing system, and operating it next door to the machine room with a window in the connecting wall has proven successful. Such a station is ready to function even when the communications network or the line computer fails, and can operate a quick printer or magnetic tape at full speed.

Dialog terminals and express stations make similar demands in terms of continuity and security as real-time systems. Short-term and medium-term data retention on direct access storage devices must be given special attention. But the operation of remote job entry stations from the point of view of systems usage planning is a variant of a normal batch mode system, because the entire systems input does not run centrally over one job preparation. In order to avoid surprises, especially in a well-planned and well-utilized EDP system, only short programs should be run in this manner. Today's operating systems support control of the limited resource demands. Since large programs are combined with large input/output volumes, the relatively slow communication line represents a limiting factor. The situation is different in pure service centers such as universities and research institutes, where strictly scheduled jobs are less predominant and the input/output less extensive than in commercial computer centers.

### 3.4.2.6 Time-Sharing Dialog Systems

When separating task setting and machine operations, certain difficulties emerge that negatively influence program tests. Among other things this was the cause for the development of special operations that permit open job runs on data terminals despite a closed shop operation. Because it allows conversations between terminal operators and the EDP system it is known as a "dialog operation."

In this operation, terminals (teleprinters, electric typewriters, or video display terminals) are directly hooked up to the EDP system. Now a program can be developed and tested in a dialog between man and machine. This is called "time-sharing." The program runs of specific applications jobs can be observed as well; this is a "partnership operation." Examples are booking and information systems.

Dialog operations do not differ from remote job entry in the conditions they impose on the computer center. In terms of hardware the EDP system must be equipped for dialog terminal hookups. Systems usage planning must ensure that the jobs that are brought to the EDP system do not run over normal systems input. It goes without saying that with teleperiphery hookups programmers do not operate equipment independently.

Since dialog operation generally does not require operators (tapes and plotters are not absolutely necessary, and certain dialog languages do not permit their use), it can be made available as an additional computer center service even during unattended periods. There is no increased risk even if the equipment runs on nights and weekends with the paper periphery turned off, as long as appropriate automatic control measures are used.

### 3.4.2.7 Computer Networks

Publications about computer networks have increased significantly during the past few years, but for the most part only technical problems have been considered. However, organizational problems in this form of data processing are no less important and frequently do not correspond to the technical possibilities. It is not only a question of breaking through psychological barriers among the users in programming and individual departments who prefer local EDP capacity, but of solving a number of other problems as well:

Usage times must be agreed upon

Usage charges must be calculated

A network advisory service should be developed

Availability is to be guaranteed

The special characteristics of all groups must be considered

The communication system of both parties involved is of special importance. The problems of operating line computers which from a technical point of view belong to the network but do not represent separate EDP systems for the user are considerably less complex.

In using the term "network" the question of whether the systems involved are operated under one or several organizations initially remains open. The operations organization of the entire network needs to be developed accordingly. The types of systems used result in a further subdivision:

Identical data processing systems are linked to identical operating systems.

Identical data processing systems are linked to different operating systems.

Different systems of different manufacturers are linked together.

The reasons for a computer network, which have been examined initially only in reference to the simplest cases can, however, be expanded and applied more generally. The following considerations emerge with respect to the operations organization:

*System availability*: Switchover capability in case of partial failure, available via terminals and data administration, etc.

*Capacity expansion*: Realizeable in small increments and adapted to applications requirements.

*Distribution of computer center services over several systems*: For example one system can only perform batch operations, the other only dialog operations.

*Maximum suitability of special services*: Not all partial systems need costly and rarely used software components for their implementation.

*Shared expenditures*.

Thus the realization of a computer network is essentially determined by a concrete cost-benefit analysis which may affect the characteristics of the operations organization. Systems operation may be over shared consoles, and hardware and software debugging requires special techniques.

### 3.4.3 Job Descriptions of Computer Operations

This section focuses exclusively on the technical prerequisites for machine operation. The central tasks of operating fall into two qualitatively distinct groups:

- In systems operations via console the operator is responsible for the entire system of that particular shift.
- Auxiliary services are performed only by special instructions (change paper, adjust printer, insert tapes, etc.)

The tendency is to decrease the activities of the second group or shift them over to the users, while the qualitative requirements imposed on the first group are on the increase. Requirements pertaining to the operating system are to be derived from the manufacturer's literature; they are included in these organizational considerations only in an overall sense.

The operation of applications programs running over the EDP system will be discussed in conjunction with program description and job documentation in section 3.5.2. All this forms the basis for machine operation. Technical operating instructions are compiled in a manual located near the console, and should be familiar to operating personnel in all its details.

Operating instructions for applications programs are made available in job preparation to keep them handy during program runs. In the case of programmed interruptions (announced by console printout), machine operators must react according to operating instructions. This means that the documentation should include measures to be taken for each interruption.

Programmed interruptions of applications programs are distinguished from systems interruptions. If these interruptions can be handled without influencing the program run (such as failure of a tape unit), operators should remedy the problem while maintaining all necessary safety precautions, for example, by declaring the unit as unknown and changing the definition. In the case of more critical systems interruptions, such as the failure of a main storage module, the run may have to be terminated. At any rate a report must be made to systems support, job preparation, and the chief operator.

### 3.4.3.1 Console Operations

In EDP systems of the first and second generation machines were operated from the console just as they are today. But as soon as a program run is supported by an operating system the EDP system is only indirectly operated over the operator control panel: actual operation occurs by means of the operating system. This differentiates the range of tasks of the console operators in the two cases. Operation of the engineering panel does not count among the operator's actual tasks.

Hardly any other interface between the operating system and its environment is accompanied by as many technial problems as machine operation. This is due to the fact that in general there is no vocational training for machine operators. If one considers two identical EDP systems which are run by two different operating systems (for example IBM 3031 with operating systems DOS and OS), it is evident that machine operation from the operator control panel differs in essential points. The reason for this is that essential components of the EDP equipment are operated over the operating system. Even identical operating systems manifest differences not only in their configuration but in the organizational structure of the computer center.

A description of machine operation over an operating system must differentiate between two different types of operating activities. In the first, the initiative comes from the operator: this is the rare case. The following activities are included:

- Turning on the entire EDP system (cold start, warm restart, autoload, initial program load). This is usually in conjunction with determining the initial values of the systems parameters that describe the condition of the system.

- Shutting off the entire system. The problems involved in starting and stopping the system are discussed separately in section 3.4.3.4, along with the role of the operating system.

- Operator-initiated termination of a job or run, for various reasons. Generally a personal decision on the part of the operator or supervisor is the determining factor.

- Inspection of queues or tables within the operating system.
- Inspection of individual program runs. This can be handled by the console operators, as in general there is no output of all details, and video display consoles do not require information on prior results.
- Alternative solutions, to be found in case of system components failure. If a disk unit fails it must be reported to the operating system, for example by means of a down report.
- Establishment or alteration of program priorities.
- A repeat of the primary systems output in multiprogram installations. This can be requested, possibly depending on specific job instructions. An example could be a multiple printing process if copies cannot be made otherwise.
- Starting foreground and background programs, such as SPOOL programs.

In the second type, the initiative comes from the operating system. Since the operating system itself generates many reports on the internal process to the operator, either on the screen or the keyboard of the control panel, it is necessary to have these reports specifically identified. The operating system OS/370 accomplishes this with an action indicator that is the last letter of a six-digit report code. Differences in activities to be anticipated can thus be identified as follows:

- Pure information, but for a specific reason, such as use of the wrong program name.
- An expected operator activity without response at the operator console, for example if the printer is not turned on or not operational.
- An expected operator activity with response at the console; example: a tape mark is to be overwritten.
- An expected operator activity with response at the console; example: a tape is requested and must be mounted and allocated from the console.
- Reports on program terminations, for example in case of specific machine defects.

This type of machine operation via console will be illustrated by means of two operating systems.

**Example 1:** Operating system OS/370 with different action indicators

**A** (await action). Operator intervention is required before the program can be continued, for example: IBC158A WRONG TAPE ON cuu. MOUNT PROPER TAPE

**D** (await decision). Operator intervention is required before the program can be continued, for example: IEC601P Mddd ser REPLY = SKIP VOL OR MOUNTING

**I** (information message). The console output gives only information and requires no operator activity, for example: IEF1421 PGNAME MORE THAN 8 CHAR

**S** (processing stopped). Processing is interrupted because of a machine error

**W** (wait). The processing of specific programs is delayed until the operator has performed the required activity, for example: IEF402W SELECTED UNIT INVALID

**Example 2:** Operating system MASTER of the CDC3300 with report types

**D** (destructive). Information on program termination, for example: D Job 1 DEF 63

**I** (informative). Program run information, for example: 1 EXEC 171 DP...

**A** (operator action). Operator intervention is required before the program run can be continued, for example: A EXEC 103...

**R** (operator action with response). Operator intervention with response is required before the program can be continued, for example: R SINT 007 (DATE)

These brief examples demonstrate the extent of machine operations available at the console with the support of an operating system and the significant degree of difference between systems. Reference to manufacturers' operating guides is strongly recommended, therefore, even though sometimes they have the disadvantage of not containing the special systems adaptations of respective installations. Usually special console manuals need to be developed for each system, which can also be used as training manuals.

The trend with operating systems is clearly in the direction of relieving operators to an increasing degree. There is little opportunity for relief in the operation of peripherals—for example, in changing forms, feeding punched cards, or putting on tapes; improvements in this area are slow to develop through technical innovations such as self-loading tapes or disk packs. This type of situation causes a great discrepancy between the quick but intellectually little challenged operational aide and the systems operator. It is the goal of computer center organization to diminish this gap by providing opportunities for advancement in the computer center. The installation of secondary consoles for special tasks such as the allocation of peripheral alternate storage devices is a first step in this direction.

One special feature of console operation deserves mentioning: the systems restart procedures after a possible systems failure. In a pure batch processing operation, systems terminations and restarts are relatively simple. The terminated programs just have to be reloaded and their data files returned to the condition existing prior to the terminated process. In the case of sequential files this means repositioning the input files and erasing the output files; the incomplete lists of the terminated job have to be destroyed. The situation is different in online systems with random access data files, because the data are continuously accessed and subject to constant alteration. Added to this are other problems:

Several parallel transactions may process the same files.

Systems input may not be in the form of a file that can be positioned and read at will but the handiwork of many users. Repeat runs of such input is not only an unreasonable expectation but may lead to entirely different results

The online system must be available at short notice

Even though the development of suitable restart methods is the responsibility of systems development, the computer center management needs to be concerned with making appropriate standardized restart methods available. It is here that the service performance of a computer center vis-à-vis its users is noticeable—in the degree of systems availablility.

### 3.4.3.2 Magnetic Media Handling

The extremely varying qualities of these devices make a general description rather difficult. Nevertheless, some general statements on the operation of devices with magnetic media are needed. For detailed specifications the manufacturer's literature should be consulted. Together, the general and the specific information form the basis for written periphery operating instructions. Magnetic tape operators frequently work at separate stations (secondary consoles), which indicate only the messages relevant to their specific tasks.

#### Magnetic Drums

Magnetic drums require practically no operator because the storage medium is not removable and the high rotational speed of drum units does not allow the device to be turned off, generally even during nonworking hours.

#### Magnetic Tape Units

Magnetic tape units require particularly conscientious operation, as unclean and careless work causes immediate operational disturbances and significantly increases the rate of read-write errors. The following guidelines should be observed in the operation and care of magnetic tape units:

Insertion of tapes into the units designated by the console operator.

Identification of output tapes by means of labels, and removal of the write-enable rings.

Removal of defective tape segments at the beginning of reels.

Identification of tape units for specific functions or status, for example, off-line spool units.

Regular cleaning of tape units, generally every 8–10 operating hours; read-write heads, vacuum shafts, and feed mechanisms must be cleaned with a special cleaning fluid such as isopropyl alcohol and dust-free dry rags (tissue or leather). The entire area should be gone over a second time with a leather rag to remove all alcohol traces. The capstan rolls should only be cleaned with leather. Cleaning activities must be recorded in a log (Figure 3.22).

There are numerous references in the literature pertaining to the handling of magnetic tapes. They are briefly summarized here, even though they are not all equally important or applicable, especially with self-feeding devices:

Tape reels should be removed from their plastic containers only prior to loading; the containers should then be closed to keep them dust-free.

If the spool has been secured with a ring lock it should not be released until the tape has been loaded (not applicable to self-feeding devices).

**Machine Cleaning Log**

**Device:** **Month:**

| Day | Shift | | Cleaning Per Shift | | | | | | | | | | Quick Printers | | Cleaning Per Day | | | | |
|---|---|---|---|---|---|---|---|---|---|---|---|---|---|---|---|---|---|---|---|
| | | | Magnetic Tape Units | | | | | | | | | | | | Punched Cards Entry | Punched Cards Exit | Page Printer | | |
| | | | 00 | 01 | 02 | 03 | 04 | 05 | 06 | 07 | 08 | 09 | L1 | L2 | | | | | |
| 16. | 1 | | | | | | | | | | | | | | | | | | |
| | 2 | | | | | | | | | | | | | | | | | | |
| | 3 | | | | | | | | | | | | | | | | | | |
| 17. | 1 | | | | | | | | | | | | | | | | | | |
| | 2 | | | | | | | | | | | | | | | | | | |
| | 3 | | | | | | | | | | | | | | | | | | |
| 18. | 1 | | | | | | | | | | | | | | | | | | |
| | 2 | | | | | | | | | | | | | | | | | | |
| | 3 | | | | | | | | | | | | | | | | | | |
| 19. | 1 | | | | | | | | | | | | | | | | | | |
| | 2 | | | | | | | | | | | | | | | | | | |
| | 3 | | | | | | | | | | | | | | | | | | |
| 20. | | | | | | | | | | | | | | | | | | | |
| | 2 | | | | | | | | | | | | | | | | | | |
| | 3 | | | | | | | | | | | | | | | | | | |

**Figure 3.22** Log for Regular Cleaning of Peripherals during Operating Hours

Tape spools must not be pressed but should be handled by placing the thumb in the center and 4 fingers lightly around the rim.

Care should be taken to avoid dropping the ends of tapes or entire reels.

When loading a tape, press down firmly on the core of the spool.

Soiled tapes should be cleaned with a nonshredding fabric and special cleaning fluid.

Magnetic tapes should not be touched after loading; if this cannot be prevented, care should be taken not to touch the rough side.

When removing a tape, the tape unit should not be opened until the entire tape has been unloaded.

When the tape is unwound from the loaded reel, the reel should always be turned by the finger sprockets to avoid bending the tape edges.

Before returning a reel to its container, the outer tape layer (i.e. the beginning of the tape) should always be fastened with a piece of foam rubber.

Tapes should be returned to their containers immediately after use; the container is to be closed at once.

Tapes are not to be placed on warm surfaces such as card or tape units.

Tapes should under no circumstances be bent.

Tape units are to be cleaned regularly—for example, once per shift or per day, according to the cleaning instructions in the operating manual.

Operating and maintenance personnel should not wear garments with shredding fibers, such as fuzzy sweaters.

Tapes should be tested for read-write errors at regular intervals and cut if necessary (scratch tapes approximately every two weeks, tapes in storage every 6–9 months).

Reflector markers are to be attached approximately 8–10 turns from the beginning; they must under no circumstances protrude.

Tapes must be stored upright in closed containers or with ring locks in place; storage cabinets must be dirt- and dust-free.

Air-conditioning requirements during storage should be carefully maintained (for Mylar: 20–80% relative humidity, 10–20°C; for HD 20–80% relative humidity, 4–50°C).

Smoking should not be allowed in rooms where magnetic tapes are used.

Prior to usage, tapes must be stored at the prescribed climatic conditions for at least 24 hours.

Inscribed tapes must not be exposed to magnetic fields; the permitted maximum is 50 oersted (for example, a 4 cm distance from a 1000 ampere power line). Danger of destruction exists primarily during transport in cars, where tapes should not be placed near the ignition coil.

The plastic tape containers should be checked for dirt and dust and cleaned regularly.

During transport tapes should be protected against shock, dust, magnetic fields, and rapid temperature changes.

Special tape cleaning devices have proven very successful. Cleaning is recommended after approximately every 100 runs. This figure is based on observed error susceptibility in actual tape usage (Figure 3.23). A number of operating systems support tape cleaning activities by generating cleaning instructions at the console according to preestablished criteria.

The time periods for individual operating tasks with no self-feeding tape units are as follow:

| | |
|---|---|
| Insert or remove tape: | 2 minutes per spool |
| Change tape: | 3 minutes per spool |
| Rewind tape at 30 KB: | up to 5 minutes per tape |
| Rewind tape at 120 KB: | up to 1.2 minutes per tape |

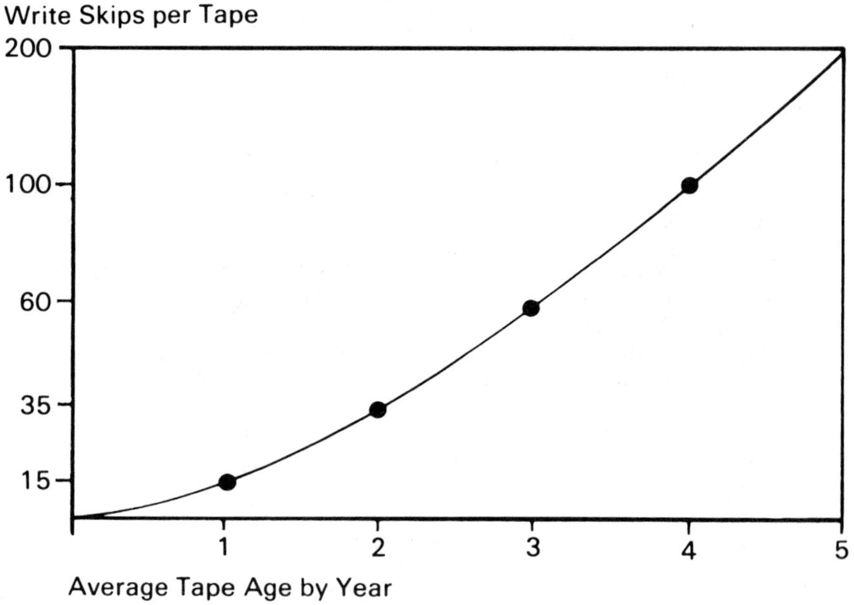


**Figure 3.23** Observations on Error Susceptibility of Magnetic Tapes

Obviously these times are guidelines only for conventional tape devices and deviations are possible in individual cases. Beyond that, time required in handling magnetic tapes depends largely on the personal qualities of the operators. Operating time in self-feeding tape stations which are widely used today is reduced to about one-fourth, without considering the time needed for administrative tasks in conjunction with tape set-up activities.

#### Magnetic Disk Devices

The operation of disk devices is generally simpler than that of tape devices. In addition, data media exchange usually does not occur as frequently and today's large-capacity disks no longer have that capability. In general, the following activities belong to the operation and maintenance of magnetic disk devices:

Disks are to be inserted into the units specified by the console operator.

Disk units should be identified with the volume number of the inserted disk.

Cleaning of disk devices is frequently handled by technical maintenance personnel during regular preventive maintenance calls.

Prior to loading a disk pack a brief visual control should be conducted, with special emphasis on the following points:

- External damage
- Scratches on the disk surface
- Contamination of the disk surface
- Condition of the air filter on the underside
- Condition of the thread around the bolt which fastens the disk to the device

Occurrences of read-write errors in a disk pack are under no circumstances to be corrected by changing the device; it increases the danger of transferring the error undeteced to other devices. Instead, the error is to be corrected through control and by cleaning the disk pack on the same device.

Operating times of magnetic disk devices are as follows:

| | |
|---|---|
| Insert disk pack: | 1 minute per pack |
| Change disk pack: | 3 minutes per pack |

A number of guidelines exist for handling magnetic disk packs, of which the following are generally valid:

Disks must be stored horizontally.

Cleanliness is absolutely essential.

Disk containers are to be kept scrupulously clean.

The disk storage lid must remain closed, regardless of whether or not a disk pack is in place.

Disk packs should never be stored outside of the disk drive except in their plastic containers.

Disk packs that have been damaged externally or dropped (even slightly) must be checked by a technician before reuse.

Disk packs should not be exposed to strong magnetic fields to prevent destruction of data.

Smoking should not be permitted in work areas involving magnetic disks; cigarette ashes may damage the read-write heads.

Disk packs should not be stored on top of each other, but rather side by side.

Disk packs should be placed only on level surfaces, as an uneven surface may cause deformities.

Disk packs should be stored at machine room temperature of 18–28°C and 10–80% relative humidity.

Following transport a disk pack should be allowed a period of at least 2 hours to adjust to the climatic conditions of the machine room.

Disk packs are to be stored in clean and locked metal cabinets or other fireproof containers; they should never be exposed to direct sunlight.

Disk packs are to be cleaned approximately every 4 weeks as follows:

1. Clean bulbs and inside of sleeve with a nonshredding cloth, cotton swab, or the like.
2. Insert disk pack in the turned-off storage device.
3. Wrap a clean, nonshredding cloth around a plastic pin, and moisten with isopropyl alcohol (do not soak the cloth).
4. Turn the disk pack manually and insert the pin between the disks, continue turning while cleaning upper and lower surfaces. Remove pin while continuing to turn.
5. Repeat this process with a dry, nonshredding cloth wrapped around a plastic pin.
6. Repeat steps 3–5 until all disk surfaces are clean.
7. Clean the upper and lower surfaces of the disk pack with a nonshredding cloth and isopropyl alcohol.
8. If necessary, clean the cartridge with nonshredding cloth and isopropyl alcohol.
9. Remove disk pack and insert in cartridge.

The condition of the air filter on the underside of the disk pack must be checked at regular intervals. A clean filter is white in appearance, a soiled one dark gray. A heavily soiled filter interferes with the air stream that carries the read-write heads, causing them to rub against the disks and damaging the magnetic layer and heads. Soiled filters must be removed promptly as follows:

1. Remove the bottom of the cartridge.
2. Pull the rubber ring from the hub of the disk pack; this ring contains the filter.
3. Exchange filter.
4. Return the rubber ring to its position around the hub.
5. Replace the bottom of the cartridge.

Even though magnetic disks are less susceptible to soilage than tapes, these guidelines should be upheld, since damage to disks is considerably more costly than damage to tapes.

#### Mass Storage Systems

These require virtually no specific operational expenditure and are therefore extremely suitable when introducing unattended operation.

#### Diskettes

Diskettes are used by all systems with intelligent terminals and distributed data processing. In this context they are important for the operation of EDP main systems because data input is particularly simple. For this reason diskette stations are rarely found in the machine rooms of central systems. Diskettes can easily be mailed.

### 3.4.3.3 Paper Periphery Operation

The operation of paper periphery such as card readers, card punchers, quick printers, perforated tape readers, and plotters still represents a significant portion of total operating expenditures. Occasionally, however, a trend away from paper is noticeable. Punched cards are becoming rare, and the increasing use of COM and video display terminals will definitely result in a decrease in machine operation. Paper periphery is frequently located in separate rooms because of the amount of dust produced.

#### Punched Card Readers

Punched card readers generally do not pose any special operating demands. Instructions are to be derived from the technical manual. A number of correctional measures can be taken in case of error reports. Card jams are almost always handled by operating personnel. The device must then be turned off and in most cases the carrier shaft has to be turned manually. Punched card readers should be serviced according to manufacturer's instructions.

The handling of punched cards, as any other data media, is governed by a series of rules. Even though they are equally valid for job preparation and data entry they are mentioned at this point for the sake of completeness, as follows:

New cards are to remain in their original cartons or in specially designated containers until needed for keypunching.

Punched cards should never lie around openly.

Punched cards that are being worked on are best kept in tubs.

No more than two cartons should be stacked on top of each other, otherwise the cards in the bottom carton will bend.

Before processing, cards should be stored under the climatic conditions of the machine room for 5 days.

Data cards must be properly identified.

Cards no longer in use should be removed from the machine room immediately.

Before processing, the card packs should be loosened up in order to remove dust or possible electrical charges.

Cards that need to be duplicated following a jam must be stored (with proper labeling) until the job with the duplicate card has been satisfactorily completed.

#### Card Punches

Card jams in card punches need to be treated more carefully than jams in readers. Depending on the frequency of use, punched card samples are to be checked periodically by means of a card gauge. Cleanup duties include regular removal of paper waste.

#### Quick Printers

The paper output of EDP systems is not likely to disappear in the next several years; the qualitative demands of the users are the determining factor here. The following activities belong to the operation and maintenance of quick printers:

The insertion of continuous tabulating paper or continuous form paper is one of the routine tasks of quick printer operations. The paper is fed into the device so that the form feed is properly adjusted and entries print out in their respective fields. The programs must run a sample printout for verification which has to be repeated until the adjustment is correct to within exactly 1 mm. Approximately 3 minutes are allocated for paper changes.

Paper must be replaced as soon as it runs out. An open carton of paper should be kept ready for that purpose.

Carriage control tapes are mounted according to program requirements.

Carriage control paper tapes must be prepared. These tapes should be checked regularly for signs of wear and tear. A replacement tape must be kept ready at all times.

The print chain must be checked to ensure that the type slugs always correspond to the program requirements.

Paper alignment and print display must be controlled. If incorrect, maintenance technicians must be notified.

The copies of multiple-ply output paper must be checked.

Changing the ribbon is also part of quick printer operations. It should be checked regularly for signs of wear and tear and replaced to avoid unusable output. This precaution reduces duplication of effort.

Quick printer lists must be separated and identified.

Corrections must be made when errors are indicated.

Printing units must be cleaned (once a day).

The operation of quick printers is associated with physical labor (transporting paper cartons) for which not everyone is suited. Paper transport, which at times is handled with dollies, is an integral part of printer operation.

#### Paper Tape

Paper tape is a very old data medium. Nevertheless it does not enjoy great popularity because it is not as easily handled as punched cards. The operation of paper tape devices includes the following tasks:

Paper tape insertion—the preparation of a paper tape reader for the read-in process requires approximately 3 minutes per spool; the same applies for the preparation of output devices

Adjustment of units to tape dimensions

Checking tape beginnings and sorting sequences

Handling correction when errors are indicated

Patching tapes when torn or damaged

Cleaning tape devices, including the perforator and its waste basket

As a general rule, breakdowns and defects to all peripheral devices must be reported to the shift supervisor.

The list of guidelines for the treatment and storage of paper tapes is not as extensive as that for magnetic data media. The following recommendations are made:

Perforated tapes should be rolled up and stored in transparent plastic containers.

All containers must be appropriately labeled.

Oiled tapes should not be allowed to come in contact with optical read stations. Therefore, oiled and plain tapes must be handled separately.

Tape containers must always be clearly labeled, including the file and job names as well as the beginning and end.

### 3.4.3.4 Start-Up and Shut-Down Procedures

Since EDP systems are generally operated around the clock, start-up and shut-down activities are not among the daily recurring duties of machine operations. Therefore special care should be taken in developing instructions for power-on and power-off procedures of the total system, which will then be incorporated into the console manual. The points listed here should be understood as guidelines which must be adapted to the specific configuration of a particular computer center. In large centers it is advisable to add a room diagram identifying all items in question in numerical order, including switches, doors, etc.

*System Start-Up*

Obtain key for power supply at designated place

Turn on air-conditioning if necessary

Check climatic conditions by means of thermograph and hydrograph

Unlock and switch on power supply

Check power supply; usually a bell rings when the tolerance is impaired

Switch on the console and peripheral devices; usually there is a prescribed sequence

Cold start (Autoload, IPL); generally this is handled by a detailed but operating system-dependent procedural description

Enter in shift log (record machine counter number)

*System Shut-Down*

Enter commands for shutdown or transfer to unattended operation at the console

Start final jobs (salvage accounting or error logs)

Unload and switch off magnetic tape units, put away all tapes and disks —under no circumstances should units containing loaded tapes be switched off

Check card readers and punches for cards remaining in the tracks, put away all cards, including blanks, and empty wastebaskets

Remove the final printout and console output and staple together; shut off printer

Switch off power supply at the console

Switch off and lock main power supply

If required, adjust air conditioning, or shut off

Shut off printing card punch, if any, in the machine room

Enter in shift log (record machine counter number)

Make sure cabinets and devices are locked

Turn off lights

Make a final acoustic check: is everything quiet?

Lock room and deposit key at the designated place

A special protocol may be maintained on systems shutdown, which can serve as a completeness check for all prescribed activities as well. Moreover, such procedural descriptions can be developed for transitions to or from unattended operations and added to the console manual. Before the operators leave after completing their shift and the system runs unattended, it is necessary to prevent unplanned stops during the night, start background loads, expand output files, shut off other devices, and report this to system control so as to avoid unnecessary "hanging parties."

## 3.4.4 Shift Organization

It is one of the characteristics of a computer center that the EDP systems, which constitute a sizeable investment, should be operated around the clock, i.e., in three shifts with a possible fourth shift on weekends, for economic reasons. Shift operations in and of themselves are not at all unusual, but the shift operations of a computer center differ from traditional shifts insofar as highly qualified specialists who usually work normal and regular hours must work alternating shifts here. Thus the organization of a shift operation must especially consider the human angle.

Opinions differ as to the inclusion of older employees in computer center shifts. One attempts to avoid it instinctively, but other and positive points of view exist, especially where only two attended shifts are planned with unattended operations on nights and weekends. In any case care must be taken when setting up employment contracts for operators to allow for possible shift work. Details on personnel selection for such operations have been published extensively in scientific investigations and are available in the form of practical checklists.

Shift schedules, i.e., the assignment of operators to specific time intervals, are developed monthly by the chief operator. Operators who work well together as a team should, if at all possible, remain together in shift work. Changes in personnel composition have generally not proven successful in actual practice.

Shift changes are commonly scheduled for 6 A.M., 2 P.M. and 10 P.M. The shifts must overlap in such a way that an orderly transfer of work is guaranteed, usually by 20–30 minutes. Cyclic rotation usually occurs every weekend, although doctors and psychologists recommend longer turns per cycle. Turns of less than one week are not recommended. Experiences with two-week turns have proven very successful.

In a three-shift operation, rotation should be made from night shift to graveyard shift and from graveyard to morning shift. This has the advantage that operators changing from day shift to night shift have a long weekend, namely from Friday afternoon until Monday evening.

Shift schedules should contain information on absences due to vacation or participation in training programs, and should identify the shift supervisor and the individual responsible for order and cleanliness in the machine room. In addition, contingency plans should be made. Deviations from this schedule must have the approval of the computer center manager.

A shift protocol is necessary to ensure orderly shift changes. An example in the form of a numbered page from a shift log is provided in Figure 3.24. Sequential numbering of pages has proven successful for determining if pages have been removed. The following information is assembled in a shift log:

Shift name (morning, night, graveyard)

Date and time of start of shift

Shift was taken over from...

Shift was transferred to...

Page number of log at time of transfer

Entry for key transfer

Machine room personnel present, including times present; names and times of visitors expected, including reason for each visit

Shift Log No. **194**

| Protocol | Shift<br>I ☐ II ☐ III ☐<br>From To | Date Shift Begins<br>________ |
|---|---|---|

1. Attendance
Computer Center Personnel

| Name | From | To | Name | From | To |
|---|---|---|---|---|---|
| | | | | | |
| | | | | | |
| | | | | | |
| | | | | | |

Customers, Personnel, and Dept.

| Name, Firm, Department | From | To | Name, Firm, Department | From | To |
|---|---|---|---|---|---|
| | | | | | |
| | | | | | |
| | | | | | |
| | | | | | |
| | | | | | |
| | | | | | |

2 Remarks (special occurrences)

Machine not/Conditionally Operational

| From | To | Reason |
|---|---|---|
| | | |
| | | |
| | | |
| | | |
| | | |
| | | |
| | | |
| | | |
| | | |
| | | |

| Keys to Key Cabinet | |
|---|---|
| | Handed to ... |
| | Received from ... |

| | | |
|---|---|---|
| Taken over ________<br>Transferred ________ | Operating System Log No. ____<br>Operating System Log No. ____ | Computer Center Manager<br>________ |

**Figure 3.24** Page from a Shift Log used at Siemens

Machine cleaning protocol in a running operation, such as magnetic tapes, printers, card readers, card punches, printer keyboards

Records of the time started, standard starting time, and completion time for all jobs

Records of short-term changes in machine usage planning

Special occurrences, for example breakdowns, cold starts, restarts, and their causes

Remarks on system shutdown

Machine counter number at startup and shutdown

Initials of the computer center manager

When work is transferred at shift change, the outgoing and incoming shift supervisors should take inventory by means of a checklist and confirm the transfer of the system by signing the protocol. The check list may contain the following:

Forms and papers on hand

Imprinted punched cards on hand

Print cloths on hand

Magnetic tape coupling bars and loops on hand

Tools for daily use

In addition to the sample in Figure 3.24 the transfer of special keys may be noted, and the log may have a special column for visitors to the machine room. The notation of machine counter numbers is a precaution against unauthorized and uncontrolled use of the system outside of working hours (for example after the console files have been emptied).

### 3.4.5 Logbook Control Procedures

Operations control is handled by means of a usage report that contains information on run times and materials requirements of individual programs. This is commonly known as a log. Since it contains documentation on the actual run of programs in the system, errors and irregularities must be reported in it.

In principal two types of logs are maintained: one is kept manually by machine operations, the other automatically through the operating system. The form and content of manual logs in installations without operating systems differ from those which are maintained over the control panel of the operating system. They may accordingly appear in the following formats:

- Logs may be a collection of single, sequentially numbered pages, forms, or blank. They are usually in a punchable format for subsequent accounting purposes.
- Manual logs can also be developed in the form of bound books; in this manner single pages are less easily lost or misplaced. Format and entries correspond to the individual forms.
- Information may be logged automatically over the printer keyboard. Unfortunately, the reporting procedures among the various operating systems are not all alike. The operating system itself reports all errors and irregularities. Since most interventions are handled by the operator over the console, these are logged as well. If continuous forms are used for this purpose the pages should still be numbered. The operating system reports should indicate the materials requested for each job but not used. The log records of prior days may additionally be made available to the users (programmers); this eliminates further questions. Logs are saved for a minimum of 6 months. Usually only larger systems collect and store logging information in mass storage as well. The filing of logging information on copy is very popular and highly recommended. This way possibly longer storage periods can be planned.
- Large installations are equipped with video display consoles, and logging information is exclusively kept in direct access mass storage. That way one can bring up the records of the past 12–24 hours on the screen (usually since the last dead start). Older information is transferred to magnetic tape. Since this method is less convenient for the user, a list of logging files is occasionally made available. In addition, some operating systems print the logging information at the end of each job following the output on the quick-printer, so that every programmer receives it at the same time as the program output (see Figure 9.3).

## 3.5 Program and Data Archives

The task areas coming up for discussion here do not all belong to the fulfillment of primary data processing responsibilities. As a result, the scope of tasks may vary considerably among different computer centers. Since they are in part based on diverse methods of archive maintenance, a closer analysis of this area is necessary, preferably beginning with a consideration of general objectives. This also serves as the basis for an evaluation of automated archive systems, because once such a system has been introduced one has to live with it for a good number of years.

### 3.5.1 Objectives of Computer Center Archives

Technical considerations alone dictate that data maintenance belongs among the tasks of a computer center, as data media need to be stored under specific climatic conditions and to be available for use without notice. Archival tasks include prearranged security measures as a computer center service. Since the demands in this respect are often diverse—the higher the demands, the greater the expenditures—data security will be discussed in a separate chapter (Chapter 4).

The archives of large computer centers may contain upwards of 50,000 magnetic tapes and hundreds of disks. The entire system of electronic data processing is based on these data files. Because of the pivotal significance of this area, special consideration must be given to dependable, clear, and competent methods of archive management.

This area is generally subdivided into four categories:

Data media administration

Space management

Catalog administration

Program management

Many large computer centers have organized their archives along these categories.

The first three of these categories are closely interrelated and will therefore not be separated for the time being. Program management is separated into coding and documentation. An examination of the individual functions of archive management results in approximately the following breakdown:

- Active machine programs and data files must be kept up to date at all times.
- Quick and easy access to each partial volume of an archive must be guaranteed, so that the release of specific programs and files required for processing can be handled promptly and efficiently.
- Program documentation must be up to date, complete, and correspond to the requirements of optimal job preparation and smooth program runs.
- Symbolic programs must be managed by means of appropriate service programs, for example UPDATE or COSY in batch processing or an editor in dialog operations.
- Inactive machine programs and files from prior work periods must be retained as long as they are needed for special security evaluations or auditing purposes. In the same context retention times must be closely observed, and the data media released at prearranged schedules.

- The technical condition of programs and files must be such that they allow for trouble-free processing by the EDP systems.
- Archive management is responsible for making a sufficient number of spare data media available for ongoing postprocessing activities.
- Spare capacity volumes must be clearly recognizable.
- Shipments of data media, for example to other computer centers or for off-premise jobs, should not impair control over or quick access to a particular file; their return must be ensured according to predetermined deadlines, if necessary by way of reminders.
- Archive management must at all times be in a position to provide information on the location of files and media under its control.
- Data security measures must be observed.

In connection with the guidelines for the handling of data media the guidelines for data media storage have already been mentioned. Archive management is responsible for observing these as well, in addition to safety precautions against fire, theft, misuse, etc., and security measures for the protection of the privacy and confidentiality of data entrusted to the computer center.

Archive management differs widely in different computer centers and with respect to different data media; this is contingent on the various job profiles of each computer center. Consequently, the tasks of archive management are occasionally performed by job preparation—for example in commercial computer centers with small data volumes—or even by machine operations, such as in educational and research institutions.

The greater the volume of data to be administered, the more economical and automated archive management tasks can become, as, for example, in catalog administration and reminders. Program-supported methods have in recent times increased significantly for managing magnetic tape and disk files.

## 3.5.2 Program Documentation

Program documentation is primarily the responsibility of programming and appears in more detail in the literature on programming. Of interest in connection with the computer center, however, is the practical side of programming—that is, the question as to the manner in which program documentation supports program flow. For that reason it is most often referred to as job documentation. The computer center considers the following 5 points:

Instructions for job documentation

Instructions for machine operations

Instructions for postprocessing

Operating instructions for special devices (COM, plotters, etc.)

Instructions for emergency situations

Program documentation must be examined from this point of view at the time it is handed over to the computer center by programming. Differences in documentation are based on the specifications of different installations and operating systems.

The job file, which is the operations-related part of the program file, contains the following information on the program:

Program name and version

Cost center number, account number, job number

Brief description of program function

Program and data media form

Program originator, or manufacturer's name and date of purchase with purchased or leased standard applications programs or program products

Creation data and dates of alterations

Flowchart

Control statements—description and instructions for creating control statements

Header cards or procedural parameters

Description of program input and completion control methods

Description of program tasks—for example, list sample output and describe where files are created; the description of program tasks serves as the first completion control on the machine as well as determining supplies such as punched cards, forms, and tapes

Complete listing of machine stops and error messages with corresponding instructions on activities to be expected by machine operations

Restart possibilities

Materials requirements, possibly contingent on data volume to be processed; this is especially valuable for job preparation and systems usage planning and includes machine usage schedules

Security measures (passwords, etc.)

It should be noticed that documentation does not include the post list, more specific program runs and the like. These portions of documentation are purposely restricted to programming. They are not kept in the computer center in order to prevent intervention with programs on the part of the center and above all in error situations. The program files of all programs are administered by the computer center. Large files can be distributed to individuals, usually be department.

As already mentioned, documentation in general and handling instructions in particular depend on the specific task spectrum and characteristics of a particular installation.

The takeover of documentation from programming is an essential component of program documentation management in the computer center, which is handled by so-called program transfer sheets (Figure 3.25). When a new task or program is taken over by the computer center for processing, two things must be ascertained: the documentation included must allow for trouble-free processing, and the various points in the computer center must be supplied with the appopriate documents necessary for production in a timely manner. A consultation is usually combined with the transfer of documentation in order to ensure that the programs are adapted to the run as much as possible.

An essential aid in a successful program takeover is the existence of appropriate developmental guidelines and programming standards. Since the computer center must be involved in their formulation, the following criteria should be considered:

Integrity (compatibility with current procedures)

Hardware component requirements

Software component requirements

Maintenance of budgeted values (especially for run times and storage requirements)

Test completion and release to users

Process documentation

Data security

Input programs

Restart options

Error routines and error messages

Retention period and safety measures

JCL instructions (utilizing available options)

| Siemens Data Processing | Program Transfer Protocol |
|---|---|

Program Transfer to ______________________________

Program Identification ______________________________

Program Number ____________________ Data Processing System ____________________

The following documents are transferred: 1)

| | | | |
|---|---|---|---|
| 1 Program | 1.1 Symbolic Program | ☐ | 2) |
| | 1.2 Machine Program | ☐ | ?) |
| | 1.3 Systems Control Cards | ☐ | Total Number ________ |
| 2. Handling Folder | 2.1 Handling Instructions | ☐ | |
| | 2.2 Work Flowchart | ☐ | |
| | 2.3 Form Movement | ☐ | |
| 3. Program Folder | 3.1 Specification of Duties | ☐ | |
| | 3.2 Data Flowchart | ☐ | |
| | 3.3 Description | ☐ | |
| | 3.4 Program Flowcharts | ☐ | |
| | 3.5 Translate Protocol | ☐ | |
| | 3.6 Testing Documents | ☐ | |
| | 3.7 Program Data Sheet | To Data Processing Office | Transferred ☐ |

| Account at Time of Transfer | Cost Center | % | Cost Center | % | Cost Center | % | Cost Center | % | Cost Center | % |
|---|---|---|---|---|---|---|---|---|---|---|

Add'l Questions re Program ______________________________

Remarks

Program Released by ______________________________

1) Check if Applicable ☒ Enter Remarks, if Any
2) List Data Media

| Submitted | Verified | Accepted |
|---|---|---|
| Department | Department | Department |
| Date / Signature | Date / Signature | Date / Signature |

**Figure 3.25** Sample Program Transfer Protocol

Ease of handling by operators

Suitability for unattended operation on nights and weekends

Clarity of operating instructions

In addition, the checklists used in programming are valuable instruments for documentation transfers. Since they provide valuable suggestions for the computer center, a brief summary follows:

Are program chains possible?

Are the devices in program chains allocated in such a way that media need not be changed?

Are line-up routines provided for?

Are printed forms provided with adjustment markers?

Are standardized feeder tapes used?

Are protocols issued in standardized form?

Are only standardized responses allowed at the console?

Are program stops avoided as much as possible?

Are program restarts provided for?

Are labels used in data management?

Are handling instructions checked by machine?

Can useful alternating units be employed?

Do only protocols for machine operations appear on the printer keyboard?

Are handling procedures provided for each program or program chain?

Has the updating of procedural parameters been clearly established?

Can procedural parameters be replaced by program routines?

Are punched cards used to input procedural parameters?

Can data media such as punched cards or perforated tapes be checked for completeness?

Have symbolic names been used for I/O devices?

Are no unauthorized activities requested of machine operations, such as manipulating the service field?

Do handling instructions correspond to existing usage?

Are costly activities assigned to small programs? This should be avoided.

Are handling procedures checked when punched card input errors occur?

A completeness control of all individual program documentation segments should be incorporated into this checklist. But documentation management in the computer center must correspondingly exercise care in updating services as well. Undocumented or insufficiently documented programs should not be accepted for regular jobs.

## 3.5.3 Program Libraries

The maintenance of program libraries is an additional computer center responsibility. Operating systems and service programs are operational aids that allow the computer center to maintain a large number of different program libraries. One commonly differentiates among the following types of program libraries:

- In source module libraries each data record on the magnetic tape or disk corresponds to a program card. Service programs such as UPDATE or COSY allow for easy handling of such libraries which can be used to great advantage in dialog or test operations. Generally, however, the entire program library of the computer center is kept in this form.
- Program libraries with programs in translated but unlinked form are suitable for all programs that are used by a variety of different tasks. One usually differentiates between libraries for main programs, secondary programs, and macros.
- Program libraries with programs in linked form are most suitable for practical routine jobs. Job preparation in this case only needs to prepare the control statement records, if necessary by means of catalog procedures, and the data to be processed. Since the maintenance of such libraries is associated with higher expenditures—library administration as well as translating and binding services—changes in the program library should take place only at set time periods. On the other hand, the rapid integration of programs into this library obviously facilitates security in processing. Programs at the time of takeover into the library must be fully tested, and test run results should be presented for this purpose.
- The systems library generally holds portions of the operating system, service programs, and those applications programs which rarely change but are frequently used. The option of keeping applications programs as such in the systems library is chosen less often. Library maintenance jobs are usually handled by the systems software group, and commonly includes real-time programs and online data entry programs.

Program library maintenance is carried out by the archive or by job preparation. At least the two last versions of a library must be retained for security reasons. Frequently the penultimate program versions are kept in a separate archive for the purpose of reconstruction runs for audits and reviews. Care is to be taken to properly identify the different versions. When establishing a new version of a library a new catalog and table of contents must be set up as well. In addition to the name, the version, and the storage requirement, the location of each program in the library should be indicated. This is especially important with program libraries on magnetic tape. A record of maintenance work should be kept on a separate list, generally including the following information:

References to the library, such as name and version

Date when the library was established

Deletions of programs vis-à-vis prior versions

New programs taken over into the new version

Archive number of the original data medium

Archive number of the duplicate data medium

Name of computer center employee responsible for assembling the library

In addition to the standard programs provided by systems manufacturers, a series of individual developments are utilized in program administration. The developments in this area indicate that over the years program administration in computer centers has grown to considerable proportions. Since job preparation is essentially dependent upon a good program administration system, decisions in this area are of special importance. However, nowadays one is no longer dependent on individual solutions but has the option of using commercially available products.

The program library in the computer centers of universities and scientific research institutes plays a special role. The computer center statutes usually require that the largest possible selection of standard applications programs be maintained. The special feature of these libraries is that a wide spectrum of procedure-oriented programs (occasionally even method banks) must be maintained in such a generally valid manner that every user is able to call up and use one of these programs. This requires not only a high degree of universality and accuracy but also precise documentation, systematic information, and substantial advisory expenditures.

A number of computer centers have developed various documentation procedures in this context, but unfortunately none of them have been integrated into operating systems in standardized form. In these systems the control statements are able to call up the following:

Lists of program titles in the form of a mini-directory

Directories of brief program descriptions

Detailed program descriptions with or without source program

Programs in translated form

Since all of these programs serve the purpose of education and research, they are universally applicable and made available to the users of university and research computer centers without charge. However, this complex will soon have to be integrated into the accounting system. The use of video display terminals corresponds to the modern point of view.

The assignment of program names in the different libraries should be handled through guidelines, so that duplications and infractions against these restrictions by the library maintenance program can be avoided. This can be more easily accomplished in commercial computer centers with uniform job preparation than in service computer centers which have to assemble the programs of a heterogeneous user circle. The confidentiality of the administered programs must be guaranteed, for example through a security code or password. Frequently the use of special applications programs is restricted to certain terminals, so that unauthorized use is avoided as much as possible.

Catalogs of outside program libraries such as manufacturer's libraries are also under the care of the computer center's library administration, as are a wide variety of standard applications programs developed in the past several years. Even though the selection of standard applications programs is not made by the computer center itself, it should act in an advisory position because it is to a large degree involved in the care and maintenance of these programs. In service computer centers this task area can nowadays grow to such proportions that a special team is assigned to it. This is also partly true of university and research computer centers engaged in an exchange of applications programs.

An important question must be asked in this context: Who adjusts the job documentation of commercially bought programs? In most cases it is handled by job preparation, as this area subsequently has to work with these documents.

## 3.5.4 Punched Card File Archives

Punched card archives are occasionally still maintained today, especially in conjunction with programs, but data files are rarely kept on punched cards any longer. Since punched card technology was introduced some decades ago but has diminished in importance in modern computer centers, it will not be further discussed here. Suggestions for setting up a punched card archive are available in the literature.

## 3.5.5 Magnetic Tape Archives

Computer centers are responsible for setting up archives for the steadily growing flood of data and for maintaining them ready for use. Magnetic tapes have moved into a leading position as long-term archive media for this constantly increasing mass of data. Although magnetic disks are superior in processing, the tapes still occupy first place in the computer center. Accordingly, several procedures for archive maintenance will be considered.

The objective of archive management in general and the treatment of magnetic tapes in particular has already been mentioned elsewhere. Here it is essentially a question of keeping an archive with data media of this specific type. Such systems can by analogy be constructed for other media as well, such as magnetic disks or strips. In organizing a magnetic tape archive system, however, allowances must be made for the growing demand for data media exchange by means of magnetic tapes. A solution via telecommunication is not always recommended because of the large volumes of data involved.

Since automated archive systems are not as yet generally used in computer centers, the basic concepts underlying magnetic tape archives will be discussed insofar as the procedural problems are brought into the foreground and an evaluation of automated systems is thus facilitated.

### 3.5.5.1 Master Records

A number of different systems are in use for the management of magnetic tape archives, but independently of the various administrative systems a uniform method of tape reel identification has developed. New magnetic tapes are assigned an archive master number which is attached on the reel by means of a reel label. At the same time this number is attached to the reel container in such a manner that it is easily legible when stored upright in the archive. The archive master number is also recorded on the identifying volume label when labeling the tape. Archive master numbers are assigned sequentially. The standard code regulations should be consulted for technical details.

In conjunction with this reel identification, a card or master record is created in practically all of the archive systems to be discussed. This card serves to inventory the new tapes and can be used for other purposes, depending on individual requirements. Although tapes are generally considered the consumer materials of data processing, such archive systems become well established for the purpose of identifying errors and losses more easily. The following items may be listed in such master records:

Archive master number

Owner's name

Date of purchase

Manufacturer

Supplier

Tape length

Changes in tape length

Number of runs to date

Number of tracks (verified/used)

Character density (verified)

Usage and releases

Loans

Cleaning

The extent of information in a master record is contingent upon the working methods of the archive. Occasionally the above information is kept on lists as well.

### 3.5.5.2 Archives as the Responsibility of the Programmer

A relatively simple archive system is most often used in educational and research computer centers but also in service centers. When a job originator needs a magnetic tape for his processing task, he requests it from the computer center archive. The allocation of tapes for specific purposes can be for a limited or unlimited period of time depending on the request. The tape is removed from the collection of available tapes, is assigned a file number and a job label containing project and file name. At the same time the allocation is recorded in the archive listing (Figure 3.26). After processing is completed, filing occurs according to the file number. In many cases the file number and archive number are identical.

In this procedure the individual in charge of the project is responsible for the tapes thus allocated. He must know which tapes can be requested for processing his program. The tapes need not be made available through job preparation but can be obtained on request from the console over the tape operator. The tape user (i.e. the programmer) sets up a list for recording the usage of tapes.

Such a list, which the computer center can distribute to its users, may contain the following information in tabular form:

Archive master number of tape

Sequential number of data files on the tape

Recording data of each file

File name, version number, and number of records

Retention periods

Information on assignment to a task area

| Archive Number | 7/9 Track | File Number | Name/Project | Allocation | | Release | |
|---|---|---|---|---|---|---|---|
| | | | | Date | Archivist's Initials | Date | Archivist's Initials |
| | | | | | | | |

**Figure 3.26** Archive Listing of Tapes at the Programmer's or Department's Responsibility

It is relatively simple to set up an accounting system for the data media required by a project for the allocation periods involved by recording the tape usage times on a monthly basis on an archive data file which is incorporated into an accounting program. This is usually a small disk file accessed by the tape administrator via terminal. If during the period of allocation a large number of read or write errors occur, the tape listed under that particular file number is exchanged after transferring the contents to the next tape and erasing the defective tape. However, this rarely happens. The main disadvantage of this archive system is that tapes allocated for unlimited periods must be released by the project leader or programmer, and that they themselves must keep records on their tape inventory. This may mean an unnecessarily large total tape inventory for the computer center.

### 3.5.5.3 Application-Dependent Archives

In another and equally simple system, tapes are filed in the archive by task area. There is no particular system within each area, except that the various generations of a data file are placed next to one another. The job label, which is color coordinated by task area, contains above all the data identification which also designates the task area. Compared to the system mentioned earlier this procedure has the advantage that the tapes of a specific task area are filed together as a group and can easily be made available for processing by job preparation. It is relatively simple to inventory such a tape archive as long as it is divided into the following four categories:

Magnetic tapes assigned to task areas

Magnetic tapes currently off the premises

Scratch tapes

Blank or released tapes

### 3.5.5.4 Archives Organized by Data File

The archives discussed thus far dealt above all with individual data media and neglected the relationship between data medium and data files. It is for this reason that in many cases these systems have proven insufficient. The actual use of individual tapes is not clear enough, and frequently arising additional questions are not answered satisfactorily.

Sometimes the actual inventory procedure is separated from the allocation file in the sense that a tape reel file is kept as well. A reel card or reel record is generated for each tape reel and contains the following items:

Archive master number

Name of data file and versions

Reel number, i.e., which reel in a file extending over several tapes

Allocation date

Release date

The individual reels can now be filed in the archive according to their archive master numbers. This is especially useful with very extensive magnetic tape archives. In addition, tape management in a great many archives is handled by means of so-called tape data file records. A data file record is set up for each tape file and administered separately by file name. Such an administrative file serves as a record for all tapes in current use as files or in processing activities.

A so-called release file may be kept as well for the purpose of supervising tape releases. It essentially corresponds to a calendar in which on given days the archive master numbers to be released are recorded. At the same time, releases are entered on the tape reel file. Inventory is simplified insofar as filing is organized by archive master numbers which are sequentially assigned. Tapes missing at inventory should not be replaced immediately. Instead, the gaps should be allowed to remain for a period of time to avoid duplication in case the missing tapes are found.

### 3.5.5.5 Programmed Archive Systems

The archive systems discussed thus far illustrate that a dependable system is usually costly in terms of personnel. In addition to that, personnel-related activities are associated with a relatively high error rate. Small and seemingly insignificant errors in tape management sometimes result in a significant number of repeat runs. This is wasted data processing capacity and steps should be taken to prevent it. The following factors may be decisive:

Accidental erasure of magnetic tapes

Mixing up of tapes

Allocation errors caused by entering the wrong tape number (usually involving transposition of numbers)

Insufficient overview with large tape inventories

Errors in manual preparation and archive maintenance

Poor coordination between job preparation and operating

Lack of maximum tape reserves caused by poor overview (there may be a sudden shortage of blank tapes)

Numerous read/write repeats caused by unsystematic tape cleaning practice and poor quality control of tapes in use

Because of these deficiencies the first automated tape archives were introduced a number of years ago.

There is a variety of standard systems on the market today, so that custom-made procedures are no longer economical. When deciding on a system for practical application, it is advisable to check for fulfillment of the following minimum requirements:

- Archive administration should be possible by tape number and by area of application.
- An automated tape administration system should develop in a step-by-step procedure so that switchover expenditures are kept to a minimum.
- The transition from test files on magnetic disks to work files on tape should be simple.
- Tapes in operation should automatically be checked for version, file generation sequence, and reel sequence by virtue of the identification label (i.e. multireel tapes must be possible).
- Processing should be refused in each error occurrence and the cause of error should be indicated.
- In order to minimize changeover expenditures user-owned identification labels should be accepted in addition to standard labels.
- The JCL possibilities must not be restricted.
- Application in batch and dialog operations should be possible.
- The desired general overview should be made available by video display terminal.
- The use of magnetic tape modules should be restricted to the times when the file is actually open (i.e., between the OPEN and CLOSE statement).

- Open assignment to tape modules must be supported for preparatory set-up activities.
- Data security regulations must be observed, for example by file duplication on tapes or disks.
- Integration into a total system of computer center software should easily be accomplished.

Figure 3.27 demonstrates the variety of different systems that can be utilized in a computer center, as well as the close connection between tape administration and job preparation. The individual components should form a total concept.

Checklists are available for a concrete evaluation of software products which can be consulted if necessary. The control statements of the Dynamic Tape Administration System (TAS) are reproduced in Figure 3.28 as an example and overview of the capacity offered by current standard software products.

The variety of parameters possible within the various control statements cannot be addressed in the context of this overview.

An essential organizational advantage of automated tape administration systems should be mentioned at this point: Job preparation transmits only the tape requirements to operating in the form of a list, and no longer the tapes themselves. The operators personally get the tapes from the archive and return them after use.

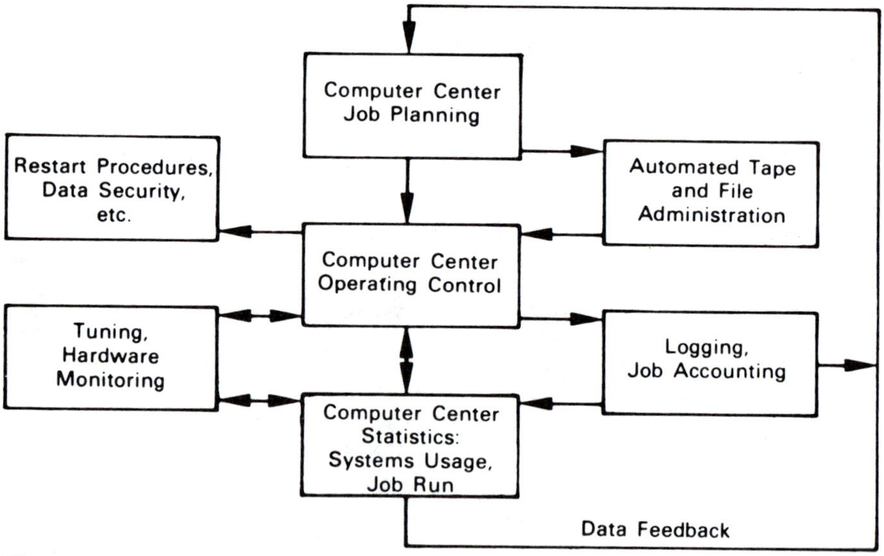


**Figure 3.27** Relationship between Software Packages and Adjoining Work Areas

## Tape Administration Maintenance Program TASMAINT

**Control Card Format:**

b Operation  b (Operand)  or
b Operation  b (Operand)  (. . . .) (Operand)  b Comment
Card maximum including column 71
Column 72 continuation card identifier (if required)
Column 73-80 identification of continuation numbers

Continuation Cards

Column 1-15 must be b
Columns 16-80 as above

b stands for blank

| Operations Code | | Function |
|---|---|---|
| 1. ADDA | = | Add reel to TAS file |
| 2. DELA | = | Delete reel in TAS file |
| 3. REPA | = | Replace statistical fields |
| 4. ADDF | = | Add a file to TAS inventory |
| 5. DELF | = | Delete a file from TAS inventory |
| 6. REPF | = | Replace fields in TAS file |
| 7. RENAME | = | Rename an item in the catalog |
| 8. FILELIST | = | Print list of total inventory |
| 9. FILESORT | = | Print list of inventory with standard sort |
| 10. FULLIST | = | Print list of all tapes |
| 11. FULLSORT | = | Print list of all inventory with standard sort |
| 12. LABLIST | = | Print labels |
| 13. LABSORT | = | Print list of all inventory with standard sort |
| 14. REORG | = | Erase/Replace the latest n generation |
| 15. COPYSAVE | = | Overall change of retention period |
| 16. SAVE | = | Save TAS file |
| 17. RESTORE | = | Restore a TAS file |
| 18. MERGE | = | Merge with a new TAS file |
| 19. ALLOC | = | Set up a TAS file |
| 20. OPTION | = | Set standard options for TAS system |
| 21. STATUS | = | Print usage list of TAS file |

## Possible Parameters and Their Symbols

| | |
|---|---|
| BLKSIZE = nnK | Blocksize of an inventory in K; one or two numerals followed by K; Op. Code 4,6 |
| BLKCNT = nnnnnnn | Number of physical blocks in this file; 1-7 numerals; Op. Code 4,6 |
| CLEAR = yy/dd | Cleaning date with year and day of year; Op. Code 3 |
| CLASS = xx | Specification of a tape class for printer dump |
| CORE = nnnnnn | Number of places in main storage; 1-6 numerical symbols; Op. Code 7,9 |
| CRT = yy/ddd | Origination date, year (2 digits), day (3 digits) separated by /; Op. Code 4,6 |
| DATE = yy/ddd / Real | Form of date; REAL = day of year; Op Code 7,8,9,10,11 |
| DECRET = nnnn | Number of days by which copyright is decreased; Op. Code 13 |
| DELETE = nnnn | Erases the latest nnnn generation of an inventory; Op. Code 13 |
| DENS = 800/1600/6250 | Recording density; one of the three must be used; Op. Code 4,6 |
| EPATCOMP = Yes/No | TLBL in Epat format changed to TAX format; erases the latest nnn |
| ERASE = Yes/No | Indicates whether certain generations should be erased or declared expired; Op. Code 13 |
| EXP = yy/dd | Release date (see CRT); Op. Code 4,6,9,10 |
| FF = cyl (trk) | Size for TAS file; Op. Code 18 |
| FILE = Tape / Disk | File specification for backup file; Op. Code 13,14 |
| FORCEBL = Yes/No | DTFs without ID are to be converted to DTF code; Op. Code 20 |
| FREETAPE = No/Yes | Special identification of free tapes; Op. Code 9,10<br>Yes = only free tape reels<br>No = all tape reels |
| FROM = yyddd/hhmm | Time limits for tape label printing; Op. Code 11,12 |
| GEN = No/Yes | Specifies whether version identical with generation in REORG function; Op. Code 13 |
| HDRINFO = Yes/No | Identifying labels to be printed; Op. Code 20 |
| ID = 'x. . . . . x' | Name of inventory up to 17 digits; inside apostrophes any value is allowed; Op. Code 4,5,6,7,20 |
| IGNMPS = No/Yes | Allows multiprogramming during formalization of TAS files; Op. Code 18 |
| INCRET = nnnn | Number of days by which copyright is to be increased, 1–4 digits numerical; Op. Code 13,14 |
| INPEXPCH = Yes/No | Allows to change copyright of inventory; Op. Code 20 |
| NEWID = 'xxx. . . x' | Like ID parameters; Op. Code 7 |
| NEWVL = gggg (/gg) | Like VL parameter; Op. Code 7 |
| ONEDAY = No/Yes | Printing of tapes with a specific release date; Op. Code 9,10 |
| PROG = xxxxxxxx | Program to be developed; 1-8 alpha numeric characters; Op. Code 4,6 |
| RETAIN = nnnn | Retains the newest generation of an inventory; Op. Code 13 |
| RETPER = nnnn | 1-4 digit numeric code to retrieve copyrighted tapes |
| SINGLE = No/Yes | Only newest generation per inventory to be printed; Op. Code 8 |

**Figure 3.28**

JUDAS 18 73.338 7:26 a.m.

## Tapes in use

| Record Name Number | Volume Number | Job | Creation Date | Release Date | Prod. Date | Catalog | Short-age | Label | Last Processing | | Date Used | User ID | Total Users |
|---|---|---|---|---|---|---|---|---|---|---|---|---|---|
| R.FB550200.G0001V00 | 0 002057 | JR551010 | 73.334 | 73.333 | Free Tape | | | SL | U | 73.334 | 66.311 | 23 | 34 0 |
| R.FB130002.G0027V00 | 0 002058 | | 72.329 | 99.359 | | 50 R | | SL | | | 66.311 | 3 | 3 0 |
| R.FB211802 | 0 002059 | JR211423 | 73.338 | | | 50 R | | SL | K | 73.338 | 66.353 | 3 | 38 0 |
| R.FB182021.G0013V00 | 0 002061 | JR186020 | 73.288 | 74.013 | | 50 RV | | SL | K | 73.318 | 66.353 | 19 | 19 0 |
| R.FB130002.G0065V00 | 0 002064 | JD251003 | 72.318 | | 74.300 | 50 R | | SL | K | 73.012 | 66.353 | 2 | 2 0 |
| R.FB174030.G0004V00 | 0 002065 | JR174030 | 73.306 | 74.031 | | 50 R | | SL | C | 73.306 | 66.353 | 5 | 35 0 |
| R.FB175022.G0009V00 | 0 002066 | | 72.305 | 99.359 | | 50 RV | | SL | K | 73.053 | 66.353 | 7 | 7 0 |
| R.FB130002.G0076V00 | 0 002067 | | 72.305 | 99.359 | | 50 R | | SL | S | 72.302 | 66.353 | | 0 |
| R.FS990222.G0551V00 | 0 002068 | JDDMP | 73.338 | 73.340 | | 50 R | -1 | SL | C | 73.338 | 66.353 | 19 | 19 0 |
| R.FB175022.G0027V00 | 0 002070 | JR175021 | 72.357 | 73.357 | | 50 RSV | | SL | K | 73.003 | 66.353 | 9 | 9 0 |
| R.FB130002.G0054V00 | 0 002072 | | 72.305 | 99.359 | | 50 R | | SL | S | 72.302 | 66.353 | | 0 |
| R.FB130002.G0062V00 | 1 002073 | JD251003 | 72.318 | | 74.300 | 50 R | | SL | K | 73.012 | 66.353 | 2 | 2 0 |
| R.FB175022.G0105V00 | 1 002075 | JR175021 | 73.236 | 74.236 | | 50 RSV | | SL | K | 73.248 | 66.353 | 11 | 11 0 |
| R.FB213034.G0014V00 | 1 002076 | JR213030 | 73.324 | 74.049 | | 50 R | | SL | K | 73.328 | 66.353 | 30 | 30 0 |
| R.FB130002.G0071V00 | 0 002079 | | 72.305 | 99.359 | | 50 R | | SL | S | 72.302 | 66.353 | | 0 |
| R.FB130002.G0006V00 | 0 002080 | | 72.314 | 99.359 | | 50 R | | SL | | | 66.353 | 2 | 2 0 |
| R.FB175022.G0085V00 | 0 002082 | JR175021 | 73.177 | 74.177 | | 50 RSV | | SL | K | 73.191 | 66.353 | 31 | 31 0 |
| R.FB712020.G0007V00 | 0 002089 | JR700015 | 73.278 | 73.338 | 73.293 | 50 R | | SL | K | 73.284 | 66.353 | 14 | 44 0 |
| R.FS550000.G0064V00 | 0 002091 | JR550027 | 73.335 | 74.000 | 73.345 | 50 R | -1 | SL | K | 73.335 | 66.353 | 32 | 32 0 |
| R.FB175022.G0114V00 | 0 002093 | JR175021 | 73.261 | 74.261 | | 50 RSV | | SL | K | 73.279 | 66.353 | 15 | 15 0 |
| R.FB212049 | 0 002094 | JR212041 | 73.279 | 73.339 | | 50 R | | SL | K | 73.332 | 66.353 | 22 | 22 0 |
| R.FB213034.G0012V00 | 2 002095 | JR213030 | 73.264 | 73.354 | | 50 R | | SL | K | 73.265 | 66.353 | 31 | 31 0 |
| R.FB175021.G0248V00 | 0 002097 | JR175020 | 73.313 | 73.345 | 73.323 | 50 R | | SL | K | 73.319 | 66.353 | 24 | 24 0 |
| R.FB146021.G0095V00 | 0 002098 | JR142010 | 73.314 | 73.334 | 73.337 | 50 R | | SL | U | 73.327 | 66.353 | 19 | 19 0 |
| R.FB217080.G0010V00 | 0 002099 | JR217070 | 73.320 | 74.315 | | 50 R | | SL | K | 73.327 | 66.353 | 20 | 20 0 |
| R.FS511015.G0033V00 | 0 002101 | JD990120 | 72.365 | 74.195 | 74.198 | R | | SL | K | 73.004 | 66.353 | 10 | 10 0 |
| R.FS990221.G0549V00 | 0 002102 | JDDMP | 73.333 | 73.335 | | 50 R | -1 | SL | C | 73.333 | 66.353 | 10 | 10 0 |
| R.FB146021.G0097V00 | 0 002105 | JR142010 | 73.320 | 73.340 | 73.337 | 50 R | | SL | U | 73.327 | 67.043 | 26 | 26 0 |
| R.FB175041.G0002V00 | 3 002106 | JR175052 | 72.356 | 74.326 | | 50 R | | SL | K | 73.026 | 67.043 | 10 | 10 0 |
| R.FB211600.G0020V00 | 0 002107 | JR211600 | 73.327 | 74.022 | | 50 R | | SL | K | 73.330 | 67.043 | 2 | 34 0 |
| R.FS550000.G0063V00 | 0 002108 | JR550027 | 73.327 | 73.357 | 73.337 | 50 R | -1 | SL | K | 73.327 | | 15 | 15 0 |
| R.FB582030.G0024V00 | 0 002112 | JR582030 | 73.278 | 73.338 | | 50 R | | SL | K | 73.314 | 67.043 | 24 | 24 0 |
| R.FB175022.G0017V00 | 0 002114 | JR175021 | 72.326 | 73.326 | | 50 RSV | | SL | K | 73.053 | 67.043 | 8 | 8 0 |
| R.FB213013.G0013V00 | 0 002115 | JR218013 | 73.320 | 74.015 | | 50 R | | SL | K | 73.320 | 67.043 | 21 | 21 0 |
| R.FS550001.G0063V00 | 0 002116 | JR550027 | 73.327 | 73.357 | | 50 R | -1 | SL | C | 73.327 | 67.043 | 2 | 34 0 |
| R.FB175022.G0079V00 | 0 002117 | JR175021 | 73.157 | 74.157 | | 50 RSV | | SL | R | 73.191 | 67.043 | 25 | 25 0 |
| R.FB175022.G0111V00 | 0 002119 | JR175021 | 73.251 | 74.251 | | 50 RSV | | SL | K | 73.279 | 67.043 | 22 | 52 0 |
| R.FB122014.G0244V00 | 0 002120 | JR122010 | 73.320 | 73.324 | 73.330 | 50 R | | SL | U | 73.320 | 67.043 | 27 | 27 0 |
| R.FS112000.G0018V00 | 1 002122 | JR177120 | 73.314 | 74.039 | | 50 R | -0 | SL | K | 73.329 | 67.043 | 24 | 24 0 |
| R.FB186031.G0002V00 | 0 002123 | JR186012 | 72.302 | 74.292 | | 50 R | | SL | K | 73.283 | 67.043 | 12 | 12 0 |
| R.FB171021.G0013V00 | 0 002124 | JR175030 | 73.307 | 74.002 | | 50 RV | | SL | K | 73.333 | 66.342 | 31 | 31 0 |
| R.FB135023.G0011V00 | 1 002125 | JR135021 | 73.284 | 73.314 | | 50 R | | SL | K | 73.296 | 67.043 | 13 | 44 0 |
| Y.FBCLASS0 | 0 002126 | JDDATE | 72.318 | | 99.365 | | | NL | S | 72.341 | 67.043 | 3 | 3 0 |
| R.FB322051.G0008V00 | 0 002127 | JR322020 | 73.297 | 73.347 | | 50 R | -0 | SL | R | 73.320 | 67.043 | 25 | 25 0 |
| T.FT137076 | 1 002129 | JT137075 | 73.334 | | 73.344 | 50 T | | SL | C | 73.334 | 67.043 | 10 | 40 0 |
| R.FB135023.G0011V00 | 0 002130 | JR135021 | 73.284 | 73.314 | | 50 R | | SL | R | 73.296 | 67.043 | 11 | 11 0 |
| R.FB174038.G0014V00 | 0 002132 | JR174030 | 73.335 | 74.030 | | 50 R | -0 | SL | C | 73.335 | 67.043 | 19 | 19 0 |
| R.FB175022.G0022V00 | 1 002133 | JR175021 | 72.341 | 73.341 | | 50 RSV | | SL | K | 73.063 | 67.043 | 7 | 7 0 |
| R.FB130002.G0082V00 | 1 002135 | | 72.305 | 99.359 | | 50 R | | SL | S | 72.302 | 67.043 | | 0 |

**Figure 3.29** List of Tapes in Use in a Programmed Archive (System: JUDAS)

Tape handling is thus simplified and therefore safer. Figure 3.29 presents a view into an automatically produced tape archive catalog in the form of a page segment. Such inventory lists produced by the program can:

Indicate the total inventory by spool numbers

Provide a file overview with or without generation references

Provide an overview of tapes in storage (possibly by date)

Provide an overview of all free tapes

Provide an overview of the frequency of utilization (possibly with information on programs requesting tapes)

Finally, automated archive systems should be analyzed from an economic point of view. In actual practice it has been found that in some cases the initial investment was amortized within 1–2 years, primarily as a result of considerable savings in personnel expenditures. Savings in terms of reduced repeat runs, set-up times and better equipment utilization cannot be as easily documented. The following are among the essential cost factors:

Software purchase price

Software support and/or adaptation

Changeover expenditures including operator training

Demands on EDP resources (CPU time, disk protection for administrative files, channel allocation, list output, and possibly terminal hookup)

Personnel expenditures

In addition to that there are certain usage factors in scheduling and data security to which a monetary value cannot be assigned in a simple manner. Further advantages may be gained in considering an overall data administration system that includes tape management but also covers disk files.

## 3.5.6 Magnetic Disk Archives

The procedures for setting up magnetic disk archives are essentially the same as for magnetic tapes. Since disk archives are less extensive than tape archives and disks rarely leave the premises, there are correspondingly fewer problems in archive organization. Unfortunately it is not as easy to label disks and disk containers as is the case with tape reels and tape containers. Once a disk pack has been mounted on the module it is impossible to determine during operating which pack is on standby.

**Department Computer Center**

(Sequential) Number

**Return to**

Subject: **House Cleaning**

The Jobs Listed below Are To Be Carried Out

| *) | (from) Library | Member | (to) Library | Rename |
|---|---|---|---|---|
| | | | | |
| | | | | |
| | | | | |
| | | | | |
| | | | | |
| | | | | |
| | | | | |
| | | | | |

| Requested by | | Completed by | |
|---|---|---|---|
| Date | Project Leader | Date | Job Preparation Supervisor |

*) S = SCRATCH, C = COPY/SCRATCH, R = RENAME

**Figure 3.30** Sample Housekeeping Form

Identifying cards can be inserted into frames, for which some manufacturers provide sample forms. Once the disk pack has been mounted, most of the operating systems are able to read the labels and display them on the systems console.

Housecleaning presents a special problem. Data and programs no longer needed are to be deleted from the disks at regular intervals, and the vacated areas made available for processing. As shown in Figure 3.30, these activities can be combined with renaming and consolidation. These tasks are generally handled by job preparation.

## 3.5.7 General Archive Administration

The multitude of different data media and their proportionate physical volume have in many computer centers resulted in assigning a superior position to space management.

A space allocation plan is set up for all magnetic data media, especially those with a high investment value such as drums and disks. Each required space must be requested from space management. This is generally done by means of a form; however, consultation combined with an evaluation of the request usually results in maximum space utilization. Editing and test files for dialog operations occupy a special position. Small blocks of space are allocated to and administered by the users themselves in this case.

The special significance of maximum management of direct access space also affects online and dialog processing from another side: here it is not only a question of disk space utilization but of data path designs as well. Many dialog systems are equipped with insufficient channel capacity, and this negatively affects response times.

While section 3.3.7 already referred to the problems of updating services in the total area of job preparation, changeover planning in mass storage realization will briefly be discussed again here. Experience has shown that in this context an initial investment of 1–2 man years will have to be considered, especially in changeovers to new technologies. Among the most important activities are:

Development of a JCL changeover program

Design of new mass storage for data to be entered

Adjustment of currently operating systems, including their corresponding management system, to the new mass storage

Try-out period for the new mass storage with continuous test

Operator training

Programmer instruction

Changeover strategy for test and routine jobs

An overall space management system such as this usually also assumes the function of disk archive, so that space management is handled according to uniform procedures. Figure 3.31 illustrates the operation of such a space management system used by Lufthansa Airlines. The market for system-related standard application software has adjusted to these demands. For example, the demands of tape and disk management for operating systems DOS/VS(E) are both covered by the program package CADYNAME/FI, after separate programs for each task (CA-DYNAM/D for disks and CA-DYNAM/T for tapes) had already been available for some time.

## 3.6 Documentation Systems

Commercial computer centers in most cases are subject to adjusting their internal documentation systems to that of the company. Since this system is not generally suitable for the specific characteristics of the computer center, the necessity of undertaking a corresponding expansion may arise. A similar situation exists in computer centers of the public domain.

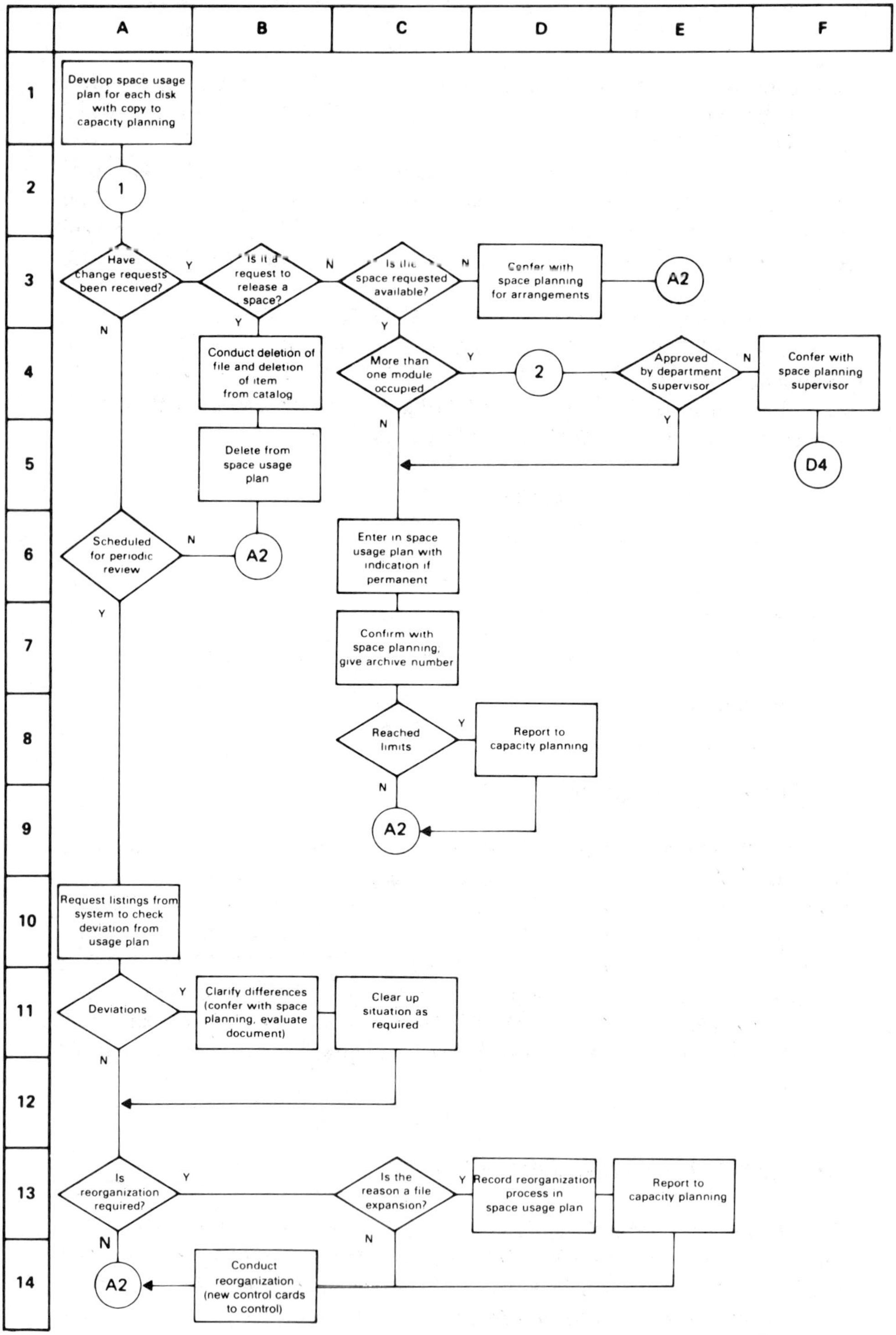


**Figure 3.31** Graphic Overview of Space Management Functions

A somewhat different situation prevails in service computer centers and university and research computer centers. Here the opportunity of designing a documentation system custom-made for the computer frequently exists. The following system is particularly meant to provide suggestions for these two computer center types. It is a new and independent system which was successfully initiated at the Center for Data Processing at Tübingen University some years ago. Naturally, only the overall scheme is reproduced here. Individual cases will require farther expansion and refinement as demanded by specific situations.

0. General EDP Affairs
0.0 General remarks
0.1 The foundation of EDP (e.g. standard forms)
0.2 Professional/occupational affairs (training in EDP occupations)
0.3 External events, conferences, seminars, workshops
0.4 Relations with other computer centers
0.5 Relations to professional organizations
0.6 Questionnaires and statistics
0.7 Relations with advisory firms
0.8 Public relations, press (see section 6.7)
0.9 Miscellaneous
1. Departmental Administration
1.0 General remarks
1.1 Legal status (official regulation, signature authorization, interface to individual departments)
1.2 Internal organization:
- Data Processing Committee, long-term planning
- Reports and statistics from the computer center
- Library of professional literature
- Job instructions
- Publicity
- EDP handbook
- Organization of daily routine
- Paperwork administration
- Company events

1.3 Buildings and offices
- Property management, house rules
- Heating
- Air conditioning
- Closing schedule, key allocation
- Space requirements and space planning
- Construction plans (expansions, new buildings)
- Office and machine room furnishings (items other than EDP)
- Telephone and teletype
- Intercom

- Copy machines
- Vending machines
- Janitorial
- Traffic Control

2. Personnel
2.0 General remarks
2.1 General regulations
- Salaries and wages
- Employee organization
- Relocation expenses
- Accidents
- Meal subsidies

2.2 Working hours
- Vacations and vacation requests
- Overtime
- Shift schedules
- Illness and substitute planning

2.3 Training and continuing education
- Travel regulations
- Training and continuing education planning
- Travel expense accounting

2.4 Staff planning and job descriptions
2.5 Personnel files (active, in alphabetic sequence)
2.6 Personnel files (inactive, in alphabetic sequence)
2.7 Job advertisements and applications for employment
3. Budget and Accounting
3.0 General remarks
3.1 Budget and accounting regulations
3.2 Budget plan and budgetary requests
3.3 Budget execution
- Management
- Exceeding the budget
- Nonscheduled expenses
- Annual report

3.4 Income
3.5 Tariffs and taxes
3.6 Accounting and budget control
4. EDP Systems and Computer Center Equipment
4.0 General remarks
4.1 EDP installation, Type A
- Rent/lease payments
- Maintenance
- Insurance

- Purchase agreement
- System software and tuning
- Manufacturer's training
- Manufacturer's literature
- User meetings
- Usage statistics

4.2 EDP installation, Type B (same breakdown as Type A)
4.3 Capacity definition and expansion
4.4 Data entry:

- On OCR documents
- On diskettes
- On data collection systems
- On line

4.5 Applications software
4.6 Relations with manufacturers and second-hand market
4.7 Remote processing and terminals

- Node computers
- Dialog terminals
- RJE terminals
- Telecommunications installations
- Computer networks
- Telephone
- Mail

5. Use of the Computer Center
5.0 General remarks
5.1 Regulations governing use
5.2 Fees
5.3 Relations with users
5.3 Relations with users
5.4 Account numbers
5.5 Planning orders

## 3.7 Materials Management

It has already been mentioned that as a rule computer center services include the provision of all data processing materials. Since materials disposition is not a specific data processing task, only a brief sketch will be presented here.

Material management is divided functionally into three areas:

Inventory management

Stockroom management

Materials procurement

The entire supply and movement of punched cards, forms ribbons, perforated tapes, and the like must be recorded on a card file. Usage may also be determined retroactively, i.e., by monthly inventory controls.

Even though materials usage in computer centers has declined in proportion to the increase in online jobs, materials management is occasionally automated and incorporated into the computerized accounting system. Since the operating system reports on the need to change forms on the printer, related magnetic tapes, or other materials consumption, this information needs to be assembled only insofar as to provide additional information not registered up until that point. If by the same token materials procurement or the recording of delivered supplies is hooked into the system, the entire concept of automated materials management along with inventory control and shortage reports (with respect to prescribed minimum balance) is only a short step away. Figure 3.32 is an example of an automated inventory report of the AGENA accounting system.

As a rule, the minimum quantities ordered cover quarterly needs, with the exception of rarely used items which are ordered annually. Orders can also be placed as the need arises, but this should be discussed with the department in question. Sufficient reserves should at any rate be kept on hand, preferably twice the amount needed for a processing period in case a production run needs to be repeated.

All supply orders are recorded in an order book for the control of expected deliveries and shipping schedules.

The storage of data media above all requires strict observation of handling instructions (section 3.4.3). Materials must be put away as quickly as possible upon delivery, not only for the purpose of maintaining order but for the protection of data media as well.

The check-out of supplies must be supervised. Unusual rates of consumption should be reported to stockroom management, possibly by means of a specially

AGENA Inc. Computer Center Accounting—Monthly Report April 1980, List 2B, page 6

Delivery to Mayer Co. Materials Movements Agena, Inc. 15/04/30 02/05/80-000

| Form No. / | Item Name | | Per Carton | Price | Unit Price | Beginning Balance | Units Received | Usage Quantity Units | | Cost |
|---|---|---|---|---|---|---|---|---|---|---|
| 3752 | Tabular Paper | 375-12-2 | 1000 | 34,95 | 1000 | 0 | 0 | 4687 | 4,68 | 163,81 |
| 3753 | Tabular Paper | 375-12-3 | 600 | 55,80 | 1000 | 0 | 0 | 9114 | 15,19 | 508,56 |
| 3754 | Tabular Paper | 375-12-4 | 500 | 77,60 | 1000 | 19066 | 0 | 2892 | 5,78 | 224,41 |
| | On hand, new | 16147<br>32,3<br>1255,10 | | | | | | | | |
| 3758 | | | 0 | 0,00 | 0 | 0 | 0 | 2431 | | 0,00 |

**Figure 3.32** Monthly Report on Materials Movements (AGENA Accounting System)

designed form. This applies especially to materials stored near terminal printers and RJE stations.

It is useful to keep a daily supply of forms and punched cards in the machine room. Requisitioned materials should be made available on schedule. Stockroom personnel must take care to release those supplies which have been in storage the longest—that is, earlier before more recent deliveries. Machine operators are responsible for transporting their materials from and to the data processing devices.

Inventory of all supplies on hand (punched cards, forms, etc.) should be taken regularly, for example once a month, for the purpose of determining total usage. If materials are left with other cost centers, such as data media in decentralized entry operations, the cost should be transferred.

Materials requirements are to be discussed with job preparation and systems planning. Requests for changes, for example in form design, are usually based on suggestions made by individual departments. Samples and proofs should therefore be reviewed by these departments prior to approval.

Because of the narrow tolerances and often widely divergent prices, the purchase of data processing materials sometimes requires decision making that is beyond the competency of normal materials purchasing personnel. The following guidelines are offered for this purpose:

Has the computer center clearly defined the item or service that was ordered?

Has the computer center been informed of new developments among the known supplies (date of order)?

Is the quantity ordered practical in view of price development?

Has the computer center been informed about offers from hitherto unknown suppliers (date of order)?

If the computer center requests purchases from a specific supplier:

- does the quality of supplies meet expectations?
- are these the best prices under the circumstances?
- are supplies delivered on schedule?

Has the computer center been informed of changes in delivery schedules?

Did the previous contract with the suppliers in question occur more than 6 months ago?

If the supplier has raised prices,

- have attempts been made to obtain a concession?
- have attempts been made to contradict the supplier's arguments?

Have several or all suppliers raised their prices?

## 3.8 The Disaster Handbook

The organizational guidelines elaborated thus far concern normal work routines in the computer center. In concluding this chapter, situations that may be referred to as "disasters" will be addressed. The procedures discussed are partly based on building safety measures (fire alarm box, fire extinguishers, etc.) which are treated separately in section 8.5.

This section deals with the organizational concept in the form of a so-called "Disaster Handbook" introduced in a large manufacturer's computer center. In practice, large computer centers are more likely to have such handbooks than smaller ones. The disaster plan presented here is a guide for dealing with a variety of emergencies; all supervisors should familiarize themselves with the plan and share this information with their co-workers. One of the essential objectives of this handbook is to test the disaster plan at regular intervals (every 1–2 years) for current and functional capability. Equally important is a clear description of contents and applications on the fly leaf. There is no doubt that total protection against danger is technically and organizationally impossible; the goal is maximum protection against risk and danger at affordable cost.

The arrangement may look as follows:

1. General objectives and operational areas
2. Emergency plan: In case of emergency the manager or a substitute assumes responsibility for action or appoints a suitable co-worker. Important telephone numbers are recorded on an emergency listing:
   Fire
   Accident
   Ambulance
   Hospital
   Police
   Emergency number for the building
   In addition, the person to be notified in the organization is to be contacted immediately.
3. Immediate measures

3.1 All employees assemble outside, for example in the parking lot
3.2 All personnel must be accounted for
3.3 A command post is set up (room, telephone, private automobile)
3.4 The following are to be notified about the location and extent of the disaster and the location of the command post...
3.5 Arrangements for suitable work facilities...
3.6 Determination of possible causes.

4. Persons responsible for and authorized to make decisions
5. Actions to be taken in case of fire, natural or other disasters:

Reports via telephone or fire alarm box
Turn off machinery
Turn off air conditioning
Report to supervisor
Put out fires with fire extinguisher—use only $CO_2$ extinguishers in the machine room
Persons not involved are to leave the building
Avoid drafts—keep doors and windows closed
The fire department must be given directions and alerted about special dangers
Fire fighters must not be obstructed

6. Serious accidents
Report accident
Call ambulance, if required
Report location and nature of injuries
Rescue and give first aid to injured persons
Do not disturb scene of accident
Direct medical personnel to scene of accident
Determine witnesses
Keep unauthorized persons and curiosity seekers away; eyewitnesses should be interviewed privately
Note down eyewitness reports
Sketch scene of accident, if necessary, as well as other important data
Serious and fatal accidents are investigated by the employee organization, factory inspection, and the police
7. Unrest
In case of danger from outside through demonstrations and the like all rooms and entrances are to be locked at once
Work in endangered rooms is to be stopped and lights are to be switched off; workers should assemble in safe areas
The following persons are to be notified...
No active resistance should be attempted nor should any attempts be made to intervene.
8. Layout of buildings (should contain the following)
Escape routes
Fire extinguishers
Hydrants
First aid stations
First aid cabinets
Emergency exits
9. Temporary arrangements
10. Materials procurement
11. Important addresses

# FOUR

# DATA PROTECTION AND DATA SECURITY

## 4.1 General Remarks

The computer center is the nerve center of an enterprise or government agency. Its efficiency is therefore a decisive prerequisite for the users' job performance. The higher the degree of automation—i.e., the number of job runs taken over by data processing—the greater are the consequences for the user in case of breakdowns or interruptions.

The computer concentrates hardware, software, data, and highly specialized personnel in a small area, a situation which renders it vulnerable to diverse kinds of disturbances. Considerations such as these have in the past led to reflections on how effectively to protect such installations. The need for protection and security developed along two lines, protection against damage and destruction from inside or outside causes, and protection of data against misuse or corruption. These concerns gave rise to the terms "privacy" and "data security."

Privacy protects the individual against misuse of personal data in the course of data processing. It includes all measures taken to safeguard against any type of undesirable data processing or the undesired results thereof. Undesirable is everything that stands in contradiction to personal, legal, and political objectives, such as the confidentiality of medical records.

Data security is responsible for protecting the condition and contents of data and consists of procedures to prevent damage during storage, alteration, or processing. Such damage could occur through

Processing errors

Misuse of data or systems

Destruction through natural disaster.

Privacy of personal information is primarily in the interests of the individual involved; data security is primarily in the interests of the user. Data security represents the technical side of privacy and is thus closely linked with it. There can be no privacy without security because the technical invulnerability of the data is not guaranteed. Data security goes beyond privacy in the sense that it also protects nonpersonal data.

## 4.2 Methods of Data Protection

### 4.2.1 General Remarks

There are three areas of protection:

- Preventive measures for the purpose of avoiding errors, falsification, and losses as much as possible. Such controls require constant or periodic supervision of work processes and receive special attention here.
- Subsequent review of orderly data processing procedures, thus also review of data for accuracy. This area, which can be summarized as "auditing procedures" is discussed in detail in section 7.5. Since it is more a question of planning and review of operations than of operations organization as such, a separation of the two is technically justified. Auditing is a review of completed processes and includes monitoring the effects of controls.
- Insurance measures, which do not serve to prevent damage but are prior agreements for handling damage once it has occurred. For that reason they are discussed in conjunction with other agreements pertaining to computer centers.

It has already been mentioned that data and programs are not handed over to the computer center prior to each processing run but in general are stored in the archives after testing and documentation. The user must be able to depend on the computer center's security measures to safeguard data in its care in accordance with the user's preconceptions. This is especially the case for service centers that concurrently serve a variety of independent or interdependent users, and for that very reason service centers are usually trend-setting in solving data security problems.

Data and programs entrusted to the computer center must be protected along the following guidelines:

- *Erroneous selection*. This pertains to negligence in selecting correct data sets, as for example in accidentally allowing punched cards to get into the wrong set or selecting the wrong tape. It is characteristic of this type of error that it is not automatically detected without special security measures, and that it is caused by inattention, unreliability, or ignorance.
- *Erroneous or impaired processing controls*. This includes primarily operating and technical errors and does not initially assume deliberate tampering. Examples are console operating errors, unauthorized program termination, and erroneous introduction of fall-back plans in partial failures. Technical errors may be power failures, equipment failures, or air-conditioning breakdowns. Efficient operating systems are designed to recognize and to report such errors. Error reports must always be verified; completeness verification of finished runs is included here.
- *Misuse of data and programs*. This includes not only unauthorized access but unauthorized alteration of data and programs, and constitutes a criminal offense.
- *Loss of data and programs*. This includes losses incurred through deliberate theft or the intervention of a higher power—for example, fire, water, or radioactive damage. Data may also be lost through power outages or technical breakdowns such as the head crash of a magnetic disk.

It is imperative in any case to treat data and programs in such a way as to prevent the above situations; errors of the first three categories should never occur without detection. In addition, security measures should also include recovery and repair procedures at minimal cost. While the major part of this section concerns data security, a brief reference is made to the problem involved in reorganizing data files, since a number of data security measures must be coordinated with it.

In comparing the goals of data security with methods generally in use three principal areas emerge which cover security requirements:

- *Mechanical-technical measures*. These include parity bits, error correction codes (ECC), storage protection, machine lock-up (i.e., consoles), reported irregularities in power, and air-conditioning supply.
- *Technical program measures*. This includes all measures pertaining to the operating systems and application programs, for example file labels, completeness and reasonableness checks, check digits, sequence control, summation checks, and prefix checks. These measures are of primary concern in programming and systems analysis and do not directly involve

activities in the computer center, where the operating system plays an increasingly important role.

- *Organizational measures*. These are divided into internal and external controls and will be more fully discussed below.

Even though technical program measures are to be given preference, it is impossible to get along without controls in the computer center itself as well as in contacts with the outside world. The increasing size of EDP systems and of the functional scope of operating systems encourages programmed controls, which for the computer center means a growing importance of organizational controls owing to their key positions in the total security concept. Before detailing the functions of data security it is useful to list the following general guidelines:

The eyes-only principle applies to controls carried out by individuals.

All in-person controls must be examined and verified.

Methods of error correction must be in writing.

For the purpose of coordinating data security controls and reconstructing data at minimal cost, all checks and controls should be under one central supervision.

Operators should not be permitted to interrupt programs unsupervised or contrary to operating instructions.

Extreme caution is in order when handling data media not in use.

Only data files with identifying labels should be used, even if certain operating systems allow processing without labels.

There should be a separate documentation for all technical program security measures according to task specification. This documentation should not be stored in the computer center.

Security measures should be coordinated with the various areas of operation as control chains of specific density.

Density of control does not need to be equally intensive for all areas and time periods.

Strict separation of functions such as in programming, document development, data collection, operations scheduling, machine operation, data revision, and control provides the best opportunities for data security.

In order to forestall fatigue, frustration, and deliberate malicious action with maximum effectiveness, as many controls as possible should be beyond human intervention.

## 4.2.2 Data Security in Acquisition and Entry

On delivery of source documents the computer center takes responsibility for entry and processing. This interface with outside is therefore an important security factor. In the days of punched cards this meant a relatively simple procedure, but today the great variety of technical possibilities requires a correspondingly broad spectrum of security measures. In order to utilize these technical possibilities the entire data acquisition system can be divided into six security areas with mutually coordinated controls:

Data are recorded on receipts.

Receipts are collected and sorted.

Receipts are transferred to data entry.

The data on receipts are transferred to a machine readable medium (data acquisition in the narrower sense).

Data are converted to compatible media.

Data are collected directly via online devices.

The first two areas do not directly concern the computer center. Since data acquisition is frequently handled centrally by the computer center, the security system goes into effect upon transfer of the receipts. Transfers should be handled through waybills, transfer records, and written agreements as shown in Figures 3.8 and 3.10. It is essential that care be taken on agreements pertaining to completeness controls.

Offline entry via data media such as punched cards, punched tape, and magnetic tape generally requires additional verification which should not be handled by the personnel involved. The entered receipts should be identified by data entry operators to avoid duplicate or missing entries. Examples of identification are stamping or perforation. Technical problems of data entry devices can be avoided by equipment checks during shift changes; such checks are to be recorded. Technical problems occurring during the work process should be reported immediately, even if they do not interfere with the work at hand. In addition to that there are a number of checking features built into the more advanced entry devices, for example automatic counters and computation and comparison of check characters.

Direct entry on terminals often requires additional security measures because data go directly into the system. As long as the same types of receipts are used as in more conventional systems these methods can be retained. In addition there is a wide variety of reasonableness controls as well as lock-up of entry devices and key control. The required level of security is usually achieved by the following combination:

Hardware security devices (storage protection, cable protection, and monitoring for taps)

Access check (passwords)

Numerical I.D. code (to be changed periodically)

Since data processing as a whole cannot be more secure than permitted by data acquisition and entry security, each system should have alternate security measures at its disposal. This ensures the desired security level in terms of time and material.

## 4.2.3 Data Security in Processing Sequential Files

Even though sequential files are primarily thought of in terms of magnetic tapes, punched cards should be briefly mentioned here.

Data stored on punched cards are technically protected against overstorage, but security measures are needed to prevent falsification during the key punching process, usually in the form of operating instructions. Outdated cards or already processed transaction file cards should not be destroyed but stored in case reconstruction is necessary. Since punched card technology has been in use for the past 80 years a number of proven techniques are available for safe storage, including water- and fireproof cabinets. Unauthorized addition or removal of cards can be handled by locks, and systems planning should provide programs for detecting this type of falsification through identification of card type, sequence, number, and the like.

A number of programable security measures exist to protect data stored on magnetic tape. Only those which directly affect the work process in the computer center will be mentioned here.

Input and output data files should always be stored separately to prevent overstorage of the original data.

In practice the generation principle has proved to be very useful (Figure 4.1). The input file is referred to as "father" and the output file as "son." In the next transaction cycle the former "son" becomes the "father" and the former "father" is now the "grandfather." In cases where a "grandfather" already exists from a prior processing cycle it may be released as "son." The advantage of this principle is that tapes containing old records will not be accidentally released. If the storage medium needs to be exchanged on account of permanent read/write errors, it should be erased before release.

Occasionally more than three generations need to be stored. Overrides of such tapes can be prevented by physically removing the write-enable ring from the tape. Depending on processing frequency all surplus recovery tapes should period-

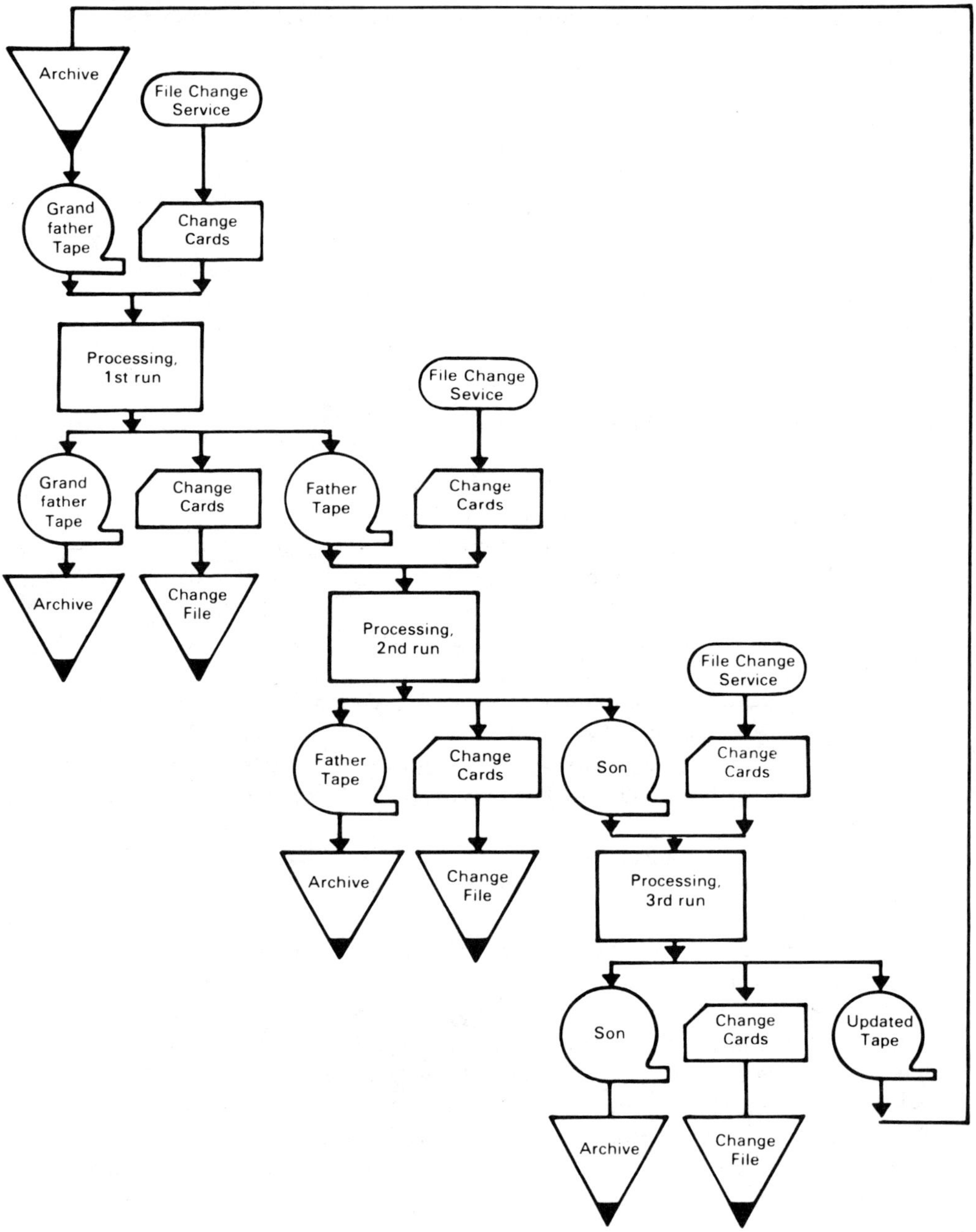


**Figure 4.1** The Generation Principle: Magnetic Tape Security

ically be moved to the archives or stored off-site for security against natural disaster.

Sequential data files are occasionally duplicated, especially when there is sufficient space for physical storage and duplication is handled concurrently in a multiprogramming operation. Otherwise the system may become overburdened. It will at any rate increase the demand on magnetic tape unit availability.

### 4.2.4 Data Security in Random Access

This concerns files stored on magnetic disks or drums. If sequentially processed, the generation principle can be applied to these media as well. In the case of nonremovable media the various generations or even the duplicate file are kept on the same medium. Even though this procedure enhances the security factor it cannot be recommended because the entire file becomes unavailable in case of breakdowns. Since most operating systems can, if necessary, function without file labels, data security through technical program measures is more reliable.

The generation principle cannot be applied to random access files in which individual records are changed without changing the entire file, because the original records are deleted in the overprinting process. In this case a duplicate tape should be made before processing.

In continuous processing such files are usually copied at regular intervals. The copying frequently depends on the frequency of file changes per unit of time and can range from once every hour to once a week. For budgetary reasons it is recommended to store the data to be secured on magnetic tape. The transactions are secured separately, for example, by means of a log file which records the changes chronologically by date.

Since copying increases machine demand, security measures built into the development of work processes are often preferable. The use of log files mentoned above is one example of such integrated security measures.

Finally, mention should be made of duplicate data storage in which duplicate files are maintained parallel to each other, and file changes are entered simultaneously on both copies. With an efficient configuration this method of data security requires practically no extra machine time but is otherwise rather costly because it involves a doubling of media and runtime units.

### 4.2.5 Data Security During Program Runs

Numerous opportunities for falsification of data or misuse of programs exist during program flow, and the entire organization of machine operations must be coordinated for this eventuality. In spite of all possible security measures there is general agreement among computer center managers that it is impossible to be fully secured against breach of confidence on the part of employees. For that reason security measures should be directed primarily against negligence without, however, interfering with normal work processes.

In processing especially confidential or valuable data, stricter than normal guidelines must naturally be followed. One example of this might be having two operators in the machine room at all times. Some computer centers have made this a general rule. Special guidelines must be applied to documentation as well: all interventions must be documented in a log with numbered pages. Moreover, data files must be securely locked. Loss of data because of machine-caused termination can be prevented through checkpoint restart programs.

A particular problem at this point is to safeguard against unauthorized use of programs and data. There are safety measures available to protect against even criminal actions; one is the use of passwords in addition to account numbers, program numbers, and file names. Passwords are not reproduced on lists, and the control cards containing passwords are removed immediately after each use so that repeated access can only be gained with new password cards. This principle can be combined with randomly selected code numbers.

Each project leader's data and programs should be listed periodically in such a way that each authorized or unauthorized use is readily recognizable. This also makes it possible to recognize program run under false account numbers. The disadvantage is that complaints can only be registered retroactively. Preventive measures such as programmed reasonableness checks of job numbers and program names through the operations system are to be preferred. Smaller installations can check the log manually. Finally, misuse of false account numbers can be detected by allowing only authorized individuals access to exit pockets.

### 4.2.6 Data Security in Postprocessing

All work processes related to processed materials and the results of program runs are included here. For security reasons it is important to have data preparation and postprocessing jobs performed by different groups. The results of production runs are to be differentiated from those of test runs.

Verification of completeness should be recorded and receipted for all production results at the time of transfer. In shipping, the general guidelines for the care of data media prevail (temperature, electromagnetic disturbances, etc.). Empty media such as tapes or disks should be demagnetized before shipping and this activity should be recorded in writing.

Data security is equally essential in the organization of archives and data preparation, and includes measures such as locking cabinets. Key transfers during shift changes should be receipted. Occasionally cabinets requiring two keys are used so that the "eyes-only" principle cannot be violated. Also included here are water and fire safety measures which will not be discussed in further detail.

Security measures cannot always be uniformly applied without considerably interfering with the test process. Therefore testing should not include the use of real and confidential data; instead, test data generators should be used. Besides, exit pockets for the results of test runs can be locked from outside.

Finally, the use of waste baskets in the computer center may increase the possibility of security leaks. As a result many computer centers have switched to shredders or burners.

### 4.2.7 Reorganization of Data Files

As already mentioned, security measures must include provisions for possible recovery. The extent to which such measures are feasible as well as the extent of foreseeable damage are decisive factors in the choice of guidelines. Generally, recovery includes reruns of prior work and the determination of checkpoints. Recovery begins at the last rerun point. Occasionally the extent of lost data has to be determined through control and analysis of batch totals. The recovered file should be duplicated before processing resumes because errors are frequent in such situations.

Optimal checkpoint frequency depends on the efforts necessary for data recovery. It is generally practical to set checkpoint frequencies after work has begun rather than during pretests, and to begin with a rough estimate, keeping in mind that optimal processing intervals and program run times need to be estimated as well. The results of these experiments can then be brought into harmony with theoretical formulas and appropriately adapted by modifying the checkpoint frequency. These corrections should be carried out in a consistent manner to avoid potentially significant loss of time.

In simple runs with sequential processing of external files a record counter determines checkpoint frequency. When processing large sequential files involving many tape reels it is more practical to set the checkpoints at the theoretical optimum in such a way that they coincide with the end of each spool.

Direct recovery poses a difficult problem that cannot necessarily be solved with conventional checkpoint techniques. With extremely large files (master files extending over several disk packs), only program-specific solutions are possible in which the prevailing condition of the file in question must be analyzed beforehand. In most applications, however, especially in scientific-technical areas, only small files fall into this category, in which case a modified version of conventional checkpoint techniques can be applied. At the time of setting the checkpoints the affected disks and the main storage must be saved, i.e. transferred to other media. Because of these difficulties most data bank systems have instituted specific checkpoint restart routines under the supervision of the data bank administrator.

Other programs are designed to combine files of a duplicate set into one error-free copy, based on the assumption that two copies of a duplicate set rarely contain read errors at exactly the same place.

A final point that needs mentioning here is that security measures should not only be developed but checked and practiced periodically. A number of computer centers have instituted unannounced emergency drills (perhaps every two or three years) in which designated files and programs are declared lost. Since such a hypothetical alarm can be deliberately aimed at traditionally touchy points in the system without causing much damage, it aids in determining weaknesses in data security.

## 4.3 Guidelines for Data Protection in Top-Level Security Computer Centers

### 4.3.1 Machine Room, Job Preparation, and Archives

All individuals with access to this area must take measures to prevent misuse of data media or destruction of or damage to devices and equipment.

The machine room, the job preparation area, and the archives are classified as top security areas. Access is restricted to

- Machine operators
- Job preparation employees
- The systems group
- Data entry operators if required by a task
- The computer center manager
- The data security officer

Exceptions may be made by the respective supervisors and must be documented.

Access to the machine room is through job preparation. Doors to this area are to remain closed at all times.

Every time a door is opened from the machine room, authorization must be verified, possibly via intercom.

Visitors are admitted only if accompanied by someone authorized to enter. When large groups visit, data media, lists, and forms should not be lying around.

A visitor log must be maintained.

Parcels or bags must be kept outside this area except when required by the job.

Maintenance technicians from outside must show identification; identities should be verified by calling the technician's firm.

The computer center's own technicians as well as janitorial staffs must show I.D. cards unless they are known to computer center personnel.

Strangers and unauthorized persons must not be admitted. In cases where entry has been obtained they are to be removed from the area immediately, if necessary by plant security or the police.

All individuals in these areas must familiarize themselves with fire prevention measures.

At least two persons must be present at any one time in the machine room and job preparation area. Exceptions are to be made only in special cases. Maintenance and cleaning personnel must be accompanied by at least one computer center employee.

### 4.3.2 Data Security

Data in random access storage belonging to the public or private sector are stored by systems operations; they are copied on magnetic tape and kept in the computer center safe. There are four types of backups:

Daily

Weekly

Monthly

Annual

All backups must be checked out and duplicated by systems operations. The duplicates should be stored in a safe area away from the computer center.

*Daily backups*: All files that have been changed since the previous check are put on tape and kept for at least one week.

*Weekly backups*: All files that have been changed since the last monthly check are put on tape and saved at least one month.

*Monthly backups*: All files are put on tape and saved at least three months.

*Annual backups*: All files are put on tape and saved at least two years.

Users are responsible for backups of private volume data.

### 4.3.3 Storage Media Exchange

Transfer of media to and from the computer center is to be handled exclusively by operations scheduling and must be signed for. This ensures proof of completeness. Operations scheduling must verify authorization to receive media in transfers out of the computer center.

The following items are to be listed on the form:

- User's name
- Date
- Time
- Data media number
- User's I.D.
- Listing of personal/confidential data files
- Information on physical deletion of tapes using programs furnished by the computer center
- User's signature
- Initials of the operations scheduling employee who transfers data to media in and out

For personal/confidential data the following items should be added:

- Source or receiver of the data
- Listing of contents
- Legal specifications allowing data transfer

The completeness of incoming and outgoing forms for personal/confidential data is to be checked by operations scheduling by means of bills of lading. Errors are to be traced immediately. The type and extent of lists should be noted on the bill of lading.

Forms, lists, and media shipped by courier are to be handed over only to authorized persons. Couriers not known to operations scheduling should be checked for authorization, if necessary by telephone. In case of doubt no transfer should be made.

Lists, forms, and media with personal/confidential information should be transported in locked containers.

Precautions should be taken to ensure that tapes released from the computer center are deleted in such a way that no data other than those actually necessary exist on them. Tapes used for media exchange must have been deleted prior to recording.

Loan tapes may be requested only through the computer center's tape management services. Authorization for use should be verified by systems operations. Tapes with sensitive data must be provided with a password.

Discarded material that is going off the premises should not contain personal/confidential data and must be checked out by the systems group prior to release.

## 4.3.4 Programming, Production, and Data Entry

All user identifications are to be assigned passwords that change periodically.

Data files with personal/confidential information should also be given such passwords. These files are not to be shared. Exceptions can be made only by the data security officer.

Test files should not contain actual personal information and must be recognizable as test files. When altering real data for test purposes no clues to personal identies should be allowed to remain.

Lists and forms with personal/confidential data, especially medical information, should not be accessible except in top security areas. They are to be destroyed when no longer needed.

Lists and forms with personal/confidential data may be shipped only to authorized destinations or should be kept in locked shipping containers.

Private volumes released by the user are to be physically deleted by systems operations with programs provided by the computer center.

Information on personal data stored in the computer center is not to be divulged to outsiders. Such information can only be given by the "storing party."

Agreements are necessary for the return of processed documents, which should not be stored in the computer center for any length of time.

User identification passwords should be known only to the systems group. Should others purposely or accidentally come into possession of such passwords, the systems group leader must be notified.

Additions, deletions, and alterations of personal/confidential files pertinent to the existing privacy acts are to be reported to the data security officer as follows:

- Extent of data records
- Persons or group affected
- Origin of data
- Judicial guidelines

Only those files for which these conditions are absolutely necessary should be shared.

Only absolutely essential tapes should be located in the tape management system. A password is recommended if these tapes are made shareable. Personal/confidential tapes should have passwords in addition to and different from general file passwords.

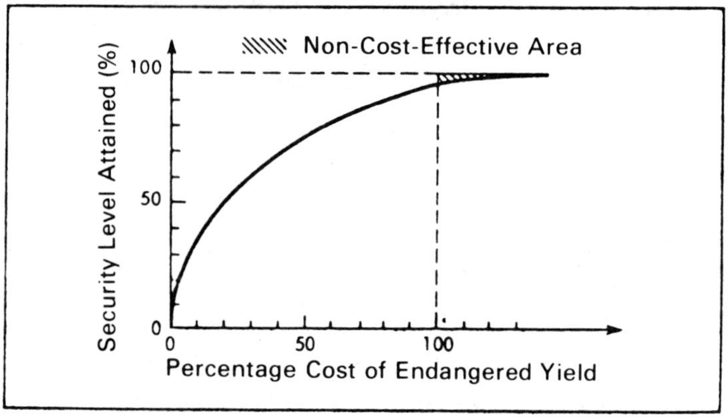


**Figure 4.2** Efficiency Benefit Function in Data Security

## 4.4 Cost of Data Security

A general guideline in choosing suitable methods is:

"Security measures must be financially feasible."

This means that a reasonable ratio should exist between security costs and the cost of possible damage (Figure 4.2). No general figures can be given, as each case must be evaluated differently. The respective costs must, however, be closely scrutinized. A differentiation along the following lines is possible:

The cost of systems planning and necessary investments relative to estimated service life

Running operating costs of security measures such as equipment, personnel, and rental value

Running operating costs of partial systems affected by security measures

In each case a detailed cost-benefit analysis should be made for every security measure to be installed.

Finally, the cost of organizational security measures is defined less by pro rata systems planning costs than by running operating costs, especially personnel expenditures. Programmed security measures are higher initially but more cost-efficient operationally.

## 4.5 Security of the Operating System

While there is no longer any question about the necessity for technical, organizational, and personnel security measures, the problem is just beginning to be recognized in the systems software area. Many operating systems today can only be called "open systems":

- Unauthorized persons can have untraceable access to stored files and programs via switched facilities.
- Files can be deliberately or accidentally altered or erased.

Pressures on the part of customers have caused most manufacturers to correct weak areas in systems software security. The security factor dependent on other modes (time sharing, batch processing, console operations) has been examined and discussed with respect to BS 2000 (Siemans,), RACF-MVS (IBM) and SECURE (ESC) in an effort to improve the operating systems.

The security concept of most operating systems is based on a more or less complete password structure. The Siemans system BS 2000, for example, offers the following security functions:

A password provides access protection for user identification.

Data stored under a certain code can be accessed by other codes only by permission of the owner.

Owners can specify read-only or write-only access.

Passwords can be assigned for read, write, and program invitation functions.

Tape files can be protected by passwords.

Access to specific tapes can be restricted to owner's I.D.

Passwords can be coded so that they will not appear in legible form in dumps or data media.

Computer centers should expect the following security measures in future operating systems:

Limited access to user identification codes on terminals restricted to specific tasks

Graduated limitation of user circles for data access beyond password range

Recording and control of unauthorized attempts to access passwords and data files

Alert signal on systems console in specific cases

FIVE

# COMPUTER CENTER PERSONNEL

The computer center is a service operation that performs production or test jobs on one or more data processing systems, the results of which are to be delivered to the job originators by a predetermined schedule. Today this requires a broad spectrum of service functions which at times may be extremely personnel-intensive. In addition, the computer center performs an advisory function in programming and in the development of new processes.

While Chapter 2 discussed the functions and tasks of individual areas, this chapter focuses on the distribution of tasks over specific personnel groups. The type and scope of the assigned tasks have resulted in a work-related personnel structure and the formation of differentiated occupational groups with clearly defined job characteristics.

Figure 5.1 illustrates the personnel organization of a medium-sized computer center as a starting point for subsequent job descriptions. Organization, systems analysis, and programming were deliberately excluded. While they belong to the area of data processing, they do not form part of the computer center in terms of the above definition.

## 5.1 Computer Center Personnel and Job Descriptions

The job descriptions presented in sections 5.1.1 through 5.1.16 show how computer center tasks can be distributed over individual personnel groups in a mean-

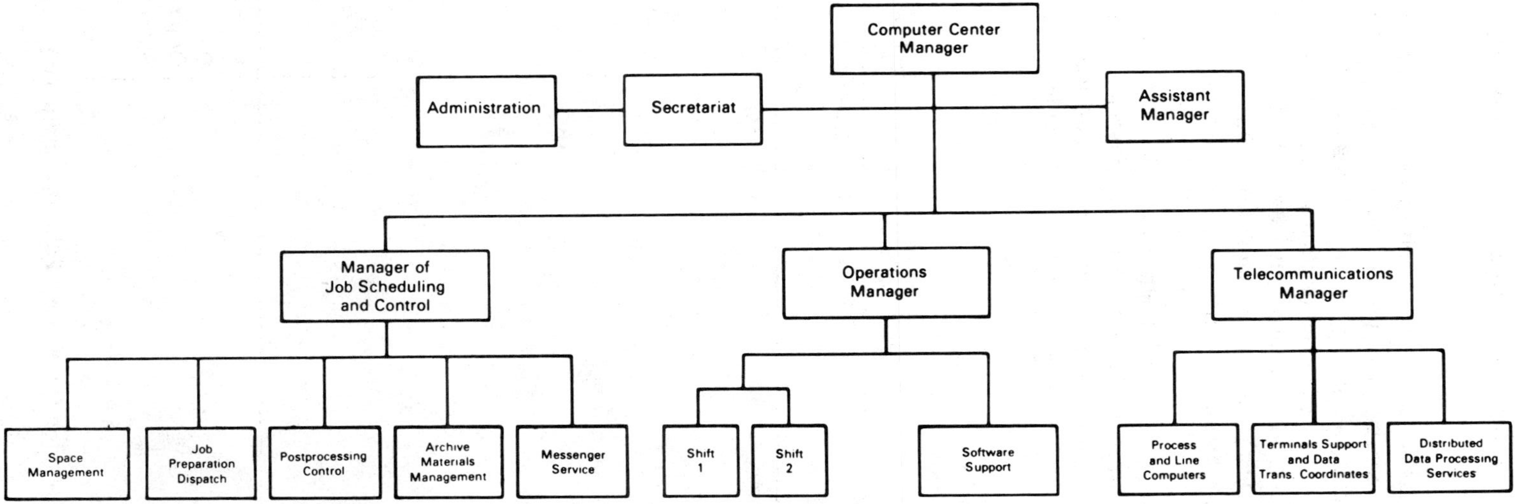


**Figure 5.1** Organization of a Medium-Sized Computer Center

ingful manner. This allocation of tasks and personnel is not intended to be either complete or exclusive, but rather presents one of the possibilities which has proven itself in actual practice. It applies to a medium-sized computer center with approximately 15–59 employees (section 2.3.1.2); the personnel functions in decidedly large computer centers will have to be further subdivided (section 2.3.1.3). The inclusion of telecommunications and distributed data processing with the attendant planning activities creates staff functions in addition to production functions.

The structure is based on a hierarchical order largely along the principle of "management by exception." Closed shop and partly automated operations impose additional demands on management in terms of employee motivation. A printed form serves as the basis for a job description, as it does in other areas (Figure 5.2).

**Job Description**

Department:
Position:

Number:

| | |
|---|---|
| Reports to | In Charge of |
| Is Represented by | Represents |
| **Objectives**<br><br>**Individual Tasks** | Assignment No./<br>Work Sequence |
| **Authorizations** | Classification<br>Date:<br>Organizer:<br>Approved by: |

**Figure 5.2** Sample Job Description Form (Integrata Co.)

A critical point—and this applies not only to the computer center—is the handling of representation or substitution, i.e., the answer to the question of who represents whom. In principle the following three variations are possible:

Representation by the next higher superior (substitution upward)

Representation by a co-worker on the same level (lateral substitution)

Representation by an especially qualified and experienced subordinate (substitution downward)

Computer centers generally prefer the third possibility of appointing the most experienced subordinate as a representative. This method motivates capable employees to greater achievements by assigning additional responsibilities, and represents part of their professional advancement. At the same time it is the best guarantee for a smooth continuation of operational processes. Special care should be taken to avoid conflict situations. If, for example, the chief of systems support is appointed acting computer center manager, the danger arises that systems tasks in certain situations are given unjustified priorities at the expense of routine operations.

One additional point of view in personnel organization should briefly be pointed out: within the framework of uniformity in data processing, computer center personnel and development personnel are often considered under one common denominator.

## 5.1.1 The Computer Center Manager

The computer center manager bears total responsibility for personnel, equipment, and the proper execution of all jobs. He is the central figure in the computer center and his personality determines the atmosphere, style, and work methods of this area. He is responsible for the professional motivation of his employees. The position and its demands are sketched below. The technical range of responsibilities is broader for managers of smaller computer centers than for managers of large installations, whose tasks are more along the lines of leadership and coordination. But this job profile is subject to fluctuation as well.

*Job Description*

| | |
|---|---|
| Organizational unit: | Computer center (department or division) |
| Position title: | Computer center manager |
| Reports to: | Director of the organization and data processing |
| Acts on behalf of: | Director of the total organization and data processing in the data processing division |

| | |
|---|---|
| In charge of: | Computer center group leaders and computer center management |
| Is represented by: | A directly subordinate manager, usually the job preparation and coordination manager. |

QUALIFICATIONS

*Personal Qualifications*

Personal leadership ability and the ability to represent the organization on the outside

Understanding for human concerns

Ability to establish and maintain contacts

Initiative

Administrative talent, ability to improvise, flexible work style

Ability to succeed in objectives, skillful negotiator, convincing personality

Ability to work under pressure

Sense of responsibility

Ability to make judgments

Ability to recognize complex relationships of abstract circumstances quickly and accurately

Highly developed ability for logical reasoning

*Professional Qualifications*

College graduate (for example, in information science, economics, business management, communication, physics, or mathematics), or corresponding professional experience

Thorough background and diversified experience in EDP operations and applications

Ability to evaluate hardware and software systems, including developing tendencies

Knowledge of effective utilization of systems and applications software

Practical experience in the management and control of computer center operations by means of standards and work instruction

Professional recognition both within and outside of the computer center

*Responsibilities*

Is responsible for personnel, space, devices, and other computer center resources

Is responsible for business management, operations, and execution of appropriate controls

Is responsible for personnel planning, selection, and utilization

Selects and assigns data processing personnel

Is responsible for providing leadership, information, advice, and motivation for all employees

Plans and supervises employee training and continuing education

Plans and supervises the organization and operation of all computer center work, with special consideration of economic factors (materials disposition, effective utilization, optimum operating conditions)

Handles the business management of the computer center budget, operational cost accounting, cost and efficiency planning, cost control, performance

Handles decisions on accepting or rejecting job orders based on current possibilities and computer center workload

Determines operational philosophy as part of the total organization, including project planning and control

Determines systems configuration and systems election in hardware and software

Negotiates with manufacturers; designs the technological aspect of contracts and certificates of inspection

Continuously observes and is informed about hardware and software developments in the systems and application area

Issues and supervises operational regulations, for example working instructions, user allocation, safety regulations, and house rules

Represents the computer center on the outside

Exchanges information with superiors and subordinates

Exchanges information or collaborates with other computer centers

Advises and supports other organizational units in questions concerning data processing

## 5.1.2 The Assistant Manager

The assistant has a staff function and supports the manager in carrying out his duties. This position imposes especially high demands in terms of personal qualifications, since the assistant can decisively influence work atmosphere. The job tenure of an assistant is frequently considered as limited in duration (a stepping stone position), and promotion to managerial ranks usually follows after several years of satisfactory service (Figure 5.5). It should be mentioned here that assistants are rarely found in medium-sized computer centers and not often in large ones, even though this position can be very useful.

*Job Description*

| | |
|---|---|
| Organizational unit: | Computer center |
| Position title: | Assistant manager |
| Reports to: | Computer center manager |
| Accounts on behalf of: | — |
| In charge of: | — |
| Is represented by: | Business manager (if appropriate) |

QUALIFICATIONS

*Personal Qualifications*

Ability to learn quickly and think logically

Sense of responsibility and ability to work under pressure

Ability to adjust and improvise; flexible work style

*Professional Qualifications*

College or professional school graduate in information science or economics

Basic familiarity with programming and the utilization of EDP devices and systems

Ability to assume full responsibility of accounting systems

Familiarity with all regulations pertaining to computer center operations

Ability to write technical reports

*Responsibilities*

Supports the computer center manager in executing his tasks

Administers all contracts and agreements pertaining to computer center devices and installations

Supervises reports on utilization and capacity planning of EDP equipment and auxilliary devices

Supervises the computer center accounting department (financial accounting, cost accounting)

Is responsible for budget, cost, and performance planning

Organizes training and continuing education programs for computer center personnel

Develops reports, statistics, etc. for computer center informational publications

Handles routine correspondence

Prepares discussions, meetings, conferences

Prepares negotiations with sales representatives

Organizes and conducts computer center tours

## 5.1.3 Executive Secretary

*Job Description*

| | |
|---|---|
| Organizational unit: | Computer center |
| Position title: | Executive secretary |
| Reports to: | Computer center manager |
| Acts on behalf of: | — |
| In charge of: | Clerical workers and typists |
| Is represented by: | Secretarial assistant |

Qualifications

*Personal Qualifications*

Ability to grasp abstract relationships

Ability to make independent decisions

Ability to adjust and work under pressure

Sense of responsibility

Tact and sensitivity

*Professional Qualifications*

Proficient in all aspects of office and administrative work

*Responsibilities*

Administers and supervises the computer center secretarial pool, including files and switchboards

Handles all clerical and copying tasks

Plans and schedules appointments for the computer center manager

### 5.1.4 Systems Software Support

Systems software support is often referred to as systems programming. However, an applications-oriented computer center is not responsible for developing systems; this is a task for the manufacturer. What it means, therefore, is that in contrast to applications programmers, the systems software manager's staff must be thoroughly familiar with the design and characteristics of all systems software. Individuals with a formal background in information science are best suited for positions as systems programmers

*Job Description*

| | |
|---|---|
| Organizational unit: | Computer center |
| Position title: | Systems software manager |
| Reports to: | Computer center manager |
| Acts on behalf of: | — |
| In charge of: | Systems programmers |
| Represented by: | Computer center manager or systems programmer |

QUALIFICATIONS

*Personal Qualifications*

Outstanding ability for logical and analytical thought

Ability to grasp and analyze complex abstract relationships under pressure; ability to concentrate

Ability to grasp and solve unanticipated problems rapidly

Systematic work habits

Ability to improvise in emergencies

Initiative, persuasive ability, and willingness to work as part of a team

Sense of responsibility

*Professional Qualifications*

Practical experience in systems programming

Expertise in all systems programs of the computer center

Expert command of machine language and the most essential higher programming language of the system

Excellent understanding of machine operation

*Responsibilities*

Selects systems programs suitable for the EDP system and its tasks

Generates and maintains the operating system

Ensures continuous systems readiness with respect to systems programs

Plans and executes systems software changes and additions

Designs and administers the systems library

Supports machine operations through training; resolves error situations

Provides user training and consultation

Keeps the computer center manager informed on systems software

Administers the library of technical literature

Provides training and continuing education for operators

Advises in evaluating standard systems software

### 5.1.5 Manager of Job Scheduling and Control

In the sense that the computer center is an EDP production plant, the job scheduling manager occupies a central position. During periods of transition to teleprocessing and distributed data processing he must take special care to stay in firm control of a changing task spectrum (section 3.3). An essential function in this respect is the maintenance of contacts with the individual departments—a good relationship based on mutual understanding is instrumental in successfully motivating computer center personnel.

*Job Description*

| | |
|---|---|
| Organizational unit: | Computer center |
| Position title: | Manager of job scheduling and control |
| Reports to: | Computer center manager |
| Acts on behalf of: | Computer center manager |
| In charge of: | Job scheduling, archives, dispatch |
| Represented by: | Job scheduling employee |

QUALIFICATIONS

*Personal Qualifications*

Ability to maintain control over a variety of simultaneous and complex operations

Sense of responsibility; orderliness and conscientiousness

Ability to work under physical and psychological pressure

Ability to grasp relationships quickly and accurately

Ability to establish and maintain contacts

*Professional Qualifications*

Long-term and successful background in job scheduling and machine operation

Knowledge of the operating system, JCL, and programming languages

Working knowledge of applicable and applied job scheduling software

Knowledge of data structure and data storage procedures

Understanding of special processing tasks

*Responsibilities*

Supervises and coordinates special jobs runs in the computer center

Makes decisions with regard to reruns

Controls systems usage and utilization

Controls incoming and outgoing program and data runs and their preparation prior to processing

Controls postprocessing

Analyzes and corrects above average systems run times

Participates in program documentation, especially with purchased standard systems software

Prepares guidelines for data and program documentation

Supervises program and data storage, especially with respect to maintaining documentation guidelines

Controls program additions and changes

Participates in selecting standard applications software

Suggests uses of automated computer center software to increase performance, simplify operating, and increase data security

Supervises the use and design of forms

Controls the job reporting for cost-effective operations

Keeps the computer center manager informed, especially with respect to operating irregularities

Establishes and maintains contact with individual departments

Is responsible for data privacy and security

## 5.1.6 Job Coordinator

*Job Description*

| | |
|---|---|
| Organizational unit: | Computer center |
| Job Title: | Job coordinator |
| Reports to: | Job scheduling and control manager |
| Represents: | Job scheduling and control manager |
| In charge of: | — |
| Represented by: | — |

QUALIFICATIONS

*Personal Qualifications*

Independent, reliable, and systematic work habits

Ability to grasp relationships quickly and accurately

Ability and willingness to make decisions

Ability to work under pressure

Ability to maintain control over a variety of simultaneous processes

Ability to establish and maintain contacts

*Professional Qualifications*

Knowledge of operating and programming data processing systems

Thorough familiarity with the operating system and its JCL

Familiarity with computer center work routines

Familiarity with the uses and design of job coordination forms

Knowledge of modern planning resources

*Responsibilities*

Assembles jobs for processing; develops appropriate job control instructions

Labels data media

Plans job schedules, maintenance, test runs

Supervises schedule due dates

Determines optimum job input flow

Develops systems usage plans (short and medium range)

Receives job instructions from programming and coordinates them with the requirements of computer center operations

Keeps the job scheduling and control manager informed on coordination processes

Resolves errors in daily operations

Is responsible for proper data media and address labeling for shipping

Manages computer center job documentation

Takes on new tasks, programs, and documentation

## 5.1.7 Library Administrator

This presupposes that programs and data are catalogued along traditional methods. In automated library systems the job description should be adjusted accordingly. In general this position includes disk space management (programs and data).

*Job Description*

| | |
|---|---|
| Organizational unit: | Computer center |
| Job title: | Library administrator |
| Reports to: | Job scheduling and control manager |
| Represents: | — |
| In charge of: | — |
| Represented by: | Job coordinator or machine room supervisor |

QUALIFICATIONS

*Personal Qualifications*

Independent and reliable work habits

Systematic and conscientious personality

Ability to establish and maintain contacts

*Professional Qualifications*

Familiarity with operating and programming a data processing system

Thorough familiarity with auxiliary programs applicable to this area

Knowledge of computer center work routines

Familiarity with the uses of applicable forms

*Responsibilities*

Makes data available for processing

Manages the archive

Administers the archive master file and tape file

Prepares documentation for archive services accounting (possibly via automated inclusion in the accounting system)

Is responsible for accurate data media labeling

Takes inventory at regular intervals

Allocates and releases data files and media

Manages the program library in source and object form

Administers job documentation

Manages disk space allocation

Ensures data security

## 5.1.8 Data Base Administrator

Within the framework of increasing specialization and qualification of computer center personnel a new function has developed which has found its way into computer center organization. In this context data base management should be considered from two aspects: on the one hand it deals with general data base tasks which require the addition of an advisory and supervisory staff position for tasks and data base systems, and on the other it concerns project-related tasks that need not be discussed here.

*Job Description*

| | |
|---|---|
| Organizational unit: | Computer center |
| Position title: | Data base administrator |
| Reports to: | Systems group manager or computer center manager |
| Represents: | Systems support |
| In charge of: | — |
| Represented by: | Systems support |

QUALIFICATIONS

*Personal Qualifications*

Familiarity with organizational structure

Diplomatic skills

Conscientiousness, orderliness, sense of responsibility

Mathematical and combinatory ability

*Professional Qualifications*

Solid data processing background (for example a degree in information science)

Thorough familiarity with data base applications

Long-term experience in systems programming

Commanding knowledge of relevant systems programs

Thorough familiarity with data base software

Knowledge of national and international data base norms

*Responsibilities*

Manages and services the data base

Optimizes the data base

Analyzes data base utilization

Plans data base operational modes

Supervises data base recovery and restart

Designs emergency and security measures

Determines security requirements

Supports and advises in data base design for different applications

Determines data base performance criteria

Executes performance estimates

Resolves incompatibilities between different data base applications

## 5.1.9 Administrator

*Job Description*

| | |
|---|---|
| Organizational unit: | Computer center |
| Position title: | Administrator |
| Reports to: | Job scheduling manager |
| Represents: | — |
| In charge of: | Clerical/technical employees |
| Represented by: | Assistant manager |

QUALIFICATIONS

*Personal Qualifications*

Conscientiousness, sense of responsibility and orderliness

Business ability

Ability to delegate and improvise

*Professional Qualifications*

Formal educational background in business management

Thorough familiarity with accounting and purchasing practice in computer centers

*Responsibilities*

Manages the computer center accounting department (financial, expense, cost accounting)

Supervises purchasing, especially supplies

Handles inventory management and control

## 5.1.10 Dispatcher

*Job Description*

| | |
|---|---|
| Organizational unit: | Computer center |
| Position title: | Dispatcher (I/O controller) |
| Reports to: | Manager of scheduling and control |
| Represents: | — |
| In charge of: | — |
| Represented by: | Job coordinator |

QUALIFICATIONS

*Personal Qualifications*

Independent and reliable work habits

Ability to grasp relationships quickly and accurately

Ability to get along with people, especially users

*Professional Qualifications*

Thorough familiarity with operating and programming techniques

Knowledge of computer center work routines

Familiarity with the uses of applicable forms

*Responsibilities*

Checks incoming data for accuracy and completeness

Checks finished jobs for completeness

Submits finished and verified jobs to job originators

Rejects incorrect input data or results

Investigates and clarifies errors (in consultation with submitting departments or programming)

Plans and supervises scheduling

Reports completion deadlines (or deviations from schedules) to submitting departments or programming

Maintains a log for errors and delays

Disseminates information on the run status of jobs

Maintains contact with the job scheduling manager

## 5.1.11 Operations Manager

The operations manager (chief operator or machine room supervisor) is directly responsible for the operation of EDP systems. The chief operator must therefore be thoroughly familiar with the operation of the entire system. For this reason—and in deviation from the principle of representation stressed thus far—the chief operator should stand in for a shift supervisor from time to time. With the transition of a maximum of four attended shifts to unattended operation during nights and on weekends, the tasks of the machine room supervisor are increasingly transferred to the two remaining shift supervisors. A critical analysis of this area shows that with only two attended shifts the function of a machine room supervisor is no longer justified. In actual practice worthwhile results have been achieved by combining several machine room supervisory positions into one.

*Job Description*

| | |
|---|---|
| Organizational unit: | Computer center |
| Position title: | Operations manager |
| Reports to: | Computer center manager |
| Represents: | Shift supervisors |
| In charge of: | Shift supervisors |
| Represented by: | Shift supervisors |

QUALIFICATIONS

*Personal Qualifications*

Independent and reliable work habits

Conscientious, orderly, sense of responsibility

Ability to maintain control over a variety of complex operations

Ability to handle physical and psychological demands

Ability to delegate and improvise

Leadership ability

*Professional Qualifications*

Long-term successful experience as systems operator and shift supervisor

Thorough knowledge of data processing systems

Superior technical ability

Thorough familiarity with machine operations

Thorough familiarity with handling systems programs

Working knowledge of data processing

Working knowledge of programming

*Responsibilities*

Supervises the operation of all data processing systems

Is responsible for enforcing computer center regulations in the machine room

Plans and supervises work assignments for machine and systems operators

Develops and supervises shift schedules

Acts as contact with manufacturers' technical services

Is responsible for keeping hardware in operating condition

Organizes equipment maintenance

Reviews programs and data supplied by job scheduling

Ensures optimal machine utilization on short notice

Maintains usage statistics

Trains and supervises machine and systems operators

Keeps the computer manager up to date on the status of operations

## 5.1.12 Systems Operator/Shift Supervisor

In computer centers with only one system the shift supervisor operates the control console, thus fulfilling the functions of console operator as well. In large computer centers with several systems the functions are separated insofar as one of the systems operators takes over as shift supervisor. The responsibilities of the two are treated together here.

*Job Description*

| | |
|---|---|
| Organizational unit: | Computer center |
| Position title: | Systems operator/shift supervisor |
| Reports to: | Machine room manager |
| Represents: | Machine room manager |
| In charge of: | Machine operators |
| Represented by: | Machine operator or chief operator |

QUALIFICATIONS

*Personal Qualifications*

Independent, reliable and systematic work habits

Conscientiousness, sense of responsibility, orderliness

Ability to maintain control over a variety of complex runs

Ability to handle physical and psychological strain

Ability to delegate and improvise

In systems with a strong emphasis on teleprocessing, ability to keep operators alert even during periods of relative inactivity

Leadership ability

Unaffected by the burden of a shift operation

*Professional Qualifications*

Long-term successful experience as systems operator

Thorough familiarity with systems operation (in the case of several different systems this can not be automatically assumed)

Thorough familiarity with systems programs

Knowledge of operating system functions and control language

General background in data processing

General background in programming

*Responsibilities*

Ensures orderly work routines and observation of operating regulations for his shift

Ensures observation of security measures

Instructs and supervises all personnel on his shift in systems operation according to operating instructions and procedural instructions

Starts up equipment and initializes the system

Shuts down the system

Supervises an orderly transition to unattended operation

Checks materials submitted by job preparation during job runs and reviews them for completeness

Supervises and controls the program run at the console

Corrects minor JCL errors

Intervenes in case or irregularities and hardware malfunction or program errors

Intervenes in case of program error according to job instructions

Determines program run times (if not done by the operating system) and maintains shift log. Such tasks can establish contact between systems operators and running jobs and may serve to stimulate interest on the work at hand.

Reports to management on job flow and irregularities

Reviews output (lists, punched cards, etc.) for completeness before turning it over to dispatch

Checks energy and air-conditioning controls

Supervises shift changes and reports on current jobs and observed irregularities

Reports to superiors on systems status, with special attention to difficulties encountered

## 5.1.13 Computer Operator

A differentiation between systems or console operators and peripheral operators is applicable only in large computer centers. Nevertheless there is a growing qualitative distinction between systems operation at the console and auxiliary services at the I/O devices, with the latter decreasing in volume relative to the increase in automation. Trainees usually begin by operating the peripheral devices, but should become proficient with the entire system as quickly as possible. The division of labor essentially depends on the philosophy of the operating system in question. Shift supervisors or console operators who provide assistance in such cases are not, however, relieved of responsibility.

*Job Description*

| | |
|---|---|
| Organizational unit: | Computer center |
| Position title: | Computer operator |
| Reports to: | Shift supervisor/systems operator |
| Represents: | Shift supervisor/systems operator |
| In charge of: | — |
| Represented by: | — |

QUALIFICATIONS

*Personal Qualifications*

Independent and reliable work habits

Conscientious, thorough, with a sense of responsibility and decision-making ability

Technical skills, ability to concentrate and think logically

Ability and willingness to work as part of a team

Willingness to participate in shift work and to stand for long periods of time

*Professional Qualifications*

Proficiency in operating devices

Familiarity with systems programs (to the degree necessary for operating secondary consoles)

Basic background in data processing

Familiarity with working instructions and company regulations

*Responsibilities*

Operates peripheral devices according to operating instructions, procedural instructions, and instructions given by the shift supervisor

Operates and services peripheral devices as follows:

- Mounts magnetic tapes (or allocates tapes via console)
- Removes tapes
- Cleans tape devices and maintains a cleaning log
- Mounts and removes magnetic disks
- Inserts paper, forms, and feeder strips into quick printers
- Changes printer ribbons and maintains change log
- Checks devices for regularity of operation (paper guide, paper ejection)
- Separates lists, collects printed and punched output
- Feeds cards into card reader and card punch, removes cards
- Checks operating condition of data media

Operates additional data processing machinery

Delivers finished jobs to dispatch

Assists in simple maintenance job

Intervenes in case of irregularity of operation

Services devices and equipment and maintains a service log

## 5.1.14 Data Transmission Coordinator

In computer centers with substantial teleperiphery the tasks of servicing and coordination may assume such proportions that a separate position is justifiable. In operations of over 100 terminals this position is no longer adequate and requires a special team (section 2.4.6). It is usually not practical to combine these functions with the systems group. The prerequisites for specific hardware conditions often vary considerably, and the relationship of these functions with the systems group is essentially no different than with other groups in the computer center, such as job scheduling.

*Job Description*

| | |
|---|---|
| Organizational unit: | Computer center |
| Position title: | Data transmission coordinator (TP coordinator, network engineer, network manager) |
| Reports to: | Computer center manager |
| Represents: | — |
| In charge of: | — |
| Represented by: | Systems software support |

QUALIFICATIONS

*Personal Qualifications*

Independent and reliable work habits

Conscientious, systematic, and responsible

Ability to concentrate and think logically

Ability to work under considerable pressure (user concerns tend to be expressed rather emotionally)

Ability to get along with people

Ability to improvise in emergencies

Initiative

*Professional Qualifications*

College graduate with a background in high frequency technology or information science

Background in data communications technology and data processing

Knowledge of the legal regulations of data communications

Familiarity with data utilization of line computers

Familiarity with data terminal equipment on the market

*Responsibilities*

Develops and supervises teleprocessing

Coordinates terminal hookups and their modifications

Performs minor maintenance work in this area

In charge of handling errors occurring in the telecommunications area

Acts as liaison with manufacturers of data communication equipment

Acts as liaison with postal and telephone services

Maintains contact with users; handles complaints, wishes, and suggestions

Keeps the computer center manager informed on line and terminal utilization and network operations

## 5.1.15 Data Entry Supervisor

*Job Description*

| | |
|---|---|
| Organizational unit: | Computer center |
| Position title: | Data entry supervisor |
| Reports to: | Computer center manager |
| Represents: | Data entry operators |
| In charge of: | Data entry operators |
| Represented by: | Data entry operators |

QUALIFICATIONS

*Personal Qualifications*

Independent and reliable work habits

Conscientious, responsible, and systematic

Able to work under pressure

Leadership ability

*Professional Qualifications*

Long-term successful activity as entry operator

Thorough familiarity with device operations

Knowledge of data processing principles

Familiarity with the most important programming languages

*Responsibilities*

Responsible for dependable and error-free data entry

Manages and utilizes data entry personnel

Establishes work schedules

Develops procedural instructions and ensures that they are followed

Performs quality control activities including control of records and data media

Participates in record design

Rejects records not corresponding to agreements and regulations both in form and content

Ensures that data entry devices are in working order and ready for use

Keeps the computer center manager informed on data entry work flow

## 5.1.16 Data Entry Operator

The personal and professional qualifications of data entry operators are largely parallel to those of clerical workers, with the exception that entry operators do not need to be as proficient in spelling and grammar.

*Job Description*

| | |
|---|---|
| Organizational unit: | Computer center |
| Position title: | Data entry operator |
| Reports to: | Data entry supervisor |
| Represents: | Data entry supervisor |
| In charge of: | — |
| Represented by: | — |

QUALIFICATIONS

*Personal Qualifications*

Dependable and exact work habits

Conscientious, responsible, and systematic

Numerical ability

Ability to work under pressure

Manual dexterity and good vision

*Professional Qualifications*

Proficient in device operation

Basic knowledge of data processing

*Responsibilities*

Operates data entry device according to operating instructions

Enters numerical and alphabetic information according to data entry operating instructions

Checks numerical and alphabetical information according to working instructions

Corrects data entry errors

Observes and maintains sorting instructions for records and data media

Maintains a clean and orderly work station

Reports operational irregularities

Identifies entered records

## 5.2 Personnel Requirements

The efficiency of a computer center is not only contingent upon its technical equipment (although some financial backers still tend to think that way) but also to a large degree upon its personnel. System support and the care and adaptation of the entire software complex determine efficiency as decisively as the effectiveness of equipment utilization, the physical environment, job preparation, controls, and the multiplicity of service functions. The effectiveness of EDP systems is lowered significantly if these tasks are performed by an insufficient number of—or insufficiently qualified—employees. The result is an excessive demand for machine capacity that is tantamount to an uneconomical investment. It must be pointed out, however, that hardware and software investments can replace employees only within certain limits.

The number of employees required is essentially determined by the type and number of systems and job volume. Since this changes from case to case, no generally valid statements are possible. Therefore, the following discussion should be interpreted less in terms of an accurate set of calculations than a suggestion for further deliberations. Suggestions for personnel requirements may, however, also be derived from areas other than the computer center.

Personnel requirements in the computer center have undergone noticeable changes in the past several years. These changes have come about through the use of complex multiprogramming systems and an increase in dialog processing, distributed processing, and computer networks. They manifest themselves in a decreasing demand for semiskilled workers and an increase in tasks requiring highly qualified personnel. In addition, the use of specialists determines management style in a manner leading to the conclusion that management tasks will decrease—that is, fewer management functions will exist. Specialist functions, on the other hand, will continue to increase in the future.

### 5.2.1 Batch Processing Personnel

In this area it is still possible to build on past experience.

$$\text{Number of computer operators} = \text{NS}\left(1 + \frac{\text{OS}}{2} + \frac{\text{NM}}{30} + \sqrt[3]{0.2 \times \text{JB}}\right)$$

NS = Number of shifts
OS = 0 with sequential operation
= 1 with simple multiprogramming
= 2 with multiprogramming in a large operation
NM = Number of tape and disk mounting per hour
JB = Average number of jobs per hour

Although this formula does not account for certain details, such as the number of form changes, practical experiences have more or less confirmed it. Others have made similar attempts to calculate personnel requirements by means of a formula.

Personnel requirements in job scheduling above all depend on the tasks and scheduling aids in use. Generally, however, there is a parallel between operational expenses for the data processing system and job scheduling expenditures. Programs requiring large operational expenditures also require large expenditures in job preparation, scheduling, and postprocessing. Pure job preparation and scheduling require about half as many employees as operations for these tasks. But even this value depends on the degree of automation in preparation and scheduling. Postprocessing may require twice as many employees, if time-consuming tasks occur (separating, cutting, binding, etc.).

Since exact calculations are not possible, some specific configurations will be discussed which may prove helpful in determining personnel requirements in individual cases.

### Small Batch Processing Installations

One operator per shift is sufficient for a relatively small batch operation. One additional employee should be trained for this position as a stand-in in case of illness, termination, or vacation. It should be noted that punched cards are now rarely used here (usually only for tax purposes) and magnetic tapes are used primarily for archive purposes or off-site storage (data security).

### Large Batch Processing Installations

Two to three operators per shift are generally required for large installations with tape/disk periphery and other special peripheral devices. In addition, a stand-in operator should be available for the machine room supervisor. Personnel expenditures can be reduced by shifting certain tasks to terminal operation or—in very large systems of several installations—to joint operation of homogeneous periphery (such as a printer), or to an EDP systems network.

### Archives

Personnel requirements here not only depend on the number of tapes and disks but also the extent of archive management and the type of archive system in use. Automated archive systems usually require one administrator and one alternate. Smaller archives (1000–2000 tapes) are managed by job scheduling or machine operations. Tasks associated with off-site storage of data for security reasons must be included in personnel requirement estimates.

#### Job Scheduling

$$\text{Number of Employees} = 1/1000\,(3 \times PE + 50 \times PN)$$

PE = number of existing programs

PN = Number of programs added annually

The term "program" in this context is to be understood as programs of medium size.

#### Data Entry

Personnel estimates are based on expected performance and calculated as follows:

2 to 2.5 characters per second equals 7000–9000 characters per hour for entry and verification tasks

3 characters per second equals 10,000–12,000 characters per hour for online data entry and data logging.

A relief operator for every 10–12 typists should be included in personnel planning, as well as a generous allowance for breaks (at least 15 minutes every 2 hours).

#### Auxiliary Personnel

Each computer center should plan for 1–2 additional employees for transportation, errands, minor repairs, cutting, separating, etc. With large postprocessing volumes (stuffing envelopes, stamping, shipping) personnel requirements must be calculated separately from mechanical equipment. It is recommended that retired persons be hired for these positions during labor shortages.

### 5.2.2 Online Operations Personnel

Personnel requirements are not as easily estimated here as in batch processing, because a number of special functions must be covered by corresponding specialists. The extent of these tasks is determined not only by their size and nature but by operational philosophy as well. Thus it becomes the responsibility of the computer center manager to decide whether to acquire the necessary capacity for systems or telecommunications maintenance via external service contracts (as is commonly the case for hardware maintenance) or whether to train internal personnel for specific teams.

Personnel requirements basically divide into three levels:

- *Basic requirements*: This pertains to the minimum number of employees required to operate an EDP system on two shifts. This concept generally corresponds to the old batch computer center. In each case the tasks must be handled by the computer center's own personnel.
- *Normal requirements*: This pertains to the minimum number of employees required for competent fulfillment of computer center tasks in the area of application. Normal requirements include systems operation as well as capacity availability for job processes. This concept largely corresponds to the scope of tasks of today's service computer center which not only disburses funds (for service contracts) but transacts concrete jobs through work contracts.
- *Real requirements*: This allows for support of special fields and tasks and the additional demands on coordination and service imposed by distributed data processing in addition to normal personnel requirements. What this means is that the utilization of data processing capacity outside the computer center requires personnel on the inside as well.

It is impossible to calculate concrete personnel requirements without first analyzing all incoming tasks for each function. Personnel requirements can then be calculated separately for each task area. Three marginal conditions must be determined, however:

- Is the task area under consideration covered in case of illness or vacation time?
- Is the personnel as planned equal to the demands of peak periods? It may be necessary to cancel vacation times during peak periods.
- Is it possible to economize on personnel by consolidating task areas? This objective is especially important for small computer centers.

### Basic Requirements

a. *Systems operation*: Regardless of the size of an installation, one console operator for each of two shifts must be available. A third shift necessitates a chief operator or machine room supervisor for management and coordination tasks. The need for a third shift is contingent upon work volume. Today one generally attempts to run the night shift unattended. Provisions must be made for absences (illness, vacation).

b. *Operation*: Punched card input/output is hardly a factor any longer in personnel planning. Many computer centers today exist without punched card I/O devices. Quick printers not requiring too many form changes can be operated at the rate of one person per 4 printers. Magnetic disk changes occur so rarely that they do not represent a personnel factor. Magnetic tape changes exceeding 15 per hour require a second operator. Less than 15 changes per hour (i.e. 120 changes per shift) are handled by the systems operator.

Generally the determining factors in this area are:

Number of shifts

Number of large terminals

Number of jobs per hour

Volume of printer output

Number of form changes

Average number of tape and disk setups per hour

Size of archive

Systems support

Spatial arrangement

Special I/O periphery

When several systems are in operation, personnel requirements for machine operators cannot be estimated by simple multiplication with the number of systems. Organizational tasks and the operation of I/O devices can possibly be combined. But one operator per console must be provided for, regardless of the circumstances. One should definitely avoid having one person operating several consoles, especially with systems of different manufacturers.

c. *Systems software support*: Calculations should be based on the assumption that each system requires two software support specialists. The operating system should never be without a support specialist at any time. Smaller systems can manage with one such employee, in which case this task area is covered through a service contract with the manufacturer. Teleprocessing in each case requires one additional software support specialist. It should be pointed out that there is no linear relationship between size of installation and the number of support specialists required.

The determining factors for personnel planning are:

Type of operating system

Number of compilers and service programs

Quality and extent of manufacturer's support

Type and extent of teleprocessing

Number of active users (because of consultation functions)

Number of machine operators

d. *Job scheduling and controls*: Although this task area is typical for batch processing, at least one employee should be available in a mixed batch-online operation, which means that at least two positions need to be planned for. One should also consider that usage control is part of this function and forms the basis for usage planning scheduling. This task area has increased in importance with today's data processing systems.

The determining factors for personnel planning are:

Number of existing active programs

Number of program changes per year

Number of program additions per year

Possibilities of using outside software

Operating system support

Type and extent of task area

Scope of controls to be executed

e. *Computer center administration*: Since administrative work accumulates parallel with the operation of the EDP system, even smaller computer centers should make provisions for at least one secretarial employee. An additional employee is needed for cost allocation and larger bookkeeping tasks. The determining factors for administrative expenditures are:

Number of computer center employees

Number of active users

Fee schedules and type of accounting system

Degree of support from other departments

Extent of report system

f. *Teleperiphery and computer network*: Tasks in this area begin with the hookup of even a single line, but they are handled by systems support as long as the volume is low. With 10 to 20 lines, however, the volume of work may increase to the point where an additional employee is needed. In the absence of manufacturer's support and participation in large-scale networks, or substantial utilization of distributed data processing, teams with 4–5 employees may have to be formed.

The following factors influence personnel requirements:

Extent of local network

Participation in regional and supraregional networks

Characteristics of teleperiphery user circles

Manufacturer's support

Uniformity of teleperipheral installations

g. *Auxiliary services*: Every computer center needs at least one employee for services required at regular and irregular intervals (transport, errands, minor repairs, and small general maintenance jobs). This position often decisively influences users' attitudes towards the quality of computer center services.

h. *Management and coordination*: A separate manager is usually required for these tasks. Management and coordination handled jointly by a group of employees in supervisory positions is found rarely, and then only in small computer centers. Additional management tasks are size-dependent. Depending on the variety of tasks, one usually plans one managerial position for every 10–12 employees. However, this position is usually not entirely managerial but covers other responsibilities as well. Additional managerial positions must correspondingly be planned with growing personnel demands in expanding computer centers.

1. *Additional personnel requirements*: Over and above normal requirements additional personnel demands may arise which must in each case be analyzed on a workload basis:

Data entry

Training

Consultation

Technical services (air conditioning, electricity, water supply, janitorial, etc.)

Repair and maintenance of devices (usually through manufacturers' service contracts)

These considerations illustrate the fact that it is no longer possible to compare the personnel requirements of two different computer centers in a simple manner. It is possible to manage with a minimum of personnel as long as only few and standard jobs are performed, one does not intend to use the EDP system to full capacity, additional tasks are subcontracted via separate contracts, and user support is restricted to a minimum. However, this lowest personnel boundary is unrealistic for practical reasons.

### 5.2.3 Personnel Planning for a New or Expanding Computer Center

The qualifications of personnel employed in the data processing division are a decisive influence on the cost-effectiveness of an EDP installation. Careful personnel planning is therefore essential when designing a new center or expanding an existing data processing department. Planning can and must never be on a short-term basis; instead, a long-term design for personnel requirements should be developed that includes time periods scheduled for job descriptions.

Deliberations on the following questions are unavoidable and should take place at an early stage in planning:

What human resources are available, and where?

What is the background required?

What is the time frame for hiring?

How is continuing training and education of new or existing personnel to be handled?

What concepts have been developed on the future expansion of the data processing department?

How does the personnel design to be developed fit into these concepts?

In order to answer these questions, both short-term and long-term plans should be developed. These plans will illustrate the time frame as well as the quantitative and qualitative features of personnel acquisition. Figure 5.3 represents a sample of such a plan. The following questions should then be asked:

*Time Frame for Personnel Acquisition*

How much time is available for search and selection?

How is notice of termination to be handled?

Does new personnel require training prior to starting work?

*Personnel Selection*

Does administrative management agree with planned personnel changes and/or new hiring?

How is a personnel search to be conducted?

What are the selection criteria?

It is important not only to concentrate on designing a harmonious job hierarchy but to consider the future distribution of tasks inside the computer center

| Position Title | Months Prior to Installation | | | | | | | | | | | | |
|---|---|---|---|---|---|---|---|---|---|---|---|---|---|
| | 18 | 17 | 16 | 15 | 14 | 13 | 12 | 11 | 10 | 9 | 8 | 7 | 6 |
| Data Processing Manager | 1 | | | | | | | | | | | | |
| Job Scheduling | 1 | | | | | | | | | | | | |
| Systems Support | | | | | | | 1 | | | | | | |
| Organization | | | 2 | | | | | | | | | | |
| Programming | | | | 2 | | | 2 | | | | 2 | | |
| Machine Operations | | | | 1 | | | | | | | | | 2 |
| Archive | | | | | | | | | | 1 | | | |
| Card Punch Personnel | | | | 1 | | | 3 | | | | | | 3 |
| Auxiliary Personnel | | | | | | | | | | 1 | | | 1 |

**Figure 5.3** Planning for Personnel Needs

at the same time. Manpower-saving measures can then be realized to an increasing extent. The danger exists that in medium-range planning too many auxiliary workers and I/O operators exist and too few specialists.

## 5.3 Personnel Acquisition and Selection

### 5.3.1 Methods of Personnel Acquisition

Once the responsibilities and the personal and professional qualifications have been established for computer center management and personnel, the problem of personnel acquisition remains to be solved. This is not a specific data processing problem but is commonly considered separately because it involves a number of unique characteristics. Some of the possibilities are:

TRAINING EXISTING MEMBERS OF THE FIRM

This procedure offers numerous advantages:

- The personal and professional qualifications of employees are already known.
- Departmental personnel are usually more inclined to work with former colleagues than with newcomers.

Internal employees are already familiar with the characteristics, problems, and possibilities of the firm; this can be a significant advantage, especially during the introductory phase of data processing.

- Internal employees are usually less costly than personnel hired away from other firms.

These advantages stand in contrast to the following disadvantages:

- Only highly qualified employees should be selected for data processing; the gaps created in individual departments are often difficult to close.
- A certain number of blind spots have been observed in conjuntion with internal acquisition; employees are often incapable of evaluating the firm and work procedures objectively.
- Internal employees are often difficult to fit into the computer center hierarchy; they tend to expect managerial positions because of their long years of service to the firm and are not inclined to accept newcomers in superior positions. On the other hand, the newcomers, who are usually experienced specialists, are not willing to accept beginners in managerial positions.

A combination of both is probably the best practical solution. Internal employees should build up the computer center together with specialists hired from manufacturers or other firms. Special care must be taken to assemble a good team: in addition to professional qualifications, the personal characteristics of employees are an important factor, and friction between highly qualified and ambitious colleagues is not an uncommon occurrence.

#### Recruitment by Advertising

This method produces a selection from a broad target area but is associated with considerable costs. Advertisements can be placed in regional and supraregional newspapers or trade publications. The extent of advertising also depends on the type of personnel requirements, the time frame for assembling the computer center, and the means at one's disposal. An advertisement represents the company's calling card and must give a clear description of duties and responsibilities; salaries should not be discussed until the interview. With the exception of very large companies it is not advisable to run an advertising campaign for more than 3–4 weeks. Lengthy and repeated advertising leads to the suspicion that earlier applicants withdrew from competition for very definite reasons.

#### Positions Wanted Ads

This method is associated with minimal cost for the company but is suitable only for completing an already existing team.

#### Recruitment at Educational Institutions

A further opportunity for contacting possible future employees is recruitment at colleges, universities, technical schools, and other institutions specializing in training data processing personnel. Large firms and public institutions often avail themselves of this opportunity by organizing company tours and conducting interviews with students in their final semester. Occasionally research and developmental projects are conducted jointly by industry and education, which open job opportunities for participating students in the firms involved. The practice of offering internships to students in technical fields is highly recommended. This enables the company to build a pool of possible future employees.

#### Personal Relationships

In this method, internal computer center personnel recommend possible employees from their circle of acquaintances. This necessitates working from the top down, that is, first a computer center manager has to be found, who in turn suggests a specialist for systems support; the support specialist brings along the chief operator, who in turn suggests some of his colleagues. Personal relationships have a distinct advantage: managerial staffs do not have co-workers forced upon them but are able to select them personally. This usually creates a homogeneous group and good teamwork. In this procedure the selection of the computer center manager is of particularly critical importance: he puts his stamp on the entire department, either positively or negatively. One inherent problem is the danger of cliques, and external consultation is recommended in such a decision.

## 5.3.2 Personnel Acquisition and Selection

The fundamental importance of personnel selection is self-evident: a computer center can only produce the results anticipated if every position is filled with a qualified person trained for that particular task. The professional qualifications of management are of equal importance with leadership ability and the employees' ability and willingness to work as a team. Data processing specialists often have strong achievement-oriented personalities and as such are not necessarily easy to lead.

The computer center manager especially must be selected from a professional point of view as well as for his leadership qualities. Extreme caution must be exercised so as not to entrust this position to an eccentric theoretician or an all around manager with only a two-week data processing course to his credit. Computer center employees are specialists in their field and can themselves only respect other specialists.

Research in industrial psychology has shown that it is extremely difficult to motivate computer center employees for programming and other services in other departments. In the computer center itself employees are guided by professional conviction. This does not mean that the computer center manager should work as a programmer or operate machinery—this is not part of his responsibilities. But he should project the image of a data processing professional, know computer center tasks from practical experience, and speak the language current in the profession. The lines of responsibility and competence are clearly drawn, and within this area he should be given a free hand and decision-making authority. An essential prerequisite, however, is a relationship of mutual trust and ongoing exchange of information with company management. This in turn obligates the specialist to convey information in terms comprehensible to the laymen.

Section 5.1 lists the personal and professional qualifications for each position in conjunction with job descriptions. When making selections among candidates it is essential to determine whether and to which degree they possess the desired characteristics. This is most easily done when internal employees are trained for data processing positions. It is still relatively simple when a candidate is known to one or more employees (personal acquisition) or has been recommended by a trustworthy third party. However, an evaluation becomes difficult when interviews are based solely on a written application backed up by supporting documents. The capabilities of personnel directors are not in question here—an interview certainly does convey certain impressions, and supporting documentation such as resumes, transcripts, and the like does have a certain value. But in actual practice numerous false decisions have demonstrated the impossibility of formulating an accurate evaluation of a candidate in the course of an interview. In an effort to obtain as much information as possible about a candidate in the shortest possible time many firms have resorted to more or less extensive tests. However, the results should be evaluated with a good deal of caution because test taking is subject to numerous external influences that are not always taken into account. No specific aptitude tests are known for machine operators, but testing materials are available for key entry operators. In each instance one should consider whether the candidate is an experienced test taker or whether this is a first experience. But by no means should a decision be based exclusively on test results. In the case of candidates with identical professional qualifications, personal impressions should be the decisive factor for purposes of congenial coopration on the job.

## 5.4 Training and Continuing Education

Training and continuing education is accorded greater significance in the computer center than it is in many other professions because there is a greater tendency toward rapid changes in the field of computing. As important as a certain amount of changes may be for a sound operation, the cost factor should not be ignored. According to a 1971 study the cost of retraining a programmer came to roughly $15,000, and an experienced machine operator would probably cost a similar amount. Besides, the job profiles often lacking in a computer center can only be alleviated through systematic continuing education, because nobody profits from employees who are no longer able to cope with increasing technical demands. Therefore special importance should be attached to training and continuing education, although it is sometimes a problem with older employees.

## 5.4.1 Training Opportunities

"Knowledge is the data processor's capital." This slogan illustrates that a data processing professional is incapable of producing anticipated results without solid and up-to-date technical know-how. Rapid developments in the data processing field demand significant expenditures and personal interest in training and continuing education. Anyone who believes that a once completed course of study —including a degree in information science—is sufficient for a lifetime will soon discover that this investment has become virtually worthless a few years down the road. On the other hand, the intensive evolution of data processing exercises a compelling fascination on many people.

Many opportunities for training and continuing education are available, even though they are fewer in number for computer center employees than for programmers and analysts. On-the-job training can only be considered as an educational supplement—not as a valid training method.

### Data Processing Schools

Numerous private and public educational institutions offer data processing training in the basics as well as special continuing education seminars. A course of study at a manufacturer-independent school avoids the danger of concentration on a specific product but can involve significant costs. Contact with colleagues at other firms and an exchange of experiences with users of products from different manufacturers can also be very helpful.

### Colleges and Technical Schools

The qualitative demands made on computer center employees have risen to the point where college and technical school graduates are now the preferred candidates for computer center jobs. A college education in information science is at any rate manufacturer-independent and qualitatively superior. Degrees in data processing are not uniformly offered in institutions of higher education, but the computer centers of some colleges without a curriculum in information science can offer certain training opportunities.

### Manufacturers Training Centers

All major manufacturers have established effective training centers for the purpose of schooling their own as well as their customers' personnel. Many firms are also willing to admit employees of potential customers to their seminars. This is always especially advantageous when a decision has been made in favor of a specific product. Training and continuing education should at any rate be included in the purchase agreements or leases of new equipment. A great deal can be accomplished in terms of training opportunities through the use of individualized purchase contracts of lease agreements.

### Internal Training

Large-volume data processing installations are switching increasingly to internal training and continuing education for their own personnel. This is by far the most economical method for companies with several hundred data processing employees; it provides an opportunity to school specific groups for a specific purpose by combining purely technical instruction with operations-internal information in preparation for future responsibilities. In this type of situation detailed and long-range training programs must be developed. Two advantages are the possibility of supervising the rate of achievement and the avoidance of out-of-town travel. Some manufacturer-independent schools also offer to provide operation-internal training, a policy which manufacturers have pursued since the early years of data processing.

Internal training can only be successful if the participants are freed from daily routine jobs and are left undisturbed during the training sessions. A certificate of completion should be awarded even for internal training. It should be emphasized at this point that training materials developed by manufacturers may be a worthwhile basis for internal operator training. Product-oriented training is not necessarily a hindrance in this respect since machine operation by its very nature is still extremely product-related.

### Self-Study and Team Instruction

This avenue deserves mention as well. In the early stages of data processing there were no choices other than laborious self-study from often inadequate manuals. Today a number of excellent self-study materials are available and manufacturers' literature has improved significantly. However, training should not be restricted to self-study but should rather be viewed as an adjunct to formal training and a deepening of knowledge through applied work processes. This is where information exchanges between team members are extremely valuable.

A team leader is responsible for the training of weaker or less experienced workers through personal instruction. An experienced chief operator, for example, is the best teacher for operator trainees. Audio-visual self-training programs are used as well.

### Computer-Assisted Instruction

With the growing use of dialog terminals the video display screen enjoys increasing popularity as an educational tool. Standard systems offer widely divergent possibilities here. Positive experiences with this method have recently been reported. The advantages are obvious:

- Individuals or small groups can begin a course at any time, thus eliminating the necessity of having to wait for a sufficient number of participants in order to justify an instructor.
- The courses are available to all computer center employees upon their completion of the training sequence, so that specific portions can be repeated or practiced again when an actual problem discussed in such a course occurs. It can also be utilized effectively to fill out work stoppages due to machine failure, for example.
- Those who include an interactive training program in their education will usually choose a beginning work level which most rapidly leads to the greatest possible utilization of this medium.
- Training costs can be reduced if simulated functions of machines and devices are offered by the training system instead of having to make real machine available. This is an especially important point during periods of conversion, when new systems can be practiced via simulation prior to installation.

Optimal training is reached when a central office, for example a training department, develops an educational curriculum for every employee. Thus a definite goal is presented along with the opportunity to prepare for the individual training sequences. Successful completion of each sequence should be acknowledged by means of a certificate so as not to devalue in-house training compared to manufacturers' courses.

A curriculum must be developed together with the employee and should include the following:

- *Personal goals*: One of the basic principles of modern personnel management is to put the right man in the right place. This means that personal interests and inclinations need to be considered.
- *Aptitude*: Another point to be considered is an individual's suitability for specific training or continuing education. Employees often overestimate

their capabilities, and false ambitions cause them to strive for positions they cannot realistically expect to attain, regardless of effort. It has been observed time after time that an excellent computer operator educates himself into a weak programmer.

A training program for systems operators is proposed below. The program clearly shows the interchange between internal and external schooling and a deepening of knowledge through practical work on the equipment. The same is illustrated by the graphic overview in Figure 5.4.

## 5.4.2 Systems Operator Training

*Training Plan*

1. Introduction — 1–2 days
   - 1.1 Introduction to the firm and its products
   - 1.2 Introduction to the department
   - 1.3 Introduction to installation and to computer center tasks
   - 1.4 Distribution of the data processing handbook
2. Concepts of automatic processing and technical installation
   - 2.1 Principles of EDP — 1–2 weeks
3. Principles of programming — 1–4 weeks
   - 3.1 Lectures on machine language and assembler programs
   - 3.2 Short overview of higher programming languages
   - 3.3 Writing and testing short programs
4. Principles of data storage — 2–4 weeks
   - 4.1 Data media
   - 4.2 Access methods
   - 4.3 Data dictionary statements
   - 4.4 Data administration and library systems
   - 4.5 Data security and confidentiality
5. Operation of peripheral devices — 1–2 weeks
   - 5.1 Data archive
   - 5.2 Peripheral device technology
   - 5.3 Lectures and demonstration of operation
   - 5.4 Individual practice on devices
   - 5.5 Function and operation of a remote system console
   - 5.6 Operation of a remote system console
6. Operation of a small system — 1–4 weeks
   - 6.1 Lectures and demonstration
   - 6.2 Analysis of secondary devices
   - 6.3 Individual practice
   - 6.4 Principles of distributed data processing on small systems

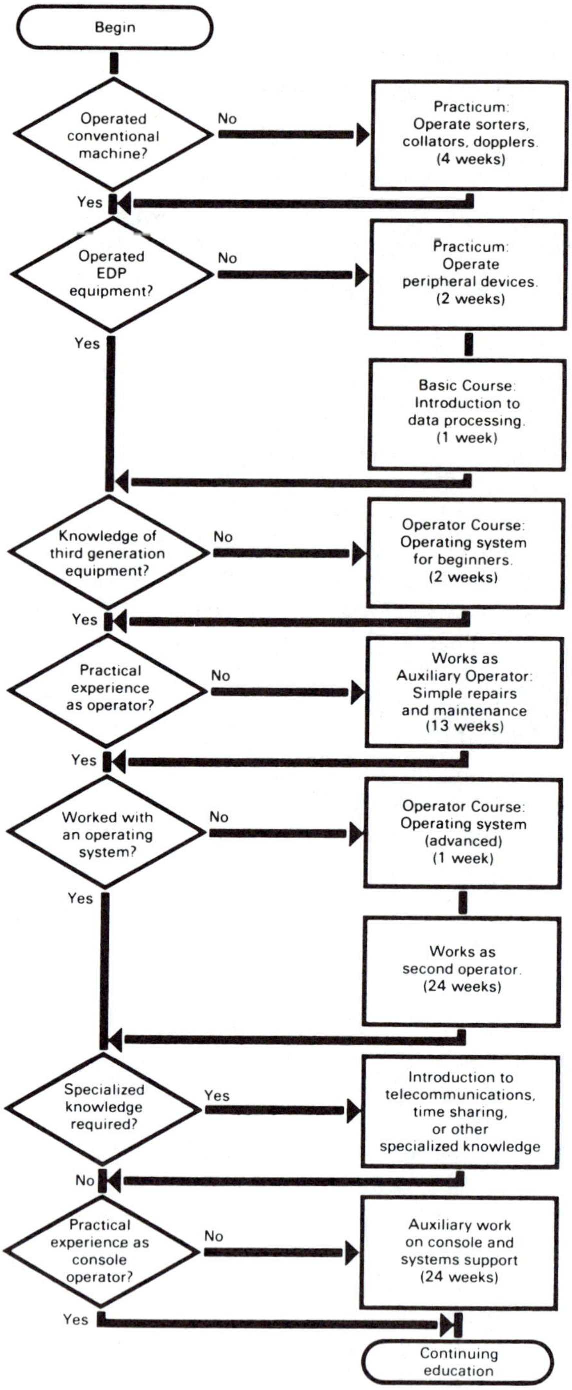


**Figure 5.4** Computer Operator Training Sequence

| | |
|---|---|
| 7. Introduction to the operating system | 4–6 weeks |
| 7.1 System services | |
| 7.2 Control statements | |
| 7.3 Console operation | |
| 7.4 Cold start | |
| 7.5 Logging and accounting | |
| 7.6 Reconfigurations | |
| 8. Operating the central processing unit | 2–8 weeks |
| 8.1 Theoretical introduction | |
| 8.2 Small group demonstration | |
| 8.3 Individual practice | |
| 9. Execution of control functions | 1–4 weeks |
| 9.1 Introduction to planning | |
| 9.2 Materials requisition | |
| 9.3 Participation in scheduling tasks | |
| 10. Principles of teleprocessing | 4–6 weeks |
| 10.1 Telecommunications technology | |
| 10.2 Remotes and terminal operation | |
| 10.3 Functions of online processing | |
| 11. Other computer center tasks | runs concurrently |
| Total: | 17–40 weeks |

The concept of internal training can be summarized in four categories:

1. *Overview (theory)*: The overview outlines the theoretical training activities (such as courses) to be carried out for each function with corresponding hands-on experiences.

2. *Training profile*: The profile determines which prerequisites are needed for each activity, the time frame for practical experiences, and the accompanying theoretical courses.

3. *Training checklist*: The checklist serves as a guideline of points to be emphasized for the instructor. It essentially represents the training content in abbreviated form.

4. *Tests*: Tests at the conclusion of each training segment allow management and trainee to evaluate the training results. They are also an opportunity to direct the employee's career in the computer center, if aptitude for more advanced activities is evident.

Since IBM installations with DOS are widely used, a few sample test items for this system are listed here:

1. ADD and DEL instructions can be entered in any sequence, but it is better to enter any kind of DEL instruction before ADD instructions.

   A. True
   B. False

2. More than one unit can be removed by entering a DEL instruction with several operands.

   A. True
   B. False

3. All operands of a SET instruction are possible in job control, but in IPL only DATE, CLOCK, and RF are possible operands.

   A. True
   B. False

4. The operands of the job control instruction SET can be entered in any sequence.

   A. True
   B. False

5. When the system for 1370 has been generated, the recorder file can be ignored by entering the SET instruction with the RF = NO operands.

   A. True
   B. False

## 5.4.3 Continuing Systems Operation Training

Continuing education is as important as training; this is often neglected, especially with machine operators. Formerly this group had the image of button pushers, that is, a purely mechanical activity not requiring any specific qualifications. As a result the best operators usually drifted over into programming, but this has changed in the past several years. The operator's job profile has become expanded to "systems operator" and his image upgraded.

Obviously numerous auxiliary functions need to be carried out in machine operation, and there will always be operators who are content with this type of activity. But for those who wish to advance, step-by-step training opportunities in data processing should be made available, and attempts should be made to retain an employee in systems operation by conferring greater responsibilities, such as advancement to senior operator or shift supervisor. Familiarity with programming gives the operator not only a better professional understanding of his work but also a feeling of being on an equal level with a programmer. Figure 5.5 illustrates

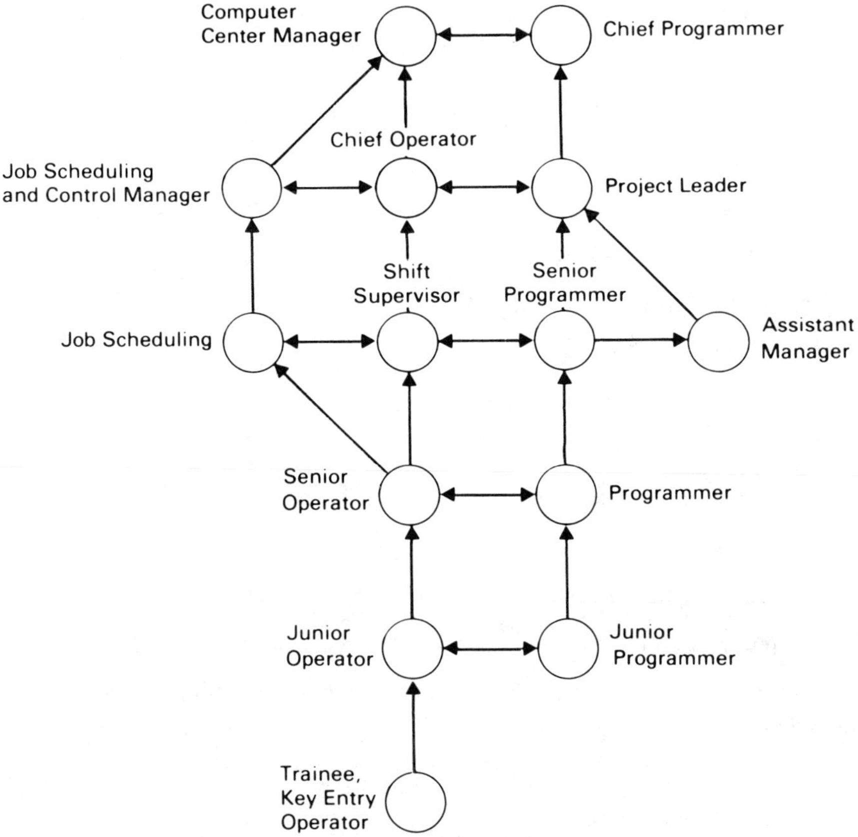


**Figure 5.5** Training Opportunities for Operators

different possibilities for machine operators for further education and development. Continued training can, for example, be conducted during maintenance periods. Dialog-oriented training systems support such efforts. Problems possibly occurring in shift operation can be resolved if approached with a certain amount of ingenuity.

## 5.4.4 Training for Coordination, Scheduling, and Control

Training and continuing education for coordination, scheduling, and control are a special problem. Some computer centers regard this area as a stepping stone for systems operators, but employees from other departments can be successfully used here as well after specialized training.

If training for job coordination is viewed as a possible form of continuing education for console operators it should include roughly the following:

Application of protocols, forms, and statistics

Accounting and machine usage control

Performance

Shift transfer guidelines

Production planning methods

Fundamentals of fields of operations

Job cycles (theory and hands-on experience)

Expanded JCL application

Methods of job scheduling

Principles of priority assignment

Methods of postprocessing

Job preparation and postprocessing with Time sharing option (TSO)

Overview and principles of other automated job scheduling and control systems

Restart

Automated job release

Principles and practices of archive management

Data security and confidentiality

Auxiliary and utility programs

Backup procedures.

Training should alternate between theory and practice. A time frame for the duration of training is difficult to plan because training is contingent on the often varied professional backgrounds and computer center tasks.

## 5.4.5 Progress Evaluation

The considerable investment made by management for purposes of training and continuing education demands ongoing supervision and evaluation of progress. It is therefore essential to prevent course and seminar participation from becoming a type of "extra vacation." This can be avoided if achievement tests are administered during and upon completion of courses and evaluations are prepared at regular intervals by the course instructor. These evaluations should be discussed with the employee so as to give him an opportunity to present his point of view. They also serve to clear up misunderstandings, modify training goals, and thus consider the interests of the employee. An employee often realizes himself that a chosen training project does not, after all, correspond to his preconceptions and abilities; if not, skillful psychological intervention becomes the training supervisor's responsibility.

Above and beyond that, trainees should have the opportunity for critical evaluation of the training curriculum, scheduled events, and instructional personnel and thus contribute to improving the instructional program.

## 5.4.6 The Training Plan

The establishment or expansion of a computer center requires careful instructional planning within the framework of personnel planning. At the point where production begins each employee should be sufficiently proficient and trained to be able to fulfill all necessary job requirements. Figures 5.6 and 5.7 present corresponding guidelines.

| Training | Standard | Months Prior to Installation | | | | | | | | | | | | | | | |
|---|---|---|---|---|---|---|---|---|---|---|---|---|---|---|---|---|---|
| | Actual | 18 | 17 | 16 | 15 | 14 | 13 | 12 | 11 | 10 | 9 | 8 | 7 | 6 | 5 | | |
| General Organization | Standard | 1 | 2 | 2 | 2 | 2 | 2 | 2 | 2 | 2 | 2 | 2 | 2 | 2 | | | |
| | Actual | | | | | | | | | | | | | | | | |
| EDP Organization | Standard | | | 3 | 3 | 3 | 3 | 3 | 3 | 1 | 1 | 1 | 1 | 1 | 1 | | |
| | Actual | | | | | | | | | | | | | | | | |
| Operating Systems | Standard | | | | | 2 | 2 | 2 | 2 | 2 | 3 | 3 | 3 | 3 | 3 | | |
| | Actual | | | | | | | | | | | | | | | | |
| Machine Operation | Standard | | | | | | | 1 | 3 | 3 | 3 | 3 | 3 | 6 | 6 | | |
| | Actual | | | | | | | | | | | | | | | | |
| COBOL | Standard | | | | | | | | | 4 | 4 | 4 | 4 | 6 | 6 | | |
| | Actual | | | | | | | | | | | | | | | | |
| ASSEMBLER | Standard | | | | | | | 3 | 3 | 3 | 4 | 4 | 4 | 4 | 4 | | |
| | Actual | | | | | | | | | | | | | | | | |
| Orientation, Individual Departments | | | | | | | | | | | 12 | 15 | 15 | 18 | 18 | | |

**Figure 5.6** Training Prior to Installation

| Training | Standard / Actual | Teams (Time in Weeks): Organization | Programming | Job Scheduling | Computer Operation | Auxiliary Machines | System Support | Audit/ Control | |
|---|---|---|---|---|---|---|---|---|---|
| General Organization | Standard | 16 | | | | | | 6 | |
| | Actual | | | | | | | | |
| EDP Organization | Standard | 12 | 8 | 4 | | | | 6 | |
| | Actual | | | | | | | | |
| Operating Systems | Standard | | 12 | 8 | 10 | 6 | 18 | 6 | |
| | Actual | | | | | | | | |
| Machine Room | Standard | | | | 16 | 8 | 8 | | |
| | Actual | | | | | | | | |
| COBOL | Standard | | 12 | | | | | 4 | |
| | Actual | | | | | | | | |
| ASSEMBLER | Standard | | 12 | | | | 12 | | |
| | Actual | | | | | | | | |

**Figure 5.7** Training Plan for EDP Personnel

## 5.5 Employee Performance Evaluation

An enterprise generally endeavors to fill management positions from the inside, which means that the appropriate information must be available on each employee. Thus an employee profile counts among the most important components of a personnel information system and should be organized with special care. Errors in appointments to management positions can cause considerable damage, especially in a computer center, when they result in passive resistance among justifiably dissatisfied colleagues.

Ewers, in reporting on EDP manager evaluation, considers the manager in rather general terms and less as one of the leading positions in the computer center, but points out the difficulties in this area. The questionnaire he recommends provides valuable suggestions, especially in emphasizing the importance of instructional planning.

An employee profile should be developed through an annual review by the immediate superior, and, in order to avoid subjective criteria, by the next higher superior as well. The main component of a review is a performance evaluation conducted for all employees according to a binding system. A number of sample criteria for an evaluation system and a sample evaluation form are listed below.

*Evaluation System*

Achieved volume
- Insufficient
- Slow
- Unable to work independently
- Good performance
- Rapid worker
- High achievement even under pressure
- Excellent achievement

Achieved quality
- Superficial with numerous errors
- Regularly needs to be corrected and repeated
- Generally good with occasional errors
- Practically always error-free

Professional qualifications
- Insufficient
- Good general background
- Well-rounded technical qualifications in a specialty

Work habits
- Passive and uninterested in the job
- Identifies with tasks
- Willing and ready team worker

Leadership qualities
- Initiative
- Ability to make the right decisions at the right time
- Personal leadership ability

Potential
- Interested in the company and its operation
- Interested in further training and education
- Aptitude for further training.

Figure 5.8 represents an evaluation form developed at Integrata (Germany). Figure 5.9 is a similar design.

## Personnel Review Form

Department:
Position:

Date

Name (Applicant):
Current Position:
Since:

Reason for Review

Evaluated by
a) Committee
b) Direct Supervisor
c) How long have you been this employee's supervisor?

Percent Suitability

| REQUIREMENTS | | Value of Work (Job Requirements) | | | Production Value | |
|---|---|---|---|---|---|---|
| | | Weight | Points | Value | Relative | Absolute |
| **1. Education and Training** 1.1 Formal Education : | High School (3), Junior College (6), General Technical School (8), College (9) | | | | | |
| 1.2 Professional Training : | Practicum (3), Job-Oriented Technical School/College (6) | | | | | |
| 1.3 Specialized Training : | General (3), Programming (3), Management and Organization (3), Other | | | | | |
| **2. Output** 2.1 Quality : | Needs Reworking (3), Usable (6), Can pass without inspection (9) | | | | | |
| 2.2 Quantity : | Slow (3), Steady and rapid (6), Above average (9) | | | | | |
| **3. Attitude** 3.1 Interest : | Considers EDP a job (3), a serious job (6), a hobby (9) | | | | | |
| 3.2 Willingness to Learn : | Existing (3), Highly developed (6), Studies on own time (9) | | | | | |
| 3.3 Effort : | Limited (3), Only under pressure (6), Self-motivated (9) | | | | | |
| 3.4 Responsibility : | Playing it safe (3), For own work (6), For the team (9) | | | | | |
| 3.5 Cost Awareness : | Limited (3), For own work (6), In every respect (9) | | | | | |
| **4. Mental Capacity** 4.1 Comprehension : | Rapid but inaccurate (3), Slow but sure (6), Rapid and accurate (9) | | | | | |
| 4.2 Reason and Judgment : | Common sense (3), Finds new and useful solutions (6), Creative (9) | | | | | |
| 4.3 Specialized Knowledge (Management and Organization) : | Beginner (3), Advanced (6), Specialist (9) | | | | | |
| 4.4 Specialized Knowledge (Programming) : | Beginner (3), Advanced (6), Specialist (9) | | | | | |

**Figure 5.8** Personnel Evaluation Form (Front of Form).

| REQUIREMENTS | | Value of Work (job requirements): Weight | Points | Value | Production Value: Relative | Absolute |
|---|---|---|---|---|---|---|
| **5. Personal Qualities**<br>5.1 Self-Conduct : | Serious minded (3), Secure but passive (6), Actively secure (9) | | | | | |
| 5.2 Decision-Making Ability : | Avoids decisions (3), Postpones decisions occasionally (6), Initiates decisions (9) | | | | | |
| 5.3 Reliability : | Needs checking (3), Occasionally needs checking (6), Rarely needs checking (9) | | | | | |
| 5.4 Conduct Toward Colleagues : | Loner (3), Makes friends easily (6), Excellent team spirit (9) | | | | | |
| 5.5 Conduct Toward Superiors : | Forward but otherwise correct (3), Correct (6), Rational and open (9) | | | | | |
| **6. Leadership Qualities**<br>6.1 Conduct Toward Subordinates : | Friendly and companionable (3), Leadership as an equal (6), Motivates others (9) | | | | | |
| 6.2 Planning and Dispositon : | Applies methods and regulations (3), Applies them with confidence (6), Improves them (9) | | | | | |

**7. Summary of Employee's Development to Date**

**8. Evaluation of Employee's Future Potential**

How do you judge the individual's potential in your area?
Do you see any personal limitations for further development?
Could this employee be better utilized at another job?
What kind of training would be necessary for advancement?

This evaluation was/was not discussed with the employee.

Date: By:

Integrata (Germany)

**Figure 5.8** Continued (Back of Form).

## Personnel Review Form

Department
Position

Name (Applicant)
Evaluated by — Date
Percent Suitability

| REQUIREMENTS | Value of Work | | | Production Value | |
|---|---|---|---|---|---|
| | Points | Weight | Value | Relative | Absolute |
| **Formal Education**<br>High school graduate (3), Junior college graduate (6), Technical college graduate—general subjects (8), College graduate—General subjects (9) | | | | | |
| **Professional Training**<br>Practicum (3), Technical or 4-year college with specialization (6), Additional training (1-3) | | | | | |
| **Practical Experience**<br>Per year of experience (1), Maximum (10) | | | | | |
| **Specialization**<br>Beginner (3), Advanced (6), Specialist (9) | | | | | |
| **Flexibility, Intellectual Capacity**<br>Qualified for Activities: With instructions (0), Routine (3), Independent (6), Independent problem solving (9) | | | | | |
| **Work Load Capability, Endurance**<br>None (0), Minor (3), Medium (6), High (9) | | | | | |
| **Leadership Ability, Responsibility**<br>Unreliable (0), At own job (3), With group or team (6), Within department (9) | | | | | |
| **Personal Impression**<br>(Application, Appearance, Personal Conduct)<br>Unsatisfactory (0), Adequate (3), Satisfactory (6), Excellent (9) | | | | | |
| Weight: 1-10<br>Points: 1-10 | | | | | |

**Figure 5.9** Sample Personnel Review Form

# SIX

# ASPECTS OF COMMUNICATION

## 6.1 General Aspects

Communication both within the computer center and with the outside world can take many forms because the computer center's primary task of storing and processing information is contingent on a further, more peripheral flow of information.

- Computer center employees must keep themselves informed on the efficiency and operation of their data processing systems with a view towards future developments.
- Computer center employees must keep each other informed on the operational process and coordinate their efforts.
- Users must be informed as to the organization, efficiency, limits of capability, and operational process of the computer center.
- Management must be informed of results and operational processes.
- Information must be exchanged with hardware and software manufacturers.
- Experiences must be shared with other computer centers on membership in professional and user organizations.

The computer center is an organizational system with diverse internal and external communication tasks. The task of effectively establishing these relationships leads to characteristic difficulties based in the nature of the computer center itself. These difficulties increase in proportion to the size and complexity of the total system.

The following examples illustrate the point:

- Users complain about requiring too much information in order to be able to work with the data processing system.
- Users complain about inadequately prepared informational literature—that is, they do not want to be bothered with professional jargon.
- Users are confronted with organizational and technical changes and complain about insufficient information.
- Management complains that data processing is too expensive.
- Operations errors are noticed too late by those affected by them.
- The computer center is overtaxed by unexpected and unplanned jobs.
- Users of remote stations feel cut off from contact with the computer center.
- Changes in the operational system require unexpected organizational innovations.

Some of these difficulties are characteristic only of large computer centers, but even a one-man operation without internal communication problems must at least establish a clear understanding with its job originators.

It is possible to determine a number of the common characteristics of the total system—consisting of user and computer center with their respective communication systems—without going into the details of computer center structure.

The system is of some complexity because of the mutual dependency between users and management. It is subject to strong environmental influences such as manufacturers, customers, financial backers, or competitors. It must therefore be considered an open system rather than a closed one, and its communication interfaces with the environment warrant a closer examination.

The specific features of a communication system are noticeably evident for the users of a service center. In comparison to other service operations, the computer center user must absorb a relatively large amount of information that is far in excess of the technical and information demands, for example, for transportation systems, new transmissions, or bank transactions from the point of view of the customer. Users must therefore be provided with correspondingly specific instructions.

If the users of a computer center are expected to work with a minimum of inconvenience they must have at their disposal a handbook of the programming language or the program listing, a control language manual of the operations system, guidelines on program sequence, files, prices, and allocations. The depth of detail required ties in with the volume of information to be transmitted, as even packaged user programs presuppose detailed knowledge of the parameters involved.

Large service centers such as college computer centers are faced with the special problems of having to keep large numbers of users up to date on a broad technical field that is not only subject to constant change but also is not their primary area of expertise.

This breadth and detail of information to be conveyed means that the methods of communication—for example, the urgency with which instructions from one sender within the system can be transmitted to a receiver—vary sharply. Information on systems breakdowns should immediately reach all users running jobs that do not automatically restart. On the other hand, information regarding the release of user packages may safely be delayed for days or even weeks.

The varying degrees of motivation and technical knowledge of the originators and receivers in this communication system also deserve attention, including their often divergent characteristics as persons and machines. This latter circumstance accounts for the considerable volume and detail of information needed, because the interface of man and machine as a rule demands greater detail of information than the interface between human beings. The focus is often less on quantity than quality.

A second group of characteristic features appears when one attempts to design and define rules for a communications network. In traditional organizational theory it was considered an advantage to have communications guidelines dovetail as much as possible with the lines of authority of the operations organization. This was completely successful only in rare cases. In the usual staff-line organization it often resulted in unnecessarily long and complex lines of communication. Identical lines of authority and communication are at any rate an advantage, and the line-of-authority system provides a framework to be expanded by the addition of lines of communication. In reality, however, such lines of authority are often lacking at decisive points in the communication system under consideration here, especially in the relationship between the computer center and the user. The emphasis on a line-of-authority structure can actually be detrimental to effective communication at certain points in the computer center, because a good deal of information is exchanged informally between specialists. In summary, the line-of-authority system of the operations organization is of little advantage in terms of designing and supporting the communication system of the computer center.

This relates to the fact that because of the large degree of detailed technical information, much of which is of an ad hoc nature, informal lines of communication are easily formed between computer center employees. The advantages and disadvantages of informal communication cannot be discussed in this context, but it is important to recognize how much this freedom of communication can contribute to the necessary learning processes and how far it can be allowed to go without adversely affecting efficiency. Experiments on the structural and functional characteristics of communication networks suggest that, in systems subject to frequent modification, adjustments are facilitated by greater freedom of communication. However, considering the breadth of information transmitted in a computer center, a certain amount of coordination and control is necessary.

To summarize briefly, then, the complex organization system of a computer center contains a communication system that differs from other communication systems in the following ways: breadth and detail of information to be transmitted, significant differences in the degree of urgency of transmission, and the characteristics of originators and receivers. Because of these factors, the operations organization is of little value in the design of a communication system.

The following sections will describe certain essential components of a computer center communication system, with special emphasis on the various forms of communication.

## 6.2 Library

Since one of the most important principles of data processing is to keep all personnel up to date on the rapid technological developments of this field, it is in the interest of management to provide an opportunity for continuing education with a library of specially selected technical literature. This is all the more important because by far the largest part of training and continuing education takes place in the computer center itself. Additionally, references in the technical literature serve to answer open questions more rapidly than recourse to long discussions on the subject of suppositions.

The necessity of a technical library is generally recognized and recommended by manufacturers. What remains open is whether each computer center should have its own library. Experience has shown that for practical purposes the entire data processing area—including the functions of the computer center, data collection, systems analysis, and programming—should share one library.

As far as the computer center is concerned, the volume and contents of such a library essentially depend on the following factors:

Type of computer center

Size of computer center

Scope of computer center tasks

There should at any rate be a reference library from which books and periodicals cannot be checked out at all, or can be checked out only on weekends.

It is difficult to give general suggestions on the type of literature to be made available, as this depends on the special characteristics of the computer center in question. For example, books on numerical processes are not absolutely essential in a commercially oriented computer center. However, a computer center handling technical and scientific tasks will require specialized literature on the field for the purpose of developing and maintaining a program library. In general the following suggestions can be made about what the computer center library should contain:

A complete set of the latest manufacturers' manuals pertaining to the equipment in use

Introductory books and documents, such as programmed instructions, for the purpose of

- Education of trainees and interns
- Information for technical personnel

Manuals for continuing education, including not only books on programming languages but basic as well as specific texts

Periodicals reporting on the latest EDP developments

Magazines published regularly by manufacturers. These are usually free of charge, and since they provide information on available innovations they are especially recommended for a library. Examples are:

- *IBM News*
- IBM: *Perspectives in Computing*
- UNIVAC: *Datascope*
- CDC: *Real Time*
- *Hewlett Packard Journal*

Technical dictionaries and data processing encyclopedias.

A staff member—usually a systems programmer—should be responsible for library maintenance. The following functions are included in library maintenance:

Suggestions on acquisition of books and periodicals

Maintenance of at least two card catalogs, one alphabetical and one by subject. An automated catalog system is recommended for large libraries.

Keeping all computer center or departmental personnel (in the case of shared library facilities including systems analysis/programming) informed about new publications and pertinent articles.

Taking measures to ensure against loss of library materials. Many employees seem of the opinion that unlimited loans of manufacturer's publications constitute a pardonable offense. There is no general solution to this problem, but a certain degree of order can be maintained if the library is kept in a room that also serves as office for a staff member and if check-out duties are rotated.

## 6.3 Meetings and Conferences

Personal discussions are an essential organizational aid for the computer center. The advantages of project discussions in systems analysis/programming are well-known. A member of the computer center should be present at these discussions so that the problems involved in project realization can be taken into consideration.

In a shift-oriented computer center, meetings of the shift supervisors are important. They serve to discuss work schedules, work transter at shift change, error situations, security systems, and the particulars of individual job processes. In addition there is the general exchange of experiences. In a two-shift operation such discussions are best scheduled at the time of shift change. A three or more shift operation requires special scheduling because at least one shift supervisor has to come in for that purpose. Such discussions will therefore not occur with great frequency, usually once a month or under special circumstances.

Meetings of department heads are customary in large computer centers. In company computer centers with central systems analysis/programming these meetings include the entire data processing area. Minutes must be taken of all agreements and points made in discussions, just as in meetings of technical departments. This means that a responsible secretary must be appointed. Since in the formulation of minutes the facts are sometimes somewhat obscured, it is important to have the concurrence of all participants at a later date. This can be accomplished either by reviewing the minutes at the next meeting or by setting a deadline for corrections.

It must be pointed out that meetings and discussions represent an absolutely essential area of communication. However, excessive discussions have a negative effect on work in the computer center. The computer center manager should be responsible for determining a reasonable average.

## 6.4 Personnel Communications

In choosing equipment, minor differences in efficiency are often the decisive factor for or against a manufacturer. In general, however, no consideration is given to the fact that once the equipment is installed even a few repeat runs can carry this decision-making factor to the point of absurdity. Repeat runs are usually caused by error, and errors are usually caused by ignorance. Maximum efficiency of data processing systems usually presupposes therefore that computer center personnel as well as users are fully informed about the current situation and the technical capabilities of the computer center. Even though this forms a part of training and continuing education (section 5.4), mention must be made at this point that information pertaining to modifications, innovations, and elimination of possibilities must be disseminated quickly and accurately.

This goal can be reached if the system group of the computer center develops and distributes information on the current system. The activity must necessarily originate with the systems group because it is the one best informed about the frequently occurring software changes. Officially this information is usually published by the computer center manager. This procedure has the advantage that other topics, such as organizational announcements, can be included.

## 6.4.1 Content of Reports

While it is not possible to provide a full listing here, the following topics should be included in reports:

Hardware configuration and modifications (in the form of tables and outlines).

Information on available software and modifications (not all existing possibilities need to be listed); systems software supplements or new versions of the operating system may have been added. In particular this could have an effect on:

- New error reports
- New service program features
- Error conditions that have not yet been corrected—for example, a console command that no longer functions adequately with a new operating system
- Control statement changes—for example, new or different options
- Console command changes
- New or different service programs
- Compiler changes
- Recommendations on which functions of the operating system are less preferable because they work inefficiently

Information on organizational changes, such as new maintenance schedules, new forms.

Information on new or different allocations or materials.

## 6.4.2 Form of Reports

In general communications of this type appear at irregular intervals and with varying length. They are frequently single sheets which are added to binders and serve to document the current situation. Many of these communications are later incorporated into operating instructions. Such loose-leaf collections should be numbered continuously, for example: MEMO 5/83, p. 1 of 3. This refers to the first of three pages of the fifth memo in 1983. All communications should be dated and signed.

Other communications to personnel include printouts of current information or messages posted on terminals. Such possibilities require support from the operating system and are only conditionally applicable. Nevertheless they should be given greater support.

### 6.4.3 Distribution of Reports

It has already been mentioned that reports are produced at various points in the computer center but are issued by the computer center manager. Connected with this is the practice of keeping a distribution register to indicate which staff members have received which communications. New employees should receive memos retroactively if the contents are pertinent to their jobs. One employee should be responsible for distribution.

## 6.5 Reports to the User

The discussion of communications to personnel also applies to the user, particularly in view of the fact that accurate and timely information eliminates error and results in greater systems efficiency. Accurate information also means satisfied users. Considering the service character of the computer center and the ratio of efficiency to total operating expenses this represents a valid argument for a company computer center.

The users of the computer center include the systems analysts and programmers on the one hand (this includes centralized programming) and on the other the non-EDP departments which furnish the data and receive the results.

### 6.5.1 Reports to Non-EDP Departments

These reports should include the following points:

Cost, including cost adjustments

Changes in type of service—for example, changes in effect as of a particular date:

- Cassette tapes are available for data collection
- Time sharing is available
- Special mailing or transportation services are offered

Communications on goal setting in systems planning

Communications to requisitioners (originators) do not generally justify a separate publication, since they often contain information of interest to other groups. They are usually integrated with general user bulletins, perhaps under a special heading.

### 6.5.2 Reports to Systems Analysts

These reports may include the following:

Systems configuration and modification; this should include data efficiency measures such as changes in disk capacity

Introduction of new and different data media; this may include references to the possibility of using nine-track tapes in addition to seven-track tapes, or making greater use of minireels

Change of operating hours—for example, task planning now works a full second shift; test jobs can now be run until 8 p.m. instead of 6 p.m.

Changes in type of service, such as changes in the archives system or data revision

Modification and/or expansion of software; this may include reports on new operating systems or generally accessible applications program packages

Library news, such as changes in hours or announcements of new subscriptions

### 6.5.3 Reports to Programmers

The points cited in section 6.5 apply to programmers as well. However, additional information should be supplied, such as:

Modification and/or expansion of systems software (details on compilers, service programs, or standard subprogram libraries)

Detailed error descriptions, such as compiler errors

Programming suggestions optimizing systems software use

Organizational changes and information on the use of data processing systems such as tests or routine tasks

Announcements of new programming materials

Announcements of courses and workshops

This is not intended to be a complete listing. Computer center personnel are aware that effective communication with users contributes significantly towards improving their relations with the computer center.

## 6.5.4 Form of User Reports

Typewritten copies have in the past proved most practical in getting reports to the user as quickly as possible. When several news items coincide for one issue, it is best to have them listed in a table of contents. Figure 6.1 is an example of the title page of such a report from the Center of Data Processing at the University of Tübingen.

It stands to reason that user reports are posted on the computer center bulletin board and at various work stations. Since it is part of human nature to pay little attention to items on the bulletin board it is not only important to find appropriate locations for them (for example near the input/output of test programs) but to give them a relevant design. A computer center employee such as the manager's secretary should be responsible for this.

A further possibility is the title page of the systems output of a program run shown in Figure 6.2. However, this addresses only the users who currently have programs running. Because of space limitation—only the latest news should be disseminated in this way—the problem is not completely solved by simply collecting the program leaders. At the very least the various news items should be numbered consecutively.

Unfortunately this type of communication is not generally supported by today's operating systems and not every computer center is able to write special programs for it. A further disadvantage is that the print is not exactly pleasant to the eye and that it means additional work for the printers.

If one is willing to accept these disadvantages, the bulletins can also be made available through a machine program. This has the advantage of minimizing the extra load on the printer because each bulletin is printed only once for each user. Addressing is by means of a stored user file. Such files exist in every computer center anyway for purposes of production accounting. This should also answer the question of distribution: everyone assigning tasks to the computer center, including every programmer, receives a user report. These reports should list the following:

Computer center name

Name of computer center manager

Name of person responsible for the report

Computer center address (city, street, etc.)

Telephone and telex numbers

Current report number

Date

Brief table of contents

Bank affiliation (also for computer centers running outside jobs).

# Center for Data Processing

*University of Tubingen*

Director: Dr. Martin A. Graef

No. 6
May 1972

REPORT
To Our Users

**Contents:**



---

Tubingen, Kollestrasse 1  Telephone:  Telex:

**Figure 6.1** Title Page of a User Report with Table of Contents

```
*********News Bulletin*********No. 8*********August 21, 1972*******************************************
Subj.: Operations
Assignment of mnemotechnical equipment names (AO, GI, etc) is no longer
possible.
Subj.: German Computer Center Programs
As of today German computer center programs are available only on large discs
under volume name "GP009."
Subj.: SPSS
As of today SPSS requires 195K. Brochure on treatment of labeled tapes available
at dispatch.
```

**Figure 6.2** A News Bulletin in the Leader of a Program Printout

Terminal operations have the option of a special type of user report: a mass storage device may contain the total information including technical and organizational references—see, for example, the information system of CDC data services (Figure 6.3). The control statement SYSINFO provides all the information on file; SYSINFO (NEWS) releases only the latest bulletins. Further parameters provide access to various subsections of user reports (Figure 6.4) so that, for example, updates can be released effective as of a specific date or can be transferred to personal files. Bulletins of special current value can also automatically appear on the screen after logging on.

Depending on the terminal, the output can be in the form of a printout or on screen. On-screen output has the advantage of providing users with the latest information instead of possibly outdated lists, but this presupposes an efficient update service.

This brings us to the question of who should be responsible for user reports. In general this task is delegated to the assistant manager or a member of systems support.

## 6.6 Reports to Company Employees

In company computer centers employees outside of data processing should be informed of developments of the data processing department, usually through a

```
PAGE    2 (VOL  2) DATE 02-17-71.  SYSTEM BULLETIN

                    CDC DATA SERVICES / GERMANY


THIS BULLETIN WILL KEEP YOU INFORMED ON THE STATUS AND AVAILABILITY OF OUR
SOFTWARE AND APPLICATIONS PACKAGES. IT WILL ALSO CONTAIN USEFUL INFORMATION
RELATED TO KNOWN (AND SUSPECTED) PROBLEMS, AND PROGRAMMING HINTS TO HELP OUR
CUSTOMERS. CONTRIBUTIONS TO THE BULLETIN ARE MADE BY OUR STAFF AND OUR
CUSTOMERS. HOW YOU CAN CONTRIBUTE TO THE BULLETIN IS DESCRIBED IN THE SYSINFO
REFERENCE BULLETIN.
```

**Figure 6.3** Example of a User Report in a Terminal Operation (Systems Information Headline of a CDC Computer Center)

```
          $SEQUENCE,NNN.
          $CHARGE,SNNNN.
          BULLS,CM7000.
          SYSINFO(PARAMETERS)

THE SYSINFO PARAMETERS WILL ENABLE THE USER TO SELECT ONLY THE
NECESSARY PARTS OF THE MATERIAL PROVIDED. THESE PARAMETERS ARE


SYSINFO.   OR   SYSINFO(NEWS)
          THE NEWS BULLETIN IS A SPECIAL BULLETIN CONTAINING
          INFORMATION LIKE

          KNOWN (AND SUSPECTED) HARDWARE AND SOFTWARE PROBLEMS (IF
          THEY CAN AFFECT THE USER IN A NEGATIVE WAY).
          ANOUNCEMENTS OF NEW FEATURES AND SERVICES.
          ANOUNCEMENTS OF EXPECTED LIMITATIONS.
          A TABLE REFLECTING THE CURRENT STATUS OF OUR SYSTEM.
          A TABLE REFLECTING THE STATUS OF THIS BULLETIN.


          THE NEWS BULLETIN IS DEFAULT AND ADDED TO ANY BULLETIN
          REQUEST MADE TO SYSINFO. NOTE, HOWEVER, THAT THE DATE
          PARAMETER WILL PROTECT YOU FROM OBTAINING A NEWS BULLETIN
          YOU ALREADY RECEIVED.

SYSINFO(ALL)
          THE ALL PARAMETER ENABLES YOU TO GET THE COMPLETE SYSTEM
          BULLETIN WITHOUT HAVING TO EXPLICITLY SELECT THE ITEMS
          COVERED. THE USER MAY SPECIFY ≠ALL≠ IN COMBINATION WITH
          THE DATE PARAMETER TO KEEP HIS SYSTEM BULLETIN COMPLETE
          AND UPDATED.

SYSINFO(SUBJECT)
          THIS PARAMETER ENABLES THE USER TO SELECT (A) SUBJECT(S)
          LISTED IN THE NEWS BULLETIN THAT HE MAY CONSIDER OF
          INTEREST TO HIM. TO OBTAIN A COPY OF THIS SYSINFO
          DESCRIPTION, ONE WOULD SPECIFY ≠SYSINFO(SYSINFO)≠

SYSINFO(ALL,SUBJECT)   OR   SYSINFO(SUBJECT,ALL)
          THIS COMBINATION WILL PROVIDE YOU WITH ALL BULLETINS,
          EXCEPT FOR THE SELECTED BULLETINS. IF THE SELECTED
          BULLETIN IS NEWS, HOWEVER, THIS WILL BE IGNORED.

SYSINFO(D=YYMMDD)
          THE DATE PARAMETER IS A TOOL YOU CAN USE TO PREVENT
          YOURSELF FROM RECEIVING INFORMATION YOU ALREADY HAVE. ALL
          BULLETINS ARE EQUIPPED WITH A DATE. THIS DATE IS USED
          ACCORDING TO THE STATEMENT
               IF(BULLETINDATE.LT.PARAMETERDATE)RETURN
          THE DATE MUST BE SPECIFIED AS YEAR-MONTH-DAY IN 6 DIGITS.

SYSINFO(L=FILENAME)
          THIS PARAMETER ENABLES THE USER TO SPECIFY A 1-7
          ALPHANUMERIC CHARACTERS NAME TO BE USED AS IDENTIFIER FOR
          A FILE RECEIVING THE SYSINFO OUTPUT. THE DEFAULT FILENAME
          WILL BE ≠OUTPUT≠.
```

**Figure 6.4** Parameters of a User Information System in a CDC Computer Center house organ reporting on events and planning in the organization. Information of this type is best prepared by the director of training programs. In the absence of such a position, an employee capable of writing a clear and concise text (for example the director of task planning activities) should have this responsibility. The psychological value of this type of preparatory work is not to be underestimated, both in terms of potential new tasks and the computer center's position as the focal point of criticism. In this respect an employee-directed instructional policy can only have positive effects.

## 6.7 Public Relations

Public relations is as important to a computer center service division as in-house publications are to the personnel of a company computer center, and both should be concerned with the choice of information reaching the public as well as the methods used to accomplish this. Computer centers at universities and research institutes are best served by the public information offices of their institutions. New methods of application or new machine configurations are generally the subject of press releases because they are of interest to the public and create an understanding and awareness of the work performed by computer centers. Creating and maintaining an image facilitates the work inside.

It should be kept in mind that besides professional publications there are information bulletins on the market which can play an important part in public relations in terms of more specific and detailed reports on advisory experiences, contracts, or products.

## 6.8 Association Members

The necessity of forming professional associations for specific interest groups has been known for centuries. As long ago as the Middle Ages the guilds acted as spokesmen to the outside world as well as providing a forum for an exchange of information among the various professional groups. These associations proved themselves especially in the apprenticeship trades which had developed over centuries and were not receptive to innovation. Such organizations are even more essential for data processing personnel because often definite job descriptions are nonexistent in the computer center and innovations and improvements are subject to immediate application.

## 6.9 Complaint Book

A consideration of computer center relations with the environment would be incomplete without a report on a safety valve through which all those in contact with the computer center can voice their criticism.

It can take the form of a suggestion box or a publicly displayed complaint book where everyone can freely criticize, unless a personal confrontation or some other form of written communication is preferred. This complaint book should be kept in a location where users pick up their results, such as the output room.

Even if the task planning and machine operations managers regularly check on the types of criticism received in that manner and take appropriate action, it is also the responsibility of the computer center manager to examine the complaint book personally. This is the only assurance that the computer center provides its users with maximum support. It has proven generally helpful to have complaints acknowledged in writing after action has been taken on them.

SEVEN

# PLANNING AND CONTROL

The growing importance of planning and control goes hand in hand with an increase in the volume and complexity of computer center tasks. A number of large computer centers have, in fact, already formed special teams for this purpose. Another factor to be considered is that the additional planning tasks cause an expansion of staff functions in the production operation referred to as the "computer center." In changeovers to large-scale distributed data processing this aspect takes on special significance.

## 7.1 Goals and Methods of Production Planning

Laymen often express their attitude towards electronic data processing by wondering why EDP requires so much personnel, considering that all the work is done by sophisticated machinery. The specialist may find this reproach rather absurd at first, but it should be taken seriously, although from a different vantage point. Data processing professionals should constantly be alert to the question of whether or not too much personnel is employed as a result of improper planning and organization. On the other hand, the computer center performs a service function, which by its very nature heavily depends on manpower. This means that planning and advisory tasks must be considered separately from production.

Industrial manufacturing provides a good example for the goals and methods of a computer center which is, after all, a production plant. The concept that available operational resources can only be fully utilized with appropriate operations scheduling and planning was slow to take hold in industrial manufacturing. But since the assumptions here have always proceeded from the concrete situation of manufacturing, no uniform definition has developed for the concept of operations scheduling in the industrial management literature. If one includes EDP production, the conceptual framework is expanded even further, sometimes to the extent that the transportation of data media to the computer is included.

From the computer center point of view the following definition is a useful prerequisite for these considerations:

> ***Operations scheduling constitutes the totality of measures, including the development of all required documents and operational devices, that are necessary to guarantee production at minimum expenditure through planning, control, and supervision.***

The total complex of activities preparatory to production can be divided into long-term and short-term planning measures. The long-term portion is more concerned with general measures and usually only determines the production outline. By and large it consists of the following components:

- *Product development.* This pertains to the quality of production—that is, which goods to produce at a later date. In conjunction with EDP, it means which tasks of an enterprise should be performed by electronic data processing. The necessary planning activities are generally carried out by a coordinating EDP committee and approved by management (section 2.3.4).
- *Resource development.* In the computer center this means above all the development of a quantitative framework—that is, a master plan for stationary operating devices. If in the first step numerous and extensive tasks were planned for production, EDP capability must be adjusted or expanded accordingly. This can mean greater computational capability, channel capability, printer output, or expanded storage; on the other hand it may also necessitate additional systems components such as plotters, OCR readers or video display screens. This shift from quantity—in the sense of increased EDP systems ouput—to quality is characteristic of EDP and is particularly noticeable in software, because program availability forms a part of resource development. This point can be further divided into the alternatives between application and system software and the various possibilities of software availability, for example internally developed programs versus purchased programs. Production planning involves the computer center primarily in terms of configuration design and system software, whereby the latter is not made available by the computer center itself but must be included in the

overall plan (section 2.5.3). The development of application software is often so extensive that a separate department for systems analysis and programming is established. In addition, resource development includes building and space planning (Chapter 8).

- *Organizational development*. The planning components here pertain primarily to the details of the operations organization. The material presented in Chapter 3 on operations organization should be understood in this sense. In this context it involves only the preparatory portion of job preparation and scheduling for each task. Production organization is not a static component but is subject to a continuous development both in the sense of ongoing production planning and in production improvement, since each planning step represents a continuing function of corresponding demands.
- *Planning coordination*. One of the characteristics of long-term planning is that it must be in harmony with all the other planning activities of the enterprise. In the computer center this coordination is handled by the EDP commission (section 2.3.4) and/or a central office of the organization.
- *Cooperation with accounting*. Since in EDP essential accounting components are contained in the accounting system, this general characteristic of a manufacturing operation is not as evident to the outside in the specific case of a computer center. However, coordination of the automated accounting program with the internal accounting system of the enterprise is essential. Large computer centers with different data processing systems have established a separate usage administration area within job scheduling for this purpose.

Short-term planning, on the other hand, includes all activities specifically related to production. It is divided into three parts, all of which represent distinct functions in the computer center.

- *Job program design*. This determines which products are to be manufactured according to which schedule. Applied to the computer center this means which programs must be available for which data processing according to a predetermined timetable. This aspect of planning will be discussed in section 7.3. In the computer center it is realized in a so-called medium-range systems usage plan which is essentially based on the long-term outline.
- *Job output*. In the computer center this refers to the sequence in which application programs are to run on the EDP systems; it is linked to the task area of short-term systems usage planning and includes the necessary job administration. For purposes of a comprehensive overview of usage planning, long-term, short-term, and medium-range planning will be discussed together in section 7.3. The task-related component—job administration—was

discussed within the framework of functions pertaining to the operations organization in section 3.3.3. This division corresponds to the concept of classifying actual planning tasks as staff functions.

- *Supervision of production execution*. In the computer center this pertains not only to audit but to the entire reporting system on equipment utilization and the broad area of coordination and controls. Since reports on equipment utilization are of special significance, they will be discussed separately. Time studies are generally the most important basis for decision-making in job scheduling.

It has already been pointed out that from an organization point of view job scheduling is classified as a staff function on account of its pronounced planning characteristics. But since the computer center as a service center is equipped with an installation capable of processing a large variety of differentiated tasks, job scheduling is a separate group. Organizational theory is maintained insofar as the tasks of production control are occasionally given a separate slot (Figures 2.9 and 2.12)

The goals of production planning in a computer center can be summarized as follows:

- Only the specifically desired products should be manufactured—that is, production errors requiring reruns are to be avoided if at all possible, not to mention the consequences in terms of damage caused by errors.
- The desired products should be manufactured on schedule; this can only be accomplished with accurate time planning.
- Production should be as cost-effective as possible; this means optimal utilizational of available capacity and avoidance of overcapacity.
- Simplification of work flow by means of production control feedback must be the overall goal of planning—that is personnel and equipment expenditures should be reduced wherever possible.

Planning is not a one-time process but may be a regularly recurring time-oriented process or a project-oriented activity that recurs only in partial tasks. The concept of controlling, now a part of computer center management, developed in the past several years from originally empirical planning methods. Its basic idea is the design of a formalized planning, control, and information system, and its utilization in order to achieve the economic goals of data processing. However, control focuses primarily on effective planning procedures which later serve as a preparation for auditing.

Once planning proceeds to the realization phase, the actual data must be entered. The very extensive accounting data of a DP system furnish computer center control with a tool for production planning and production control. The actual data must be compared with planning data for purposes of correcting possible undesirable developments. The activities of computer center control are, as a result, predominantly action-oriented. The reporting system is therefore subject to ongoing revision and needs to be adjusted to each particular situation in order to avoid unnecessary accumulations of data. This applies not only to the dynamic aspect of computer center production but also to the static component of system configuration.

## 7.2 Computer Operations Reports

Regularly scheduled reports provide information on achieved output and the efficiency and cost-effectiveness of a computer center. A conscientious report system exercises control and guidance functions. Errors and nonproductive situations are recognized and eliminated, and a comprehensive overview of all computer center functions allows for organizational changes and improvements.

Short-term and medium-range usage reports are generally distinguished from problem reports. Standard software products are used to derive information reports from the accounting data. IBM systems, for example, offer RMF (Resource Measurement Facility), but even there an effort has to be made to achieve an optimum between detailed reports with a great deal of information but an insufficient overview, and reduced reports with a good overview but little information. The time periods covered by reports must also be chosen for maximum utility.

### 7.2.1 Preventive and Corrective Maintenance

Since EDP systems consist of many individual components of limited longevity, it is in the interests of maximum operational efficiency to prevent malfunction by replacing weak components before their service life expires. This purpose is achieved through regular preventive maintenance at considerable cost which must be absorbed by the computer center. A feature depending exclusively on the operational readiness of its EDP system and representing a significant item in the computer center budget should constantly be scrutinized and improved.

Because of its increase in volume and importance, system software requires maintenance as well. The maintenance costs of system programs (operating systems, compilers) are listed separately in service contracts. This trend of separating hardware from software maintenance will be observed here as well.

#### 7.2.1.1 Systems Availability

The informative value of report data will be discussed in more detail in section 7.2.2.2. At this point, however, it is important to begin with two concepts that provide information on malfunctioning systems such as EDP systems.

***Availability is generally understood as the relationship between actual and planned usage time.***

It is important to emphasize the "planned service life," rather than calendar time, serves as the reference value. This means that systems availability can be increased by scheduling necessary maintenance for time periods not intended for usage. The result is that a system that tends to malfunction has greater availability than a failure-proof system, because maintenance and repair services have been scheduled for different time periods, usually during the early morning hours or on weekends.

Since a DP system consists of many different components it is advisable to increase the reliability of critical components through parallel connection of several identical functional units. At the same time it should be kept in mind that sequential connection of these components reduces reliability, although this cannot always be avoided with very complex systems.

The concept of reliability is derived from mathematical statistics and can be defined in this context as follows:

***Reliability is the probability that a data processing system or components thereof will not fail through error function within a predetermined period of time.***

The earlier definition of availability pointed out that it is a question of point of view. Accordingly, a differentiation is made in the computer center between the following types of availability:

- *System availability* includes start-up time and considers all unplanned malfunctions requiring warm restart or cold start.
- *Teleprocessing availability* is restricted to the time periods of systems operation during which teleprocessing is to be available.
- *Application availability* is the central availability of an individual teleprocessing application.
- *Line availability* includes the availability of all individual teleprocessing components from the central control unit by means of modems, lines, and line computers to decentralized control units.
- *User availability* refers to the operational readiness of an individual user terminal.

It must be the goal of computer center management to provide the greatest possible availability for individual applications, usually by means of statistical calculations, despite the tendency of some system components to malfunction. The practical measures for ascertaining application availability will be discussed in section 7.2.3.5 in the context of installation management, a procedure that has received favorable notice. Occasionally valuable suggestions can be obtained from online computer centers in which, for example, industrial processes are hooked up directly to the EDP system; these can be expected to provide particularly effective application availability.

### 7.2.1.2 Hardware Maintenance

Preventive maintenance of data processing systems has undergone a fundamental change in recent years. The reduced cost of circuit technology has made error correction codes affordable, with the result that one-bit errors cannot only be registered but corrected. The devices continue running despite occurring errors and produce correct results for the applications while the technicians are able to observe how often and at which points in the system errors occurred. Monitoring is handled by a maintenance processor, which in most cases is connected to the manufacturer's own maintenance network.

In most installations the continued presence of a maintenance technician is no longer required, thus none are permanently stationed there any longer. Only large installations have the advantage of being able to set up a maintenance base. Maintenance technicians take advantage of teleservice only in particularly critical situations, but service through maintenance via telephone is not inferior where smaller installations are concerned.

The era of setting aside daily or weekly blocks of time for preventive maintenance is past. Now it is a matter of a few hours per month, depending on the type and size of the installation, and this means an increase in system availability. However, corrective maintenance remains a factor. Thus the degree of automation provided by manufacturers or maintenance services should not entirely be ranked among the advantages of computer centers.

The problem of preventive maintenance is not solved simply by making available appropriate segments of time. Reports on the quality of preventive and corrective maintenance should be prepared and verified at regular intervals. The technicians enter their work in such maintenance reports. The chief operator then evaluates the quality of maintenance services performed—this is the only method for recognizing inadequacies. The reports produced automatically by the maintenance processor constitute an important supplement.

As already mentioned, a distinction is made between preventive and corrective maintenance. A number of computer centers have made it a practice not to schedule repairs during the time periods alloted to preventive maintenance, based on the opinion that a reduction in preventive maintenance increases down time. However, a statistical examination of 49 reports on the utilization of EDP installations did not support this opinion. Figure 7.1 shows the relationship between the percentage of unavailability—consisting of preventive and emergency maintenance time—and the percentage of purely preventive maintenance. It clearly demonstrates

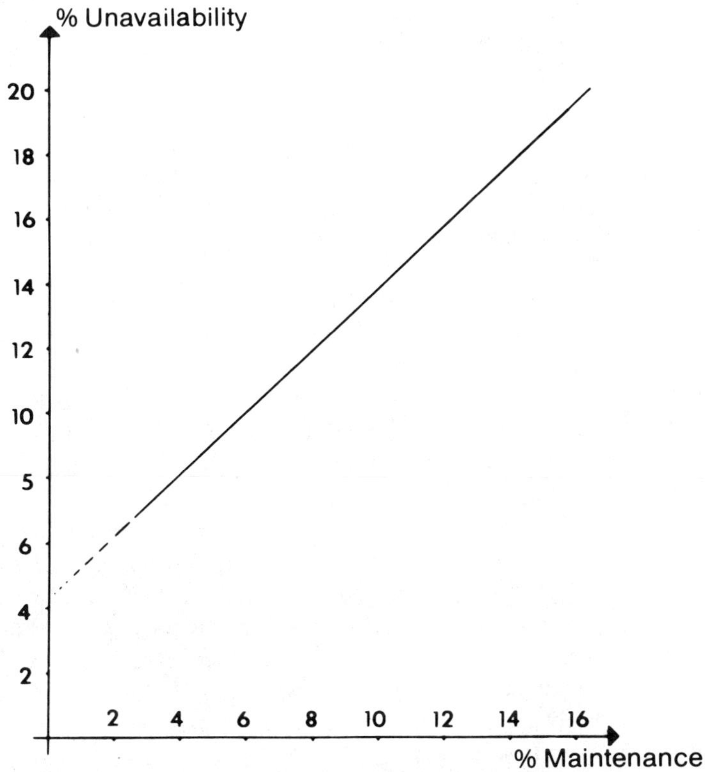


**Figure 7.1** Percentage of EDP Unavailability (Maintenance and Malfunction) and Its Relationship to the Percentage of Preventive Maintenance during Total Operating Time (statistically derived from 49 annual reports).

that in actual experience installation availability cannot be increased through an increase in the proportion of preventive maintenance. On the contrary, the almost 45-degree angle of the diagonal shows that the proportion of unavailability is increased almost exactly by the proportion of preventive maintenance, and that there is practically no relationship between down time due to malfunction and time spent on maintenance. The computed relationship of

$$F = 4.25 - 0.022\ M$$

confirms this. F represents the percentage of malfunction relative to total operating time, and M the percentage of preventive maintenance. There has been no corresponding analysis of the most recent maintenance technologies.

An examination of preventive maintenance reports shows practically no relationship between the percentage of malfunction (F) and total operating time T:

$$F = 4.5 - 0.00006\,T$$

Figure 7.2 is an illustration of the time dimension in terms of hours. The diagonal represents malfunction as a percentage of total operating time, showing that independent of operating time a 4.5% failure factor can be expected. Larger deviations are possible, however.

These considerations show that preventive maintenance is a matter of quality rather than quantity. Some courageous computer center managers have attempted to do entirely without preventive maintenance, restricting themselves to maintenance on call. This procedure is common with process computers and has shown positive results. However, to date there has been no comprehensive comparative analysis. Satisfactory experiences have been reported in individual cases where availability was improved by 4–5% in this manner.

Manufacturers of EDP installations have in recent times themselves undertaken considerations of this type, with the result that EDP installations are increasingly designed in such a way that only partial shutdowns are required for maintenance while the rest of the system continues operating. This includes partial shutdown not only of peripherals, but also of internal modules such as storage modules.

The preventive maintenance problem can also be solved by using a financially and otherwise more advantageous independent maintenance service instead of service provided by the manufacturer.

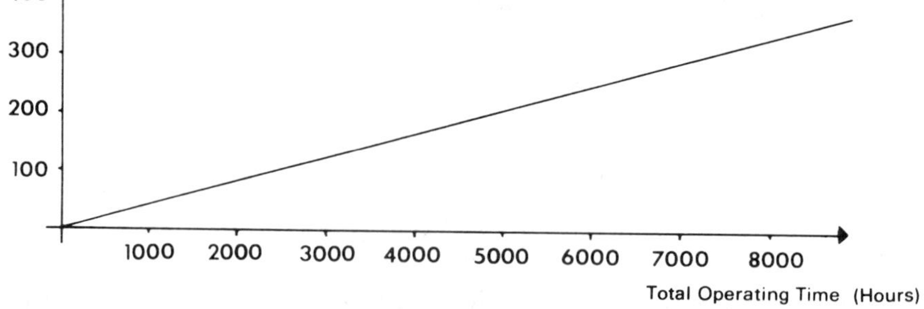


**Figure 7.2** Relationship of Malfunction (in hours) to Total Operating Time over a One-Year Period.

Data Processing Failure Report No 39102

**Customer**: ABC Computer Center **Equipment Type**: 4004/45 **Number**: 1

☐ Check Where Applicable

Customer/Operator Entry

☐ Total Breakdown
☐ Core
☐ Error Following Power Outage
☐ Printer Device **Gerät** ______
☐ Tape Device **Gerät** ______
☒ Storage Device 564C **Gerät** 564 C
☐ Paper Tape Device **Gerät** ______
☐ Punched Cards Device **Gerät** ______
☐ ______

Program, Program Section A 2423 1

Remarks Read Error

To Be Corrected
☒ At Once
☐ During Next Maintenance
☐ On 4/14/84 at 4/44 P M

Failure Reported To H Frantz

Date ______ Time ______ Signed ______

Maintenance Personnel Entry

☒ Technical Breakdown
☐ Error Caused By Power Supply
☐ Error Nonreproducible
☐ Error Caused by Air Conditioning
☐ Operating Error
☐ Program Error
☐ ______

Remarks on Cause of Error Dirty Write Head

Error/Malfunction
☒ Corrected
☐ Temporarily Corrected
☐ Not Corrected

Date ______ Time ______ Signed ______

Equipment taken over by Customer/Operator

Equipment is ☐ fully operational ☐ partly operational

Date Time Signed

**Figure 7.3** Error Evaluation of IBM/360-50 Magnetic Tapes

In order to ensure maintenance of the highest quality, operating systems should also generate trouble reports for the maintenance technicians. These will vary significantly from system to system. Figure 7.3 is an example of a trouble report for an IBM/360-50 system. If the operating system does not generate trouble reports, they must be produced manually by the operators. Otherwise this is only required in cases of errors that the system is unable to detect. Figure 7.4 represents a failure report form, which on the left contains the entry made by the operator who discovered the error, and on the right that of the maintenance technician who corrected it. Since not all errors register automatically, the practice of manual error protocols is occasionally maintained. If properly designed, these protocols can be made available directly to data entry. This also allows for entries for and about malfunctioning system components, an important consideration in terms of computer center control.

Generally speaking, maintenance reports contain references to the frequency and distribution of errors and indicate how quickly they were corrected. Based on such reports, the computer center is able to schedule an effective and not unnecessarily excessive preventive maintenance plan. Proper reaction to hardware and software errors is a vital necessity for the computer center and is contingent upon suitable organizational guidelines.

Error Evaluation of IBM/360-50 Magnetic Tapes

| VOLUME SERIAL | CPU ID | MOD NO | RECORDS | TEMP READ | TEMP WRITE | PERM READ | PERM WRITE | NOISE BLOCKS | EREASE GAPS | CLEANER ACTIONS | USAGE (SIO#S) | PERFORMANCE FACTOR |
|---|---|---|---|---|---|---|---|---|---|---|---|---|
| 002035 | JI | 50 | 1 | 0/ 0 | 3/ 3 | 0/ 0 | 0/ 0 | 0 | 3 | 0 | 1620 | 1620 |
| 002043 | JI | 50 | 1 | 0/ 0 | 11/ 11 | 0/ 0 | 0/ 0 | 0 | 14 | 0 | 582 | 582 |
| 002048 | JI | 50 | 1 | 0/ 0 | 2/ 2 | 0/ 0 | 0/ 0 | 0 | 2 | 0 | 705 | 705 |
| 002052 | JI | 50 | 2 | 0/ 0 | 6/ 3 | 0/ 0 | 0/ 0 | 0 | 7 | 0 | 1281 | 640 |
| 002057 | JI | 50 | 2 | 0/ 0 | 6/ 3 | 0/ 0 | 0/ 0 | 0 | 6 | 0 | 771 | 385 |
| 002065 | JI | 50 | 1 | 0/ 0 | 1/ 1 | 0/ 0 | 0/ 0 | 0 | 1 | 0 | 657 | 657 |
| 002068 | JI | 50 | 2 | 0/ 0 | 37/ 18 | 0/ 0 | 0/ 0 | 0 | 53 | 0 | 1931 | 965 |
| 002071 | JI | 50 | 3 | 0/ 0 | 10/ 3 | 0/ 0 | 0/ 0 | 0 | 10 | 0 | 1533 | 511 |
| 002076 | JI | 50 | 4 | 0/ 0 | 56/ 14 | 0/ 0 | 0/ 0 | 0 | 60 | 0 | 3009 | 752 |
| 002081 | JI | 50 | 2 | 0/ 0 | 10/ 5 | 0/ 0 | 0/ 0 | 0 | 10 | 0 | 1454 | 727 |
| 002090 | JI | 50 | 1 | 0/ 0 | 1/ 1 | 0/ 0 | 0/ 0 | 0 | 1 | 0 | 60 | 60 |
| 002091 | JI | 50 | 1 | 0/ 0 | 1/ 1 | 0/ 0 | 0/ 0 | 0 | 1 | 0 | 654 | 654 |
| 002097 | JI | 50 | 1 | 0/ 0 | 7/ 7 | 0/ 0 | 0/ 0 | 0 | 7 | 0 | 379 | 379 |
| 002098 | JI | 50 | 2 | 0/ 0 | 5/ 2 | 0/ 0 | 0/ 0 | 0 | 5 | 0 | 1063 | 531 |
| 002099 | JI | 50 | 1 | 0/ 0 | 3/ 3 | 0/ 0 | 0/ 0 | 0 | 3 | 0 | 1811 | 1811 |
| 002102 | JI | 50 | 4 | 0/ 0 | 29/ 7 | 0/ 0 | 0/ 0 | 0 | 31 | 0 | 1518 | 379 |
| 002105 | JI | 50 | 1 | 0/ 0 | 1/ 1 | 0/ 0 | 0/ 0 | 0 | 1 | 0 | 439 | 439 |
| 002107 | JI | 50 | 4 | 1/ 0 | 49/ 12 | 0/ 0 | 0/ 0 | 0 | 63 | 0 | 3774 | 943 |
| 002108 | JI | 50 | 2 | 0/ 0 | 27/ 13 | 0/ 0 | 0/ 0 | 0 | 27 | 0 | 2956 | 1478 |
| 002109 | JI | 50 | 2 | 0/ 0 | 23/ 11 | 0/ 0 | 0/ 0 | 0 | 23 | 0 | 1545 | 772 |
| 002115 | JI | 50 | 1 | 0/ 0 | 3/ 3 | 0/ 0 | 0/ 0 | 0 | 3 | 0 | 377 | 377 |
| 002116 | JI | 50 | 3 | 0/ 0 | 61/ 20 | 0/ 0 | 0/ 0 | 0 | 62 | 0 | 1185 | 395 |
| 002118 | JI | 50 | 3 | 0/ 0 | 9/ 3 | 0/ 0 | 0/ 0 | 0 | 10 | 0 | 1254 | 418 |
| 002120 | JI | 50 | 1 | 0/ 0 | 3/ 3 | 0/ 0 | 0/ 0 | 0 | 3 | 0 | 223 | 223 |
| 002122 | JI | 50 | 1 | 0/ 0 | 4/ 4 | 0/ 0 | 0/ 0 | 0 | 4 | 0 | 3124 | 3124 |
| 002124 | JI | 50 | 1 | 0/ 0 | 33/ 33 | 0/ 0 | 0/ 0 | 0 | 34 | 0 | 1519 | 1519 |
| 002128 | JI | 50 | 1 | 0/ 0 | 12/ 12 | 0/ 0 | 0/ 0 | 0 | 12 | 0 | 607 | 607 |
| 002129 | JI | 50 | 1 | 0/ 0 | 3/ 3 | 0/ 0 | 0/ 0 | 0 | 4 | 0 | 620 | 620 |
| 002131 | JI | 50 | 1 | 0/ 0 | 1/ 1 | 0/ 0 | 0/ 0 | 0 | 1 | 0 | 219 | 219 |
| 002132 | JI | 50 | 2 | 0/ 0 | 5/ 2 | 0/ 0 | 0/ 0 | 0 | 6 | 0 | 947 | 473 |
| 002139 | JI | 50 | 2 | 0/ 0 | 28/ 14 | 0/ 0 | 0/ 0 | 0 | 28 | 0 | 1275 | 637 |
| 002146 | JI | 50 | 1 | 1/ 1 | 0/ 0 | 0/ 0 | 0/ 0 | 0 | 0 | 0 | 406 | 406 |
| 002151 | JI | 50 | 1 | 0/ 0 | 24/ 24 | 0/ 0 | 0/ 0 | 0 | 29 | 0 | 503 | 503 |
| 002156 | JI | 50 | 1 | 0/ 0 | 1/ 1 | 0/ 0 | 0/ 0 | 0 | 1 | 0 | 998 | 998 |
| 002157 | JI | 50 | 1 | 0/ 0 | 1/ 1 | 0/ 0 | 0/ 0 | 0 | 1 | 0 | 125 | 125 |
| 002166 | JI | 50 | 1 | 0/ 0 | 1/ 1 | 0/ 0 | 0/ 0 | 0 | 1 | 0 | 961 | 961 |
| 002168 | JI | 50 | 1 | 3/ 3 | 0/ 0 | 0/ 0 | 0/ 0 | 0 | 0 | 0 | 310 | 310 |
| 002177 | JI | 50 | 2 | 0/ 0 | 32/ 16 | 0/ 0 | 0/ 0 | 0 | 32 | 0 | 669 | 334 |
| 002178 | JI | 50 | 1 | 0/ 0 | 14/ 14 | 0/ 0 | 0/ 0 | 0 | 17 | 0 | 1752 | 1752 |
| 002181 | JI | 50 | 1 | 0/ 0 | 14/ 14 | 0/ 0 | 0/ 0 | 0 | 14 | 0 | 536 | 536 |
| 002186 | JI | 50 | 2 | 0/ 0 | 42/ 21 | 0/ 0 | 0/ 0 | 0 | 43 | 0 | 1587 | 793 |
| 002188 | JI | 50 | 1 | 0/ 0 | 14/ 14 | 0/ 0 | 0/ 0 | 0 | 16 | 0 | 398 | 398 |
| 002192 | JI | 50 | 1 | 0/ 0 | 12/ 12 | 0/ 0 | 0/ 0 | 0 | 12 | 0 | 685 | 685 |
| 002196 | JI | 50 | 2 | 0/ 0 | 14/ 7 | 0/ 0 | 0/ 0 | 0 | 14 | 0 | 1255 | 627 |
| 002197 | JI | 50 | 2 | 0/ 0 | 4/ 2 | 0/ 0 | 0/ 0 | 0 | 4 | 0 | 949 | 474 |
| 002215 | JI | 50 | 1 | 0/ 0 | 3/ 3 | 0/ 0 | 0/ 0 | 0 | 3 | 0 | 1049 | 1049 |
| 002220 | JI | 50 | 2 | 0/ 0 | 42/ 21 | 0/ 0 | 0/ 0 | 0 | 54 | 0 | 2089 | 1044 |
| 002226 | JI | 50 | 1 | 0/ 0 | 1/ 1 | 0/ 0 | 0/ 0 | 0 | 1 | 0 | 173 | 176 |
| 002230 | JI | 50 | 1 | 0/ 0 | 7/ 7 | 0/ 0 | 0/ 0 | 0 | 7 | 0 | 1332 | 1332 |
| 002233 | JI | 50 | 4 | 0/ 0 | 37/ 9 | 0/ 0 | 0/ 0 | 0 | 47 | 0 | 1954 | 488 |

Total Evaluation of IBM/360-50 Magnetic Tapes

| | | | |
|---|---|---|---|
| TOTAL RECORDS | 9924 = 100 % | ERROR RECORDS | 1754 = 17 % |
| TOTAL VOLUMES | 1408 = 100 % | ERROR VOLUMES | 974 = 69 % |

**Figure 7.4** Sample Failure Report

#### 7.2.1.3 Software Maintenance

The dynamic character of software increasingly results in the necessity for system software maintenance. This includes not only error correction but supplementing and introducing new versions of the operating system. Manufacturers handle these tasks through system engineers, and users through system software specialists. As with hardware, excessive maintenance is not recommended. Since software, unlike hardware, is not subject to wear and tear, maintenance is generally not handled through regularly scheduled machine time. Night or weekend time periods are particularly appropriate in order to interfere as little as possible with normal operations. Virtual systems are especially responsive to maintenance.

The quantity and quality of software maintenance must be reported in the same manner as hardware maintenance. Under no circumstances should system programmers abuse their status in the computer center to run maintenance jobs durings normal operating hours, except in emergencies. It should always be kept in mind that the computer center exists for the purpose of production rather than for running system jobs. A special problem in this area is the constant change of operating system versions; these changes force the computer center to undertake substantial changeovers once or twice a year. Although one is always interested in improvements, a certain amount of restraint is recommended. It is sufficient to handle a changeover to a new version only once a year during a period of low productivity such as summer vacations. This must be acceptable to the manufacturer and the project leader of the system group, both of whom naturally would like to have innovations as quickly as possible.

### 7.2.2 Hardware Utilization Reports

From the user's point of view, the partial performance of the total system in processing a specific data set or program run is of immediate interest. This will be further discussed in the context of performance evaluation in section 9.4. The emphasis here is on providing an overview of the total EDP system utilization independent of individual tasks. For this purpose the summary reports will be discussed first, followed by a discussion of these reports as instruments of operations control.

Before going into detail it must be emphasized that the individual report systems should not exist independently of each other. On the other hand, it is rarely possible to cover every need (and needs vary considerably between computer centers) in a single system. The reasons for a total system are briefly listed here for the purpose of reaching a reasonable compromise:

- Isolated statistical systems can cause inconsistencies in results.
- Expenditures are higher for software and data maintenance of several systems.

- A uniform system requires a better conceptual base; thus the statistical results are stated with greater precision.
- If the uniform system can be designed independently of the equipment, a comparison of operations statistics of different EDP systems is facilitated.
- Expenditures in software adjustments are reduced when the operating system is changed.

Finally, the subject of report systems must be considered in terms of increasing standard system software availability and utilization.

#### 7.2.2.1 Significant Report Data

The report system of a computer center must be geared to summarizing significant data—that is, data with an articulative value. Thus one should always question the reason for the inclusion of certain data in a report. The most common tasks of operations statistics in a computer center can be summarized as follows:

Information on the data processing capacities taken up by individual users

Overview on the type and extent of tasks performed

Requisitions and use of resources and materials (including those independent of user allocation, for example in terms of time)

Analysis of customary usage (data volume, schedule requests, security requests, resource requisitions)

Analysis of system or component availability or reliability

Observation of operator conduct and its influence on operational efficiency

Analysis of system throughput in normal operations

Observation of the system with a view toward desirable or already executed system modifications

Recognition of bottlenecks or excess capacity

Error analysis of all components, individually or relative to each other

The information required must be gathered from logs and shift manuals as well as from different statistical error reports. It is important to consider that these data must be collected in part automatically by the operating system, but also manually by the system operators. Therefore, care should be taken to prevent the report system from becoming too costly. It is certainly inappropriate to develop a report system that occupies an entire team in the computer center. An increase in expenditure only rarely means a proportionate increase in the effects of a report system.

The following characteristics of an operation must be gathered—some at regular intervals, some in relation to events—in order to obtain a serviceable control of utilization:

System start-up and shut-down times

Time and cause of cold starts and warm starts (deadstarts, autoloads, or initial program loads)

Usage times for resources used independently in multiprogramming operations, such as CPU, central storage, peripheral storage, data channels, paper periphery; total usage time is a composite of individual resource allocations

Paging rate

Program residence times—that is, the difference between program start and finish

Run times of incorrect programs; rerun times should not be registered, because it is not the rerun but the incorrect run that was unproductive (error causes must be included in the registration)

Read and write retry times of peripheral storage devices and data transmission lines

Terminal start-up times

System and standard application program requests.

In addition, a variety of other information on the practical operation of the system can be gathered, such as the number of set-up procedures for peripheral devices, but these data are not always registered by the operating system. The question of whether the expenditure of manual logging is worthwhile must be taken into consideration.

### 7.2.2.2 Batch Processing Reports

Simple allocation diagrams are usually sufficient for older and smaller equipment. In this case the manual entries in the log are coded, and the allocation matrix is developed by means of a program. Such allocation plans are very practical, especially since the daily percentage utilization is shown separately. Start and stop times are usually rounded off to the nearest five minutes.

In multiprogram operations the control of EDP utilization is expanded to a control of the individual resources. Because of the variety of interdependencies, it is sufficient to evaluate the utilization of devices independently of each other. As a result, the report format design is correspondingly more difficult.

A report on pure system utilization should include the following characteristics of the operation, derived from the report data already mentioned:

T = *Total power-on time*. This refers to the entire time during which the equipment was turned on and includes idle time and time out for servicing. Malfunction periods are usually included on the assumption that work was available during that time. Not included are:

R = *Rest condition*.

C = *Calendar time*, which is a composite of total power-on time and rest.

I = *Idle time*, with an explanation, such as no work was available. In single program, operations idle times are identified as such in the log and are therefore easy to determine. In multiprogramming, the CPU stop times do not count, but rather the time periods during which no executable program is in the system. Therefore I/O time and I/O stand-by time do not count as idle time because there is a program in the system. Idle times in this case can be determined from the start and finish times of the program in the log.

M = *Maintenance time*, during which the system cannot be used for production

D = *Down time*, during which the system does not operate for technical reasons, even though programs are available. This includes, for example, malfunction, air-conditioning problems, and retrofit periods.

O = *Time off*, during which no production takes place due to technical or operating errors and a rerun has to be started. The reason for the rerun must be indicated, possibly with a percentage distribution of its frequency.

P = *Production time*, which is determined as follows:

$$T = C - R$$
$$P = T - I - D - O - M$$

U = *Turnaround time of programs*—that is, the difference between start and finish

F = *Multiprogramming factor*—the number of parallel programs that have been run in a multiprogramming operation, calculated as follows:

$$\text{Multiprogramming factor} = \frac{\text{Sum of program turnaround times}}{\text{Total power-on time} - \text{down times} - \text{maintenance times}}$$

This factor often provides a great deal of information on the utilization of EDP systems and has the advantage of being able to be determined via programs. Although it often does not measure above 2.5, the system can still be assumed to be well utilized due to task profile and the specifics of configuration. Large average factors of 6 or 8 are common. This usually means large main storage capacity or utilization of virtual storage. Standard program systems (for example CICS and POWER in the IBM-DOS) are not counted as separate programs in this context.

CPU UTILIZATION

$$C = \frac{\text{Sum of CPU usage times} \times 100}{\text{Total operating time} - \text{down time}}$$

C calculates utilization in percentage points. With exclusively I/O intensive programs it may well be under 15%, but mathematical and technical programs can go as high as 80%. In both cases no information is provided on periphery utilization. Moreover, the proportionate share of the operating system, which may be 10–30%, is often excluded. If the operating times of peripheral devices are recorded, their utilization can be calculated in this manner as well. Since in present day installations the CPU no longer needs to be the most expensive resource, it is recommended that the utilization of other resources be recorded. The main storage occupies a special position, because other free partial capacities can only be used when several programs are simultaneously executable. This, however, means an increase of the multiprogramming factor and thus an increase in main storage.

A mean error interval is a good yardstick for determining the failure rate of EDP systems. The sum of down times alone does not give any clue as to whether it is a matter of a few long or a great many short down times caused by frequent errors. Mean error intervals can be determined separately for individual components. A mean rate of 100 hours can be considered acceptable.

Figure 7.5 represents an example of a batch processing report for a Siemans 4004-45 system. The right-hand field illustrates the separation into test and production runs; the causes for errors are broken down into 5 categories. It is an advantage to provide a brief description of the configuration, as in the lower left-hand field. Not only is this important for computer centers with many systems, but it can give information on utilization possibilities as well as allowing for comparisons with other computer centers.

### 7.2.2.3 Time-Sharing Reports

The report system in time sharing differs from batch operations insofar as information must be provided on the number of active terminals, response times, and line utilization. Figure 7.6 is an example of a utilization report designed to be particularly simple, so as to furnish the user with an overview of the time intervals during

| To | From | Notice of receipt |
|---|---|---|
| Z2BO 42 | Computer Center, Furth | |
| Munich W | Telephone | |
| | Employee: Riemann — Extension: 359 | |
| Your reference and communication of: 6. 200. 1 | Our reference: SYB/Rie/Bu — Location and date, Furth, 1/18/71 | |

System utilization for the period from 10/1/84 to 12/31/84 (= 64 working days)

Computer Center F, System 4004/45-17

**Total time breakdown**

| | Std. | % |
|---|---|---|
| Total time | 2208 | 100 % |
| ./. Nonoperating time | 546 | 25 |
| - Operating time | 1662 | 75 |
| ./. Maintenance | 37 | 2 |
| ./. Repairs | 71 | 3 |
| ./. Malfunction | 1 | 0 |
| ./. Retrofit | 6 | 0 |
| ./. No work | - | - |
| - System run time | 1547 | 70 |

| | |
|---|---|
| Outside jobs, external | - |
| Outside jobs, internal | - |

**Run time breakdown**

| | % |
|---|---|
| Production runs | 80 |
| + Test runs | 13 |
| - Base performance | 93 |
| + Error runs due to hardware errors | 3 |
| Data errors | - |
| Program errors | 1 |
| Operating system errors | - |
| Handling errors | 1 |
| + Other program run times | 2 |
| - Program run time | 100 % |

**Configuration**

| | Number |
|---|---|
| Type 4004/45 F | 1 |
| Magnetic tape devices 442-2-9 | 4 |
| Tape control units | 1 |
| Large capacity storage | 5 |
| Storage control units | 1 |
| Printers and card punch devices | 3 |
| Other devices | - |

**Device failure**

| Number of failures | Hours |
|---|---|
| 8 | 21 |
| 21 | 51 |
| 2 | 2 |
| 5 | 14 |
| 10 | 33 |
| 20 | 71 |
| 6 | 15 |

**Figure 7.5** System Utilization Report in a Batch Processing Operation

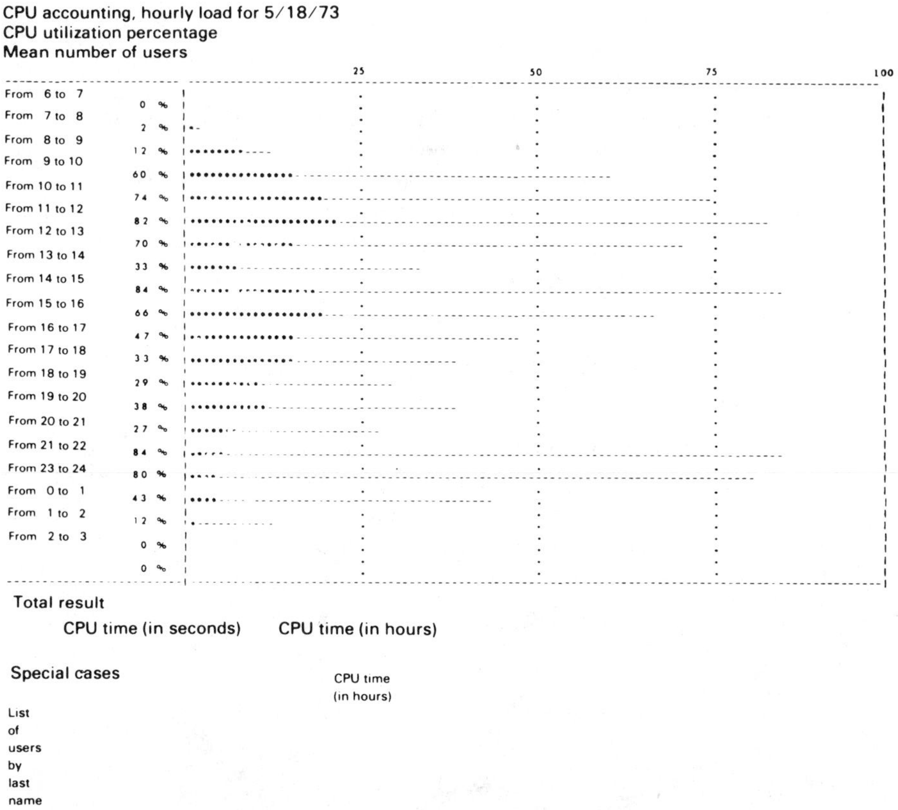


**Figure 7.6** Utilization Matrix of a Time-Sharing System, Using an IBM/360-67 in the Department of Computer Science at the Technical University of Berlin, W. Germany

which a great many or very few terminals were active. This information allows the computer center to schedule a more evenly spaced utilization of its periphery. The number of dialogs in this context is less informative.

Reports on a single day naturally have the disadvantage of being too closely linked to specific results. Reports for specific time periods, possibly for each day of the week, are more informative. In order to point out the characteristic behavior of individual users, unusually long start-up times and the corresponding CPU times are listed separately at the bottom of the diagram. In especially critical cases such as with inquiry systems for large data volumes, statistical report methods have proven to be effective.

Aside from terminal malfunctions, failures in the transmission units must be recorded in terminal operations. A large number of problems can be traced back to that. Interactive systems generally require special management. The information gathered on the dialog operation of the total system may be made available to the users on request. In one particular situation a "discomfort index" was introduced —that is, users could request an index over the terminal that represented the type of situation to be expected with a particular workload. Some of the improvement suggestions can, however, only be realized in a manufacturer's computer center, which does not address the problem of the special report system necessitated by parallel batch and dialog operations. Figure 7.7 demonstrates, by way of a concrete example, how the value of a mixed batch-dialog operation is maximized through an examination of the relationship between terminal start-up and response time. Figure 7.8 shows this value to lie at a CPU utilization of about 70%.

#### 7.2.2.4 Significant Indices on the Overall Performance of a Computer Center

In sequential or single programming operations the report data discussed thus far provide an excellent insight into system utilization. But in complex multiprogramming operations the question of how efficiently the overall system is utilized in its relationship of configuration to actual workload remains open.

The question of overall system efficiency can be answered by means of

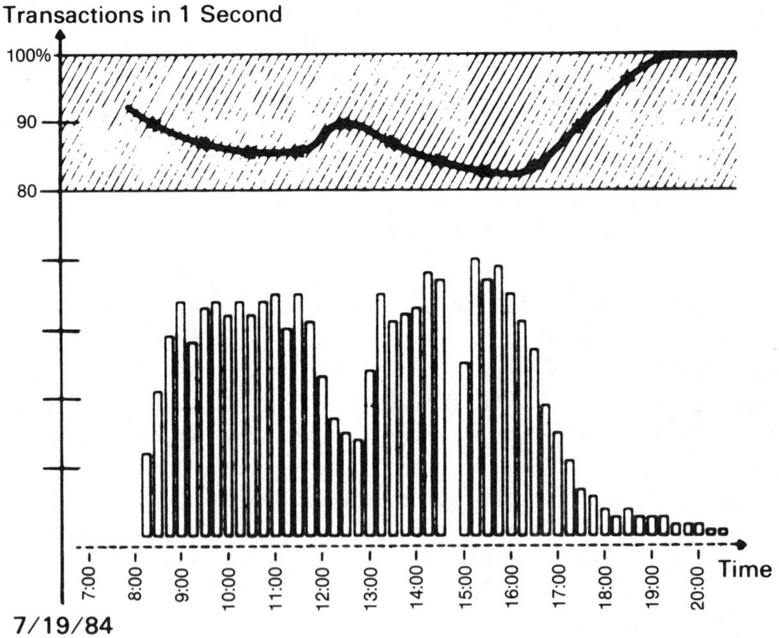


**Figure 7.7** Terminal Connect Time and Response Time Relationship From Siebert: *Informatics Bulletin* No. 2, p. 70 Springer Publishing Co., Heidelberg, 1975

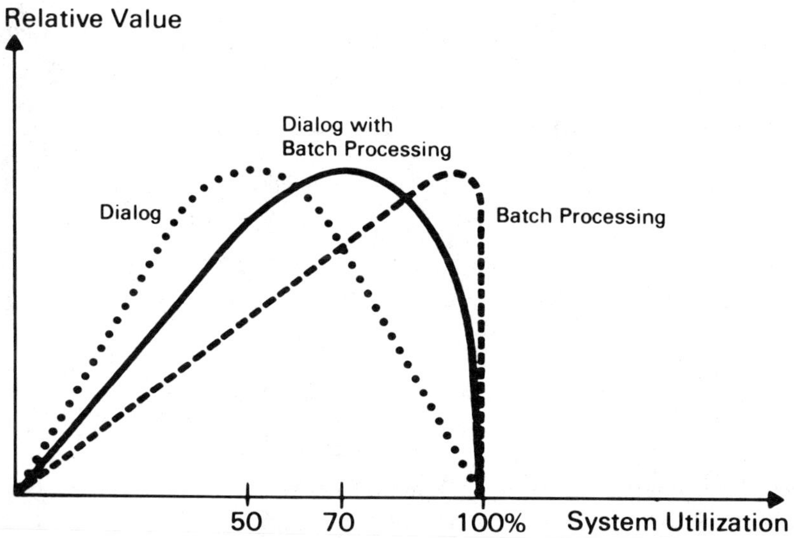


**Figure 7.8** The Value of Data Processing from Sieberg: *Informatics Bulletin* No. 2, p. 69, Springer Publishing Co., Heidelberg, 1975

throughput per unit of time. For the sake of simplicity it will be assumed that the EDP system consists of three components:

CPU

Main storage

Periphery

The efficiency rate of each component must first be determined separately, and is defined as the maximum performance rate expected of a component.

The efficiency rate of the CPU is determined analogous with the computation of CPU utilization C,

$$e_R = \frac{1}{P} \sum_{i=1}^{n} t_{R,i}$$

where e = efficiency rate
where R = CPU
where P = production time
where i = $N^{th}$ program in a sequence
where n = number of programs
where t = task performance of component

P represents the already mentioned production time of the n programs considered here for the period of observation, and i occupies the CPU for $t_{Ri}$ units of time

The efficiency rate of the main storage is calculated as follows:

$$e_H = \frac{E_H}{K_{max}} = \frac{1}{p \times K_{max}} \times \sum_{i=1}^{n} K_i \times t_{H,i}$$

where H = main storage
where E = efficiency
where $K_{max}$ = maximum available main storage

$K_i$ represents the storage requirement (in words, bytes, or pages) of the $N^{th}$ program or program segment (depending on the measuring accuracy of the operating system), which occupies the main storage portion for exactly $t_{Hi}$ units of time. Since turnaround time amounts to

$$E_H = \frac{1}{P} \times \sum_{i=1}^{n} K_i \times t_{H,i}$$

it is assumed that these times are available. The efficiency rate of the main storage component is now calculated as

$$V = \sum_{i=1}^{n} t_{H,i}$$

where V = turnaround time
where H = main storage

with $K_{max}$ the maximum available main storage. Consider the following concrete examples:

Three programs, each with a main storage requirement of 400 KB, are run on two systems.

System 1: Main storage capacity 400 KB.
Run time per program is three hours.

$$e_H = \frac{1}{9 \times 400} \times (400 \times 3 + 400 \times 3 + 400 \times 3) = 1$$

System 2: Main storage capacity 1.2 MB.
Run time per program is one hour because the CPU is three times as fast.
Assumption: All three programs run simultaneously without extension factor.

$$e_H = \frac{1}{1200 \times 1} \times (400 \times 3 + 400 \times 3 + 400 \times 3) = 1$$

The technical literature should be consulted with regard to the delay factor, inasmuch as insertion of the measured values into these formulas automatically produces the correct results. However, it becomes problematic when the efficiency rates of different systems are compared with each other. The possibility exists of introducing a main storage constant by way of compensation. However, this must be determined experimentally and is, moreover, a function of program priorities. Furthermore, one needs to keep in mind that these deliberations refer to a running operation. If comparative values are desired, warm-up and run-out times should not be considered. Moreover, the efficiency rate in multiprogramming depends on the degree of skill in program composition. Skillful multiprogramming increases throughput, otherwise the efficiency rate is kept unnecessarily low.

Periphery utilization, the third performance component, remains to be considered. Assuming that the system has m different peripheral devices (whereby several devices of the same type are counted as multiples), and that $t_{Gij}$ represents the usage time of the $M^{th}$ device by the $N^{th}$ program, the periphery efficiency rate is calculated as

$$e_p = \frac{1}{m \times P} \times \sum_{i=1}^{n} \left( \sum_{j=1}^{m} \right) t_{G,i,j}$$

where e = efficiency rate
where p = periphery
where P = production time
where n = number of programs
where m = number of devices
where i = $N^{th}$ program in a sequence
where j = $M^{th}$ device of several devices
where G = device
where t = task performance of component

The parentheses represent the sum of periphery usage times for each of the n programs. Since periphery usage times are rarely determined and gathered by the operating system, one must assume that all the peripheral devices of this particular job were used during the entire program run. Periphery usage time must be determined separately with operating systems having the capability of requesting or releasing devices during the program run.

The efficiency rates thus determined, which are dimensionless qualities between 0 and 1, make it possible to judge whether a system has the proper configuration and dimension for the spectrum of its tasks. A high value for working storage throughput and a low value for periphery throughput, for example, indicate the following:

The system may have insufficient main storage capacity

The system has excessive periphery

Programs were loaded with excessive main storage

It will at any rate be impossible to do without the information provided by these components. However, it frequently happens that when the indices are compared, too much weight is given to the possibility of equipment inadequacy. But a computer center is forced, at least for a certain time, to manage its job volume with existing equipment. If one wishes to describe the performance of the entire system with the value of L, this must be considered. Various attempts have shown that this is best accomplished through a Taylor series expansion over the different efficiency rates. For the efficiency ratio of a computer center this means:

$$L = e_H + e_P + e_R - e_H \times e_P - e_H \times e_R - e_P \times e_R + e_H \times e_P \times e_R$$

This ratio can be considered in some borderline situations. First,

$$e_H = e_P = e_R = 1$$

This means that all three components are fully utilized (maximum possibility)

$$L = 1 + 1 + 1 - 1 \times 1 - 1 \times 1 - 1 \times 1 + 1 \times 1 \times 1$$
$$L = 1$$

Second,

$$e_H = e_R = 1, e_P = 0$$

This means that calculation-intensive programs fully utilize main storage and CPU, but not the peripherals. Furthermore, during the period of observation there are no programs that could utilize peripherals.

$$L = 1 + 0 + 1 - 1 \times 0 - 1 \times 1 - 0 \times 1 + 1 \times 0 \times 1$$
$$= 1 + 1 - 1$$
$$L = 1$$

Third,

$$e_H = 0,1; e_P = 0; e_R = 1$$

This means that only one program is running, which uses about 10% of the main storage. It has no input/output, but uses the entire CPU.

An even 70% utilization of all three components can be considered as good total utilization, but this value is not easy to obtain in actual practice.

$$L = 0,1 + 0 + 1 - (0,1 \times 0) - (0,1 \times 1) - (0 \times 1) + (0,1 \times 0 \times 1)$$
$$= 0,1 + 1 - 0,1$$
$$L = 1$$

Fourth,

$$e_H = 0,7; e_P = 0,7, e_R = 0,7$$
$$L = 0,7 + 0,7 + 0,7 - (0,7 \times 0,7) - (0,7 \times 0,7) - (0,7 \times 0,7) + (0,7 \times 0,7 \times 0,7)$$
$$L = 0,973$$

An efficiency ratio obtained in this way gives a good general impression; the intermediate results in the calculation point out bottlenecks in the configuration. If an exact insight into the periphery is required, it will be necessary to go into detail. This should easily be accomplished in view of the method demonstrated.

Thus far all considerations of computer center performance indices have been predicated on the work of the EDP system. However, this is no longer sufficient in view of the changes in computer center service functions. More recent considerations aim at adding the concept of quality to computer center performance in terms of the degree of agreement between required and performed services on the condition of simultaneously minimizing expenditures. The cost-effectiveness of computer center performance is then no longer a pure qualitative attribute but becomes a secondary condition of quality assurance.

Two essential aspects of this viewpoint must be kept in mind. The influences on the quality of computer center performance are partly outside of the computer center's sphere of responsibility (in user departments, in programming, or the manufacturer's hardware and software maintenance). Moreover, the qualitative attributes must be quantifiable. This includes a provision for reference values for each attribute. As long as it is a matter of function, scheduling, and availability including terminal response times, one has to rely on more or less conventional reporting methods. Thus far no method has been developed to determine user satisfaction. In evaluating the measured values individual values must not be considered in isolation, but as part of a totality the components of which mutually influence one another.

## 7.2.3 Reports as an Instrument of Control

The report periods that are established will depend on the objectives of the report. External reports and management information reports usually require large reporting periods—monthly, semiannually, or annually. Reports intended as instruments of computer center control are usually less well served by large reporting periods because most of the irregularities have been weeded out. For weekly report periods an observation at intervals of 10 or 30 minutes over a period of a day are suitable, but more detailed screening may be necessary for detecting and resolving bottlenecks in the configuration. However, the limits of utilization control should not be misunderstood in the considerations to follow.

***The technical performance data of an EDP system do not constitute reference values for planning purposes.***

It is certainly not recommended to rely too much on the subjective impressions of users. Questions about the satisfaction of computer center users may be of some help, but they are not a substitute for objective reports, since users do not have a general overview of the types of service that may be possible.

### 7.2.3.1 Reports for Monitoring Operations

In planning EDP system usage it is important to treat the workload as a time function. Since the accounting systems only record information for the individual application programs, reporting in multiprogramming operations is possible only in retrospect. The center for data processing at the University of Tübingen therefore developed a monitoring system that registers and evaluates accounting information on the MASTER operating system at regular intervals. This monitor, which registers a label every 30 minutes, costs the computer center in a 24-hour operation approximately $60 in computer time per month. Standard application software is available for this purpose for a number of systems—for example Namic—but usually a combined hardware-software system is used, such as the Tesdata system.

In contrast to reports over long time periods where in general a summation of accounting data suffices, smaller time periods require the development of a system usage model by means of the accounting data. This is handled as follows: Based on the beginning and ending times of each task, the number and type of active tasks for each time interval are recorded. Furthermore, the respective usage condition

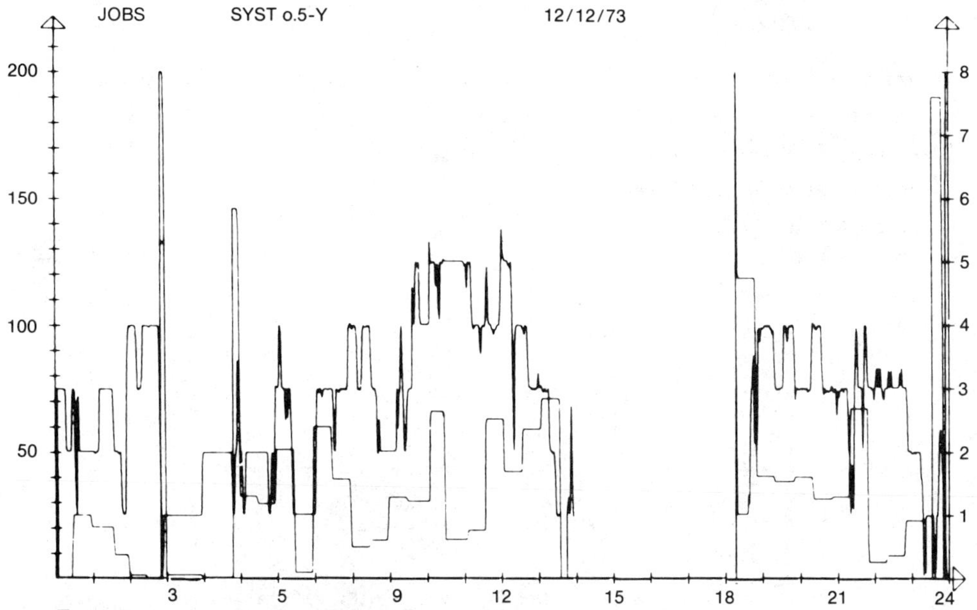


Total Power-on Time: 19 hr. 17 min. 58 sec.
Devices Used in % of Power-on Time: OP 57.8 MT504 140.0
PI3694 1.3 PLOT 0.0 MT 509 0.9 PO 3695 0.0

**Figure 7.9** CPU Usage and Multiprogramming Factor over a 24-Hour Period

can be derived from the usage times of the operating resources, including the CPU. In this manner a system usage model can be developed, which with an assumed equal distribution of resource usage within a given task describes the condition of the EDP system. In the graphic representation of such a record (Figure 7.9) it is possible, for example, to see the influence of the number of active jobs on the CPU time used by the system itself.

This time, although often neglected, is of considerable interest. The example in this case shows that with up to four active jobs, the time used by the operating system decreases proportionally, and that it increases again with a further increase in the number of parallel jobs. These critical indices vary with different operating systems.

A similar relationship exists between main storage occupancy and system time, since the paging rate increases substantially after a certain point, to the detriment of system performance. Therefore, standard application software packages should be expected to indicate the paging rate, which allows for recognizing inadequacies in job configuration at the points where there is an increase in idle loops and paging. This can be observed in Figure 7.10 in the composition of system time, which also provides information on power-on time and operating system performance.

```
DATUM      12/12/73                                   ACCOUNTING OF SYSTEM TASKS

TOTAL OF TIME COVERED  . . .     69419.000 SEC  ( = 19 STD 16 MIN 59 SEC )

CPU TIME FOR SYSTEM  . . . .     10154.358 SEC
EXEC TIME FOR SYSTEM . . . .      2213.650 SEC
CHANNEL TIME FOR SYSTEM  . .     21229.575 SEC

PERCENTAGE OF SYSTEM TIME  .        17.8    %

NUMBER OF AUTOLOADS  . . . .         1
```

| AUTOLOAD | TIME | CPU | EXEC | CHANNEL | % |
|---|---|---|---|---|---|
| | 00/24/29 | 304484 MSEC | 33158 MSEC | 426186 MSEC | 23.0 |
| | 00/54/43 | 196630 MSEC | 27564 MSEC | 297534 MSEC | 12.4 |
| | 01/32/19 | 186009 MSEC | 45318 MSEC | 503243 MSEC | 10.3 |
| | 01/56/46 | 50569 MSEC | 15919 MSEC | 84966 MSEC | 4.5 |
| | 02/26/48 | 1916 MSEC | 4800 MSEC | 5443 MSEC | 0.4 |
| | 02/56/48 | 341209 MSEC | 43734 MSEC | 10760 MSEC | 21.4 |
| | 03/26/49 | 6146 MSEC | 3508 MSEC | 835 MSEC | 0.5 |
| | 03/56/49 | 4539 MSEC | 3922 MSEC | 1283 MSEC | 0.5 |
| | 04/26/50 | 119 MSEC | 2306 MSEC | 683 MSEC | 0.9 |
| | 04/56/52 | 356127 MSEC | 82789 MSEC | 685498 MSEC | 24.4 |
| | 05/26/19 | 239371 MSEC | 40963 MSEC | 1756985 MSEC | 15.9 |
| | 05/56/22 | 219308 MSEC | 41182 MSEC | 1092865 MSEC | 14.4 |
| | 06/26/19 | 392357 MSEC | 67192 MSEC | 257546 MSEC | 25.6 |
| | 06/56/20 | 2584 MSEC | 14847 MSEC | 50954 MSEC | 1.0 |
| | 07/26/23 | 442404 MSEC | 96603 MSEC | 724143 MSEC | 29.9 |
| | 07/56/26 | 294345 MSEC | 59016 MSEC | 509024 MSEC | 19.6 |
| | 08/26/21 | 60001 MSEC | 47764 MSEC | 490057 MSEC | 6.0 |
| | 08/56/22 | 99339 MSEC | 39938 MSEC | 343819 MSEC | 7.7 |
| | 09/26/30 | 233738 MSEC | 51998 MSEC | 30283 MSEC | 15.8 |
| | 10/03/07 | 241949 MSEC | 86363 MSEC | 246049 MSEC | 14.9 |
| | 10/26/56 | 374608 MSEC | 94044 MSEC | 1491946 MSEC | 32.8 |
| | 11/03/15 | 113912 MSEC | 46180 MSEC | 2137803 MSEC | 7.3 |
| | 11/33/03 | 107186 MSEC | 63508 MSEC | 631999 MSEC | 9.5 |
| | 12/03/01 | 433221 MSEC | 129069 MSEC | 736221 MSEC | 31.3 |
| | 12/33/03 | 307381 MSEC | 74030 MSEC | 101218 MSEC | 21.2 |
| | 13/03/04 | 434356 MSEC | 94133 MSEC | 292334 MSEC | 29.3 |
| | 13/32/59 | 520280 MSEC | 116704 MSEC | 1605973 MSEC | 35.5 |
| 18/16/00 | | | | | |
| | 18/18/03 | 33417 MSEC | 8653 MSEC | 5671 MSEC | 34.2 |
| | 18/48/26 | 980941 MSEC | 94485 MSEC | 45276 MSEC | 59.0 |
| | 19/18/28 | 269804 MSEC | 94726 MSEC | 78873 MSEC | 20.2 |
| | 19/49/01 | 274068 MSEC | 76438 MSEC | 124711 MSEC | 19.1 |
| | 20/18/46 | 265736 MSEC | 95838 MSEC | 2516645 MSEC | 20.3 |
| | 20/48/23 | 206304 MSEC | 68340 MSEC | 989878 MSEC | 15.5 |
| | 21/18/16 | 213091 MSEC | 75901 MSEC | 518763 MSEC | 16.1 |
| | 21/48/13 | 524924 MSEC | 79820 MSEC | 1773047 MSEC | 33.7 |
| | 22/18/23 | 34689 MSEC | 15544 MSEC | 291552 MSEC | 2.8 |
| | 22/48/26 | 61681 MSEC | 20834 MSEC | 99407 MSEC | 4.6 |
| | 23/18/48 | 149290 MSEC | 57485 MSEC | 155684 MSEC | 11.3 |
| | 23/48/56 | 885602 MSEC | 64970 MSEC | 28653 MSEC | 52.6 |
| | 24/00/00 | 290723 MSEC | 34064 MSEC | 85765 MSEC | 48.9 |

**Figure 7.10** Composition of Operating System Times (I/O, idle time, monitoring, paging, etc.) of a CD 3300 of the MASTER Operating System. (The aggregate of 100% contains information on the workload.)

For the computer center manager, this type of report represents an overview of system utilization in retrospect and constitutes the basis for system usage planning.

In addition to improved utilization, a systematic reduction in cold and warm starts can be achieved. A report system should be introduced for each executed system above. While similar reports exist for most systems, they are not always equally informative.

Similar reports on operations control are also available for other systems; they usually have the disadvantage of being overly based on accounting data without seeing the system as a whole.

### 7.2.3.2 Bottleneck Measurement

The procedure for operations control discussed above is a general profile of system utilization and does not give much information on the utilization of individual resources. In recent years bottlenecks have been traced by means of monitors installed on operating devices. In the meantime, this field has grown to the proportion where only the principle can briefly be mentioned. For details the literature should be consulted.

#### Hardware Monitors

These are separate measuring devices that register and count impulses deriving from the events under observation. A separate entry must be available for each area in the system subject to monitoring. Depending on the scope of application, devices of lesser or greater complexity are available. The monitoring procedure may be passive (recording) or active (random sampling). Since hardware monitoring requires experienced and well-trained specialists, it will not be discussed in detail except for a brief listing of its advantages and disadvantages.

*Advantages of Hardware Monitors*

They can record almost any chosen binary signal.

They can be hooked up to almost any electronic device, thus having the capability of recording a variety of brands and models.

They produce extremely exact measurements without disturbing the timing of the signal or system being monitored.

They require no additional overhead, i.e., no storage allocation and processing time of data during the measuring phase.

They can execute measurements on almost all system components including peripherals and terminals.

They can be set for any desired time period, from microseconds to hours.

They can determine the processor time of every program, including the operating system.

They can, by means of their logic, measure several simultaneous events.

*Disadvantages of Hardware Monitors*

They have a relatively high purchasing and operating cost.

Each monitoring process requires detailed knowledge of the hardware and careful planning.

The limited number of probes, counters, timers, and other logical elements permits simultaneous measurement of only a certain number of events.

The location of an event is not always predictable with third generation installations; for example, it is not possible to determine the length of a queue.

In general it is impossible to measure activities while excluding certain individual programs, since the monitor does not recognize the connection between an action and the program responsible for it; it registers only the fact that the computer was active, but not the reason for its activity.

A learning phase is needed before usable results can be obtained.

Errors or incorrect results are obtained when probes are mounted in the wrong location.

There is a substantial overhead in connection with probes because of the time required for mounting, testing results, and deciding what to do next.

SOFTWARE MONITORS

A software monitor is a program that is interfaced to the events under observation. Software monitors in principle work like the data collection systems of accounting. Their functional design is most evident in a consideration of their advantages and disadvantages.

*Advantages of Software Monitors*

They usually cost much less than hardware monitors.

They may produce more differentiated data than hardware monitors, i.e., they can access all registers and tables, such as central storage utilization and queue length.

The technique of using software monitors is easier to learn and apply; analysis protocols are usually available less than an hour after the monitoring period and often within minutes.

Software monitors can produce far more data in less time than hardware monitors.

Software monitors are intelligent, i.e., they can distinguish between operating system components and those of the application programs.

Software monitors can make a large number of measurements at a certain point in time, while hardware monitors are usually limited to 32 counters. The software monitor CUE, for example, can monitor up to 500 events.

Software monitors possess great flexibility in their choice of parameters.

*Disadvantages of Software Monitors*

The overhead can run from 1% to 40% in exceptional cases; as a rule it is between 1% and 5%.

The overhead is most strongly felt when the job profile is most active, but measurements are of special interest at exactly those points in time.

Software monitors are dependent on the respective system software, i.e., because of market distribution they are primarily designed for IBM systems.

Software monitors as a rule cannot access information on periphery activity at the other end of the channel.

Measurement can only be as exact as the precision of the internal counter; in many cases this means a maximum precision of 1/60 second.

Delays occurring in serial measurement of the control areas make it impossible to measure overlapping activities and necessitate sequencing.

The software monitor may influence magnitudes it is supposed to measure because of its interface with the processing program.

The random sampling technique assumes a homogeneous event structure which is not always the case; the load structure must therefore be considered.

Both hardware and software monitors gather large volumes of discrete data that must be transformed via a program. Among the best known are program packages based on the SMF system.

#### 7.2.3.3 Optimizing the Systems Library

Today's operating systems work almost exclusively with system disks. Even though disk storage has eliminated long search times, it is nevertheless obvious that the read/write arm uses time for positioning itself. It is not the task of a book about computer centers to go into the details of optimizing systems libraries, especially since this is a system-dependent problem. But it is important to mention in the context of software monitors that computer center management must be

Listing No. Program Statistics March 1983 Sorted by program requests

| Program name | Program calls: GESAMT | Program calls: DAVON ABF | Total requested used: GE FORD KB | Total requested used: GE NUTZ KB | CPU: CPU time in minutes | VERRECHN: Accounted Running Time | Running Time | FAKT: CPU-Time/Error Time | KOSTEN: Total Costs | GESAMT: Total Accesses | PLATTEN: Disk Accesses | PLATTEN: Files | BAND: Accesses | BAND: STATION | DP: Accesses | DP: Files | SYSIN: Cards | SYSIN: Files | SYSOUT: Lines | SYSOUT: Files |
|---|---|---|---|---|---|---|---|---|---|---|---|---|---|---|---|---|---|---|---|---|
| IEBGENER | 2728 | 135 | 256 | 176 | 6.621 | 206.65 | 306.63 | 0.041 | 2229 | 342913 | 10551 | 4 | 59993 | 24 | 311734 | 1 | 5518 | 2 | 1892 | 3 |
| SORT | 2199 | 47 | 256 | 256 | 6.967 | 64.23 | 66.55 | 0.107 | 1535 | 98279 | 81918 | 15 | 46336 | 28 | 0 | 0 | 8601 | 2 | 654 | 3 |
| IEWL | 1856 | 852 | 256 | 160 | 0.382 | 7.02 | 10.65 | 0.054 | 162 | 11471 | 11471 | 8 | 360 | 2 | 0 | 0 | 267 | 1 | 1876 | 3 |
| IEHRPOGM | 1039 | 81 | 192 | 52 | 0.206 | 3.46 | 18.02 | 0.159 | 53 | 5596 | 5404 | 28 | 0 | 0 | 172 | 2 | 51 | 2 | 240 | 1 |
| IKFCBL00 | 754 | 474 | 160 | 104 | 4.982 | 5.94 | 16.23 | 0.838 | 321 | 2041 | 2041 | 7 | 0 | 1 | 0 | 0 | 3339 | 1 | 6692 | 2 |
| IEFGR14 | 677 | 0 | 160 | 52 | 0.000 | 0.00 | 14.63 | 0.000 | 0 | 0 | 0 | 9 | 0 | 13 | 0 | 0 | 0 | 0 | | 0 |
| PGM=*.DD | 626 | 226 | 192 | 176 | 12.569 | 16.15 | 27.07 | 0.778 | 539 | 24241 | 3232 | 9 | 24241 | 3 | 0 | 0 | 1649 | 2 | 16231 | 7 |
| IEMAA | 481 | 447 | 160 | 160 | 0.076 | 0.18 | 1.43 | 0.408 | 7 | 214 | 214 | 5 | 0 | 0 | 0 | 0 | 101 | 1 | 274 | 2 |
| IEYFORT | 442 | 81 | 256 | 160 | 3.881 | 4.61 | 21.38 | 0.840 | 183 | 1260 | 1260 | 3 | 0 | 0 | 0 | 0 | 3443 | 2 | 4651 | 2 |
| IEBUPDTE | 437 | 39 | 160 | 52 | 0.365 | 5.14 | 24.79 | 0.044 | 155 | 13335 | 13335 | 4 | 450 | 1 | 0 | 0 | 4129 | 2 | 4213 | 2 |
| IOIC | 348 | 113 | 192 | 56 | 1.356 | 5.39 | 46.97 | 0.211 | 138 | 9131 | 6693 | 5 | 4022 | 2 | 0 | 0 | 3391 | 2 | 9297 | 3 |
| EDITTIME | 331 | 0 | 160 | 52 | 0.031 | 0.10 | 0.10 | | 26 | 2 | 136 | 3 | 0 | 0 | 0 | 0 | 49 | 1 | 181 | 2 |
| IEBPTPCH | 330 | 51 | 160 | 52 | 1.348 | 19.63 | 28.50 | 0.168 | 552 | 33345 | 3346 | 3 | 18829 | 1 | 1638 | 1 | 784 | 2 | 4242 | 3 |
| LOADER | 265 | 124 | 192 | 192 | 2.65 | 6.36 | 37.47 | 0.416 | 130 | 10568 | 2771 | 23 | 10568 | 5 | 0 | 0 | 138 | 1 | 2533 | 4 |
| PMSLIN | 208 | 179 | 160 | 52 | 0.028 | 0.03 | 12.79 | 0.625 | 1 | 25 | 25 | 7 | 0 | 0 | 0 | 0 | 5 | 1 | 9 | 2 |
| EDALL | 190 | 14 | 160 | 88 | 0.101 | 0.20 | 15.29 | 0.385 | 7 | 274 | 58 | 2 | 250 | 2 | 0 | 0 | 35 | 2 | 126 | 4 |
| PROCESS | 186 | 12 | 160 | 108 | 0.582 | 4.45 | 13.78 | 0.130 | 104 | 6644 | 6045 | 11 | 1461 | 1 | 0 | 0 | 7 | 1 | 13 | 2 |
| IEQCBLOC | 179 | 179 | 0 | 0 | 0.000 | 0.00 | 0.00 | 0.000 | 0 | 0 | 0 | 0 | 0 | 0 | 0 | 0 | 0 | 0 | 0 | 0 |
| PMSINC | 172 | 6 | 160 | 52 | 0.023 | 0.02 | 2.02 | 0.793 | 1 | 25 | 25 | 4 | 0 | 0 | 0 | 0 | 9 | 1 | 36 | 3 |
| VORMELD | 171 | 5 | 160 | 52 | 0.052 | 0.51 | 15.65 | 0.101 | 24 | 848 | 848 | 4 | 0 | 0 | 0 | 0 | 1879 | 1 | 0 | .1 |
| ABMELD | 166 | 2 | 160 | 88 | 0.331 | 0.77 | 4.39 | 0.425 | 22 | 776 | 316 | 4 | 715 | 1 | 0 | 0 | 0 | 0 | 113 | 2 |
| ORDER | 155 | 55 | 160 | 96 | 0.046 | 0.21 | 1.97 | 0.211 | 5 | 296 | 296 | 10 | 0 | 0 | 0 | 0 | 0 | 0 | 0 | 1 |
| KRUPTIME | 152 | 51 | 160 | 152 | 0.700 | 4.64 | 8.25 | 0.150 | 135 | 6766 | 6766 | 17 | 0 | 0 | 0 | 0 | 0 | 0 | 6780 | 3 |
| PERTGEN | 151 | 48 | 160 | 138 | 1.436 | 3.07 | 7.37 | 0.467 | 56 | 2612 | 2279 | 8 | 1446 | 2 | 0 | 0 | 0 | 0 | 107 | 2 |
| PMSSPEC | 160 | 10 | 160 | 52 | 0.112 | 0.18 | 5.79 | 0.612 | 20 | 121 | 121 | 4 | 0 | 0 | 0 | 0 | 0 | 0 | 2107 | 3 |
| DUMMY | 159 | 2 | 160 | 52 | 0.009 | 0.00 | 10.55 | 1.000 | 0 | 0 | 0 | 5 | 0 | 0 | 0 | 0 | 0 | 1 | 0 | 7 |
| T416OVLY | 155 | 36 | 160 | 156 | 2.402 | 3.06 | 4.10 | 0.782 | 147 | 1487 | 1487 | 5 | 0 | 0 | 0 | 0 | 14 | 1 | 6806 | 7 |
| T287 | 149 | 149 | 0 | | 0.000 | 0.00 | 0.00 | 0.000 | 0 | 0 | 0 | 0 | 0 | 0 | 0 | 0 | 0 | 0 | 0 | 0 |
| IEHLIST | 144 | 5 | 160 | 52 | 0.225 | 4.08 | 13.21 | 0.055 | 84 | 6667 | 6667 | 18 | 0 | 1 | 0 | 0 | 20 | 2 | 4448 | 1 |
| ASMBLR | 140 | 5 | 160 | 160 | 8.936 | 26.29 | 42.47 | 0.339 | 837 | 29753 | 29556 | 10 | 197 | 1 | 0 | 0 | 1621 | 1 | 12614 | 2 |
| T416QL1 | 133 | 10 | 160 | 144 | 7.219 | 7.52 | 14.43 | 0.959 | 301 | 520 | 520 | 8 | 0 | 0 | 0 | 0 | 451 | 2 | 895 | 11 |
| WUC01 | 124 | 17 | 128 | 120 | 0.426 | 0.79 | 9.18 | 0.539 | 25 | 842 | 842 | 5 | 0 | 0 | 0 | 0 | 17 | 1 | 832 | 3 |
| IEBCOPY | 115 | 13 | 160 | 160 | 0.572 | 38.64 | 83.30 | 0.014 | 778 | 65263 | 65263 | 22 | 0 | 0 | 3 | 1 | 502 | 1 | 1201 | 1 |
| T589WZ | 109 | 12 | 160 | 108 | 1.280 | 1.46 | 5.05 | 0.873 | 55 | 318 | 318 | 6 | 0 | 0 | 0 | 0 | 294 | 1 | 2869 | 2 |
| T524U8 | 106 | 106 | 0 | 0 | 0.000 | 0.00 | 0.00 | 0.000 | 0 | 0 | 0 | 0 | 0 | 0 | 0 | 0 | 0 | 0 | 0 | 0 |
| F226 | 104 | 3 | 160 | 152 | 0.222 | 0.50 | 8.73 | 0.439 | 66 | 566 | 566 | 21 | 0 | 0 | 0 | 0 | 4611 | 1 | 1 | 3 |
| F188 | 102 | 5 | 160 | 52 | 1.355 | 47.54 | 112.64 | 0.028 | 483 | 79175 | 142 | 2 | 1442 | 1 | 77733 | 1 | 0 | 0 | 7420 | 3 |

**Figure 7.11** Usage Frequency of Programs in a Systems Library

informed of the frequency with which programs are requested, and to make appropriate suggestions to the systems group.

For example, programs that have not been requested for a period of 4–8 weeks do not need to be kept in direct access, but can be kept on tape and relocated as the need arises. Figure 7.11 summarizes the usage frequency of programs in a systems library. In this table the programs are listed in order of frequency, but listings by cumulative CPU time or number of processed files ar useful as well. The result of such an evaluation may be the relocation of rarely used programs or a change to an objective-based library orientation. The library can be distributed over different disks or arranged in such a way that frequently used programs are stored adjacent to each other in the middle, with the more rarely used programs on either side.

But an analysis of such statistics also permits further conclusions. For example, the number of linkage editor requests provides information on the

Listing No. 9025 Program/Job allocation, March 1983 Page No. 001 from ABMELD to B070

| PROGRAMM | JOB |
|---|---|
| ABMELD | PMSBBR |
| | PMSGBA |
| | PMSGEAN4 |
| | PMSGEA1 |
| | PMSGEA2X |
| | PMSGJA38 |
| | PMSGJA40 |
| | PMSGJA50 |
| | PMSGVK |
| | PMSHTR |
| | PMSLWR |
| | PMSSPECR |
| | PMSSPEED |
| | PMSSPEHP |
| | PMSSPELY |
| | PMSZETG |
| ASMBLR | GEHASP5 |
| | GEHASP6 |
| | GEHASP7 |
| | OSGEN15 |
| | OSGEN17 |
| | OSGEN18 |
| | OSGEN19 |
| | PLIOPT01 |
| | PLIOPT02 |
| | PLIOPT03 |
| | PLIOPT04 |
| | PLIORS02 |
| | PLIORS03 |
| | PLIORS04 |
| | PLIORS05 |
| | PLIORS06 |
| AUTOFLOW | F2003997 |
| | F79HELF1 |
| A003 | J100103 |
| A004 | EGSAC04 |
| | EGSAC07 |
| | J100103 |
| A006 | J100103 |
| A007 | EGSAC07 |
| | J100103 |
| A008 | J100103 |
| A01 | CLASS2 |
| A02 | CLASS2 |
| A021 | J100804 |
| A022 | J100804 |
| A024 | J100202 |
| A02601 | A026 |
| A02701 | A027 |

| PROGRAMM | JOB |
|---|---|
| A02702 | A027 |
| A03 | CLASS2 |
| A031 | J1010100 |
| A04 | CLASS2 |
| A05 | CLASS2 |
| A06 | CLASS2 |
| A07 | CLASS2 |
| BD01 | BD |
| BD03 | BD |
| BD06 | BD |
| BIGDATA | BEHAUFM |
| | E030B1M |
| | MABILA01 |
| BM010 | R2MEBSS8 |
| | R2MEBSS9 |
| | R2MEB1HA |
| | R2MEB1HE |
| | R2MEB1NA |
| BM062 | R2MEBSS8 |
| | R2MEBSS9 |
| | R2MEB1HE |
| | R2MEB1NA |
| BM081 | R2MEBSS8 |
| | R2MEBSS9 |
| | R2MEB1NA |
| BMOA4 | ME11 |
| | R2MET1 |
| BT005 | 001EDFF1 |
| | R21EDBR1 |
| | R21EDFR1 |
| | R21EDFR1 |
| | R2TEDLA1 |
| | R2TEDMU |
| | R21EDWF3 |
| | R21ED2HU |
| | R2TED2W1 |
| BT051 | R2TED2 |
| | R2TED2G0 |
| | R2TED2HU |
| BT072 | R2TEDGAR |
| | R2TED2GA |
| | R2TED2HU |
| | R2TED2KO |
| | R2TED2WF |
| | R3ZTRD04 |
| | R6ZTRD02 |

| PROGRAMM | JOB |
|---|---|
| BT072 | TED22BFA |
| BT077 | R2TEDBR1 |
| | R2TEDFRI |
| | R6ZTRD07 |
| BT073 | R2TED2G0 |
| BT062 | R2TED20H |
| BT086 | R2TED2 |
| | TED2WHG1 |
| BT122 | R2TEDKA1 |
| | R2TEDKA |
| | R2TEDKA1 |
| BT122A | R2TEDKA1 |
| B001 | J211403 |
| | J215403 |
| | J218403 |
| | J2914030 |
| B002 | J211403 |
| | J215403 |
| | J218403 |
| | J2914030 |
| B003 | J211403 |
| | J215403 |
| | J218403 |
| | J2914030 |
| B004 | J211404 |
| | J215404 |
| | J218404 |
| | J2914040 |
| B005 | J211403 |
| | J215403 |
| | J218403 |
| | J2914030 |
| B006 | J211413 |
| | J215413 |
| | J218413 |
| | J291413 |
| B007 | J211413 |
| | J215413 |
| | J218413 |
| | J291413 |
| B008 | J211405 |
| | J215405 |
| | J218405 |
| | J2914050 |
| B009 | J211413 |
| | J215413 |
| | J218413 |
| | J291413 |

| PROGRAMM | JOB |
|---|---|
| B010 | J211405 |
| | J215405 |
| | J218405 |
| | J2914050 |
| B011 | J211405 |
| | J215405 |
| | J218405 |
| | J2914050 |
| B012 | J211414 |
| B013 | J215414 |
| | J218414 |
| B014 | J211414 |
| | J215414 |
| | J218414 |
| B015 | J215414 |
| | J218414 |
| B016 | J211413 |
| | J291413 |
| B018 | J211131 |
| | J212103 |
| | J216103 |
| | J218103 |
| | TTKTESTK |
| B019 | J211131 |
| | J212103 |
| | J216103 |
| | J218103 |
| | TTKTESTK |
| B021 | J211132 |
| | J212103 |
| | J216103 |
| | J218103 |
| | TTKTESTK |
| B022 | J211131 |
| | J212103 |
| | J216103 |
| | J218103 |
| | TTKTESTK |
| B023 | J211133 |
| | J212103 |
| | J216103 |
| | J218103 |
| | TTKTESTK |
| B024 | J211131 |
| | J212103 |
| | J216103 |
| | J218103 |
| | TTKTESTK |
| B025 | J211132 |
| | J212103 |

| PROGRAMM | JOB |
|---|---|
| B025 | J216103 |
| | TTKTESTK |
| B026 | J211133 |
| | J212103 |
| | J216103 |
| | J218103 |
| | TTKTESTK |
| B027 | J211132 |
| | J212103 |
| | J216103 |
| | J218103 |
| | TTKTESTK |
| B028 | J211133 |
| | J212103 |
| | J216103 |
| | J218103 |
| | TTKTESTK |
| B040 | J211133 |
| | J212103 |
| | J216103 |
| | J218103 |
| | TTKTESTK |
| B041 | J211133 |
| | J212103 |
| | J216103 |
| | J218103 |
| | TTKTESTK |
| B042 | J211133 |
| | J212103 |
| | J216103 |
| | J218103 |
| | TTKTESTK |
| B045 | J212802 |
| B046 | J212802 |
| B048 | J212803 |
| B049 | J212803 |
| B050 | J211106 |
| | J212106 |
| | J216106 |
| | J218106 |
| B062 | J203002 |
| B063 | J203002 |
| B064 | J203002 |
| B065 | J203002 |
| B069 | J203502 |
| B070 | J203502 |

**Figure 7.12** Report on the Allocation of Program Requests for Requested Jobs

number of compilings. In general, optimizing the systems library is part of system tuning, which will be discussed briefly in section 7.2.3.4.

In the context of reporting program usage (and in reference to computer center security) it is also important to know which programs and files were requested by which job number (Figure 7.12).

#### 7.2.3.4 System Tuning

A term from the auto industry found its way into data processing some years ago; it pertains to the systematic improvement of a system based on experiential values.

***Tuning is defined as an improvement in the efficiency of a serially produced item.***

Tuning concerns three principal areas:

Hardware configuration

Operating Systems (system software)

Program (Application software)

The empirical changes, usually based on observation, are systematically checked for effectiveness. Tuning belongs among the tasks of the systems group, which usually utilizes a standard product. System performance is observed before and after changes have been made. The objectives of tuning can be summarized as follows:

An understanding of applied and anticipated planning and management strategies for the operating system.

An understanding of the measurement package: what is being measured and by what means?

An analysis of measurement data, recognition of data correlation, and evaluation of measurement data.

Changes in system control for purposes of optimization (the goals must be stated): when setting parameters, one needs to evaluate which are important, which are superfluous, and which are lacking.

Exchange of experiences with tuning groups of other computer centers.

Continuing work on existing procedures.

Resource expenditures are not to be underestimated. The computer center manager is responsible for keeping expenditures within a reasonable ratio to the profits anticipated by tuning. In dialog and real-time systems, increased reliability of response time can only be achieved by tuning. Synthetic load profiles hold some promise, but consideration has also been given to the possibility of introducing an "automated operator" through programming the optimization mechanism.

Some manufacturers provide handbooks for adjusting operating systems to the prevailing circumstances, but most of these cover only a portion of the total tuning area.

### 7.2.3.5 Installation Management

An examination of throughput performance is characteristic for batch processing. With today's demands on dialog operations and on consultation and support in distributed data processing and product quality, it has become essential to integrate the entire computer center report system for purposes of control. This objective has developed into the concept of installation management.

> ***Installation management is defined as the collective term for the combined use of all methods, techniques, and resources that improve data processing efficiency in its widest sense.***

The bottleneck in such improvements is generally less in the technical area than in organization and personnel, which means that installation management is not a project but a permanent process for controlling the data processing operation in all its phases. This process centers on the following points, which can be considered the goals of installation management:

Change management through improved planning and control of system modification. This was discussed in the context of operations scheduling in section 3.3.7.

Availability management through minimizing the influences of system aborts. The related report system was discussed in section 7.2.1.1.

Operations management through improved system operation.

Applications management through improved methods and procedures in realizing new applications.

Project management through improved project control.

On the organizational side, the most important tools of installation management (IM) are the management reports and weekly IM meetings, which should be attended by the various group leaders, as well as

The computer center manager (usually as chairman)

Applications programming

Systems programming

Hardware maintenance

Departmental representatives

Manufacturers' representatives

The IM meeting should be both brief and efficiently run. Problem points should be recorded in the minutes, along with the names of persons charged with resolving them, until a satisfactory solution has been achieved. In particularly problematic areas it is more important to introduce measures leading to a common goal than to look for the guilty party.

Objectives must be established in absolute values and the results measured by these values. Quantifiable objectives may be:

97% system availability

95% teleprocessing availability

A maximum response time of 3 seconds for dialog terminals

Total system down time of less than one hour

Jobs should not exceed schedules by more than one hour

Cost overrides should be kept under 2%

60% CPU utilization

Some manufacturers offer special programs in support of installation management. Figure 7.13 is a graphic demonstration of such a program package. The IM databank is the central element. Depending on user specifications, the desired information can be selected from SMF and IMS logs and stored, then organized via CRT in a TSO-related language (or in batch processing by means of control cards).

In practice, this method of centralized control through installation management based on an information system has proven successful. IM evaluation forms have been designed in support of these tasks.

## 7.2.4 Schedule Maintenance Reports

It has already been mentioned that performance rates in and of themselves do not constitute planning values; schedule maintenance is an essential performance factor as well. Adherence to schedules cannot be evaluated in terms of the certainty of binary logic (certain or not certain) but must be quantified.

The schedules agreed upon with the originating departments can be adhered to only if data are delivered on time. Statistical reports on delays must therefore differentiate among the causes for such delays. Jobs finished ahead of time may not

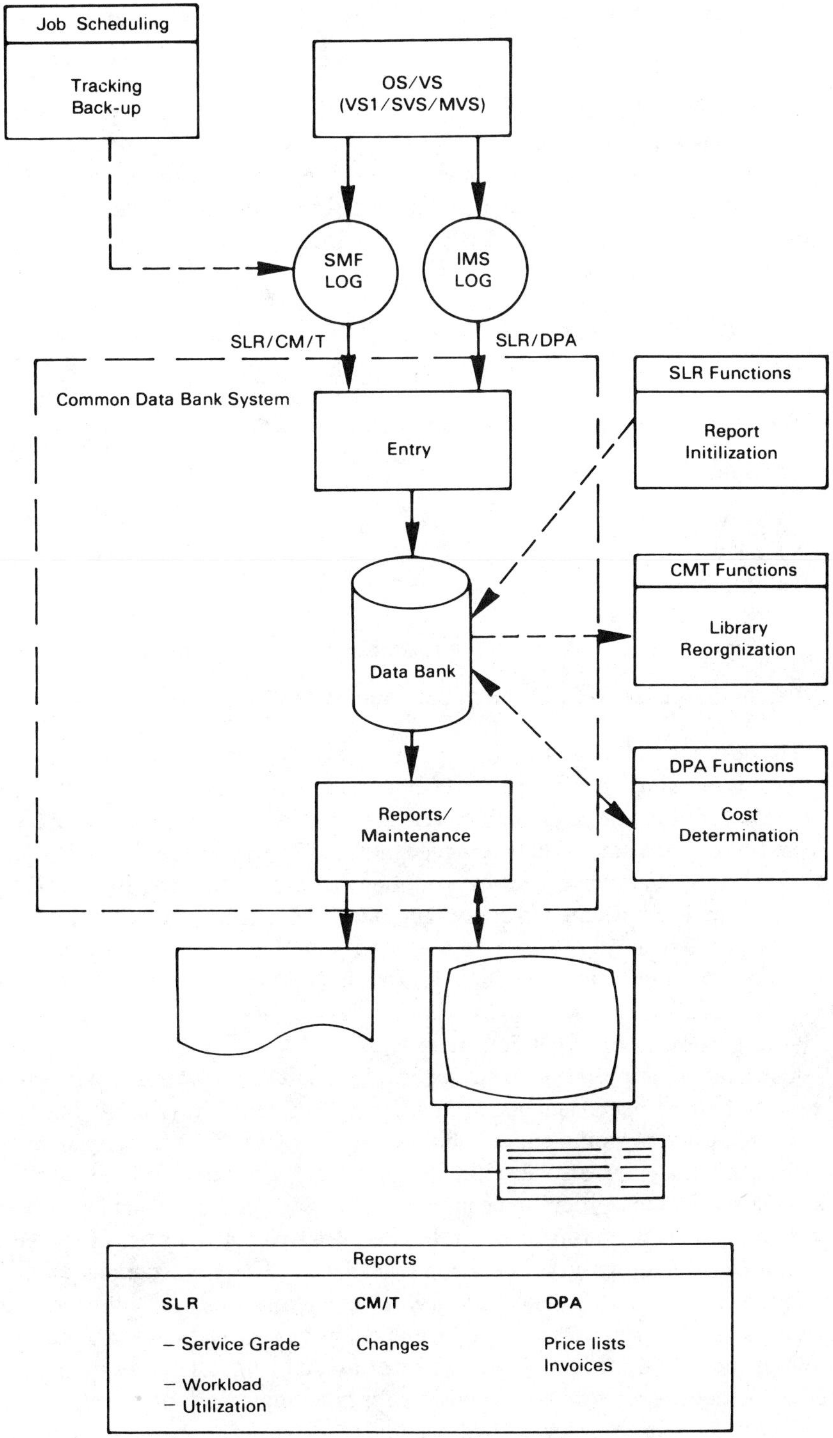


**Figure 7.13** An Overview of Installation Management and Programs

be subtracted from the delays because this would alter the punctuality profile of the computer center. As a rule, delays are examined separately by task or department because this is the easiest way of tracing their cause. In another procedure, delays are grouped together by cause and summed up separately. Experience has shown the following factors to be instrumental in causing delays, and reports on delays can be organized accordingly:

Delayed data delivery

Data deficiencies (incorrect, incomplete, illegible)

Data media deficiencies (defects, improper storage)

Program aborts due to

- Hardware error
- System software error
- Program error
- Operating error
- Processing error (incorrect control card, missing data file, etc.)

Processing delay due to aborted prerequisite run.

The question of how to develop reports on schedule maintenance at the lowest possible cost remains open for the time being. One possibility suggests itself in the schedule ticket of Figure 3.11, which juxtaposes the reference and actual values of input and output. In appropriately designed format it forms the basis for establishing data on schedule maintenance. Job scheduling can handle follow-ups via CRT so that all current data are stored in the system. It is at any rate important to reduce the flood of data and reporting costs to a minimum. Overall reviews and analyses of the scheduling situation in the computer center generally are restricted to isolated actions for budgetary reasons, and should scarcely be necessary with regular and consistent follow-ups of larger deviations.

A second point in the context of reports on schedule maintenance pertains to the exactness of estimated and planned program run times. This point is important for effective usage planning and will be discussed again in the following section. Not only percentage but also absolute deviations are a matter of interest here. A 10% error in a 10-hour program means a 1-hour change in usage planning. Errors are less critical in short runs and can be compensated for more easily. Since a consideration of all program runs in a computer center (500 plus programs per day) can rapidly result in a virtually unsurveyable volume of data, an interpreter program is used to eliminate the less interesting cases. The causes of serious deviations must be traced, so that more exact usage estimates can be made. Job scheduling should therefore be responsible for handling report analyses.

Occasionally the average turnaround time of test jobs and their minimum and maximum deviation is reported as well. This provides the computer center with documentation on the entire scheduling situation in testing, in case there are complaints by programming that test results are not received as quickly as expected. However, one should keep in mind that reports of this nature usually mean an additional time expenditure and for that reason usually are not prepared.

The reports and report analyses of rerun times constitute a problem area directly related to schedule maintenance. Some practitioners suggest special report forms for this purpose. An evaluation can proceed from standard error causes to facilitate a precoded analysis. A separation into areas of application is an important consideration and can facilitate the handling of certain dissatisfied user groups. It has been found that a rerun time analysis can not be effectively designed on the basis of operating system reports. Many programs end with an error code although they produced accurate results. Other program runs have to be repeated even though they were accurately concluded in form. A good rerun time analysis can be an important aid towards satisfactory schedule maintenance because reruns invariably affect completion deadlines.

## 7.3 System Usage Planning

The use of production resources in industry, trade, and administration must be planned with a view towards maximum efficiency. By the same token, an EDP system must not only achieve the highest possible data processing performance from an economic point of view, but at the same time must fulfill the conditions imposed by scheduling and security. Since the time factor is of special importance, the procedures used in planning a batch processing operation are highly recommended, inasmuch as they produce the highest yield for a given cost (e.g., in all service centers) or operate at least cost under a give volume (e.g., in company computer centers). All work processes in the computer center must be subjected to scheduling in order to achieve these objectives. This is the task of system usage planning, in which the individual work processes are logically sequenced. The boundaries of this procedure are determined by parallel dialog operations.

The planning tasks are repeated periodically, and different planning procedures are used depending on the length of these planning periods. This is necessitated by the fact that a certain degree of refinement in planning presupposes a certain degree of knowledge of the work processes under consideration. The further a work process is in the future, the more inexact the information about it will be. This is the starting-out concept of this section upon which the various planning methods are based.

System usage planning as a component of job scheduling comprises technical as well as budgetary tasks with correspondingly complex functional procedures. This probably explains why the use of the EDP system itself is not a simple matter in terms of solving this problem. For this reason automated planning systems are used less often than one might suppose.

## 7.3.1 Long-Range Planning

***Long-range planning is defined as rough preliminary planning, usually for a period of 1–2 years ahead.***

Planning for further ahead in the future, such as a period of 2–5 years, is rare because of an increased uncertainty factor. An updating procedure which plans ahead for 2–3 years but with a planning period of only one year has proven very useful. With ongoing planning, totally new data need to be developed only for the following year, and the plans for other years are derived by correcting the planning data of prior years (Figure 7.14). This graduated procedure not only results in a refinement of planning data and thus more closely resembles future reality, but it permits the inclusion of actual values. If, for example, the planning values for certain task areas were, commonly set too high, it is possible to compensate for this in later stages by means of lower values.

This type of long-range planning requires an annual need analysis for the following year and future years of each task area. Since the information needed is only in part available to the computer center, this procedure imposes an additional burden on the departments involved. This type of planning actually corresponds more closely to a staff function than to the function of a service center, and for that reason long-term planning tasks are usually handled by a central planning agency.

EDP capacity requirements are usually communicated to the computer center in the form of machine requirement reports. However, these reports apply to medium-range planning and require detailed knowlédge of anticipated tasks. Long-term planning data, on the other hand, are of a more fundamental nature, for example, which jobs are run during which years, or which new tasks are to be taken on. Machine capacity in this case (I/O units, storage, CPU) can only be roughly estimated but already includes the requirements for special devices (OCR readers, plotters). Secondary capacities such as channel output can at this point be

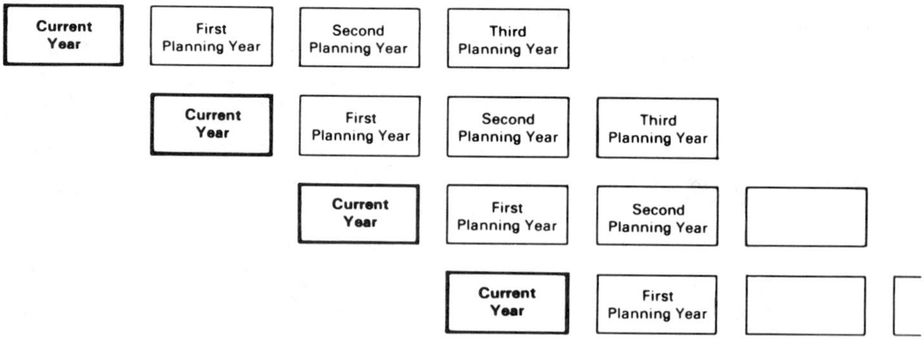


**Figure 7.14** Graduated Long-Term Planning Including Actual Values

estimated only with difficulty, and only system simulation can provide some direction.

The result of these considerations is that long-range system planning, which includes tactical management—that is, planning and control of activities within the strategic objectives—must address itself to the following areas:

Volume and high priority tasks

Application development planning

Service objectives

DP production planning

Hardware requirements

Rough network estimates, including terminals

Standard procedures

Personnel requirements, personnel deployment, and organizational planning

Training and education

Space and buildings

Financial expenditures

With respect to hardware requirements, the output of I/O devices or peripheral storage can be determined with relative accuracy and added to the requirement total. The CPU requirement is a different matter. It has become customary to plan by means of machine norms, with the currently installed equipment as a reference point. If within 3 or 4 years a multiple of the output by this machine is required, the actual situation is not changed; it is simply necessary to change the reference value with each new installation. This is handled at some additional expense by means of benchmarks that represent the task profile. If generally known machines are used for planning, it is possible to fall back on conversion factors that do not need to represent one's own task profile. A larger central unit may also become necessary as a result of expanded periphery. The degree of multiprogramming, on the other hand, probably will not play a decisive role during this phase.

If a computer center has experiential values and usage reports available from previous periods, they can serve as models for future planning. In this model the EDP system is treated as a uniform structure:

Central processing unit

Storage

I/O units

Telecommunication network

Distribution functions are assumed for the usage of the individual components, and their mean productivity is examined. This point deserves serious consideration: there is no differentiation of tasks and the scheduling situation can be disregarded. The teleprocessing share can be included only rather generally by means of a network concept. One must proceed on the assumption that there is a sufficient number of job orders on hand at all times so that it is only a matter of choosing among them for processing. This may be the case for a university computer center, but not for the very demanding deadline structure of a commercial computer center. Furthermore, the assumption of a fixed number of storage areas no longer applies to all systems.

Since long-range planning concerns itself generally with the development of EDP capacity needs within the enterprise or user circle, there is no reference to concrete installations. Statements such as "in three years we'll change from system A to system B" cannot be made because nobody knows whether system B by that time will not have been superseded by better models. It is important, however, to determine capacity limits which, when surpassed, trigger system planning activities. It has been found that an annual machine usage time of 6,696 hours represents the limit for a 4-shift operation. This figure is calculated as follows:

| | |
|---|---|
| 365 days at 24 hours/day = | 8760 hours |
| 52 Sundays (1248) | |
| 8 legal holidays (192) | |
| 8 hours weekly maintenance (416) | |
| 4 hours down time per week (202) | |
| | −2064 hours |
| Total = | 6696 hours |

Planning for a 4-shift operation has become rare, however. With fewer shifts the hourly limits are set correspondingly lower. When unattended operation is included in planning, percentage adjustments corresponding to experiential values must be made.

## 7.3.2 Medium-Range Planning

***Medium-range planning is defined as a refinement of the long-range plans already discussed, with the essential difference that the programs to be run are generally already on hand.***

In most cases, data on run times are available as well. If a new task is to be taken on by the computer center, a machine requisition is generated. There are a variety of such forms in current use. For purposes of usage planning this requisition should contain the following:

Job originator (name, department, telephone)

Task area and cost center

Priorities

Report deadline and possibly deadline for final changes (in batch processing)

Frequency—for example, once a day—and desired schedule

Expected response times in dialog operations

Job identification—for example, original, retry, conversion, testing, demonstration, training

Run time and delay factor in multiprogramming

Proportionate output (relative to the overall system) in a dialog operation

Resources required, including

- Central storage (including resident portions for dialog operations)
- Peripheral storage
- Private disks and tape files
- Disks and tape drives
- Punched card input/output
- Perforated tape input/output
- Quick printers
- Plotters
- Line terminals for teleprocessing
- Type and specifics of terminals required

Program sequence

Name of individual responsible for schedule agreement

The planning period usually extends over one week, but periods of up to 4 weeks may occur in medium-range planning. Planning for a specific task area requires the following data:

Equipment availability time (starting date)

Time necessary for each work routine

Final date for work completion

The starting and final dates are discussed with the respective departments, and agreements for periodically recurring jobs are recorded in a scheduling calendar (see Figure 3.11 for a sample schedule ticket) which forms the basis of system usage planning. Individual and special jobs are then added. For a well-balanced job throughput the schedules for all task areas must be in writing and distributed to all groups involved. These schedules are prerequisites for job coordination and medium-range usage planning. The planning specialist, who should have a good general overview of application procedures and work processes in the computer center, is responsible for continuing adjustments to new circumstances and ongoing dialog with the respective departments. Agreements on a general time frame in this context reduce administrative costs.

Planning tasks can be carried out successfully only if the times necessary for each work process can be calculated in advance with sufficient accuracy and realistic expectations. This applies to recurring jobs as well as one-time jobs in batch processing and the pro-rata teleprocessing share. Planning for recurring jobs is based on an observation of prior runs, and the volume of data to be processed is a good independent variable. Some computer centers record run times as a function of input data by means of a diagram kept in the program files. If in the course of postprocessing new run time observations are recorded, as for example via the Namic system, rather accurate estimates can be calculated for the future, and the causes of irregularities can be determined. Purely analytic calculations such as those made for card punch devices are no longer possible today. Medium-range planning is calculated to within a 15- or 30-minute range of accuracy, as fluctuations in smaller time periods are common in practical operations.

In multiprogramming, the planning and usage times must be given an empirical correction factor larger than 1. A more simplified procedure can omit this factor. This, in fact, corresponds more closely to a multiprogramming operation, because several programs run simultaneously, resulting in an overall usage time of over 24 hours per day.

Parallel processing methods always take into consideration that the sum of operating resources (printers, card readers, magnetic tape units, disks, etc.) determined by the configuration must not exceed peak values. In systems with virtual storage, the overall main storage requirement should not exceed certain experiential values, for example 1.6–1.8 times the real storage capacity, otherwise the system is uneconomical due to increased administrative costs. Set-up times are considered only for isolated high-cost jobs, because in multiprogramming they no longer result in idle time for the system.

Medium-range planning by the month is not as detailed, and tasks are calculated to within an hour of accuracy. This type of planning is most often found in computer centers with relatively small systems, where it is entirely satisfactory and reduces the time expenditures associated with medium-range planning to a minimum. In practice, a 3-shift operation should never plan more than 500 production hours per month, otherwise down times and reruns adversely affect work in the computer center. In a 2-shift operation this boundary is set at 350 hours per month; with one shift the boundary is at 180 hours.

The following is a working guide for planning specialists. It reflects a variety of external and internal influences, and is arranged in the order in which planning proceeds:

Preventive maintenance.

Programs running daily at a specific time. With a relatively small anticipated data volume such tasks can be lumped together for 2 or more days in order to reduce work expenditures.

Programs running on specific days at specific times.

Special jobs, including teleprocessing jobs.

Programs that can be run only on a specific day and time.

Programs running daily at nonspecific times.

Test jobs, especially large-scale system tests.

Buffer time. This must be included in planning because of possible reruns.

Stand-by volume. Every computer center should attempt to have a certain number of stand-by tasks ready to run in cooperation with originating departments. Often these buffer programs improve EDP utilization significantly. Overall operating time must be planned to include a percentage of time for this purpose.

The teleprocessing share is generally determined through an empirical extension factor of the program run times derived from requirement estimates.

Some computer centers use scheduling boards with card inserts for machine usage planning; different colored cards represent different areas of application. Program names and run times are recorded on each card. Boards of this type permit well-organized and easy-to-survey planning control, and facilitate alterations or modifications. Their disadvantage is that they are rarely kept up to date and cannot fully account for multiprogramming. If they are used as an additional planning aid, a job scheduling employee should be responsible for updating them. They are increasingly replaced by planning via CRT.

Since machine requirements for each task are handled by requisition forms, it is a simple matter to generate a machine usage plan via a program for either batch or dialog operations. Figure 7.15 is an example of such a machine generated plan.

Such automated planning procedures are probably on the increase, and a number of standard programs are available, such as Namic. The choice of a product suitable for one's own computer center should be made with great care.

Finally, reference should be made to computer centers with a low volume of scheduled jobs, whose main tasks consist of teleprocessing jobs, stand-by jobs, or test and conversion jobs. University and research computer centers are such an example. There is usually no medium-range machine usage planning. Short-range usage planning is for the most part handled by the scheduling algorithm of the operating system (section 7.3.4), and to a lesser degree by job scheduling, which can be handled by the machine room supervisor, because of the small volume of scheduled jobs. The fortunate situation here is that a selection can be made from a

Weekly Plan 25.02.1974 to 01.03.1974

| Job Name | Probl. NR | Type of Work | GES | Storage Data | U INT | KR Bed. | Periph. K & B | Time Span—Planning—Code # ANL. | MIN. | INT. | TAG | REG. | LFD.NR. |
|---|---|---|---|---|---|---|---|---|---|---|---|---|---|
| Friday | | | | | | | | | | | | | |
| | WS0815000 | DASI. ABN.-STAMMDATEN KUNDEN | 1 | ABN.-STAMMDATEN KUNDEN | | 50 | 1 | 1 | | 2 | 05 | 010 | 01 |
| | WS0816001 | SCRATCH ABN.-STAMMDATEN KUNDEN | 1 | ABN.-STAMMDATEN KUNDEN | | 50 | | 1 | | 2 | 05 | 010 | 01 |
| | WS0816002 | REORG. ABN.-STAMMDATEN KUNDEN | 1 | ABN.-STAMMDATEN KUNDEN | | 50 | 1 | 1 | | 2 | 05 | 010 | 03 |
| | WS0817000 | DASI. ABN.-STAMMDATEN TANKSTELLEN | 1 | ABN.-STAMMDATEN TANKST. | | 50 | 1 | 1 | | 2 | 05 | 010 | 04 |
| | WS0818001 | SCHATCH ABN.-STAMMD. TANKSTELLEN | 1 | ABN.-STAMMDATEN TANKST. | | 50 | | 1 | | 2 | 05 | 010 | 05 |
| | WS0818002 | REORG. ABN.-STAMMD. TANKSTELLEN | 1 | ABN.-STAMMDATEN TANKST. | | 50 | 1 | 1 | | 2 | 05 | 010 | 06 |
| | WS0819000 | DASI. ABN.-STAMMDATEN TK | 1 | ABNEHMER STAMMDATEN TK | | 50 | 1 | 1 | | 2 | 05 | 010 | 07 |
| | WS0820001 | SCRATCH ABNEHMER STAMMDATEN TK | 1 | ABNEHMER STAMMDATEN TK | | 50 | | 1 | | 2 | 05 | 010 | 08 |
| | WS0820002 | REORG. ABNEHMER STAMMDATEN TK | 1 | ABNEHMER STAMMDATEN TK | | 50 | 1 | 1 | | 2 | 05 | 010 | 09 |
| | WS0821000 | DATENSICHERUNG ERZEUGNISSTA.DATEN | 1 | ERZEUGNIS-STAMMDATEN | | 50 | 1 | 1 | 0010 | 2 | 05 | 010 | 10 |
| 0006 | WS0822001 | DAT.ST.SCRATCH ERZEUGNISSTA.DATEN | 1 | ERZEUGNIS-STAMMDATEN | | 50 | | 1 | 0010 | 2 | 05 | 010 | 11 |
| 0006 | WS0822002 | REORGANISATION ERZEUGNISSTA.DATEN | 1 | ERZEUGNIS-STAMMDATEN | | 50 | 1 | 1 | 0010 | 2 | 05 | 010 | 12 |
| | WS0907002 | DASI STANDARD-TABELLEN AUF BAND | 1 | STANDARD-TABELLE | | 50 | 1 | 1 | | 2 | 05 | 010 | 13 |
| | WS0908001 | SCRATCHEN STAND.TABELLE | 1 | STANDARD-TABELLEN | | 50 | | 1 | | 2 | 05 | 010 | 14 |
| | WS0908002 | REORGANISATION STAND.TABELLE | 1 | STANDARD-TABELLEN | | 50 | 1 | 1 | | 2 | 05 | 010 | 15 |
| 0063 | RZ0162000 | UEBERN. ARBEITS- U. ZEITKARTEN | 1 | | | 30 | 1 2 1 | 1 | | 5 | 01 | 011 | 01 |
| 0063 | RZ0162S100 | SORT. SA AZ FUER RZ 016300 | 1 | ARBEITSBEREICHE | | 50 | 1 | 1 | | 5 | 01 | 011 | 02 |
| 0063 | RZ0162S200 | SORT. SA AZ FUER RZ 016300 | 1 | ARBEITSBEREICHE | | 50 | 1 | 1 | | 5 | 01 | 011 | 03 |
| 0063 | RZ0163000 | AUSWERTUNG.LEISTUNGSUEB.LOCHERIN | 1 | ARBEITS-FAKTOREN-LOCHRAUM | | 30 | 2 1 | 1 | | 5 | 01 | 011 | 04 |
| 0063 | RZ0163S300 | SORT. SA AK FUER RZ 016400 | 1 | ARBEITSBEREICHE | | 50 | 1 | 1 | | 5 | 01 | 011 | 05 |
| 0063 | RZ0164000 | AUSW.LEISTUNGSUEBERSICHT PRUEFERI | 1 | ARBEITS-FAKTOREN-LOCHRAUM | | 30 | 2 1 | 1 | | 5 | 01 | 011 | 06 |
| 0063 | RZ0164S100 | SORT. SA AK FUER RZ 016500 | 1 | ARBEITSBEREICHE | | 50 | 1 | 1 | | 5 | 01 | 011 | 07 |
| 0063 | RZ0165000 | AUSW.NACH GELOCHTEN KARTENARTEN | 1 | | | 40 | 1 1 | 1 | | 5 | 01 | 011 | 08 |
| 0043 | RZ0717000 | ERST.ARB.-SAETZE A. MONATL.SMF-BA | 1 | | | 30 | 2 1 | 1 | | 5 | 01 | 011 | 09 |
| 0043 | RZ0718S000 | SORT. SA PRIMAERES FUER RZ 071800 | 1 | ARBEITSBEREICHE | | 50 | 1 | 1 | | 5 | 01 | 011 | 10 |

Figure 7.15 Machine-Generated Weekly Plan

reserve of stand-by programs. The high proportion of math-intensive programs also provides for a satisfactory overall utilization of the system, even though the response times of dialog jobs may occasionally suffer as a result.

## 7.3.3 Short-Range Planning and Priorities

In long-range planning the principal capacity requirements are determined in the absence of available programs or data. In medium-range planning the programs are available, so that resource requirements and schedules can be precisely determined. Only the data volume estimates are somewhat uncertain. Planning must include provisions for reruns and unexpected problems.

In short-range planning the work volume can be estimated fairly accurately, because programs and data are on hand. These daily estimates are, as a rule, planned to within a 5-minute range of accuracy.

From an organizational point of view this presupposes that jobs are submitted to the computer center no later than 4 P.M. on the previous day.

Daily estimates are essential for every computer center involved in running scheduled jobs and aiming for an evenly distributed utilization of the EDP system. These estimates are the basis for instructions to the shift supervisors on job sequences and short-term redispositions. It has also been found that daily written estimates tend to make operators feel more closely associated with their tasks, increase motivation, and reduce the sense of isolation common to a closed-shop operation.

The medium-range systems usage plan is the basis for daily estimates. Changes and redispositions are primarily caused by backlogs or reruns. The flowchart of Figure 7.16 is a graphic summary of production planning which includes the use of scheduled reserves. An awareness of the typical bottlenecks is essential if jobs are to be evenly distributed. Some of these bottlenecks are:

- The central processing unit, when running math-intensive jobs for engineering or operations research. Only input/output-intensive programs should be planned parallel to these jobs. Math-intensive programs have the lowest priority, because their low input/output seldom releases the CPU for other jobs.
- The printer. This is the most common bottleneck, as for example when printing invoices. In single programming operations this can only be remedied by additional printers. Spooling has also become popular. Bottlenecks in multiprogramming are avoided through automatic intermediate storage on disks. Peak loads can also be relieved by transferring printer output to COM.
- External storage devices. These can represent bottlenecks in a variety of tasks, as for example in sort programs. Storage occupancy tables have

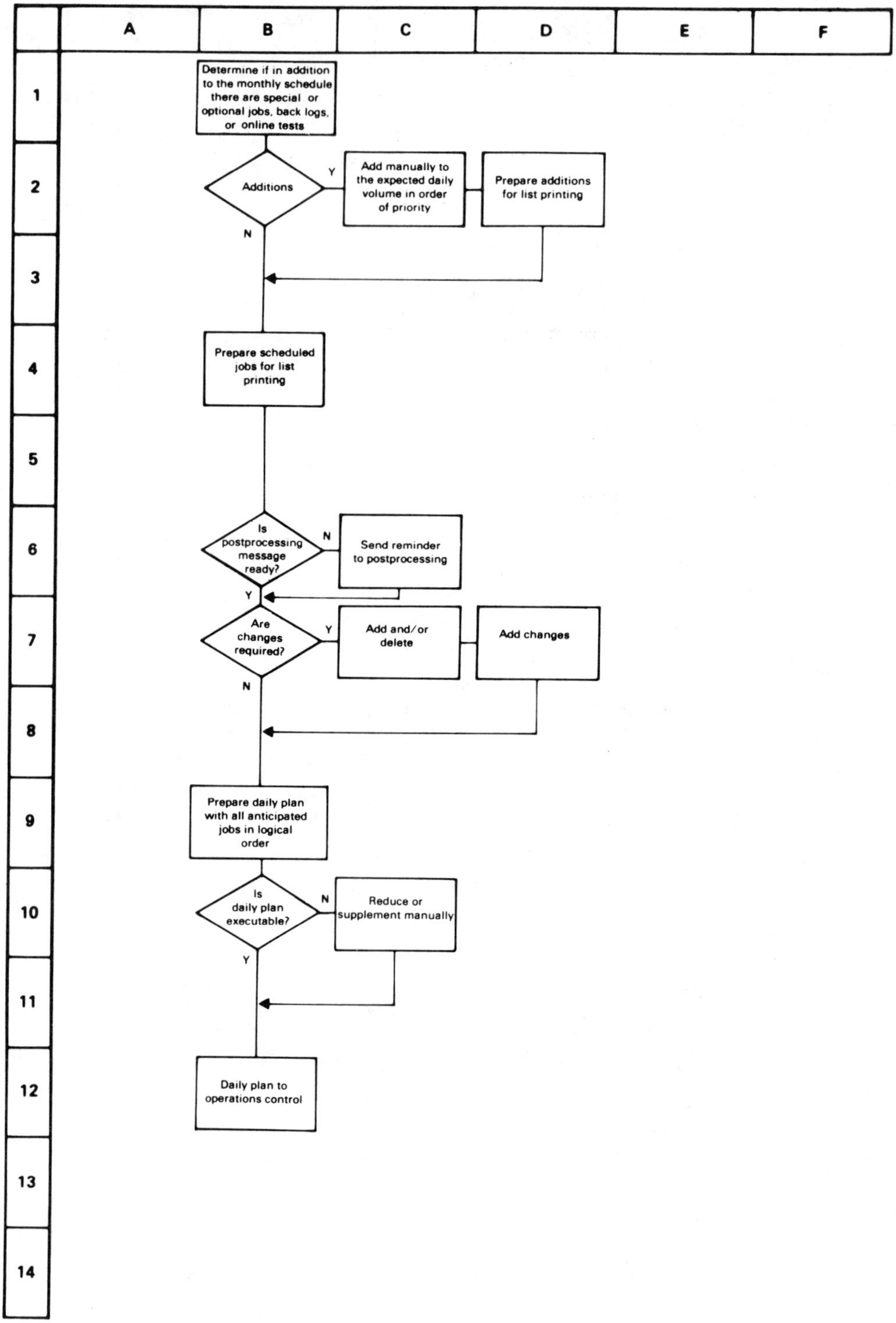


**Figure 7.16** Production Planning for a Batch Operation

proven a useful aid in usage planning. By and large, input/output-intensive programs should never have the lowest priority.

- Buffering I/O devices such as plotters and document readers. With intermediate disk storage the actual output program can utilize the maximum speed of the peripheral device if it is assigned high priority. This is recommended, because the program is given control relatively seldom and only for short periods of time because of I/O interruptions. Manual planning tasks are handled by means of forms which should be adapted to each situation.

Priority assignments, which in most operating systems can be included in the JCL statements, should observe the following sequence:

Math-intensive programs (lowest priority)

Input/output-intensive programs

Short testing and conversion jobs

Buffering periphery, which operates slowly and only rarely receives control

Highest-priority special rush jobs which must be inserted, if necessary, at the expense of other tasks. This priority should be restricted to exceptional situations.

Even if the operating system permits large-scale splitting, the sequence should be maintained except for schedule-related emergencies; otherwise the usage factor decreases rapidly with an increase in processing costs.

Large computer centers with several systems can handle daily usage planning via programs, especially when medium-range planning is already programmed. The Siemans computer centers have used such programs since 1969, and others have developed their own methods. Regrettably there has been no successful move towards standard systems for different operating systems, and standard application software is still very system-dependent.

The program specifications are stored in a separate file following entry. Copies of the program-generated system usage plans are made available to each system; the original and the job cards go to the shift supervisor.

Backlog planning is a special component of daily planning. Backlogs may be the result of reruns caused by errors or past-due program or data delivery. The gaps thus created should be used for high-priority tasks or stand-by volume. Since the original job could not be run according to the timetable, it must be rescheduled. If the delay was minor and a job scheduled for later can be moved up, the entire matter can be handled that day. In the case of longer delays, the backlog planning process goes into effect. There are basically two procedures:

- *Automatic backlog planning*: A job that cannot run on schedule for whatever reason is automatically rescheduled for the following day, i.e., the job card is added to that day's planning. This facilitates planning and saves time, but results in an excessive planning volume because there is no guarantee that the conditions on the following day will accommodate the run. Statistically this is reflected in a high rerun rate, due to multiple rearrangements.

- *Confirmed backlog planning*: The job cards of unperformed jobs are collected separately and rescheduled only upon release by the originating department or programming. This procedure may require the extra step of a confirmation, but it does result in a more realistic daily schedule.

These considerations presume that the computer center must turn out a product with maximum equipment utilization and schedule maintenance. Planning is simpler if the computer center rents block times to certain users. In that case, the daily usage plan may simply be in the form of a bar graph or table.

Usage planning that includes online jobs represents a special problem for job scheduling. Except for certain specific tasks, real-time jobs are difficult to include in system planning, because the resident portion of the operating system must be enlarged and a special area must be planned for applicaton programs. Because real-time jobs are time-dependent, they can destroy the batch processing schedule through channel or occasionally CPU occupancy. Because of this reciprocal influence and the availability of low-cost process computers, tasks of this type are usually not included in planning. On the other hand, the structure of some real-time jobs makes them unsuitable for process computers.

Dialog operations and online entry are a different matter. The discussion pertaining to main storage allocation applies here as well. Data entry, especially over intelligent terminals, makes relatively minor use of channel and CPU capacity and remains generally constant during operating hours, so that this workload can easily be included in system usage planning. Delays in overall batch processing will amount to only a few percentage points. This assumes the use of buffer terminals or even distributed data processing devices and experiential values for capacity requirement planning.

In contrast to this, the spontaneous demands made on the system by time-sharing terminals can be considerable and uneven. There are computer centers where during an operation of over 50 terminals batch processing is virtually impossible and the terminals themselves influence one another by competing for resources. In this type of situation a bottleneck analysis via hardware or software monitors becomes necessary (section 7.2.3). As a rule, the bottlenecks exist in the input/output channels or in main storage. Nevertheless, permitting critical scheduled jobs to be run at certain times of the day and during periods of intense dialog operation in order to be able to schedule and process batch jobs at other times is subject to some reservations. Whether or not dialog operation is practical during unattended operation depends on the schedule structure of batch jobs and the demands on dialog operations. As a rule, these periods are used for pure batch processing, pure teleprocessing, or a mixture of both.

Remote batch processing jobs are practically the only tasks left that are not brought to the system directly by the computer center. However, they can easily be scheduled as long as they are routine jobs. The remote terminals are usually operated by computer center employees who have been given a copy of the weekly schedule. In the case of express terminals—that is, terminals for the purpose of rapid and convenient execution of small tests and conversions—the operating system must exercise a control in order to make sure that only jobs of an agreed-upon size (for example, 1 CPU minutes, 1000 print lines, and no tape allocation) are entered and processed. These tasks can be planned by job scheduling.

Because of the difficulties mentioned above, a number of computer centers have come to the conclusion that detailed machine usage plans are superfluous, because processing is handled on a first come, first served basis anyway. This certainly does not apply to commercial computer centers with a firm deadline structure. By analogy, railroads schedule the frequency of trains based on need rather than maximum utilization of resource.

## 7.3.4 Scheduling by the Operating System

While job scheduling works very well in terms of daily usage planning, it lags behind in the moment-to-moment device distribution of multiprogramming operations. These devices run at such high internal speeds that a job running on the system can only be monitored and controlled by means of a program. Practically the entire burden of control and distribution of dialog and real-time jobs, which cannot be planned in detail by job scheduling, is on the operating system. As a result, a variety of scheduling algorithms have been analyzed scientifically, much to the benefit of batch operations. On the other hand, in some instances a certain overemphasis on this distributive function has developed in the sense that the supportive function of the operating system, which is important for daily planning and essential for commercial processing schedules, has been neglected.

This is not an attempt to treat the subject superficially and thus inadequately, but merely a means of pointing out the basic difference between the meaning of usage planning in job scheduling and scheduling by the operating system. It is, after all, one of the responsibilities of the computer center manager to guide the systems personnel in the organization in such a way as to generate the optimal scheduling procedures for a given operating system. In addition, an operating philosophy should be developed along one or more of the following suggested guidelines:

- *Scheduling accuracy*. Some operating systems have time functions that are addressable by means of parameters in the job control language in order to influence job completion deadlines through operations scheduling.
- *Maximum machine utilization*. This philosophy is associated with extremely varying queue times for different jobs. Moreover, long queues in the holding

areas offer the possibility of being able to choose the most appropriate from among a large number of jobs.

- *Maximum profit in overall performance accounting*. This pertains to priority sequencing in the fee structure rather than by job characteristics.
- *Minimizing costs per performance unit*. The definition of a performance unit remains open.
- *Precedence assignment to certain jobs*. This might include short jobs, test runs, or consideration of certain priority classes.
- *Minimizing total queue time*: This is a major aspect in dialog processing.
- *Equal consideration of job classes*. The FIFO principle is an example.

The technical literature should be consulted for details on scheduling algorithms. Reference has already been made to the fact that the extensive theoretical examinations of scheduling algorithms in dialog and real-time operations have also had an effect on batch processing. As a result, a number of theories on optimal packing can now be applied in the concrete activities of system usage planning.

Program priorities should also be mentioned in this context. Every operating system has the capability of assigning priorities to jobs via control statements. For the operating system these priorities serve as the basis for the internal processing priorities characterized by the following:

Considerably greater discrimination than program priorities

Dynamic adaptation to operating conditions, i.e., no program has to wait too long before being processed

Processing priorities adapted to processing conditions by the operating system, i.e., in waiting for specific input/output processes

Some internal priorities are reserved for operating system tasks

Since system usage planning in conjunction with priorities tends to be error-prone due to ignorance, and manifests itself in a poor performance, it is essential to educate systems personnel continuously in the mastery of the prevailing system's characteristics. Only the optimum interaction between job scheduling and the operating system can achieve an effective computer center operation which may, if necessary, be backed up by an appropriate planning system.

Since systems personnel can alter the usage strategy of an operating system (an adaptation to the spectrum of applications may be necessary), it is important not to allow too much variation in the originally developed distribution. Only an effective usage control can decide on the success of an adaptation.

## 7.3.5 Resource Allocations

One specific type of planning characteristic for computer centers in research and education warrants a brief discussion. The medium- and long-range planning methods described thus far cannot simply be taken over here, because the system tasks are less determined by recurring routing jobs (bookkeeping, inventory, billing) than by continuously changing tasks that often cannot be scheduled in advance.

Budgetary reasons alone preclude absorption costing of computer center services. Moreover, project leaders often share in investments for the computer center, and, as a result, expect financial preferences where "their" jobs are concerned. This type of situation has also promoted the opinion among many users that unlimited free capacity should be available. Only a rigorous allocation system along the following lines can handle this type of situation:

- Allocation of resources (CPU, disk storage, etc.) according to advance notification of needs and proportionate with the utilization of prior allocations. If used exclusively, this method leads to hoarding and a distortion of actual needs.
- Distribution of overall capacity by using ficticious numerical values as uniform planning factors. This procedure resembles absorption costing but cannot be interpreted as "money" because it is not convertible into any other services. The differentiated need for the resources is thus difficult to plan because, for example, sometimes there is a larger need for printing, sometimes for storage, and sometimes for computation, and each time there is the same numerical value to designate the need. On the user's part it means a limit in the ability to substitute resources. Experiences in the use of this procedure have been rather positive.
- Allocations using "real money" as a numerical reference value, whereby the fees are calculated as a share of the absorption costs. In this procedure the user can buy resources within certain limits (perhaps by voucher), but can use the money for something else as well. At any rate, this method seems to be a very cost-conscious solution to the problem without giving too much preference to the "wealthy" at the expense of the "needy." It also avoids resource hoarding, and unused capacities can be sold at market value, thus improving the computer center budget.

All these allocation methods have the disadvantage of requiring a committee to determine the relative importance of projects. This is often considered presumptuous, and the question is raised as to why the project leader cannot directly determine project costs, and why computer center use is accorded a special position.

The computer center is thus burdened with an additional and thankless job, the resolution of which may even be contradictory to the fulfillment of its actual tasks. It has been suggested that the internal problem of distribution (in the sense of optimum system utilization) be separated from the external problem, that is, the allocation of resources. The planning authority in charge of allocations in that case would have to be outside of the computer center, which would assume a staff function by describing the available resources and handling the cost accounting. Ths users solve their own optimization problems by utilizing the allocated units to best advantage. Priorities can be assigned at an additional allocation charge.

## 7.4 System Testing

Program testing has been extensively covered in the technical literature. The question to be asked here is to what extent it touches computer center planning. Program testing has two objectives:

Finding and correcting formal and logical errors

Testing the program to verify whether it meets the predetermined expectations

The program test therefore includes all the activities necessary to produce a program free of logical and formal errors. To begin with, this applies to programming, but naturally not without use of the system. Since it is not a matter of running routine jobs, and operations scheduling is not absolutely required, a separate discussion appears justified. As every practitioner knows, test runs can play havoc with deadlines. The percentage proportion of test runs depends rather heavily on the particular situation of a department; routinely it is somewhere between 5% and 20%; update services prevent it from ever sinking to 0%. Except for initialization phases, for example, the percentage rarely amounts to a significant proportion of the overall tasks. This situation justifies an organizationally separate treatment of program tests in batch operations. With large-scale testing a second system often exists for testing purposes in dialog and batch operations. While this method is advantageous from an organizational point of view, it is often considered a luxury.

### 7.4.1 Self Testing

In self testing the programmer operates the system during the test run. This is not the rule with today's systems, because it is associated with considerable budgetary and personnel problems. Self tests usually occur in conjunction with specialized problems and in small installations. Aside from the advantages and disadvantages of self testing from the programming point of view, a number of problems arise for the practical operation of the computer center. These were, in part, discussed in the context of open shop operations (section 3.4.2.1). At any rate, periodic relief of the actual operator by a programmer should be viewed negatively. It disturbs the entire work rhythm, requires transfer procedures as in a shift change, and the system must be handed over empty. Self tests should therefore be limited to exceptions. This means only by written authorization of the computer center manager, and preferably when no shifts are operating.

While programming has generally realized that self tests are not absolutely necessary for error-free programs, one area that depends on it is systems programming. Everyone agrees that a system software error must be corrected as quickly as possible, and a good many managers tend to make generous exceptions for the systems software group. It should be kept in mind that these tests especially disturb routine jobs—whose account is to be charged for reruns necessitated by such actions? An additional problem is the fact that the systems software group belongs organizationally to the computer center, and its members are often hard to convince that the EDP production center exists primarily for the purpose of running application programs while system software performs an auxiliary function. Self tests should be planned to make use of block times.

## 7.4.2 Remote Testing

In remote testing a task is brought to the computer center as if it were a one-time job. The programmer needs to decide whether a test run is worthwhile (the results are not available immediately), and whether everything has been accurately described. Since the programmer has to perform the operations scheduling activities such as program specification, control cards, header cards, documentation data and the like, special operating instructions must be provided in order to let the computer center know how the job is to be processed. Programming seldom has the opportunity to use the full range of the operating system through control statements. Therefore the best preparation for efficient production programs is the full utilization of the control language of a system through programming in the testing phase.

There are no standardized forms as yet for test instructions. Individual computer centers use forms designed for their specific needs and the requirements of the system. The programmer fills out the test instructions for each run and each conversion, and turns them over to the computer center with the rest of the testing materials. Depending on the format, reruns may or may not use the same test instructions. They go to the machine room with the test materials and are the basis for job output. This ensures that no test job gets lost and that the entire output is returned to the programmer. Dispatching usually acknowledges the run with a date and time stamp on the test instructions. If provisions are made for operator's remarks they are added in the machine room. This procedure exacts precise test descriptions which may change from one time to another, and avoids the use of no

**Test follow-up**
System 4004/15

Page No.
Date: 3/30/84

Program No. B27W　　Program Name: Evaluation of Internal Jobs

Programming Group: Accounting

| to be filled out by programmer | | | | to be filled out by operator | | | | |
|---|---|---|---|---|---|---|---|---|
| TI No.* Date | Date Received | Estimated Machine Usage Time | Programmer's Name | RT* ST* | Aborted after | Completed after | Run Date | Operator Name or Number |
| 3615 | 30.3.67 | 30 Min | | FT | 3 Min | Min. | 31.3.67 | 7. Schulz |
| 3641 | 6.4.67 | 20 Min | | FT | Min. | 15 Min. | 7.4.67 | 3. Holzmann |
| 3040 | 15.4.67 | 15 Min | | FT | Min. | 18 Min | 15.4.67 | 12. Krieger |
| | | Min | | | Min. | Min. | | |
| | | Min | | | Min. | Min. | | |
| | | Min | | | Min. | Min. | | |
| | | Min. | | | Min. | Min. | | |
| | | Min. | | | Min. | Min. | | |
| | | Min | | | Min. | Min. | | |
| | | Min. | | | Min. | Min. | | |
| | | Min. | | | Min. | Min. | | |
| | | Min. | | | Min. | Min. | | |
| | | Min | | | Min. | Min. | | |
| | | Min | | | Min. | Min. | | |
| | | Min. | | | Min. | Min. | | |
| | | Min | | | Min. | Min. | | |
| | | Min | | | Min. | Min. | | |
| | | Min | | | Min. | Min. | | |
| | | Min | | | Min. | Min | | |
| | | Min | | | Min. | Min. | | |
| | | Min. | | | Min. | Min. | | |
| | | Min. | | | Min. | Min. | | |
| | | Min | | | Min. | Min. | | |
| | | Min. | | | Min. | Min. | | |
| | | Min. | | | Min. | Min. | | |
| | | Min | | | Min. | Min. | | |

*RT Remote Test
*ST Self Test
*TI Test Information

**Figure 7.17** Follow-up Form for Remote Tests

longer applicable instructions and reruns. Follow-up forms must be used for such one-time test instructions (Figure 7.17) for purposes of later verification, such as data security.

Sophisticated operating systems can generate lists of test runs via program and a numerical accounting system (section 3.1.5.1). Figure 7.18 is an example of such a list for a MASTER CD 3300 system. Occasionally "sales receipts" are used to keep track of the cost components. This alerts programmers and team leaders to the necessity of designing cost-effective tests. In reviewing test instructions one should question the value of each item, whether it improves the job run and whether it is worth the expense.

Aside from the advantages and disadvantages of remote testing for programming, the following picture emerges:

- Since test runs generally are nonscheduled (except for multiprogramming), they represent a small buffer of stand-by jobs which can even out small fluctuations in capacity utilization.
- Testing does not need to be coordinated with the programmer's working hours, and tests can be run during the night shift.
- Remote tests can be run during the times when external devices not needed for testing are inoperable.
- In case of system failure, tests can be run on alternate equipment because they require small data volumes and usually make no special demands on resources.
- The possibilities of system software can be better utilized, especially with sophisticated operating systems, and priority assignments improve system capacity without adverse effects on scheduled jobs.
- In organizing the job input stream more attention can be given to ease of operation and thus improved operational sequence. This reduces operating

| NR | ACC.NO | JOBNAME | DAY | INIT | TERM | CPU TIME | CH. TIME | QPS | SCR | LINES | CARDS | PERIPHERAL EQUIPMENT | | | |
|---|---|---|---|---|---|---|---|---|---|---|---|---|---|---|---|
| 1 | ZRMA0001 | MA/VAO | 02/25/74 | 21/35/18 | 21/35/3[illegible] | 00/00/01 | 00/00/01 | 39 | 50 | 8 | 0 | 32: | 72 | | |
| 2 | ZRMA0001 | MA/VAO | 02/25/74 | 22/03/16 | 22/07/05 | 00/00/52 | 00/00/18 | 39 | 50 | 20 | 0 | 32: | 289 | | |
| 3 | ZRMA0001 | MA/VAO | 02/25/74 | 23/25/37 | 23/28/10 | 00/00/01 | 00/00/01 | 39 | 65 | 12 | 0 | 51: | 213 | 32: | 153 |
| 4 | ZRMA0001 | MA/VAO | 02/25/74 | 23/29/41 | 23/32/45 | 00/01/29 | 00/00/31 | 64 | 65 | 80 | 0 | 51: | 244 | 32: | 179 |
| 5 | ZRMA0001 | MA/VAO | 02/25/74 | 23/33/50 | 23/37/12 | 00/01/34 | 00/00/32 | 64 | 74 | 135 | 0 | 51: | 262 | 32: | 193 |
| 6 | ZRMA0001 | MA/VAO | 02/26/74 | 00/03/59 | 00/06/45 | 00/01/35 | 00/00/33 | 64 | 74 | 135 | 0 | 51: | 226 | 32: | 158 |
| 7 | ZRMA0001 | MA/VAO | 02/26/74 | 00/11/23 | 00/14/25 | 00/01/39 | 00/00/37 | 64 | 88 | 135 | 0 | 51: | 242 | 32: | 155 |
| 8 | ZRMA0001 | MA/VAO | 02/26/74 | 14/19/18 | 14/19/22 | 00/00/01 | 00/00/01 | 39 | 74 | 12 | 0 | 51: | 65 | 32: | 5 |
| 9 | ZRMA0001 | MA/VAO | 02/26/74 | 14/26/37 | 14/33/55 | 00/03/12 | 00/00/50 | 39 | 74 | 3113 | 0 | 51: | 498 | 32: | 200 |
| 10 | ZRMA0001 | MA/VAO | 02/26/74 | 14/45/42 | 14/57/00 | 00/05/50 | 00/01/29 | 39 | 74 | 7330 | 0 | 51: | 738 | 32: | 91 |
| 11 | ZRMA0001 | MA/VAO | 02/27/74 | 01/49/36 | 01/52/25 | 00/00/56 | 00/00/22 | 64 | 88 | 1712 | 0 | 51: | 230 | 32: | 72 |
| 12 | ZRMA0001 | MA/VAO | 02/27/74 | 02/25/55 | 02/28/52 | 00/01/05 | 00/00/30 | 64 | 88 | 2n24 | 0 | 51: | 237 | 32: | 54 |
| 13 | ZRMA0001 | MA/VAO | 02/27/74 | 05/01/19 | 05/04/05 | 00/01/06 | 00/00/27 | 64 | 88 | 2n24 | 0 | 51: | 226 | 32: | 51 |
| 14 | ZRMA0001 | MA/VAO | 02/27/74 | 05/29/26 | 05/32/06 | 00/01/02 | 00/00/35 | 64 | 88 | 2n28 | 0 | 51: | 220 | ,32: | 55 |
| 15 | ZRMA0001 | MA/VAO | 02/27/74 | 13/21/55 | 13/23/20 | 00/00/18 | 00/00/07 | 39 | 59 | 22 | 192 | 32: | 134 | | |
| 16 | ZRMA0001 | MA/VAO | 02/27/74 | 14/03/20 | 14/05/28 | 00/00/17 | 00/00/07 | 39 | 59 | 24 | 192 | 32: | 174 | | |
| 17 | ZRMA0001 | MA/VAO | 02/27/74 | 14/08/10 | 14/10/49 | 00/01/16 | 00/00/23 | 39 | 52 | 1n15 | 192 | 32: | 99 | | |
| 18 | ZRMA0001 | MA/VAO | 02/27/74 | 14/24/07 | 14/26/23 | 00/01/07 | 00/00/23 | 39 | 52 | 1n61 | 170 | 32: | 99 | | |
| 19 | ZRMA0001 | MA/VAO | 02/27/74 | 18/18/41 | 18/24/44 | 00/02/10 | 00/00/29 | 39 | 52 | 2n52 | 171 | 32: | 142 | | |
| 20 | ZRMA0001 | MA/VAO | 02/27/74 | 18/24/48 | 18/31/21 | 00/02/51 | 00/00/30 | 39 | 52 | 2351 | 193 | 32: | 111 | | |

**Figure 7.18** Machine-Generated List of Program Requests and Their Resource Usage

costs which may be considerable in many short test runs requiring frequent tape or form changes.

Despite these advantages one should not overlook the fact that programmers impatiently await their test results. Even though testing generally cannot be included in daily scheduling, some provision should be made for anticipated test volumes. For purposes of maintaining control many computer centers require test capacities to be booked in advance and included in medium-range planning. Otherwise, how is the computer center to know which projects are to be run during which periods of time and to what extent? A number of computer centers issue test allocations that can be used either in dialog or batch operations. This is decidedly advantageous for capacity planning.

One further point must be mentioned: Remote tests depend on the debugging aids of system software. The computer center manager must make sure that systems support makes serviceable debugging aids available to the users.

Since on the one hand remote tests in a closed shop are not always the perfect solution for programming, but on the other teleperiphery connections are increasingly convenient, the merits of remote job entry stations need to be evaluated for each case (section 3.4.2.5), as well as the possibility of testing programs via video display terminals or teleprinters. This is not necessarily done in the context of dialog operations (section 3.4.2.6), but by means of developing and starting batch programs from the terminal. Instead of using a specific dialog language such as APL or BASIC, the programs are written in FORTRAN or COBOL and incorporated into the routine after testing by operations scheduling. The special debugging routines of system software can be applied here.

## 7.5 Auditing Procedures

A great deal of thought has been given to the relationship between auditing and data processing. While these numerous and varied considerations will not be reviewed here, an attempt will be made to reduce the fear of an audit and promote a realistic attitude to this process. The often rather complex system of regulations is generally more closely observed when regular checks are made. Besides, an audit report is not meant to be destructive but is intended to improve the operation.

To begin with, audit and control must be delineated:

***Controls are the ongoing and effective safety measures in a processing system.***

Examples of computer center control were discussed at some length in Chapters 3 and 4. It should be emphasized in this context that a variety of controls is an essential component of an efficiently functioning computer center. But how effective are controls, and to what extent can they be verified? This leads to the concept of auditing:

***Auditing consists primarily of checking and verifying all procedures and processes with a view towards formal and factual accuracy and regularity.***

Auditing is characterized by a post factum review performed by an external expert. There are two types of audits:

- An external audit is a review of the accuracy maintained in the following processing procedures. The auditor is therefore not an employee of the enterprise. The audit is usually conducted a considerable time after the actual work process.
- An internal audit is a review of the internal concerns of an enterprise, such as computer delinquency, and organizational and budgetary efficiency.

As a result, the internal audit breaks down into three components:

Functional capability of controls

Adherence to planning and guidelines

Reliability of the information and accounting systems.

This division shows that the audit of processing procedures has a considerable effect on programming. The computer center is less affected by external audits, since it performs only an auxiliary function in the job processes of programming and individual departments. For example, questions pertaining to the retention period of data files, regardless of the media involved, apply directly to the departmental level that is responsible for reporting releases to the computer center, which is not authorized to destroy or release data belonging to a department. An audit should be designed to verify that.

Thus an audit in the computer center is restricted to a verification of functional capability, adherence to regulations, cost effectiveness, and security. This raises a question: Would the computer center rather wait for a catastrophe or an auditor, or should regular security checks be conducted internally, in which case an audit would not pose any threat? Checklists of empirical questions and comments are available as auditing aids, and an intensive study of these questions is highly recommended. A regular and self-critical review of these questions also leads to the realization that, in comparison with more traditional work methods, data processing has the capability of attaining a high level of processing security. This applies to destructive acts as well as accurate accounting methods.

The EDP system itself can be an auditing tool. However, the particulars of auditing methods go beyond the topic at hand because, unlike controls, they fall outside the province of computer center tasks. Management usually employs external auditing firms for the purpose of maintaining neutrality. The constructive criticism of an auditor's report can be an important aid in improving computer center organization.

Within the framework of critical examinations of computer center functions and operations, the concept of weak point analysis has emerged in recent years. Unlike an auditor's report, this is not restricted to a description of the weak points in the computer center but combines criticism with constructive countermeasures. Computer center managers deplore the lack of constructive suggestions not only here but in the numerous and extensive checklists available for this purpose, which contain little more than an enumeration of points to be observed. However, the examiner in most cases does not know whether to evaluate the conditions pertaining to a particular point positively or negatively, and even where reservations are in order no concrete countermeasures exist.

It is possible to suggest some systematic procedures for developing the constructive criticism necessary in an auditor's report, even though the constructive components of such a report are difficult to describe in an abstract hypothetical case. References will therefore be made to other areas of this book where concrete instructions may be found. A systematic procedure is essential, as demonstrated in Figure 7.19. There is, on the one hand, the static component of the organizational structure combined with an examination of the limits of its responsibility. This essentially pertains to the following:

Relations between the computer center and its user departments (section 2.5.1)

Organization of data entry and an examination of centralized versus decentralized entry possibilities

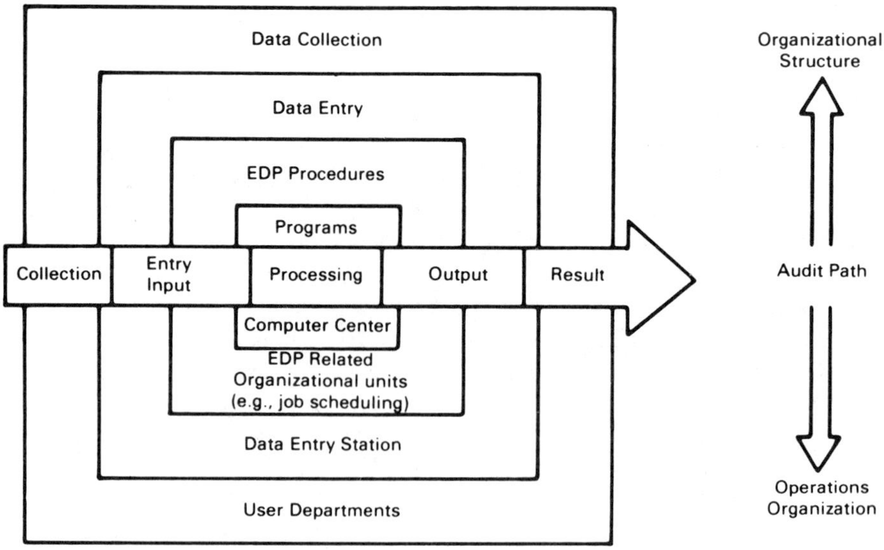


Figure 7.19 EDP Areas of Examination

Organization of operations scheduling and postprocessing, with a critical evaluation of the possibility of linking this area more closely to the user departments in teleprocessing or remote job entry.

The organizational structure in a narrower sense (section 2.4), an examination of appropriate hierarchical relations (section 2.3), the number of management levels, and the practical aspects of interrelating certain job groups

The second area of examination concerns the operations organization represented in the upper half of Figure 7.19 and subdivided as follows:

Data collection in user departments

Document processing and entry, including an analysis of work volume relative to available personnel

An examination of data processing procedures (usually considered to be separate from the actual computer center)

Program evaluation (usually closely linked to the examination of processing procedures)

An examination of computer center operations encompassing the following auditing areas:

- Operations scheduling procedures
- Records and documentation
- Update services
- Media archives
- Data protection (including tape release)
- Data security measures
- Postprocessing
- Employment and personnel qualifications (many computer centers have too many operators and not enough specialists)
- Teleprocessing

The third principal audit area concerns cost efficiency, not in the sense of general budgetary methods but with a view towards resource utilization. The effectiveness of data processing procedures must be examined apart from resource utilization. Since the computer center is not directly involved, the reader is referred to the technical literature on the subject. The consideration here applies to the operation of data processing systems in the following areas:

Critical analysis of hardware component utilization

Examination of existing hardware contracts

Critical analysis of software component utilization, including system software (e.g., compilers that were paid for but never used)

Examination of existing software contracts (occasionally, one finds that existing maintenance agreements are never utilized)

Critical evaluation of hardware service contracts (some rarely or never used devices may still be under contracts; for others maintenance on a per call basis may be sufficient)

Critical analysis of computer center budgeting (large amounts may be on the books for punched cards or other obsolete items even after conversion to dialog operations)

Critical evaluation of cost allocation or accounting methods (the total picture may be distorted where user departments participate in cost underwriting)

Critical evaluation of the cost of controls; there should be a reasonable cost-utility ratio

A listing such as this presents the essential points for organizing an audit. In evaluating cost efficiency a clear distinction must be made between cheap solutions and economic solutions. The computer center should under no circumstances be forced to invest in devices, programs, or operations that at first glance cost less but are organizationally and operationally more expensive. Finally, a word about the time element of audit reports. An audit must be comprehensive enough and timely enough for computer center operations to be able to derive direct benefits from it.

## 7.6 Capacity Planning

A discussion of computer center planning and control would be incomplete without including the complex topic of capacity planning in terms of hardware and software. The problems occurring in this context are perhaps best handled by proceeding from the question.

What gives rise to capacity planning?

EDP systems exist for the purpose of automatically processing applications from the user departments; by consequence, the causes for capacity changes do not originate in the computer center but in the applications. There are essentially two determining factors:

- The situation may exist where user departments have new tasks to process. This touches the computer center only insofar as it must answer the question of available personnel and machine capacity. This answer is based on information derived from utilization reports (section 7.2). In addition, the cost-benefit question needs to be clarified. The two answers together form the basis of management decisions on planning activities

- The second factor pertains to the running operation. Constant utilization control (section 7.2) shows that a rising data volume will have used up reserve capacity at a certain point in time. The growth of certain tasks or the increase in testing must also be considered. This is handled through preparation and analysis of accounting data.

In both cases an expansion of capacity must be planned. The computer center shares in the decision on a planning volume only to the extent of supplying technical hardware suggestions. Since the tasks of the user departments must be processed over this EDP capacity, they essentially determine the planning process. This interdependency becomes clear in a comparison of capacity planning in a commercial enterprise with the planning and selection procedures of a university computer center.

It is impossible to present in detail the entire process of capacity planning from device planning to selection in these pages. However, an attempt will be made to present a brief overview for computer center management, keeping in mind that changes in capacity (expansion or new installation) do not count among the everyday business of a computer center, and that sufficient techincal literature is available on the subject. It is for that reason that even the organizational flowcharts of large computer centers (Figures 2.9 and 5.1) lack organizational units exclusively designed for planning activities. In general, committees are formed for that purpose (sections 2.15 and 2.3.4) in which the areas affected are represented:

Company management

Relevant departments

System analysis/programming

Computer center

Legal services

Purchasing

Only very large data processing departments with the status of a major division have a separate group for the staff function of system planning. These departments need not be simultaneously charged with short- and medium-range planning tasks.

One problem must be discussed separately at this point: There are occasional concerns that the data processing side cannot be sufficiently represented on the planning committee; external EDP consultants are therefore often included. But the appointment of external consultants opens up new problems: Company management now worries about an overrepresentation on behalf of EDP, and some computer center managers interpret the appointment of an external consultant as a manifestation of distrust in their own technical competence. As a matter of fact, all cases where no separate planning authority exists are definitely underrepresented in terms of technical background and knowledge of the prevailing market. And, in planning extensive projects, suggestions and observations from neutral outsiders may be extremely valuable for the success of the outcome.

Once the decision for a capacity change has been made and a concrete proposal is at hand, a clockwork procedure is set in motion. This begins with an offer to submit bids and ends with receipt of the selected devices. The technical literature offers a variety of suggestions on the subject, but the details vary from case to case. The selection of equipment, however, is a problem of special significance.

Data processing specialists only conditionally admit to the fact that their line of reasoning is not the only decisive one. However, their role in the decision-making process is to represent the purely factual data processing side of the argument. A number of decision-making aids are available, such as detailed checklists, models, or methods for determining the performance capacity of a system. Additional functional and legal points contribute to the decision in cases where mixed hardware is being considered.

Software is often not sufficiently included in capacity planning, partly because of the difficulty of seeing it as an item distinct from hardware, and because attempts at a quantification are invariably overshadowed by a certain subjectivity. Even checklists of the type often suggested in selecting programming languages do not help to overcome this problem where system software is concerned. On the other hand, such lists are a valuable guide in making decisions on standard application software, another issue that cannot be viewed as distinct from capacity planning. Numerous information services offer detailed materials on the subject.

The following software information services are available:

West Germany, Austria, Switzerland: *ISIS Software Report*, published by Infratest Inc., Munich

France: *Guide Europeenne du Software*, published by Software International, Inc., Paris

England: *Copac-Index*, published by Software World, London

United States: *ICP Quarterly*, published by International Computer Programs, Inc., Indianapolis

*European Software Catalogue*, published by International Software Service, Zurich

One common factor is shared by the diverse planning methods and their realizations: there are no patent formulas for guaranteed satisfaction in implementation. Even the best contractual conditions cannot change that. Uniform contracts of the type used in government are a significant improvement. What remains is to learn from the experiences of others, and from consulting checklists of common errors in planning and selection.

The enormous influence of this decision-making process on the computer center becomes clear when one considers the extent to which the center is affected by such decisions: personnel and space planning (Chapters 5 and 8) must be coordinated with system planning, and the entire interface of EDP system and operation in the form of job scheduling, consultation, programming, and training is affected. Only a thorough acceptance test at the time of installation can determine whether the expectations developed in the planning process have been fulfilled. The planning phase must, therefore, include not only an assessment of needs and how they can best be met but also measures for testing the equipment for these expectations. Acceptance tests must be designed by the computer center, and should be part of the purchase contract.

EIGHT

# PLANNING AND IMPLEMENTING A COMPUTER CENTER

## 8.1 Introduction

The installation and operation of a data processing system with its peripheral devices requires numerous structural and technical preparations. It is not enough to set aside some office space—a computer system demands an environment containing specific features. Beyond that, managerial and staff offices must be designed and equipped with a view towards optimal working conditions.

It is advisable to hire a team of specialists for planning and implementing a computer center in accordance with the manufacturers' technical specifications. Another possibility is to turn the entire project over to the manufacturer. This method eliminates the often critical interface problems. Both methods have the advantage that detailed and binding cost estimates can be demanded, and that the references of the firms under consideration can be verified by visits to computer centers designed and installed by them.

## 8.2 Space Planning

### 8.2.1 Furnishings and Equipment

Space planning is determined primarily by task organization, system size, and the number of employees anticipated. The functional procedures, the hardware floor plan, and the personnel organization thus form the planning base as well as providing information on the task structure and operational procedures—for example, research center or general service center; batch, dialog, or real-time operation.

Planning should take into account the following special conditions:

Separation into air-conditioned and non-air-conditioned areas

Floor preparation for equipment installation in the air-conditioned area

Quiet zone in personnel areas (management offices, system support, operations scheduling, visiting programmers, library, conference room, coffee room)

Solid and soundproof walls (over 40 dB in passage ways) to separate air-conditioned from non-air-conditioned and noisy from quiet areas

Extensive use of moveable walls to allow for ongoing adjustments to technical and task-related developments

Inclusion of reserve space in air-conditioned and un-air-conditioned areas

Provisions for visitors so they do not disturb operations. (Many computer centers no longer permit machine room tours for security reasons, but portions of the operation may be viewed through safety glass from a gallery.)

The following guidelines should be observed in room planning and furnishing:

### Computer Room

*Space requirement*: From 400 sq. ft. to several hundred thousand sq. ft.; length-to-width ratio shuld be approximately 2:3; no long, narrow rooms.

*Room height*: 10–15 ft.

*Ceilings*: Attached light metal ceilings (dust free).

*Floor loading*: Should be sufficient, preferably with a sound-absorbent and antistatic covering.

*Air-conditioning*: Heat extraction should be 50–80 Kcal/h per square foot of equipment, with humidity controls

*Power supply*: Energy should be calculated in terms of maximum possible occupied space, using the formula 1KW = 860 Kcal/h; adjust upwards for water cooling systems.

*Water supply*: Through hookup to the industrial water supply system; many installations require additional water cooling.

*Soundproofing*: Floors, walls, and ceilings should be soundproofed; a noise level of 70 dB should not be exceeded in the machine room

*Lighting*: Adequate and glare-free.

*Draft-free work stations.*

*Automatic fire protection equipment.*

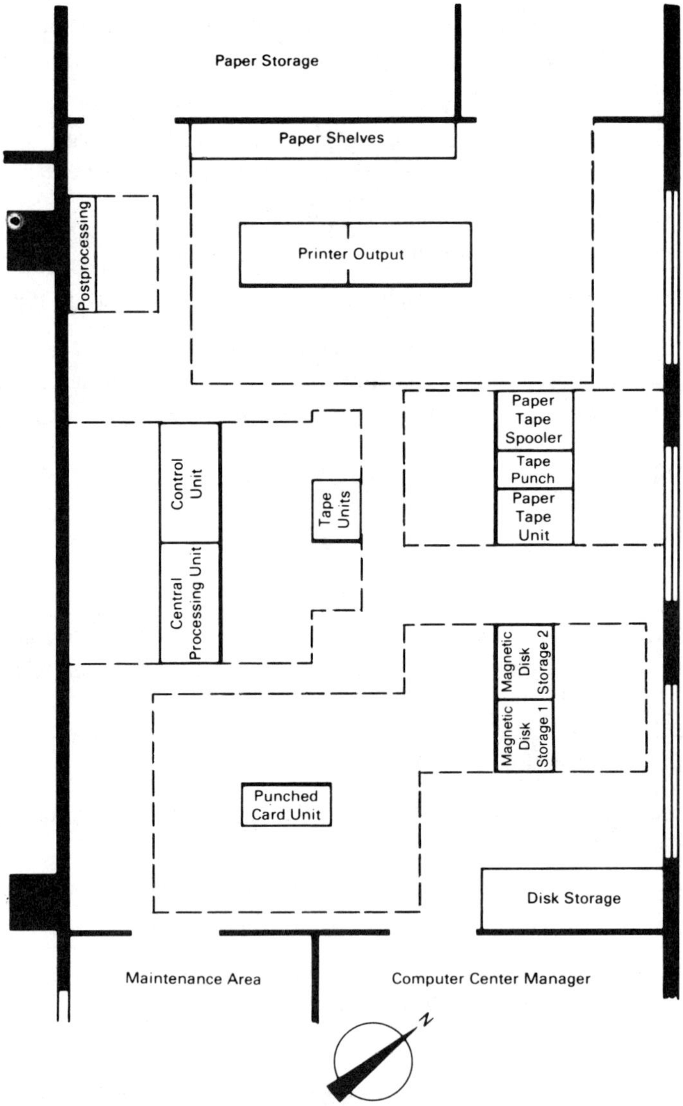


**Figure 8.1** Floor Plan for a Small System

*Special furnishings*: For punched cards, tapes, disks, paper, etc.

*Burglar alarms*.

Opinions are divided with respect to combined installations of conventional and electronic data processing devices. Many are returning to the older theory that paper processing devices should be separated, even though the opinion was long held that paper processing devices should be operated in the same room from an operations-organizational point of view. But the noise and dust factors should not be disregarded.

A hardware floor plan must be worked out prior to installation, taking into consideration the following points:

Optimum access for operators and supplies

Sufficient space for maintenance

Room for expansion without displacement of already installed devices

Figure 8.1 is a sample floor plan for the machine room of a small computer center. Figure 8.2 represents a plan for a medium-sized system—a host computer with a front-end processor and large storage periphery.

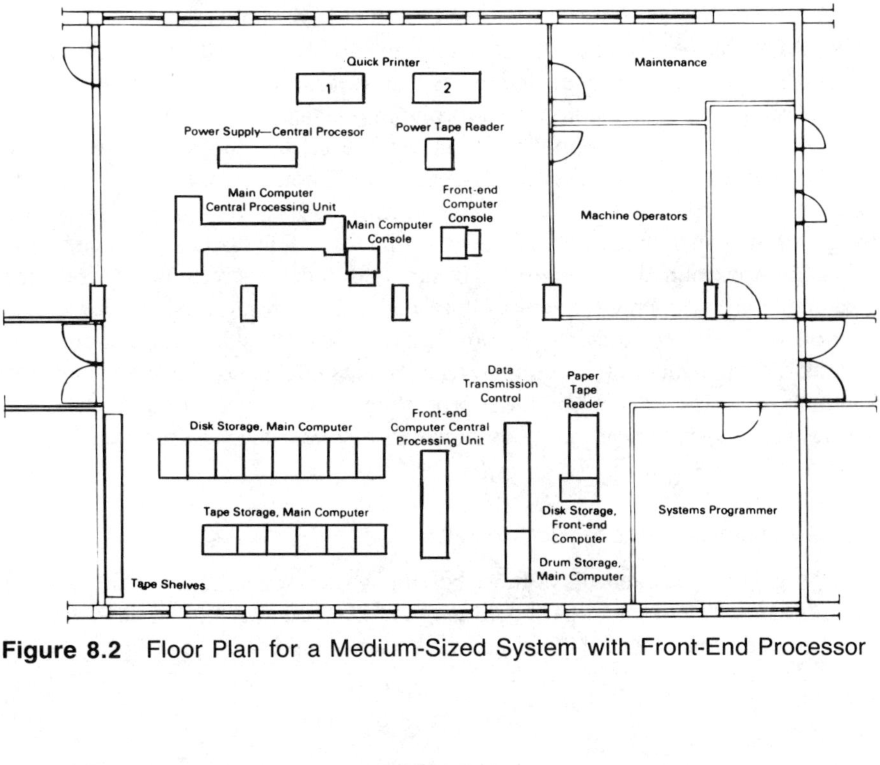


**Figure 8.2** Floor Plan for a Medium-Sized System with Front-End Processor

### Data Entry Room

The size and equipment of this room are largely determined by the data entry procedures in use. Thus entry via diskette has different prerequisites from entry via document readings. The room dimension depends on the scope of compter center tasks: a computer center for administrative tasks requires more space for data entry than a research computer center with dialog operation via VDTs. A standard size of 200–1500 sq. ft. can be assumed, with 40–50 sq. ft. per work station. A number of document readers require air-conditioning. Provisions for soundproofing should be made for these devices as well as provisions for acoustic separation from adjoining rooms. Soundproof walls in the passageways are one possible measure. Proper lighting is of special importance.

### Shipping Room

In addition to the normal work stations, this room contains a number of offline devices, such as cutters or bursters, separators or deleavors, copy machines, and automatic staplers. Air conditioning is not necessary, but soundproofing and fire protection measures should be taken. In large computer centers this room may be expanded into a mailroom, and a ramp is recommended.

### Stockroom

Despite intensive efforts to reduce the flood of paper—for example, through direct tape or disk entry or COM—paper as a data medium continues to play a major role in the computer center. It is advisable to keep at least a 4-month supply of printer paper, console paper, and forms as protection against delivery schedules and delays in new designs of printed forms. In practice, a separation into a main stockroom for long-term supply needs and an intermediate stockroom for weekly supply needs has been successful. The main stockrooms will, as a rule, require 500–1000 sq. ft., and the intermediate stockroom 150–300 sq. ft. The heavy weight of the paper stacks necessitates a sufficient ceiling load carrying capacity. The main stockroom does not need to be air-conditioned but must be dry and kept at a moderate temperature; temperature and humidity must be automatically controlled. The intermediate stockroom should be located inside the air-conditioned zone. Since the main stockroom is usually located in the basement and not continuously occupied, automatic fire protection devices are required. An efficient and reliable paper transportation system is of special value, as for example on pallets.

### Archive for Magnetic Storage Devices

Magnetic tapes and disks must be stored with special care in a dust-free environment. The usable area should measure 200–500 sq. ft. and be located in the air-conditioned zone. Tapes and disks are stored in special space-saving cabinets which ensure sufficient protection from dust. Two to three hundred tapes or 20–30 disk packs can be stored per 10 square feet of space.

OFFICES FOR ORGANIZATIONAL AND JOB CONTROL STAFFS

*Computer center manager*: 200–350 sq. ft., office furnishings to include a VDT.

*Secretary*: 200–400 sq. ft., office furnishings to include an automatic type-writer and soundproofing.

*Systems administrator and systems programmers*: 100–120 sq. ft. per person, with no more than 4 persons per room. The work of these employees demands a high degree of concentration; a larger room is less suitable because of the increase in distracting sounds such as telephones.

*Operations scheduling and control*: 150–600 sq. ft., check-out and receipt of data media, coordination and editing documents, preparation for processing

*Input/output room*: Service computer centers, which in a larger sense also include university computer centers, should have a separate input/output room. If the computer center offers consultation services, the consultation room should be in the immediate vicinity of the output room. With substantial teleperiphery a quiet room for telephone consultation has proven very practical.

*Testing area*: 200–500 sq. ft. Modern installations usually conduct program tests in dialog over VDTs; in addition, a remote batch station can be installed as an express station. For reasons of optimal device utilization and because of noise factor, especially printers, these machines should be located together in a testing room rather than the programmers' offices.

*Conference and training rooms*: 300–800 sq. ft., equipped with chalkboard, flipchart, overhead projector, slide projector, possibly film projector, terminal with monitor, public address system, and equipment for audiovisual instruction.

*Library*: 300–500 sq. ft.

*Employee lounge*: 250–500 sq. ft., equipped as a recreation room with vending machines.

*Maintenance*: Depending on computer center size, the continuous or intermittent presence of maintenance personnel is required. A room for these employees should measure 150–300 sq. ft. and be equipped in accordance with manufacturers' specifications

*Air conditioning*: Cabinet space for a one-circuit unit in a small computer center requires 150–300 sq. ft.; larger computer centers will need central two-circuit units of 800–1500 sq. ft.; the ceiling load carrying capacity should be sufficient.

*Uninterrupted power supply*: Depending on required output and technical features, approximately 200–500 sq. ft. should be planned for. A dynamic system requires more floor space than a static system.

## 8.2.2 Room Layout

Once the overall space planning phase has been completed, consideration must be given to the arrangement of rooms and offices with special attention to the following three points:

Document flow and step-by-step work sequence

Materials flow

Personnel flow

The resultant criteria are:

Central location of the computer center in a data processing department

Central location of the computer room relative to the other computer center rooms

Separation of noise-intensive from quiet work areas

Separation of operations scheduling and control from the computer room by a room for input/output and shipping

Data media archives in the proximity of the computer room and operations scheduling

Visitors' paths planned so as not to interfere with the operation

Location of secretarial and input/output rooms near the computer center entrance, so that they can be easily found by new users

Stockroom for data processing materials next to the computer room

Air-conditioning and power switching facilities should not be near quiet work areas

Separate room for dust generating devices such as paper processing devices

The following criteria apply to the computer room:

The devices should be arranged with a view towards optimal work flow.

The operator at the control panel should have an unobstructed view of all system components, especially those requiring an attendant (quick printers, plotters, magnetic tape devices).

The mechanics of magnetic storage devices (disk and tape storage) render them particularly sensitive. It is advisable, especially in large computer centers, to locate them in a separate room inside the computer room (also on account of their noisy ventilation systems).

Input/output devices should be placed near the input/output and shipping area.

Sufficient work and storage space should be provided for maintenance.

Figure 8.3 is a schematic representation of the functional units in a computer center and their interdependencies.

The extent to which these criteria can be realized depends on whether the computer center is already established in an existing building or whether new

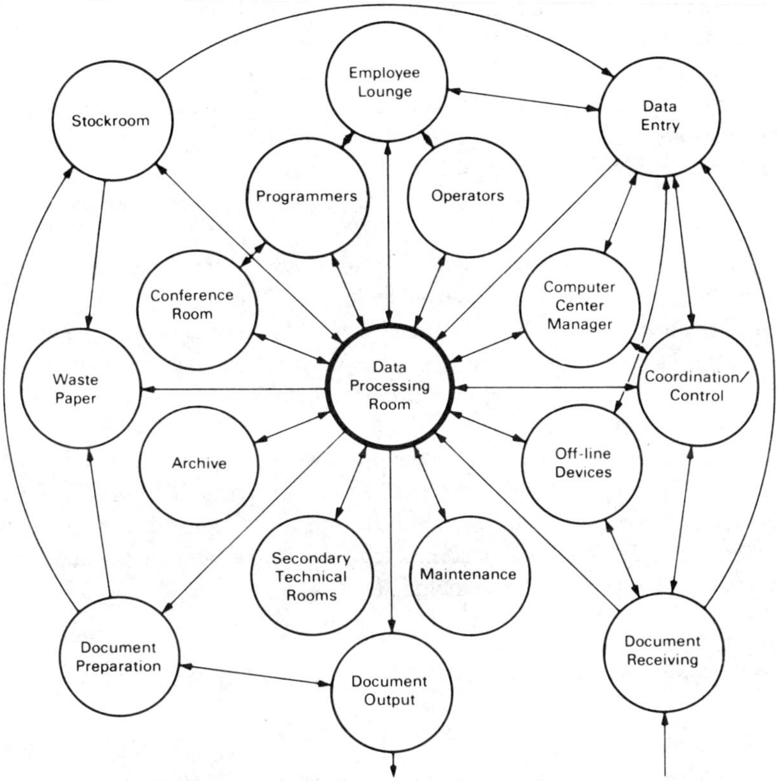


**Figure 8.3** Functional Units in a Computer Center and Their Interdependencies

construction is planned. In the latter case, the technical and organizational criteria as well as planning space for future expansion can be fully considered. In general practice, a one- to two-story building with a basement for storage, power supply, and the air-conditioning unit has been found most suitable. The building can be constructed from precast parts and should have a flexible interior with moveable walls. Single-story pavilions have also proven well-suited, because they permit a relatively large-scale realization of the concept of central function, but fire safety and air conditioning may present problems (see Figures 8.4 and 8.5).

## 8.3 Power Supply

### 8.3.1 Layout

Data processing installations are generally hooked into public power supply lines. The power load is determined by the number and size of devices to be connected and is somewhere between 5 and more than 100 kilovoltamp (kva).

During construction a separate line should be run from the main voltage distributor or transformer for the exclusive use of EDP equipment. general power-consuming devices such as electrical outlets, lighting, and especially those causing fluctuations in the power supply (elevators!) must not be connected to this line, as they may disturb the EDP equipment. Tolerances in the working voltage may normally amount to $+10\%$, but the frequency tolerance should not exceed $+0.5$ to $+1.0$.

Alternating voltages usually deviate somewhat from the strict sine-shaped movement; these distortions are caused by an overlay of sinusoidal oscillations of varying frequencies with a basic frequency of 50 Hz. For data processing devices the distortion factor, measured between two phases and between phase and center, should not exceed 5%. Special attention should be paid to proper grounding of wires, device housings, and floors.

The planning and execution of power supply installations must be continuously supervised by representatives of the EDP equipment manufacturer. A good many headaches can be avoided by assigning the job to a general contractor or the manufacturer itself, but the deadline for completion should be contractually established and a penalty clause included.

### 8.3.2 Failsafe Power Supply

While the public power supply system is largely reliable, it is not entirely trouble-free. In a 5-year period, for example, an average of 9–10 outages per year of various lengths were reported for the medium voltage networks of the West German electric power supply companies. But tolerance fluctuations lasting longer than a few milliseconds can endanger data processing operations. In some networks a frequency of 1–100 disturbances per month was registered; an average of over 90% of them were shorter than 400 ms. If a given network is found prone to excessive disturbances, uninterrupted power supply must be ensured through an additional energy storage device. Failsafe installations provide sufficient power at a constant voltage and frequency during periods of fluctuation or total outage. Different systems are utilized depending on the length of the disturbance to be compensated for—from a few milliseconds to several minutes or longer.

#### 8.3.2.1 Dynamic Systems

The simplest energy storage device for a bypass period of up to several hundred milliseconds is a flywheel that is driven by a direct current motor with a regulated rotational speed, which is coupled with a three-phase current generator. The motor receives its current from the public power supply, while the generator supplies the EDP installation with constant voltage. During short disturbances the flywheel keeps the generator in action, thus assuring a constant voltage for EDP. During longer disturbances the rotational speed of the motor and thus also of the flywheel and generator decreases; this causes a decrease in generator voltage with a corresponding decrease in the voltage supply for EDP, and shuts down the system. It has been found that this method can handle over 90% of all power fluctuations.

Batteries are an additional storage device that can extend the period of power compensation to about 10 minutes. The power supply system can also be supplemented by a diesel engine that automatically couples with the generator set. This type of emergency power supply functions indefinitely.

#### 8.3.2.2 Static Systems

The development of semiconductor electronics offers the possibility of replacing the motor and generator components with such high-voltage switching devices as thyristor-inverters and filter circuits. These installations are usually in continuous service, that is, the EDP system is constantly supplied by the inverter. The bypass time is contingent upon battery capacity. Static systems avoid rotating parts, and a trouble-free operating period is possible at a lower maintenance cost. Further advantages are: no switching process in the power supply system in case of outages, simple installation, less heat-producing, a higher efficiency rate, and lower noise level.

## 8.4 Air Conditioning

### 8.4.1 General Problems

Data processing demands air quality standards in terms of temperature, humidity, and purity that can only be met by air conditioning. An efficient ventilation system

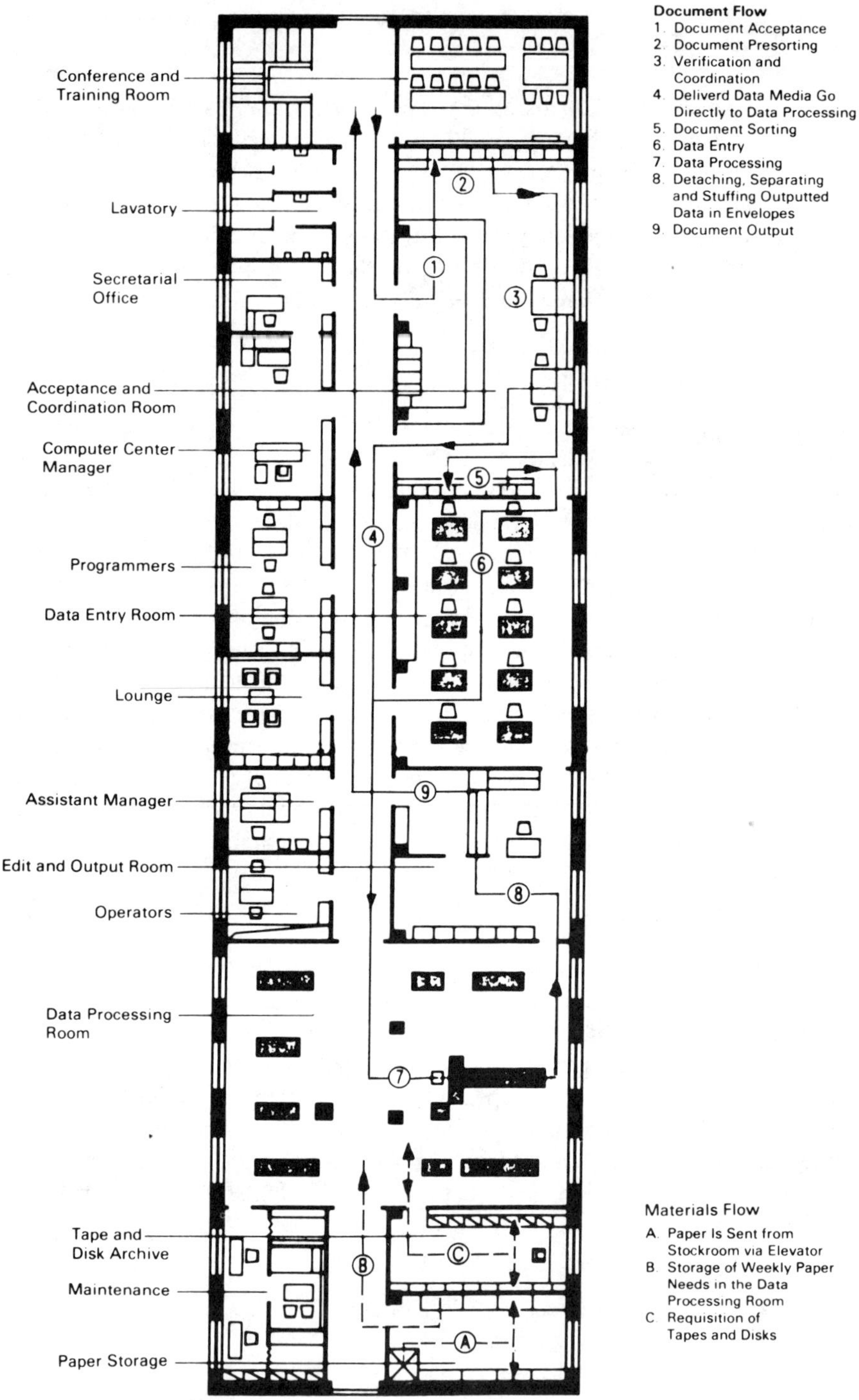


**Figure 8.4** Layout of a Single-Story Computer Center with Document and Materials Flow in a Long and Narrow Building

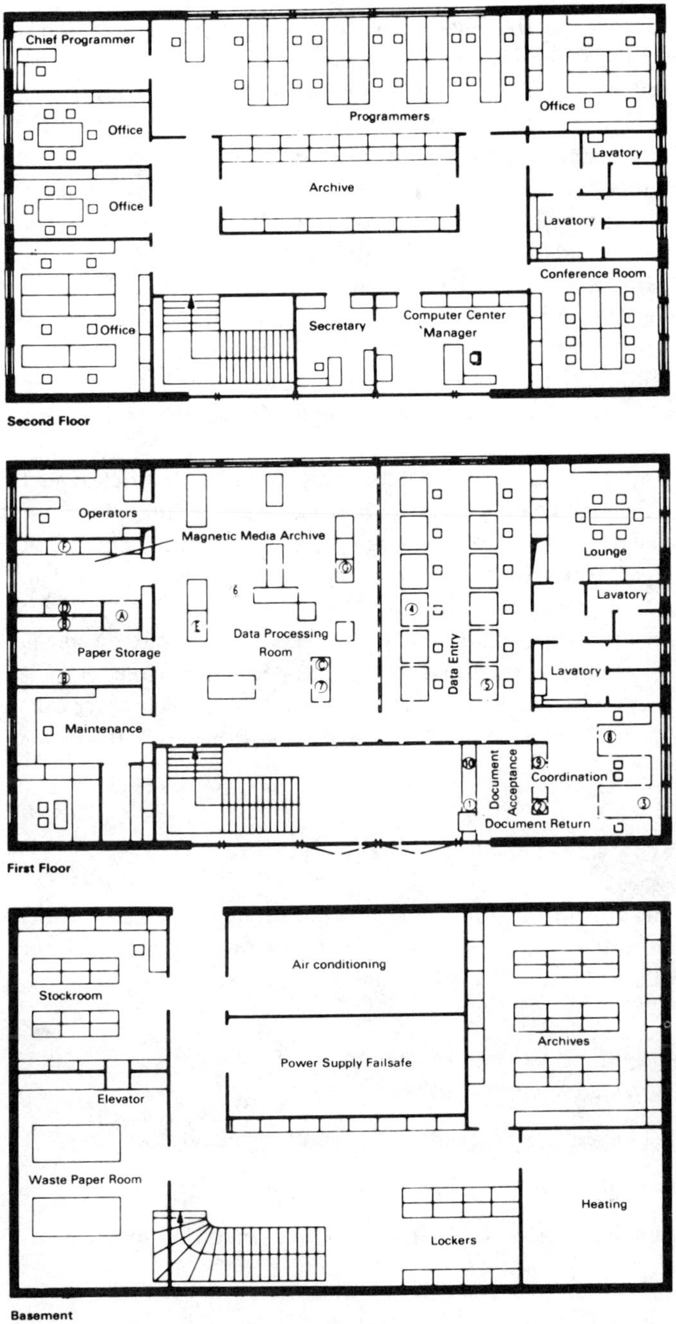


A three-story computer center with a practical room layout. The document and materials flow on the first floor has been drawn in.

**Document Flow**

1. Over the Counter Acceptance
2. Sorting and Filing
3. Document Verification
4. Data Entry
5. Data Entry Supervisor
6. Input
7. Printing
8. Output Control
9. Sorting
10. Document Return

**Material Flow**

A. Elevator
B. Paper Storage
C. Printer
D. Tape Archive
E. Tape Devices
F. Disk Archives
G. Disk Storage

**Figure 8.5** Layout of a Three-Story Computer Center

serves only for compact computers. Energy consumption in the computer center has decreased since the introduction of semiconductors and integrated circuits, but in most cases air conditioning is still a necessity. An important consideration in this context is the sensitivity of paper products to temperature and humidity, and employee efficiency is directly affected by climatic conditions. A large computer manufacturer lists the following range: Temperature: 15–32° C, relative humidity, 20–80%. Paper and personnel reduce these tolerances to a comfort range of 20–26° C for temperature and 50–65% for relative humidity.

Dust-free air is extremely important for magnetic storage devices. Aside from physical damages to these extremely thin, high-speed media, air pollution causes malfunctions in the read/write process. A speck of dust with a diameter of one-hundredth of a millimeter lodged between the read/write head and the magnetic layer of the tape can reduce the read/write amplitude of the signal by over 50%.

The chemical purity of the air is of equal importance: gaseous particles, such as sulphuric compounds which cause metals to corrode, must be filtered out.

Climate-controlled areas should be air-conditioned at a somewhat higher rate when adjacent to other areas in order to prevent an intrusion of unpurified air. This increase also handles air purification in sealed EDP systems.

Drafts should be avoided in employee work areas by maintaining an air circulation of between 15 and 20 cfm (cubic feet/minute)/occupant in the room. A complete air exchange 20–30 times per hour is considered normal in data processing rooms, but a rate of over 50 times per hour represents a significant draft.

## 8.4.2 Dimensions of Air Conditioning Systems

An air-conditioning installation requires an evaluation of all heat quantities per unit of time occurring in the area under consideration, with a view towards the maximum possible values. Further considerations are:

Heat output of lighting fixtures in the order of 30–50 Kcal/h (1000 calories/hour) per square meter of ceiling

Heat output of persons in the order of 100 Kcal/h per person

Heat intrusion through walls and windows

Heat accumulation through outside air, loss of ventilation, or other heat-producing agents

In addition, the outside air must be tested for chemical pollutants, dirt and dust.

### 8.4.3 Technical Realizations of Air Conditioning

Modern technology offers the following alternatives:

Central air conditioning or individual units

Single or dual circuit systems.

In central air conditioning the components such as ventilators, humidifiers, heaters, and coolers are independent units and ordered sequentially according to function.

In individual units all necessary components are contained in one housing.

The serialized production of air-conditioning units usually means an even quality and good maintenance services, because all units are equipped with the same or similar parts.

If an expansion becomes necessary, the existing unit can be exchanged for one that is more efficient, or an additional unit can be installed if sufficient wiring is available.

A central air-conditioning system can be expanded only up to a certain limit, unless it was originally installed with a view towards increased performance.

The installation time for a single-unit system is considerably shorter than for a central system. Central systems can be adjusted to suit the prevailing needs, but their space requirements and installation times are many times that of single units.

The ratio of price to performance is more favorable with single units.

The installation of a central air-conditioning system is preferable and economical only in very large rooms. Close to 90% of all computer centers today are air-conditioned with single units.

Practical experiences have shown that single units do not always suffice in the data processing room. Variable air currents and air distribution cause inadequate climatic conditions in the room, and the accumulation of heat above heat-intensive devices can cause uncontrollable shutdowns. The need for air conditioners requiring water installation in the computer room represents an additional danger. Single units are therefore advantageous only with small data processing systems.

In single circuit air-conditioning systems the air is blown into the room through ceiling vents. All data processing devices derive their supply of cool air from the room and return their heated air to it. This air is extracted along the ceiling, particularly above heat-intensive devices. However, a portion of the air should be extracted near the floor in order to remove floating dust particles. This procedure produces better circulation and prevents the formation of cold air pockets near the floor.

Dual circuit systems work on two separate circuits, a machine circuit and a room circuit. The machine circuit blows air through the floor directly into the data processing devices and extracts it through the ceiling. The room circuit operates like the single circuit from the ceiling, and a portion of the return air is siphoned off near the floor. Both circuits are adjustable to the prevailing circumstances; the room circuit especially can be regulated for a set number of air exchanges per hour for personal comfort. If both circuits are operated separately, one of them can function in emergencies for a period of time.

A trouble-free air-conditioning system is a prerequisite for every computer center. Temperature and humidity must constantly be controlled by measuring devices which produce optical and acoustic signals in the event of critical deviations.

In recent times energy-conserving considerations have moved into the foreground of computer center planning. The heat energy generated by a computer center, for example, does not need to be pumped back into the environment through the air-conditioning system, but should be used to heat other rooms by means of special technical devices.

If, despite careful preparations, the climate control system should turn out to be inadequate, the consequences for the failure rate of the system can be significant. In such a case it is highly advisable to arrange for a computer environment analysis with a firm of specialists.

## 8.5 Technical Safety

The considerable assets in a computer center, as well as the enormous significance of data processing in an enterprise, mandate that special attention should be given to safety precautions. There are essentially three areas:

Control of supply lines

Fire and water safety

Safety precautions outside of normal operating hours

The extent of this spectrum is reflected in the reports of insurance companies.

### 8.5.1 Safety Provisions for Electrical Equipment

The first and foremost provision is an emergency switch near the emergency exit which turns off the power for the entire installation with the exception of lighting. This switch should be easy to locate and highly visible.

Since computers operate with impulses, they are especially vulnerable to high frequency fluctuations. An effective grounding system with low resistivity is the best protection against disturbances of this type. Sheets of copper foil with edges soldered together can be installed in the false floor. The chassis of the computer and of all other devices is then connected with it by means of copper tubing. If the foil can be installed before the false floor, the floor supports and slabs necessarily serve as conductors to the foil. This creates a wide area of metallic counterweights under the devices. The entire grounding system should be connected to the conductor rail in as broad-based a manner as possible. The individual parts of the grounding system must be interconnected with the lowest possible resistivity; this requires perfect workmanship in soldering the junctions and extremely good connections of a large diameter. Grounding systems with high resistivity can transmit disturbances, thus becoming a danger factor themselves.

A less costly procedure has also proven satisfactory: Layers of foil can be attached to the underside of the floating floor, between the slabs. This establishes a good connection between the slabs and floor supports; the supports are additionally connected to the conductor rail by means of strip conductors. The upper surface of the slabs should then be covered with antistatic material which also acts as a conductor, such as carpeting with interwoven copper thread.

## 8.5.2 Safety Provisions Against Fire and Flooding

Fire hazards in the computer center can be drastically reduced by the following measures:

*Fire from outside the facility*: All outside surfaces should be built with fire retardant or fire resistant materials. Openings such as doors and air-conditioning shafts must be fireproof and must shut automatically.

*Fire in the facility*: Extensive use should be made of nonflammable or nearly nonflammable materials.

*Outside smoke and gas*: All openings leading into the facility should be provided with automatic sealing mechanisms.

*Inside smoke and gas*: The materials used should not emit noxious gases when heated.

*Water outside the facility*: Ceilings should be watertight; threshholds at a height of 2–3 in. prevent water from entering the computer room.

*Water inside the facility*: The subfloor should slant away from the building and have proper drainage to avoid flooding.

*Other precautions*: fireproof self-contained rooms for the central processing unit, conventional machines, storage and archives, keypunch, and air-conditioning are highly recommended.

Stored data should be kept in fireproof cabinets and/or in duplicate at another location. There should be smoke detectors in the false floor, at strategic points in the air-conditioning shafts, and on the ceiling.

As protection against electrical accidents, only carbon dioxide extinguishers should be used in the computer center. Only the fire department can fight fires according to its own judgment. Waste containers should be nonflammable and close automatically.

Smoking must not be permitted. Operators must be familiarized with all safety rules. The extent of damage largely depends on the measures taken in the first few seconds of a fire. Sprinklers are not recommended for the machine rooms, as smoke detectors are a more effective means of signaling a developing fire.

## 8.5.3 Protection Against Computer Crime

Data security legislation has increased an awareness for the need to protect data and devices in the computer center. Computer crime is essentially defined here as a deliberate action designed to impair computer center operations and to endanger, damage, or destroy the systems, devices, and programs through theft, burglary, sabotage, or terrorist acts.

The most effective protection against acts of this nature are controls that prevent access to sensitive areas by possible criminal elements. There should, however, be no doubt about the fact that the effectiveness of security precautions essentially depends on available financing. But no amount of money can guarantee absolute safety—it is merely a question of setting up the most effective obstacles possible.

The rooms in the computer center should be assigned to various security zones depending on their level of sensitivity. The areas requiring highest security include the computer room, operations scheduling, shipping, and media archives, unless the latter are stored off-site in burglarproof safes. The next level of security circle includes all rooms in which personnel-related and other important documents can be stored safely in locked cabinets. The security system must be designed in such a way that the obstacles become progressively more difficult to overcome on the way from the lower to the higher security areas. In addition to built-in safety measures such as burglarproof walls, shafts, cable ducts, windows, and doors, procedures controlling access to rooms and devices are of special importance.

### 8.5.3.1 Access Control

Access control must ensure that only authorized individuals have controlled access to sensitive areas. Guard personnel have been almost entirely replaced by electronic and computer-controlled devices which verify the authorization of each individual by means of coded identification cards interpreted by the system, either online or offline. The individual is then either admitted or denied access to a particular area. There are generally three categories:

General access

Access limited to certain areas

Limited-time access to sensitive areas

Combinations of the above are possible. The function of the card holder determines the degree of access to be authorized. All employees, including management, are subject to this control. Coded access cards which can also serve as identification have become widely accepted in a relatively short time, even though they have been subject to constant technological changes. The simple cards with punched or raised letter codes were replaced by cards with permanent or magnetic codes, which were superseded by cards for radio-controlled systems that by today's standards are considered virtually impossible to forge.

Since computer controlled systems are programmable at will, the control functions can be adapted to the requirements of each computer center. In addition, all system activities can be recorded—for example, all data pertaining to authorized access but also attempts at unauthorized access. If date and time are recorded as well, subsequent checks and reconstructions are greatly facilitated.

Alterations made by a security officer via console—for example, about authorization and data on time of day or doors used—can be recorded on diskettes.

The system can be programmed to perform functions other than access decisions, for example:

Print lists of lost or stolen I.D. cards

Open or close one or all doors in an emergency

Validate or cancel any authorization via console

Give an alarm signal whenever a door is opened without authorization or left open accidentally for longer than a predetermined length of time

#### 8.5.3.2 Room Security

In addition to built-in precautions, the use of electronic devices predominates here. Based on experiences made especially in the banking industry, a combination of monitors such as motion sensors and TV cameras is recommended. Motion sensors are based on radar, ultra sound, or infrared transmitters or receivers and have been used successfully in controlling windows.

Remote-controlled TV cameras with zoom lenses are especially useful if the monitor can be installed in a central observation post or in plant security. These posts should be manned around the clock. Another proven method is the use of video intercoms that permit one-way observation and speech communication with the area under observation. These devices can be coupled into monitor networks and included in already existing access control systems.

# NINE

# COST AND PRICE PLANNING

## 9.1 Organizational Prerequisites

The increase in automated work processes in an enterprise by means of data processing is reflected by a proportionate increase in cost sharing by this area. The costs of automation, however, originate only partially in the computer center itself; a significant proportion comes from systems planning, system analysis, and programming—and in distributed data processing from the user departments as well. In keeping with the concepts of this book, these costs are considered as separate items according to the areas in which they originate. Computer center jobs performed on behalf of systems analysis and programming should be charged on a separate account the same as jobs for user departments. This procedure results in the cost visibility necessary for data processing, especially considering that software is increasingly purchased rather than programmed on the premises.

This visibility is a prerequisite for cost-effective management, especially in view of the fact that the costs of a modern computer center represent a considerable share of the overall costs of an enterprise. Incompetent and uncontrolled use of the data processing system can cause additional and avoidable costs; controls in the form of a performance accounting system are therefore a necessity. The computer center should, after all, contribute to company profits.

Nevertheless the question must be asked whether cost accounting should actually be undertaken in the computer center, since many computer centers operate with established annual budgets that are administered on a cost-planning basis. The essential criterion is the organizational integration of the computer center in the enterprise. An established budget without any further cost breakdown is justifiable for an EDP system inside a department and with only one field of application, such as process computers or medium-sized installations. In all other instances an internal accounting system should be established.

A functional accounting system for computer center services presupposes certain organizational prerequisites. This applies to computer center agreements with outside agencies as well as internal organizational conditions. The costs for each fiscal year must be planned in advance. All costs occurring in the computer center and detailed in section 9.2 must be recorded and based on corresponding performance accounting systems.

Within the framework of organizational prerequisites one must also consider the close association between the accounting system of the computer center on the one hand, and operations control not only in the computer center but in all other areas as well. In the final analysis this all comes under the heading of cost control. Only effective measures can produce accurate records.

### 9.1.1 Areas of Application

Computer center performance represents only one of many items in the overall cost accounting system of an enterprise. The efforts made to achieve a technical cost effectiveness of operating resources do not count among the primary responsibilities of computer center performance accounting. This means that cost accounting excludes any consideration of whether and to what extent the operation of EDP devices is related to profit. This approach requires consideration of all factors involved in handling each individual task. These include:

Planning tasks

Systems analysis

Organization

Programming

Testing

Program acquisition

Program maintenance

Data entry

Implementation

Post processing

Data evaluation and subsequent processing

At this point the overall costs are distributed among the various cost centers in the computer center (section 9.3). Over and above that, certain indications on the economy of individual operating devices—for example, separately administered systems components—may develop in the course of profitability calculations.

Figure 9.1 shows the relationship between EDP performance accounting on the one hand, and systems planning, performance level, and price determination on the other. Figure 9.2 presents an overview of the composition of data processing costs. To begin with, this is a purely static approach. But once the time variables are included in the calculations in such a way that predictions can be made for future values by developing actual values, a direct line can be drawn to the concept of cost control mentioned in section 9.1

The design of an accounting system for EDP performance is practical only if it includes a definition of the entire area subject to this cost settlement procedure. The very complex area of EDP costs can be made more visible with separate accounts for computer center performance and systems analysis and programming, with a further separation of the proportionate share these two areas have in data processing. In developing a cost settlement system it is important to make provisions for a possible expansion of the established areas of application. Expansions should be preplanned for the following:

Additional performance types such as online entry, postprocessing, expansion of the supplies spectrum, dialog operations, or systems consultation in distributed data processing

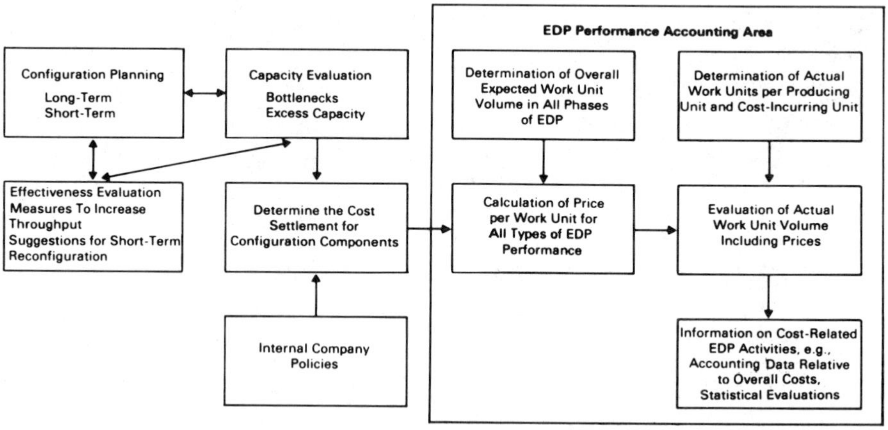


**Figure 9.1** Relationship between EDP Performance Accounting and Price Determination

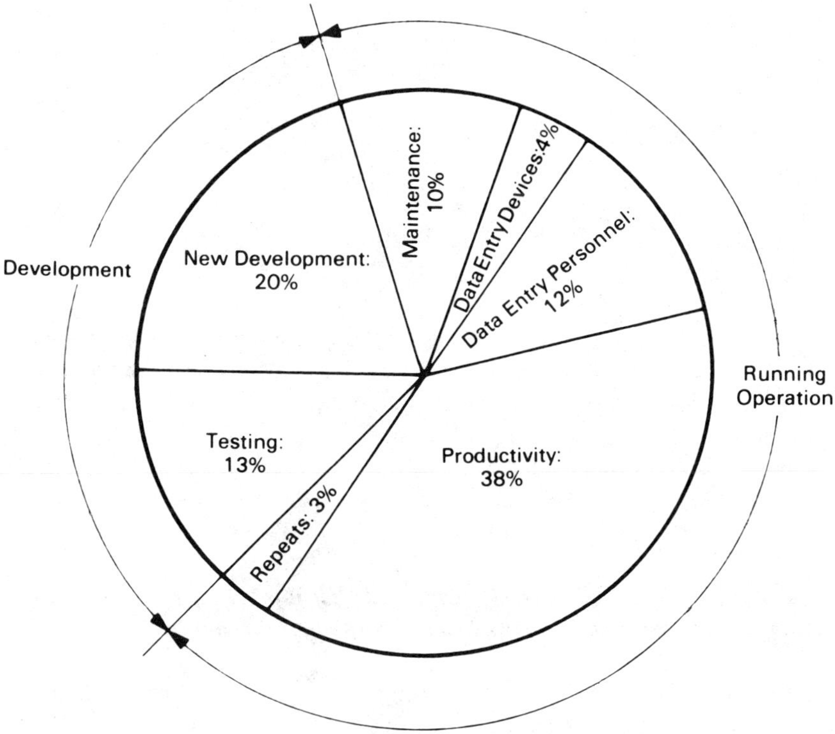


| | |
|---|---|
| Procedure Development: | 30% |
| Computer Center Costs: | 54% |
| Data Entry: | 16% |

**Figure 9.2** Composition of Data Processing Costs

Additional cost centers that are integrated with EDP or the cost accounting area of EDP performance

Enlargement of the user circle

## 9.1.2 Distribution Codes

If the costs of computer center performance need to be specified, reference must be made to the cost-incurring units.

***A cost-incurring unit is the end product of a manufacturing process in the context of its relationship with production costs.***

Cost-incurring units in EDP performance accounting are, among others:

Data entry job orders

Job runs

Printed lists

Terminal transactions

Jobs run by users

Task setting plays an important role for the computer center in this context; for example, whether a job order is received to produce a certain output, such as printing 10,000 address labels or handling 20,000 payroll accounts, or whether users are allocated certain time periods in the sense of a service order. The latter applies to all job orders handled by the users themselves. In the first example there is a relationship between the cost-incurring unit and procedures in terms of the run parameters for each program; the second example deals with resource usage times.

***A procedure is a sequence of interrelated logical processing steps that are carried out in the course of each computer center function.***

For example, the procedure following the acceptance of a job order might consist of the following steps:

Receive documents, plan job processing

Enter and verify documents

Prepare job processing

Execute processing, for example, in the following steps:

- SPOOL in
- Sort
- Update inventory
- Print

Check and separate listings

Deliver listings

The procedures in a computer center must be designed in such a way that they can be repeated at any time, either periodically or on demand as dictated by the situation. In addition, each must be nonambiguous from the processing point of view. This nonambiguity is important for cost determination as well. In dialog processing the concept of transaction is more appropriate.

***A transaction is defined as an elementary processing step in a task—beginning with online data entry and ending with the display of results at the terminal —or a request for and response to a system function in dialog. This elementary step may consist of a brief multilevel dialog.***

Each cost-incurring unit has a cost distribution code that is valid for a designated period. This code indicates which cost center assumes what percentage of the cost incurred. Each cost-incurring item must be able to have several sequential cost distribution codes. All relevant costs must be distributed according to the distribution code that was in effect on the job output data.

Administrative steps are necessary to make sure that the only cost-incurring units that appear in the cost records are those whose distribution codes have been acknowledged in writing by their respective cost centers, that is, by the users in question. This applies especially to data processing and postprocessing costs.

### 9.1.3 Impartial Error Clarification

It is common knowledge that at least one work process in the computer center will have to be repeated. Repeats are necessary for a variety of reasons, and the fault is not necessarily in the computer center itself. When an error is traced to a source outside of the computer center, the repeated operation is charged to the user's cost center as a normal work process.

The situation is different with errors caused by the computer center. It is an understandable human trait that the individual responsible for the error may attempt to disguise the fact and have the cost charged to the user. However, it is in the interests of the computer center to have these costs posted and paid out of budget; otherwise the computer center and its performance accounting system will suffer a loss of credibility.

The costs incurred by repeated processes must be added to the computer center overhead. The users as a whole bear these costs indirectly along with services used by the computer center itself, such as the library, accounting systems, or work on the operating system. It is difficult to establish a generally valid percentage basis, but 8 hours per week can be assumed to be a realistic standard in a four-shift operation. Over longer periods of time it should not exceed 10% of the total indirect cost budget. Figure 9.2 represents an overview of a realistic situation.

Individuals outside of normal production and production accounting should be in charge of error detection and clarification; this eliminates the motive for disguising errors. It is obvious at this point that accurate performance reporting and accounting can at the same time be instrumental in improving computer center efficiency. The following can be controlled and influenced for this purpose:

Utilization of the overall system and system components

Susceptibility of the overall system and system components to malfunction

Manufacturer's hardware support

Programming quality

Quality of job documentation

Personnel qualifications

Quality of delivered data

Processing quality (batch and dialog operations)

Quality of teleprocessing components

Quality of operations scheduling

Idle time in the computer room

Cost and performance comparisons with other computer centers

Budgeting for new processes to be developed

Usage and scheduling control

Diagnosis of hardware bottlenecks

Multiprocessing

Cost effectiveness of programs and procedures

## 9.1.4 Computer Center Efficiency

Efficiency in data processing can be viewed either as applying to the entire operating sequence in a user department compared to a prior manual operation, for example, or to various segments of the operation. The considerations here are limited to the segment of systems operation—in other words, to the computer center itself. For the other data processing areas (such as systems analysis or programmingl) the computer center should be viewed as the output producer with a clearly defined cost function. Empirical studies have shown that in actual practice very little thought is given to the concept of systems efficiency.

A quantitative analysis of computer center efficiency requires a closer look at the performance and cost quotient. Efficiency increases whenever performance increases but costs remain the same, or when costs decrease but performance remains the same. If only the variability of costs is considered, the data processing procedures that have been used remain excluded for the moment. It is difficult to compare the various individual performances of a computer center as separate entities within the framework of efficiency calculations—it is easier to compare the costs of a process that remains constant. An analysis of the efficiency of this process can then be added separately, but it then no longer fits into the narrow framework of an examination of computer center efficiency. It is not merely a question of economic hardware utilization, but also of the influences of systems software. The suggestions on the subject of performance evaluation offered in Chapter 7 will be discussed in greater detail in section 9.4.

It must be emphasized at this point that in comparing the efficiency of different computer centers one cannot simply undertake a comparison of computing time for identical jobs (i.e., identical performance). Speed, configuration, periphery, and systems software, among others, must be taken into consideration. Reliability and security cost money as well, and are as important as other performance criteria although less easy to calculate. This explains why the efficiency rate of different computer centers may vary by as much as 100%. Some of these differences may be due to errors in management. These cost components, often referred to as hidden costs, occur more frequently in programming than in the computer center itself. They are a problem which must be taken seriously.

Efficiency control is of special importance. This does not mean a control of computer center output produced during certain periods of time, but budget control applied to that output. Appropriate ratios can be applied for regular and periodic efficiency controls. These ratios can also be used to observe and influence the efficiency of subtasks. But efficiency is often also expressed by the dollar amount of computer center production. For the sake of clarity the two components of efficiency—cost and performance (benefit)—will be discussed separately.

## 9.2 Cost Types

Cost accounting takes place at various points in an enterprise. However, practical experiences show that these cost accounting methods cannot be taken over by the computer center without some alterations. It is for that reason that a detailed breakdown of cost types was developed which will be reproduced here to the extent that it is relevant for the computer center.

The suggested groupings are suitable for both absorption (overhead) costing and direct costing and are independent of the organizational form of the data processing station.

A cost comparison would be possible if all computer centers were to accept the grouping suggested below up to the 200 level as mandatory. All further subgroupings should be interpreted as possible examples that can be varied in each specific case. Allowances are made for operation-specific circumstances by leaving some of the cost types blank. In general such an extremely detailed system is not possible, for example if the computer center is a participant in services rendered to the entire enterprise. In most cases separate accounts for power, water, and the like are simply not feasible.

A comparison of cost types is, however, associated with certain difficulties. A comparison of cost center accounts or hourly rates might be more informative.

*Cost elements*

000 Personnel Costs
- 010 Salaries
- 020 Emoluments
- 030 Wages
- 040 Social benefits
- 050 Retirement benefits (actual), if exact figures are not available, lump sum percentages can be used
- 060 Voluntary social benefits
- 070 Other personnel costs, such as help wanted ads or personnel from other groups
- 099 Retirement benefits: the difference between actual and lump sum amounts

100 Data Processing Materials. Materials purchases may be handled via inventory accounting, in which case only actual expenditures are posted.
- 110 Simple forms
- 120 Continuous form paper
- 130 Tabular paper
- 140 Punch cards
- 150 Tapes
- 160 Disks
- 170 Diskettes
- 180 Ribbons
- 190 Other material used in data processing

200 Rent and Maintenance—Energy (utilities) and Materials
- 210 Rent for data processing equipment and moveable devices
  - 211 Data processing systems and devices (including conventional devices)
  - 212 Data entry devices
  - 213 Rented software (can be separated into system and application software)
  - 214 Other rented equipment
  - 215 Copiers
  - 216 Rent for teleprocessing lines (dedicated and switched lines)
  - 217 Data transmission devices (such as modems)
- 220 Hardware repair and maintenance by third parties. Only the maintenance costs of purchased equipment apply: the maintenance cost of leased devices is included in the rental. Included must be extraordinary repairs such as deliberate damage or maintenance on call.
  - 221 Data processing systems and devices
  - 222 System software
  - 223 Data entry devices

224 Other devices
225 Standard application software (general)
226 Special standard application software
227 Data transmission devices

230 Building and ground rental; other rental fees. Improvements which appreciate property values are considered assets and are added to the costs after depreciation

240 Building and grounds maintenance
241 Building and grounds
242 Janitorial services
243 Traffic control
249 Other

250 Heating

260 Electricity and other energy

270 Water

280 Shop tools and other supplies

290 Other operating costs
291 Vehicles
292 Groundskeeper
293 Vending machines

300 General Costs

301 Books, technical literature, newspapers, manufacturers' literature

310 Taxes

320 Fees and contributions, including auditor's fees

330 Insurance

340 Office furnishing and materials. Copying and duplicating costs are included if the computer center does not have its own machines

350 Postal and transportation expenses, not including telecommunication lines

360 Publications, such as pamphlets, operating instructions, and training materials produced by the computer center

370 Publicity

380 Travel

385 External training and education

390 Other general expenses

400 Payment for Service Received

410 Consultation

420 Acquisition of programs or program parts (without maintenance)
421 Development or purchase of programs or program parts
422 Acquisition of programs or program parts for service contracts
423 Program update service contracts

430 Manpower agency fees

440 Program update for special jobs

460 Data entry by third parties
470 Use of outside systems and devices

500 Calculated Costs

510 Depreciation of fixed assets (applicable national tax policy applies). In depreciating capital goods, the highest possible rates for straight-line depreciation permitted according to the IRS tables are recommended. Computer centers not subject to the audit office may derive suggestions for depreciation from these tables. If the actual service life is longer than provided for in the tables, the normal rate of depreciation continues for the excess time period. If the actual service life is shorter than provided for in the tables, the remaining residual value is depreciated at the rate resulting from the known actual total service life.

511 Data processing systems and devices
512 Data entry devices
513 Data transmission devices
514 Other devices and installations
515 Low cost goods
516 Automobiles
517 Programs

520 Calculated real property depreciation

530 Calculated interest. A calculated interest rate of 7% is recommended. For purposes of simplification annual interest calculations are based on average interest and using the media interest rate of the original capital. The median is calculated by the formula

$$MI = \frac{P(n+1)}{2n}$$

whereby P represents the calculated interest rate of 7%, and n the number of years to be written off. Thus the median interest at an interest rate of 7% amounts to 4.7% for a 3-year service life, 4.2% for a 5-year service life, and 3.9% for a 10-year service life.

590 Other calculated costs

591 Calculated risks
592 Calculated one-time costs, initial costs
593 Calculated value adjustments by demand

900 Other costs.

This table purposely ignores the usual breakdown into one-time and running costs because it would apply only in a rough sense. The total picture becomes unclear with a mixed installation where some systems components are leased and others purchased. But since this type of breakdown is useful for simple calculations and shared cost recovery accounting, it is worth mentioning at this point.

Among the one-time costs are those having to do with the installation and expansion of the computer center. They are for the most part listed under the calculated costs in the above list, and include the installation costs for the EDP systems (in case of purchased equipment also the purchase price), the one-time royalty fees for system software, the cost for items such as building modifications, air conditioning, office furniture and the like, training costs, and other initial costs.

There are two types of running costs:

The first type occurs regularly and independent of machine utilization. In addition to personnel costs it includes machine lease payments, maintenance costs for purchased equipment, software royalties, and building rental. This assumes that the EDP system is used only within the framework of its minimum predetermined service life. Power consumption is generally included in this type as well, even though the EDP and air-conditioning systems cannot always be shut down during off-hours for technical reasons.

The second type contains those components which are directly dependent on the service performed. This includes all materials such as punch cards, fanfold paper, ribbons, tapes, and disks, as well as additional rental and maintenance costs due to excessive machine usage (maintenance on call). Overtime, pay differentials for night shifts and wages for seasonal help may also be included.

This brief description points out the problem involved here. It is certainly possible to derive a base rate from the one-time costs and the first tye of the running costs, and add a supplementary rate based on usage derived from the second type. The procedure becomes complicated with usage in excess of the predetermined service life, because a portion of it is already contained in the base rate.

## 9.3 Cost Center Planning

EDP job accounting includes a determination of occurring costs and their treatment as follows:

- The determined costs are allocated to their cost units and distributed according to the appropriate distribution codes.
- The determined costs are credited to the producers of output—for example, machines or systems. In profit accounting these credited amounts are juxtaposed with the expenditures for each output producer.

Cost center accounting methods can be used to handle this task. The cost types are distributed over the task areas—i.e., cost centers—unless they can be directly allocated to the cost units. This is generally done on expense distribution sheets. It has already been mentioned that costs can be allocated to cost centers by means of distribution codes, so that, for example, building rentals can be allocated by square footage as well as room type.

The largest share of costs should be allocated directly to the cost units.

A portion of the costs can, however, be handled only through prorated expenses. Examples are the personnel and materials costs for secretarial services. An appropriate breakdown of cost types can facilitate a more direct allocation to the cost units.

Cost centers should be categorized along the lines of organizational units in order to facilitate an internal supervision of cost development. At the same time, this categorization should support cost allocation to cost units on the basis of a justifiably caused distribution. Both these points are largely in accord with one another and lead to the suggested minimum breakdown for cost center accounting. Expansions can be made based on individual need. Certain indirect cost departments can, if necessary, be reclassified as productive departments, for example education and training. Other indirect cost departments can be dispensed with if organizational reasons make it necessary to reassign them to a productive department.

The ordering sequence of indirect cost departments depends on the type of distribution of the costs incurred by them. The form suggested here is one of several possibilities.

## 9.3.1 Estimated costs

Physical space and appropriations

Administration and management

Education and training

Basic principles and integration

Systems jobs, such as mass planning, maintenance, project-independent software

Operations planning and technical operations scheduling

Experimentation (those excluded from actual costs for purposes of experimentation)

Form redesign

Data postprocessing

Data media archives

Data protection and security

Controls

### 9.3.2 Actual Costs

Data entry (punched cards, punched tape, magnetic tape)

Task-related operations scheduling

Job control and run control (pre, post, and simultaneous controls)

Data processing

- System A
- System B
- System C
- Component a
- Component b
- Component c

Processing on special devices

Shipping

Programming (if applicable)

The changeover from estimated to final costs depends on the special circumstances of each computer center and on task characteristics. The allocation of the costs accumulated in the productive departments to the cost units, and the associated problems of performance evaluation and performance accounting will be discussed in the following section.

## 9.4 Performance Data and Performance Evaluation

Since the performance data of the computer center play such a central role in arriving at a just cost distribution and effective efficiency control, the entire complex of logging and accounting will be briefly presented here. The basic functions of this area consist of the following components in chronological order:

Log systems activities during the production process

Edit the gathered data and convert them into proportionate subtask performance

Evaluate or adjust the proportional subtask performance by systems components, cost factor, and so forth

Calculate charges and distribute the costs over the cost units responsible for them

Prepare billing

Develop efficiency control lists and generate corrective action with a view toward optimizing the operation

### 9.4.1 General Comments on Performance Evaluation

The above comments show that an effective performance evaluation is a basic prerequisite for computer center accounting. Even though the information gained in the course of a performance evaluation depends on the special characteristics of the cost units, it is possible to arrive at a number of common characteristics that can form the basis for a coordinated performance logging system. Typical parameters which are representative for system usage should be selected for each performance type. The performance types are subjected to the decision of the accounting staff who base their decisions on the respective configuration, the operating method, and the typical application profile.

The following minimum data are required in performance accounting:

Job type

Identification of the cost unit—for example, the terminal number or system number in case of several systems, or the software used

Cost unit of the area to be charged

Name of job originator

Job name

Date

Usage time, such as program run time or beginning and ending times

The following information may be recorded if needed:

Job identification code

Operator code

Billing type—for example, rerun or billing to external users

Materials used—for example, list specification, printed lines, plotter paper

Detailed information on the usage of system resources to be administered separately (only for multiprogramming). In this case one must determine to what extent individual or groups of resources can be considered separate cost units.

Performance can be recorded in three ways:

1. Manual recording of significant data on lists or special forms. This is the simplest method and presupposes conscientious machine operation. Accurate manual recording and subsequent data entry are time consuming. The

entries are made by the machine operators, with each line corresponding to one separate operation. These time sheets are designed to simplify data entry and thus make a programmed evaluation possible.

2. Semiautomatic recording by means of a time clock. This method is less time consuming and more accurate. The beginning and ending times of each job are clocked at the top of the sheet. All other entries are made manually.
3. Automatic recording and evaluation over the logging and job accounting part of the operating system. This makes it possible to determine and log certain data of programs by machine—for example, the usage times of resources such as the arithmetic and logic unit, main storage, or data channels. Although the logging of performance data belongs among the standard jobs of the operating system, this area is usually ignored in theoretical considerations. This stepchild of systems designers can also be a source of concern for the practitioners. Data logging must be considered separate from accounting.

Since the emphasis today is on these automated logging procedures, they must be subjected to a critical analysis along the following lines before they are applied:

At what points of time are logging records made?

Are the logging records buffered in main storage?

When and where is this information saved?

Is it possible to lose the information?

Can logging records be suppressed without the intervention of the operating system?

Can user-specific records be generated and stored as well?

Can the expenditure for this information-gathering system be estimated?

What is the expenditure for generating and saving a user-owned record?

Which information is made available to the users after a run?

It is understandable that a variety of further aspects grow out of this which not only concern the form and content but also the subsequent evaluation.

Figure 9.3 is an example representing the notation of a CYBER 72-28 of a SCOPE operating system. It shows in what way the two central processors (CPA and CPB), the peripheral processors (PP), the data channels, and the main storage are occupied by the program. Corresponding performance logging systems are today planned for all multiprogram systems.

```
  02/28/73  U OF TUEBINGEN        SCOPE 3.4 02/05/73
00.00.02.JW32009
00.00.02.JOB WAS RERUN
00.00.02.IP  00003968 WORDS - FILE INPUT  , DC 00
00.00.02.JW320,CM50000,T1000,MT01,P4.
00.00.02.SETCORE.
00.00.02.REQUEST(TAPE4,HI,L,E) (2 BANDER FUR STUD
00.00.02..STAT)
00.00.09.( MT35 ASSIGNED)
00.00.09.FTN.
00.00.26.       6.361 CP SECONDS COMPILATION TIME
00.00.26.REDUCE.
00.00.26.LGO.
00.00.29.RECOVERED PARITY ERROR
00.00.29. FILE NAME  ZZZZZ04:
00.00.29. FET ADDRESS  000101
00.00.31.       5.032 RT SECONDS LOAD TIME
00.00.33.$ MT35  UNLABELLED
00.00.37.GO35.
00.01.35.LOCKIN.
00.05.22.      STOP
00.05.22.UNLOAD(TAPE4)
00.05.23.OP  00008128 WORDS - FILE OUTPUT  , DC 40
00.05.23.CPA     66.738 SEC.
00.05.23.CPB     65.216 SEC.
00.05.23.PP     288.220 SEC.
00.05.23.IO     277.054 SEC.
```

**Figure 9.3** Example of Automated Performance Logging with a Multiprocessor (CYBER 72-28) and Operating System SCOPE 3.4

A major disadvantage is associated with this type of automated logging: there is a strong dependency on the philosophy of the operating system in use. Table 9.1 juxtaposes the accounting data of different multiprogram operating systems. An examination of the parameters of the accounting routines shows significant differences. For example, in one instance the number of input/output performance data is missing or not recorded. This makes it difficult for the computer center to apply uniform accounting algorithms and thus standardize performance accounting. In introducing a new system it will at any rate be impossible to do without verifying whether and to what extent the required and desired performance data are logged. Evaluations and comparisons are nowadays facilitated by practical checklists.

The preliminary work of a computer center performance evaluation can be done today via standard application programs. The quality of some of these products on the market today may differ widely.

Because of the rather differentiated interests of different computer centers,

**Table 9.1** Logging of Multiprogram Accounting Data with Different Operating Systems (The Data were taken from manufacturer's literature.)

| **EDP System** / **Operating System** | IBM/360 DOS | IBM/370 OS (SMF) | S4004 BSV | U1100 EXEC8 | CD3300 MASTER | CD-CYBER SCOPE |
|---|---|---|---|---|---|---|
| Accounting Information | x | x | x | x | x | x |
| User ID | x | x | x | | x | x |
| CPU time | x | x | x | x | x | x |
| Main Storage Requested | | x | | | x | x |
| Main Storage Used | x | x | x | | x | x |
| ECS Requested | | x | | | | x |
| ECS Used | | x | | | | x |
| Drum Requested | | x | | x | | |
| Drum Used | | x | x | x | | |
| Drum Released | | x | | x | | |
| Disks Requested | | x | | x | x | x |
| Disks Used | | x | | x | x | x |
| Disks Released | | x | | x | | x |
| Channel Access Times | | x | x | x | | |
| Channel Usage Times | | | | | x | x |
| Tapes | x | x | x | x | x | x |
| I/O Units | x | x | x | | x | x |
| I/O Records | | x | | x | | x |
| System Time (self-caused) | x | | | | | x |
| Residence Time | x | x | x | x | x | x |
| Set-up Time | | | | | | |

standard programs are rarely offered for the final evaluation of performance data. The following criteria may, however, be considered valid:

Usage types—this includes the differentiation between production runs, test runs, reruns, and maintenance. Others may be added (Chapter 7.2.2)

Cost centers or customers

Program names or procedures

License programs used

Device utilization (bottleneck analysis)

Daily utilization

Actual and standard capacity requirements (relative to run times and schedules)

Comparison of actual and standard processing schedules

Device error statistics

Special evaluation of imperfect runs

### 9.4.2 Performance Evaluation in Data Entry

Performance evaluation in data entry can be seen from two points of view: the measurement of performance in a certain task area for the purpose of allocating the percentages of data entry costs to their respective cost units, and performance evaluation for the purpose of setting just wages for data entry typists.

Data entry performance per document type and employee should be recorded daily. This makes it possible to evaluate the data volume of each task area for cost accounting, and to have a control for the performance of each data entry worker. One factor to be considered is that the data volume may not be established until the initial entry into the system, as for example the transfer of OCR documents to magnetic tape via SPOOL.

The cost center "data entry" first has to be broken down into procedures or devices, such as:

Entry on punched cards

OCR recording

Entry on tape

Entry on magnetic tape via single devices

Entry on magnetic tape via collection systems

Entry on magnetic disk or diskette

Entry via meters

Direct input

Different performance evaluation systems are applied to these procedures.

The performance rate is calculated through division, and set-up times are added to the working hours without limitation.

The system activities occurring in connection with OCR, entry via meters, or direct input are to be recorded for the cost center "data processing."

In offline entry with key entry systems there are additional possibilities for automated performance evaluation. This applies, for example, to systems where data are entered on a central data medium by several work stations with separate storage. The stored data are then called up by the central medium by area of classification. The data entry performance at the individual work stations is recorded manually only if the recording system does not have the capability of logging their operating times per cost unit—that is, per job. It may be sufficient to add the data records entered for each cost unit if the time requirement per data record is known.

The performance evaluation procedure may also be used for purposes such as:

Cost distribution

Efficiency calculation

Schedule control

Schedule planning

Capacity planning

Control of sensitive data

These possible other factors must be considered in developing a performance evaluation system for data entry.

### 9.4.3 Performance Evaluation in Single Program Operations

Since small EDP systems today may also be controlled by one operating system with a built-in meter but without multiprogramming, performance evaluation for such systems will be briefly discussed.

The single program operation technically does not permit the use of resources not required by the currently running program, such as tape stations or main storage, by another program. Nevertheless, performance evaluation is important for operations control and accounting purposes.

Performance accounting is handled in accordance with the performance logging procedure of the operating system. The system usage times for each program are registered automatically on a separate log file either on tape or disk. This information appears simultaneously on the console printout and on the output list for control purposes. The system-internal clock produces accurate time indications. This automation no longer permits a simple allocation of idle times and set-up times to each of the program runs. It is advisable, therefore, to calculate the set-up times separately from the program run times and to use a median mark-up figure based on observation.

One point of departure can be the sum of idle times registered by the system and distributed equally among the program runs. Since this procedure is unsatisfactory with runs of greatly varying length, a proportionate figure based on time units of system usage is the only possible standard of measurement for a performance evaluation.

### 9.4.4 Performance Evaluation in Multiprogramming Operations

In multiprogramming systems a performance evaluation is more difficult insofar as the program residence time no longer represents a useful value. This time varies considerably for one and the same task, depending on which programs are running concurrently. Thus the run time of a low priority program is correspondingly longer. The time factor is also affected by the structure of a high priority program. What follows from this is that a program with the same data volume and data type may have different run times depending on its priority and the structure and characteristics of the concurrently running programs. This points to a multiplicity of random factors which influence the values of a performance evaluation and thus the allocatable costs.

This fluctuation caused by the coincidences of the multiprogramming environment cannot, in all fairness, be charged to the user cost center or computer center customers, even though it can be expected to even itself out over a period of time.

Performance evaluation and accounting in multiprogramming must therefore be based on initial values which are determined entirely or to a large extent by the demands made on the operating resources by each program run. The determining factors are the performance ratios—for example, main storage occupancy—and processor and channel usage times which, however, do not yet solve the problem. A closer examination reveals the inadequacies of the operating systems. The resulting problems are as follows: the waiting times of a program in a separately administered resource are filled out by the working times of other programs. In order to make it possible to operate with a maximum utilization of resources, waiting periods occur in a number of intermediate phases of a total job process. In recording the pure usage time of the CPU, the waiting times and thus the usage times of other resources, for example the main or peripheral storage, are not counted, even though they have a proportionate share of the total output. These waiting times are nonproductive, although resources are in use. A further disadvantage is that the logging information is not fully reproducible.

Even if at first glance a performance evaluation system that permits an accounting of all resources used per unit of time (including waiting times) appears just and suitable for multiprogramming, there is the drawback that the interdependence of jobs running concurrently in the system is not taken into account. To cite the situation already mentioned: a low-priority program has a longer turnaround time than a high-priority program. But this would cause the low-priority program to be more costly because of the additional storage occupancy time. However, the idea of multiprogramming is not to make slow jobs more costly to run than foreground programs.

In addition to these considerations there is also the problem of examining the logging dimensions, because as part of a large operation that processes 1000 or more jobs per day, an accounting system can rapidly accumulate a vast volume of data. A choice must therefore be made between a task-related and a job-related registration. This applies to dialog operations as well. Because of the increase in data volume the trend is how to move away from a purely sequential log file and towards data bank technology.

This situation has generally resulted in a compromise solution for performance accounting and thus for performance evaluation, with emphasis on the following points in multiprogramming operations:

Exclusively based on resource usage but considering the underlying causes

Simplicity of logging and accounting procedures

Consideration given to software component usage

Introduction of evaluating factors for program classifications

Allocation guidelines

Equality of cost with different systems

A number of other points could be added, but none have thus far received general recognition. The special characteristics of operating systems must in any case be considered.

Performance logging by the operating system of a multiprogramming operation should therefore be designed in such a way that subsequent accounting procedures and an evaluation for operations control are possible with the above points in view. This requires the recording of performance ratios in a log file for the following operating resources:

- *Central processor*: The beginning and ending times of each work process must be recorded with the program numbers and job type. A differentiation by jobs, tasks, and transactions leaves a certain amount of room for decisions. Information on job type must specify whether it is an applications program, an input/output program, a systems program, or idle time. Nowadays it is occasionally practical to register standard applications programs separately because they are associated with special costs. If several processors are in use they must be logged separately, even though they may later be allocated to a common cost center.
- *Peripheral processors*: These should be treated like central processors.
- *Working storage or main storage occupancy*: The size of the storage areas occupied and the usage times are recorded. This information is a part of practically all performance evaluation systems, although performance accounting is no longer reproducible because the working storage bears a share of the cost. It is important to keep in mind that the occupied storage area is subject to change during the course of a program run. The performance evaluation system must make certain allowances for that, but it increases the accounting problem, especially in the case of virtual storage. The paging rate, on the other hand, is a significance performance ratio for optimizing the computing operations.

- *Data channels*: In order to complete the picture of input/output activities, the usage times as well as the number of accesses (EXCPs) must be recorded. Unfortunately, some operating systems calculate these analytically from the I/O commands.
- *Magnetic tape units*: In addition to the pure usage times the number of set-up procedures must be recorded as well, since they represent additional work on the device. Section 9.5.4 discusses an accounting method for set-up operations.
- *Magnetic disks*: With private disks the usage time for the entire disk is recorded. If general disks contain several data files, the times during which the files were requested by a specific program are recorded. Additional parking fees for permanent files are discussed in section 9.5.7. The set-up times for pack changeovers should also be taken into account.
- *Magnetic drums*: These are treated like disks, except that there are no set-up times.
- *Input/output units*: In general only the data records are counted for card readers, card punches, quick printers, express stations, document readers, paper tape readers, and plotters. With paper tape readers the number of input digits is more informative because of the variable record length. Plotters are an exception—here the usage times are relevant, and set-up times for plotters and quick printers must be taken into account. Form and pin changes (unless automatic) must therefore be recorded.
- *Telecommunications*: In general the number of transmitted records are counted because they are usually of uniform length. The records of several varying lines cannot simply be summed up, because in accounting each line must be handled separately due to varying speeds, or differences in dial and dedicated lines which can be private or public.
- *Terminals (VDTs, teleprinters, RJE stations)*: It is customary to record the operating times separated by jobs or job numbers as significant performance indicators.

The discussion thus far presents a certain overview of possible performance data which can be registered by an appropriate system. Since these data are not exclusively meant for performance evaluation but must also be used to follow up on machine usage (section 7.2), it is not necessary to proceed from the assumption that all of them must be used for performance accounting purposes. A useful and appropriate performance accounting system is also characterized by a certain simplicity.

## 9.4.5 Evaluation of Computer Center Services

The discussion thus far has been limited to measuring the performance of the systems themselves. However, other services offered by computer centers have increased significantly during the past several years (section 2.4.8). Hardware costs, on the other hand, have fallen drastically, so that the cost of a CPU, for example, now amounts to only 15% or less of the total computer center costs.

The increase in broad-based consulting services presents a contradiction of sorts: the best type of consultation is designed to reduce the customer's data processing expenses to a minimum. But at the same time this minimizes computer center income. Consulting services can therefore not be provided free of charge indefinitely. As a result, computer center services must be included in the performance accounting system. Some attempts have been made in this direction, but thus far without satisfactory results. Some standard application systems for accounting already include service performance. Computer centers would do well to orientate themselves according to the unbundling policies of hardware and software manufacturers.

# 9.5 Accounting Methods

In the foregoing section performance evaluation methods as the basis for performance accounting were discussed. The methods of performance accounting are as valid as the performance characteristics themselves. A critical analysis of various procedures points out the inadequacies of these systems, many of which are the result of the information gathering methods of the operating system.

The choice of method depends on computer center structure, the size of the installation, the user circle, the type and accuracy of performance recording, the operating system routines available, and the funds that can or should be allocated for accounting. Added to this is the extent of available system software. Preference will most likely be given to performance-oriented procedures. Examples of self-developed systems are available in the technical literature.

The principle of absorption (total production and overhead) costing will be the starting-out point for the cost accounting methods discussed here. The cost of performance by man and machine is fully absorbed into the cost of produced output. The section on pricing (9.6) will discuss aspects of internal company policies according to which prices are determined based on known costs, and the effects of corresponding user attitudes. It is impossible to disassociate these two areas from one another.

Monthly cost accounting is the rule, but bimonthly practices occur as well in order to reduce accounting expenditures. Service computer centers prefer immediate accounting; for in-plant purposes, semiannual or annual assessments or automatic charge-offs against an annual budget allocation are sufficient.

The accounting method must be chosen in such a way that the costs for each task area can be planned in advance. The accounting procedures must generally answer to the following:

1. The system-generated job costs must have been justifiably caused.
2. The results determined by the accounting procedure must be reproducible.
3. Output and performance and their costs should, if possible, be machine-independent.
4. It should be possible to extrapolate the procedure, so that cost estimates based on experiential values can be made with some accuracy.
5. The accounting procedure must be readily understood by the user in order to facilitate optimization.
6. Prices based on politics should be used only in exceptional circumstances.
7. The system should remain stable for long periods of time so that the users can engage in long-range planning.

If a new accounting system is planned, further considerations may be added which depend on the specific situation.

## 9.5.1 Time Costing

Only the residence times of each program are used for accounting purposes. The sum of all chargeable program run times and the sum of program run times for each customer are then determined. This establishes each customer's share in the total time, and permits a semiannual or annual assessment of charges based on this share.

It should be emphasized that this procedure can also be used in multiprogramming operations. In actual practice this includes a consideration of program residence times or block times as well as CPU times. However, this procedure is not satisfactory with programs of widely divergent characteristics, such as math-intensive or I/O intensive programs.

*Advantages*

There is no need to calculate machine-hour rates or hourly rates for data entry and other devices.

The administrative accounting costs are low.

*Disadvantages*

The customer has almost no way of veryifying usage.

The programs are all evaluated equally and without any consideration of resource requirements.

The customer has only limited opportunities to reduce costs through optimization.

It is impossible to differentiate in terms of resources used by various computer center teams.

When selling computer time to outsiders, the prices charged are frequently not in line with the work performed.

Residence time costing assessments are therefore practical only in computer centers that work exclusively or at least predominantly for one job submitter. Assessments are justifable even with a few job submitters and more or less equal program characteristics, but are not applicable in computer centers operating with several divergent systems.

## 9.5.2 Lump Sum Pricing

In cases where the same program or program package is run at regular intervals —such as daily or weekly—with a more or less constant data volume, a lump sum price can be negotiated with the customer. Such prices are then independent of the monthly time or materials requirements and the costs incurred by the computer center. This procedure is generally possible only if the customer has clear-cut and relatively constant tasks to process.

The advantage of lump sum pricing is the simplicity for accounting purposes and ease of financial planning. However, there are a number of disadvantages:

The lump sum can be inflated if the computer centers includes excessive security charges.

The lump sum can be too low if the data volume increases or is subject to periodic fluctuations.

The calculated values are subject to constant verification.

Changes in the prerequisites may lead to disagreements between the customer and the computer center.

The prices may be in contradiction with the principle of underlying causes.

These disadvantages point out that lump sum pricing is not to be recommended for EDP performance.

## 9.5.3 Piecework Pricing

The lump sum method discussed above can sometimes be modified in such a way that a price is mutually agreed upon for each data record, check, address label, or invoice produced. With many programs it is relatively simple to calculate the cost associated with each piece. The overall costs of a program run (loading, set-up times) have to be apportioned to each piece as absorption (overhead) costs based on an average number of processes.

Since some operating systems do not have the capability of recording the performance of SPOOL jobs and thus do not permit a clear-cut allocation to each customer, SPOOL jobs are usually handled on a piecework basis, such as per number of printed lines, even though otherwise cost accounting is contingent upon resource usage. The same is true of reader-interpreter or writer-interpreter programs. The performance logging capability of the operating system is usually inadequate in this respect, because the administrative expenditures are considered too high.

This procedure is not only used in the accounting system for EDP performance but also in data entry. A piece price is frequently determined by means of a simple algorithm that contains the digit number, the data field characteristics of each record, and the degree of difficulty. This can also be used as the starting point for calculating piece rates for teleprocessing. In transaction-driven systems each transaction has to be defined as a product before prices can be established for each product type. Cost accounting and pricing procedures in cases of this complexity are no longer readily understood by the user.

*Advantages*

The customer has a better understanding and control of prices.

The overall price is independent of computer center operations; slowness and poor composition of parallel jobs in multiprogramming are not charged to the customer.

The computer center is forced to produce the same output every time.

The piece rate method encourages the computer center to optimize work processes and promote an economic operation.

In telecommunications systems the waiting times in queues no longer count directly as part of output production.

The output of a transaction is independent of response time.

*Disadvantages*

This accounting method cannot be used for all procedures and job types.

The reference quantities may have to be recorded additionally unless they are registered by the program or operating system.

The advantages of system optimization can no longer be directly handed down to the users.

The calculations are somewhat more difficult and costly for the computer center.

This method is suitable only if the procedures are well tested, little subject to change, and are firmly established in terms of their run times. On the other hand, it is often used for rough cost estimates when reorganizing a task area. If, for example, telephone billing is to be handled via automatic data entry on tape or diskette and with interpretation over the system, the question must be asked: What will be the accounting cost per phone call later on in the routine operation?

## 9.5.4 Hourly Rate According to Resource Utilization

In this method an hourly rate is established for the user of each resource. This has the advantage of being an accurate accounting method that can also be used in multiprogramming. However, it is costly and possible only with an efficient performance evaluation system.

To begin with, the entire EDP system can be considered a single resource. This accounting method is of particular interest insofar as data entry devices and intelligent terminals can also be considered as one single device and billed on an hourly rate basis. When applied to EDP systems, the utilization of individual resources by a particular program (main storage, periphery, etc.) is left out of consideration, but this is not relevant in a single program operation.

The cost per machine minute is calculated through division. The costs to be kept in mind include the machine lease or depreciation, maintenance, insurance, operating personnel, rent, and energy, including air conditioning. The costs which cannot be directly allocated must be assigned to the cost centers as prorated expenses. The materials costs can either be added to the overhead or charged to each individual job. However, this is possible only with appropriate performance evaluation systems and is especially easy with job-specific forms.

The details of performance evaluation systems for different models are available in the manufacturers' literature.

The calculation is based on the total number of hours of systems utilization depending on the number of shifts in operation. The chargeable hours per year are roughly:

| | |
|---|---|
| One-shift operation: | 1350 hours |
| Two-shift operation: | 2900 hours |
| Three-shift operation: | 4600 hours |
| Four-shift operation: | 6000 hours |

These figures may be interpreted as being rather high, and lower annual figures are often used as a base for calculations. The computer time used by the computer center itself is part of the overhead and does not count as chargeable time. This includes, for example, work on the system, library and accounting, and self-caused reruns. Depending on the task configuration, 3–10% of the performance total should be set aside for this purpose (Figure 9.2).

One of the advantages of considering the EDP system as a single resource is the simplicity of the performance evaluation and accounting systems. One of the drawbacks is that run times and thus the price per program can be influenced by the degree of skill on the part of the machine operators. The problems associated with multiprogramming have already been mentioned.

This method is very popular, and occasionally different tariffs are charged for day and night work.

Before going into a cost breakdown by individual resource, the method of using only CPU time as an accounting base will be discussed. The hourly rate is again determined by division. The prorated share of the costs does not differ essentially, but the annual hourly rate is much lower because EDP systems never operate with 100% CPU utilization.

The average CPU utilization now enters into the calculations for hourly rates, because the annual systems utilization hours mentioned before must be multiplied by the utilization factor of the CPU. The standard values that are given may fluctuate widely with different computer centers. When using this procedure the computer center cannot help but establish its own values based on experience. However, it can generally be assumed that

Exclusively commercial jobs as a rule have a CPU utilization rate of 10–30%

Exclusively technical/scientific jobs have a CPU utilization of 60–70% or more

The hourly rate for processors requires a corresponding performance evaluation system. The advantage here is accuracy of run-time determination and accounting which includes consideration of multiprogramming. On the other hand, however, the utilization of external devices is not taken into account. The examples provided in section 9.7 include appropriate modifications. This accounting procedure is more suitable for technical/scientific than for commercial computer centers, because in the latter case CPU time is not the only significant performance factor. Moreover, one needs to keep in mind that the CPU share of the overall computer center costs is constantly declining.

In a performance accounting system that considers each resource separately, the overall costs of a program run $K_p$ consist of the direct costs $K_i$ of each individual resource according to the following formula:

$$K_p = \sum_{i=1}^{n} K_i$$

The cost shares $K_i$ of the resources involved, which now represent individual cost centers, consist of the product of accounting units or performance ratios (such as CPU seconds), multiplicity (such as the number of magnetic tape units), and cost units or price (such as price per CPU second). Thus the costs $K_p$ of a program run using n different resource types are:

$$K_p = \sum_{i=1}^{n} m_i \times f_i \times L_i \times P_i$$

(See also section 9.5.6)

Most of the accounting systems used today differ only in the type and number of resources considered separately. The calculation of performance ratios was discussed in section 9.4. One should keep in mind that this accounting method is counterproductive unless all other computer center performances are included, because optimization invariably results in lower revenues. This form of optimization is of no interest to computer centers.

The following resources are to be treated separately as individual cost centers:

COST CENTER: CPU

In the CPU cost center identical processing units are pooled together the same way as in a single program operation, but nonidentical units are subject to separate accounting. Peripheral devices are added to this cost center if they are used exclusively by the operating system; for example:

System disks

Card readers for systems input (for control cards)

Control consoles

This also includes the portion of main storage used by the resident part of the operating system. In teleprocessing the costs for the continuously used main storage area are directly allocated to the respective applications. The composition of such a cost center warrants a special analysis for each particular case. General reflections on the subject can be used as guidelines.

It is generally assumed that programs are written in such a way that others can run parallel to them. Pricing can then be handled by categorizing the number of resources used by the program, and may, if necessary, include hourly rates. This type of cost allocation also makes allowances for the possibility that programs exceeding a certain main storage requirement receive special consideration. Such programs have adverse effects on multiprogramming because of the difficulty of finding suitable programs for parallel runs, or the paging rate may increase considerably. The resulting decline in systems utilization must then be compensated for by surcharges for the excessive program run. Moreover, the objective should be that programs of this type should be implemented only if the benefits of an overflow far exceed the disadvantages for the overall operation. The surcharges are added to the CPU time units in form of a weighting factor. The calculation of this factor F will be demonstrated in section 9.5.5. If one assumes that $F = 1$ for a normal program, the weighting factor can then rise relative to specific situations. The factor appropriate for each case is added to the CPU accounting units as follows:

Accounting units for the CPU cost center: $VE_{ZE}$

$$VE_{ZE} = VER_{ZE} + F \times T_{ZE}$$

$VER_{ZE}$ represents the number of accounting units for an average program set-up, and $T_{ZE}$ the time units used by the program run, for example CPU seconds.

In calculating the cost unit or price for CPU utilization one must consider the fact that in the course of a year programs with varying factors will be run. This results in the necessity for only a few discrete weighting factors. If one assumes 4 different factors, the result for the cost unit $KE_{ZE}$ per CPU minute is:

$$KE_{ZE} = \frac{\sum_{k=1}^{n} KZE_k}{\sum_{j} VER_{ZE} + \sum_{i,j} F_i \times ZE_i}$$

The sum in the numerator represents the overall costs of the cost center "CPU" in one year and is derived from the resource accounting records. In the denominator all set-up times and program run times are summed up separately, with the latter being grouped together by the various weighting factors. The utilization times $ZE_i$ (the index $_i$ indicates to which factor the program belongs) are obtained from the performance log of the operating system. The set-up times have to be determined separately.

Cost Center: Main Storage

As already mentioned, a separate cost center for main storage is associated with certain problems, because even inactive programs may represent a performance here. For that reason the main storage costs are usually allocated to the CPU, less the share chargeable to special applications such as teleprocessing jobs.

Occasionally it may become necessary to maintain a separate account, so that only the resident part of the operating system is allocated to the CPU costs.

In order to determine the cost units for main storage, the average utilization rate must be established from the performance log of the operating system. This is rather costly and can be handled only through a special accounting program. The calculation of the main storage utilization coefficient will be discussed again in section 9.5.5. This average utilization rate is the reference point for the cost center "main storage." Annual utilization is understood as the sum of annual usage times of the central unit, because CPU time has to be considered in addition to the number of storage locations. This avoids penalizing low priority programs with higher storage costs.

Sometimes CPU time alone is not considered sufficient. In that case, as is occasionally done elsewhere, one assumes a self-caused usage time $t_{SV}$, which in this context can be expressed as follows:

$$t_{SV} = t_{CPU} + \sum t_{Ch}$$

The channel usage times are added to CPU time. Systems that only count the number of input/output processes (EXCPs) are at a disadvantage here. The values measured in a number of IBM systems are listed in Table 9.2.

**Table 9.2** Time Usage/EXCP in Milliseconds for Calculating Self-Induced Turnaround Time in IBM Systems (1972)

| Firm | Tape | | Disk/Drum | | Card Reader | Card Punch | Printer |
|---|---|---|---|---|---|---|---|
| 1. Firm | 2420–5 | 16 | 2314 | 32 | | | |
| 2. Firm | 2401–5 | 25 | 2319 | 50 | | | |
| 3. Firm | 3420 | 12 | 2319 | 40 | 95 | 2540 200 | |
| 4. Firm | 2420–7 | 12 | 2301 | 9 | | | 60 |
| | | | 2305 | 5 | | | |
| | | | 2314 | 60 | | | |
| | | | 3330 | 30 | | | |
| 5. Firm | 2401–5 | 34 | 2314 | 34 | 0 | 0 | 0 |
| 6. Firm | 2401–3 | 35 | 2319 | 35 | 35 | 35 | 35 |
| 7. Firm | 2401–5 | 36 | 2319 | 32 | 60 | 60 | 60 |
| 8. Firm | 2420–5 | 50 | 2319 | 50 | | | |
| | | | 3330 | 50 | | | |

COST CENTER: PERIPHERAL GROUPS

The cost of all devices necessary for operating the peripherals must be added to the costs of the peripherals themselves—for example, tape control units, disk controllers, and printer control units. Data channel cost should also be considered here, even though some operating systems register channel usage separately. But this is intended more for evaluating channel utilization than for cost accounting. If time is not registered independently, the program turnaround times are used to represent periphery utilization. CPU time cannot be used here in the sense of self-induced usage because, unlike main storage, most peripheral devices do not permit parallel operations (lists must be continuous, for example).

The program run costs in this cost center are again given the symbol $K_j$, with j representing the device index for each particular case. Indices for different device categories are, for example:

$K_B$ = Magnetic tape unit cost

$K_P$ = Magnetic disk unit cost

$K_D$ = Quickprinter cost

$K_L$ = Card reader cost

$K_S$ = Card punch cost

$K_Z$ = Plotter cost

$K_M$ = Microfilm device cost

The costs are calculated as follows:

$$K_j = \frac{L_j}{1000} \times P_j$$

That is, the costs for each peripheral device are related to the mean costs $P_j$ per 1000 accesses of the device cost center j. The performance index $L_j$ essentially represents the number of accesses. If usage time is chosen as the reference value, the resulting formula is analogical to the one for the central unit:

$$L_j = p_j \times V_j \times L_{pr} + q_j \times Z_j + V_r$$

In considering this formula for the performance index $L_j$ of the device j, p, and q for the time being represent dimensionless allocation ratios:

$$p + q = 1$$

These ratios are meant to divide the accounting units representing actual performance into usage times and accesses. With sequential storage devices such as magnetic tapes, printers, and card punches which can be addressed by only one program at a time, it is advisable to use $p = q = 0.5$, and with random access storage $p = 0.2$ and $q = 0.8$. Program runs requiring only occasional access are less handicapped that way. The values for p and q should be interpreted as suggestions for personal reflections on the subject.

It has been suggested that in this context a reference should be made to the CPU times $L_{ZE}$. However, it is preferable to use the program turnaround times $L_{pr}$ because, as already mentioned, peripheral devices generally do not permit parallel operation. Disks and drums are an exception in certain operating systems. $Z_j$ indicates the number of accesses of a particular program for the peripheral device with the index j.

$V_r$ represents the accounting units for the set-up times of the devices addressed by a particular program, thus incorporating the set-up processes into performance accounting. A separate determination of set-up costs is possible only if the set-up can be recorded as a performance in a multiprogramming operation. The cost per set-up is determined from the sum of costs for set-up processes (for example, operator wages).

The mean costs $P_j$ per 1000 accesses to the peripheral device j are calculated as follows:

$$P_j = 1000 \times \frac{\sum_{\text{Year}} K_j}{\sum_{\text{Year}} Z_j + \sum_{\text{Year}} R_j}$$

The numerator represents the total annual cost of device j, which includes materials costs such as paper, ribbons, and control tape for quick printers. Data media costs will be discussed separately in section 9.5.7. The denominator for $P_j$ consists of the sum of all accesses and the sum of all set-ups per year for the device j. These values can be obtained from the performance log of the operating system.

Surcharges are recommended for cases where the number of devices addressed by a program interferes with multiprogramming operations, for example:

More than 5 magnetic tape units

More than 1 printer

However, individual circumstances should determine which program requirements can be considered an interference and which weighting factors should apply.

## 9.5.5 Evaluating the Influences on Multiprogramming

Several references have been made to the problem of how to handle the influences on multiprogramming in the context of cost accounting. A factor $F_i$ was mentioned, but no further specifications were provided. There is no absolutely accurate procedure, but the following three suggestions may be helpful.

### PROGRAM CLASSIFICATIONS

All programs are assigned to 3 or 4 classes depending on their suitability for an optimal multiprogramming operation. The classification is based on requirements for working storage and peripheral devices, with their upper limits determining the class. The example used here is a 1413 machine with 12 peripheral devices (this can be expanded to fit present-day storage capacities):

Class I: Up to 200 KB and/or up to 2 peripherals
Class II: up to 600 KB and/or up to 7 peripherals
Class III: all programs exceeding the Class II limits

Provisions must be made to ensure that the hourly rates can be applied even where there was no simultaneous operation. This is the case, for example, if the classes are set up as $F_i = 1, 2$ or 3.

Sometimes the program priorities as determined by the operating system are classified by these guidelines. However, weighting program priorities in the accounting system beyond that point is problematic. The assignment of program priorities can influence the strategy of resource distribution to the extent that on the one hand high-priority jobs are given preference, and on the other this preference negatively affects the cost-effectiveness of the system. It is therefore virtually impossible to come to terms with this economic influence in an accounting system. In actual practice fixed surcharges or separate rates are used depending on priority. Unfortunately, the differences between rates are in many cases based more on instinct than calculation.

### WEIGHTING FACTORS

The weighting procedure is a refinement of the program classification scheme. Based on the concept of section 9.5.4, it separates the capacity of a data processing system into two components:

Working storage capacity

Total peripheral capacity

and evaluates their utilization separately.

A program that fully utilizes at least one of these components blocks the entire EDP system, independently of the utilization of the other components. Programs of this type are weighted with the highest factor.

A fair cost allocation of program runs is possible only if a program that fully utilizes one of the two components is charged the full hourly rate, because it prevents a parallel run of one or more additional programs. The program is weighted through a percentage distribution of central unit and total periphery capacity. For example:

| | | |
|---|---|---|
| 1 magnetic tape | = | 5% of the total periphery |
| 1 kilobyte | = | 0.83% of available main storage capacity |

Periphery calculations can also be based on the amount of investment required. The systems utilization of each program is a percentage computation separated into working storage and periphery.

The weighting factors for working storage and periphery produce the program-specific factor according to the formula below. Multiplying this factor by the hourly rate for the system results in the program-specific hourly rate. The accounting value of the program is calculated by multiplying the program-specific hourly rate by the turnaround time of the program in the working storage. The formula for this weighting factor is:

$$b = a_0 + a_1[\,1 - \sqrt{(1-k)\,(1-p)}\,] + a_2[\,1 - \sqrt{(1-k)\,(1-p)}\,]^2$$

| | | |
|---|---|---|
| $b$ | = | weighting factor |
| $a_0$, $a_1$, $a_2$ | = | weighting coefficients |
| $k$ | = | working storage coefficient |
| $p$ | = | periphery coefficient |

The weighting coefficients may have the following meaning:

- $a_0$ Assigns a basic value to the program, which, for example, includes operation by the system. It is also meant to avoid giving very small programs extremely small values
- $a_1$ Assigns values to the devices used by the program (periphery and working storage).
- $a_2$ Represents a surcharge over and above the resources used to compensate for the interference with multiprogramming.

The working storage coefficient k consists of the quotient of the storage locations used and the storage locations made available for the program; the resident portion of the operating system is not considered.

If the entire working storage magnitude is used, the programs have lower values.

$$k = \frac{\text{Space occupied by the program}}{\text{Space available for the program}}$$

It is more difficult to determine the periphery utilization quotient, because of the difference in devices. The following is a suitable formula:

$$p = \sum_{i=1}^{n} g_i \leq 1.$$

The symbol $g_i$ stands for the valuation of the individual devices. Other representations which include the number of devices used (perhaps by establishing

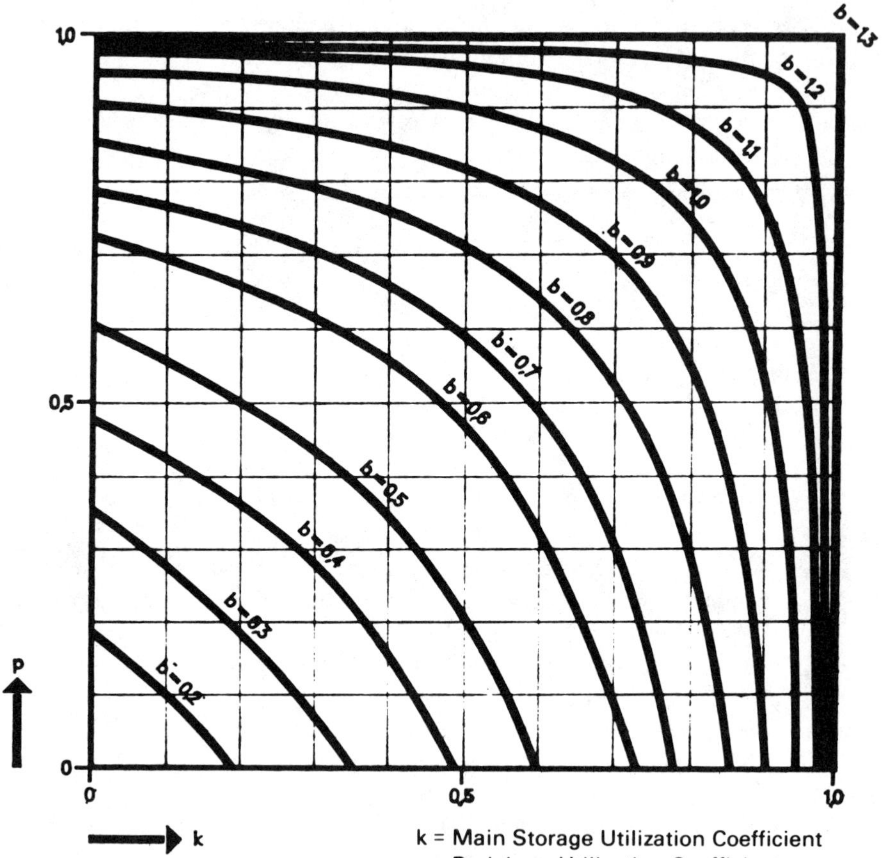


k = Main Storage Utilization Coefficient
p = Periphery Utilization Coefficient
b = Weighting Factor

**Figure 9.4** Curves of Identical Weighting Factors

their mean values), or which evaluate devices of a specific class, such as printers, result in a higher utilization coefficient but otherwise lead to more complicated computations.

Figure 9.4 represents the curves of identical weighting factors for one specific case ($a_0$ = 0.1; $a_1$ = 1; $a_2$ = 0.2).

The grid of Figure 9.5 shows the equation for the weighting factor b in a general form. Here, b as a function of k and p can be read more accurately than in the curves of identical weighting factors.

Figures 9.4 and 9.5 demonstrate that with this choice of coefficients the

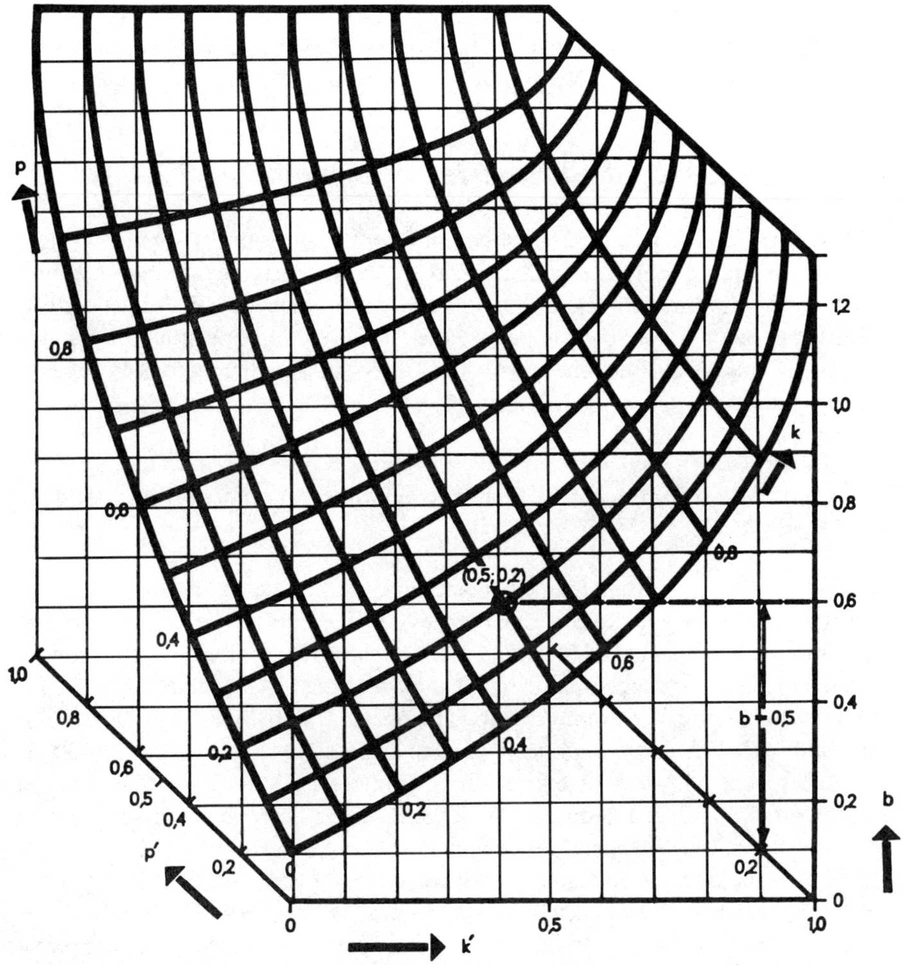


**Figure 9.5** Grid for the Equation Factor. k = 0.5; p = 0.2.
(A parallel is drawn from the coordinate point (k,p) in the curves of the grid to the k' axis. The length of the perpendicular from point 0.2 of the p' axis to the parallel corresponds to the value (0.5) of the weighting factor b.)

weighting factor for a program must be at least 0.1 and may rise to 1.3 if a program entirely hinders multiprogramming. A program whose utilization coefficients k and p are each 0.8 is assigned the value of 1. A different type of norming can easily be adapted from this model.

SIMULTANEOUS POINTS

A further possibility of honoring multiprogramming capacity is a valuation by means of simultaneous points. These points result from the different valuation of individual peripherals in terms of run time, working storage, and periphery requirement. A statistical evaluation based on the simultaneous factor of these programs in prior runs (section 7.2.2) is also possible in principal, but procedures of this type are no longer widely used today.

## 9.5.6 Evaluating the Influences of Different Machine Types

EDP systems of different sizes and often different manufacturers are increasingly used in one and the same computer center. From the customer's point of view it must be taken for granted that the cost of a program run is machine-independent. From the point of view of the computer center, however, a program must be planned and run on one system one time and on the other system another time. This leads to the principle:

***Identical EDP jobs cause reproducible identical costs. Even though one cannot always do justice to this principle, the differences must be kept as small as possible.***

An accounting system that adheres to this point of view will always more or less be based on the principle of separate device accounting. The resource utilization time (for example in CPU seconds) will now be no longer the only determining cost factor; instead, accounting is handled by so-called "work units."

In considering, for example, a specific device, the IBM 3203 Printer, it will not matter whether this printer is attached to an IBM 4341 or an IBM/370-3033. The differences will only have a bearing if printers are used that differ from the above example in cost and output. With the resource "central processing unit" a machine will have to be chosen on which one CPU second corresponds exactly to one work unit. Depending on the cost to performance ratio of this resource, other work units must be determined when other central processing units are used. Since the cost of this resource, which is considered a separate cost center here, is already incorporated in the pricing, the work units can be defined as performance ratios. The following relational numbers $f_{CPU}$ (type), which are used in the accounting algorithm, are listed by way of example.

$$f_{CPU}\,(360-\ \ 40) = 0.115$$
$$f_{CPU}\,(360-\ \ 50) = 0.275$$
$$f_{CPU}\,(360-\ \ 65) = 1.00$$
$$f_{CPU}\,(360-195) = 5.50$$
$$f_{CPU}\,(370-135) = 0.19$$
$$f_{CPU}\,(370-145) = 0.48$$
$$f_{CPU}\,(370-155) = 1.05$$
$$f_{CPU}\,(370-158) = 1.40$$
$$f_{CPU}\,(370-168) = 4.00$$

This only serves as a suggestion for further thought, and the reference to older systems does not matter, since it is not only a question of comparing systems of different sizes and manufacturers but also of comparing the characteristics application fields.

Relational figures can now be established for other resources. The formula for determining the program run costs can thus be altered as follows:

$$K_p = \sum_{i=1}^{n} m_i \times f_i \times L_i \times P_i$$

where $P_i$ = price of one work unit for the resource with the index i
where $L_i$ = the number of work units used by the index i resource for the program run
where $m_i$ = the multiplicity of the index i resource; the multiplicity must be indicated, because the resource type, not the individual resource, represents the cost center
where $f_i$ = compensation factor of the index i resource type

Other compensation factors can be used to consider the processing type (batch, dialog, or real-time)

If possible, the procedure should be refined in one area: the costs should be in reference to a program step instead of an entire program. Since this is possible only hand in hand with the operating system and its performance evaluation system, and more or less proceeds automatically in this form, the problem will not be further discussed here.

### 9.5.7 Data Archive Costs

In the context of data media archives, reference was made in section 3.5 to the fact that archive management must include an accounting system for archive performance. The performance indices are the number and capacities of the data media, or the usage times for permanently available media. A difference must be made between the removable media managed by the archive, and the permanently released random access media for specific tasks where the performance index is generally assumed to be the number of tracks. These figures are available from the archive records. It is irrelevant whether the reserved space is occupied by data or by programs.

Since the cost-related area of data archives is handled differently by different computer centers, a few of the various possibilities are briefly considered here:

- The user departments or customers purchase their own media, which can be made available for each program run or managed by the archive. The disadvantage is a poor utilization rate and higher risk; read/write errors are more frequent because of their being transported back and forth. In this case the archive does not charge for possible performance.

- The archive is a separate cost center within the computer center. The fees for making media available over a monthly period of time are calculated through division. Since the media are consumer goods, they must be depreciated over an average service life, usually 2–3 years, although this is rather pessimistic. The monthly rate for rented disks is added to the calculations as a cost factor. Purchased disks are assumed to have the same average service life as the entire system. In general only rough fee estimates can be used here per monthly usage. This procedure has the advantage that it requires only a relatively small archive and the user departments do not requisition disks unnecessarily.

- The data archive costs are not assigned directly but prorated as a share of the overhead. This simplifies accounting, but the disadvantage is that the customers are less willing to release the reserved tapes, and the archive quickly fills with so-called "corpses."

- The cost centers include the data media costs in their calculations for peripheral devices. This variation is also applicable in the context of automated archive management, where the appropriate utilization of tapes is the responsibility of the user.

### 9.5.8 Charges for Dialog Operations, Teleprocessing, and Computer Networks

A separate subcost center is usually necessary for teleprocessing, real-time processing, and dialog operations, because certain specific tasks in this area require additional resources.

If only a single such job is run next to normal batch operations, the additional costs associated with this job are charged to it as a monthly surcharge added to the normal costs of the program run (in case of monthly accounting). This cost may include the following possible resources:

Data transmission lines

Modems

Terminals

Multiplex channel usage

Additionally required resident working storage

Routed or purchased programs (for example, APL compilers)

If several jobs or the jobs of different customers are processed in this manner, these additional costs are distributed over the different jobs. A distinction must be made between resources used by only one job originator, such as a channel or terminal, and resources used concurrently by several, such as multiplexers or programs.

In general, the costs for lines, modems, and terminals are passed on directly to the tasks. If this is not possible, as in the case of several participating job originators, the number of data blocks can serve as the performance reference for accounting. This procedure is applicable in remote batch processing, where several independent jobs run over one terminal. The overhead proportion in teleprocessing (resident part of working storage, program cost, multiplexer cost) is distributed over the tasks in the form of terminal connect times by simple division. In dialog operations the rate of transmission and length of session serve as units of measure, and in transaction-driven systems it is the transaction which can be estimated with relatively good accuracy.

The normal data processing costs represent the third share of costs in this type of operation. They no longer differ from the normal batch processing costs and can be derived by the accounting procedures mentioned in section 9.5.4. It should be emphasized here that in a number of EDP systems online jobs have the highest priority; this must be considered in the cost calculations.

In this type of cost distribution for teleprocessing the nature of the task is of no consequence and may, for example, include the EDP costs of a direct data entry operation.

No specific accounting system has developed for computer networks. The extensive cost catalog, together with the difficulty in quantifying the benefits, pose a complex problem for cost accounting. The objectives of such an operation must also be considered when designing an accounting system.

### 9.5.9 Final Calculations

Final calculations are defined as the cost distribution based on accurate information on a completed job interval. Final calculations are usually omitted in accounting for computer center services because they tend to stifle the motivation for cost-effective management. Moreover, computer centers often depend on these possible surplus profits in order to finance innovations.

On the other hand, final calculations are useful for the purpose of continuously adjusting planning volumes and planning costs to actual values. The causes of excessive or insufficient cost recovery are revealed in this manner, and an accounting system that remains stable over several accounting periods can be developed.

## 9.6 Pricing Policy

Up until now the costing problem for EDP tasks was seen from the point of view of an objective determination and distribution of incurred costs, and of cost-oriented prices. The price per work unit, arrived at through division, does not pose any special problems. But one basic dilemma must be pointed out: the computer center users are interested in pricing from a problem-solving point of view, i.e., they expect product prices. The computer center, on the other hand, proceeds primarily from the concept that price represents performance; almost all accounting systems are set up in this manner. Users lack the insight for this system, and are for the most part not even interested in it.

It was already mentioned, however, that one can achieve desirable or undesirable side effects by allocating partial costs to certain cost centers. One example is the fees charged for setting up data media, which help the users in their decision for permanent files instead of files managed by the archive. This decision could be supported even further by not charging parking fees for permanent files. But since the computer center cannot allow the mass storage in the system to grow to unreasonable proportions, controls are necessary through set-up fees for overhead and parking. This raises the basic question of whether pricing should be purely computer-oriented, or whether occasionally a data-oriented method is preferable.

A second problem pertains to the difference between planned (or reserved) and actually used EDP capacity. Every time the computer center makes capacity available based on machine requisitions, there are associated costs. It is well known, however, that users do not always fully utilize the requisitioned capacities. If arrangements for other jobs can be made at short notice, no one suffers. But who is responsible for the costs if no substitution is possible?

In the light of these reflections it seems understandable that in some computer centers a machine capacity request is associated with a fee which is taken into consideration in job accounting, and which covers the costs of idle time in case the job is cancelled. The situation is even more critical in the case of "privately" reserved mass storage, whose unused portion cannot be used by anyone else because of the nature of the reservation.

An endeavor to minimize expenditures on a long-term basis requires orientation aids in order to decide whether a problem should be solved with or without the aid of the EDP system. A decision among alternatives is usually based on a comparison of operations-internal prices. These decisions are correct only if the operations-internal prices were determined by including a consideration of long-term expenditures. This means that during the introductory phase of data processing —i.e., with a minimally utilized system and relatively slow growth—the user departments of a company-internal computer center should not be charged on a cost recovery basis. In other words, the users are assessed partial costs instead of absorption (total production and overhead) costs, i.e., the computer center during the beginning phase is temporarily assigned a fixed budget. Some computer centers charge reduced prices for certain projects during that phase, but the EDP capacity allowed under this introductory price is determined in advance.

Similar considerations are in order when introducing new peripheral devices which can be fully utilized only after a corresponding program conversion and are therefore uneconomical at the beginning. One example is the transition from sequential to random access storage. In order to avoid excessive charges against the few advanced applications due to minimal utilization, the temporarily unused capacity can be charged to cost center "experimentation."

An attractive price profile can also help to increase the use of little-used but necessary components. If the EDP configuration contains systems or software components whose use is restricted to one task, the total systems component costs are customarily charged directly to that task. The same can apply to a part of the teleperiphery in cases where lines and terminals are allocated exclusively to certain tasks.

Price incentives can be instrumental in developing viable EDP solutions that require low personnel expenditures, utilize the overall system, and are easy to continue after a restart. The users should be encouraged in that direction through a reduction of computer costs for system support by program optimization.

It has already been mentioned that costs are to be calculated on an annual basis and that accounting should be handled monthly. In the computer centers of a company with branches in different locations the prices are determined per location. If significant differences exist between main office and branch office wages, these differences should also be reflected in the prices. But in each location, and independent of the machine in question, equal costs should be assessed for equal work.

In computer linkages to different locations, a politically influenced price structure is difficult to avoid where different price levels exist. While on the one hand one cannot help but equalize prices, there is the possibility of relocating certain jobs through sophisticated pricing methods. The disposal of capacity is economically sound only if the line costs can be compensated for by lower tariffs, such as night rates.

If a computer center no longer works exclusively for the parent firm, the absorption (total production and overhead) costing methods discussed thus far no longer suffice. The division into fixed and variable costs mentioned in section 9.2 offers the possibility of determining by way of a contribution margin at what point the acceptance of a job order is more profitable than its rejection, provided free capacity is available. The acceptance is more profitable as soon as at least a small contribution is made to cover the fixed costs.

If the computer center is disassociated from the parent firm as a profit center, it can continue to exist only as long as at least the costs for work performed are covered. However, this is a problem area which can not be further discussed here.

In conclusion it can be said that politically influenced pricing is at times unavoidable. Pricing, in the final analysis, is an instrument for the control of an unreasonable use of capacity and allocation systems such as exist at university computer centers. However, political prices should be avoided as much as possible because they destroy cost visibility. Permanent overcapacity is, after all, best resolved by adapting the configuration to the task spectrum rather than by price incentives for EDP applications.

## 9.7 Example of a Simple Accounting System

After discussing the broad spectrum of accounting possibilities, a few concrete examples are offered here, beginning with the cost types of a medium-sized model computer center. The monthly costs indicated are therefore only value standards and date from approximately 1981. The following abbreviations are used:

OH: Overhead share
DP: Data processing share
DE: Data entry share

1. Personnel (including social benefits)

| | | |
|---|---|---|
| 1 Computer center manager | OH | $3,200 |
| 1 Secretary | OH | 1,463 |
| 1 Operations scheduling manager | DP | 2,423 |
| 4 Operations scheduling assistants | DP | 7,771 |
| 1 Chief operator | DP | 2,422 |
| 3 Shift supervisors | DP | 6,171 |
| 6 Operators | DP | 10,286 |
| 1 Systems support specialist | DP | 2,423 |
| 2 Systems Programmers | DP | 4,114 |
| 1 Databank specialist | DP | 2,286 |
| 2 Teleprocessing specialists | DP$_4$ | 4,343 |
| 1 Data entry operator | DE | 1,463 |
| 1 Janitor | OH | 1,143 |

2. Data Processing Materials

| | | |
|---|---|---|
| Continous form | $DP_3$ | $3,200 |
| Magnetic tapes, disks, etc. | $DP_2$ | 1,371 |
| Diskettes | DE | 91 |

3. Rent, Energy, Maintenance, etc.

| | | |
|---|---|---|
| Rent | OH | $4,571 |
| Software (without teleprocessing) | DP | 5,486 |
| Teleprocessing software | $DP_4$ | 1,829 |
| 1 Data entry device | DE | 274 |
| Power, etc. | DP | 9,143 |
| Heating | DP | 1,143 |
| Maintenance (CPU) | $DP_1$ | 9,143 |
| Maintenance (tape & disk units) | $DV_2$ | 6,857 |
| Maintenance (paper periphery) | $DP_3$ | 1,829 |
| Maintenance (teleperiphery) | $DP_4$ | 4,571 |

4. General Costs

| | | |
|---|---|---|
| Office supplies, copying, telephone, etc. | OH | 549 |
| Furnishings | OH | 366 |

5. Calculated Costs

Assuming a 5-year depreciation period and a 7% interest rate.

5.1 Calculated Depreciation

| | | |
|---|---|---|
| CPU (purchase value $2.5 million) | $DP_1$ | 41,920 |
| Disk & tape units with controls (purchase value $914,286) | $DP_2$ | 15,269 |
| Paper periphery with control units (purchase value $228,571) | $DP_3$ | 3,794 |
| Teleperiphery with control units (purchase value $685,714) | $DP_4$ | 11,383 |
| Air conditioning (purchase value $437,143) | OH | 1,828 |

5.2 Calculated Interest

The calculated interest for the air-conditioning unit is included in the building rental.

| | | |
|---|---|---|
| Central processing unit | $DP_1$ | 8,800 |
| Disk and tape units | $DP_2$ | 3,200 |
| Paper periphery | $DP_3$ | 800 |
| Teleperiphery | $DP_4$ | 2,400 |

This amounts to the following total monthly costs for the model computer center:

| | |
|---|---|
| Data processing (DP) | $174,377 |
| Data entry (DE) | 1,828 |
| Overhead (OH) | 13,120 |
| Total | $189,325 |

If the overhead is proportionately divided among data processing and data entry, the monthly costs are:

| | |
|---|---|
| Data processing | $137,366 |
| Data entry | 1,959 |
| Total | $189,325 |

It is assumed that during an observed annual period the installation operated for 4800 hours with chargeable programs.

If the EDP system is considered as the only operating device, one usage hour would cost $468.42 ($187,366 × 12 ÷ 4800 hrs.). It seems contradictory to include the telecommunications portion.

If the results of the observation had been that on the long-range average the system had been operating in a batch mode with a simultaneous factor of 3.5, the result would be an hourly rate of $114.29 (excluding the telecommunications proportion). It has already been mentioned that CPU time is a fairly good accounting unit for math-intensive programs. If one were to assume an average CPU utilization of 50%, CPU time would have an hourly rate of $937.14. This would mean, however, that the calculations are based on a resource which shares only one third of the costs.

If in a more refined accounting system the data processing costs are apportioned to the 4 cost centers according to their share of the total investment,

| | | |
|---|---|---|
| Computation (CPU, working storage, etc.) | $DP_1$ | = 57.99% |
| Storage (tapes, disks, etc.) | $DP_2$ | = 21.1% |
| Input/output (paper periphery, etc.) | $DP_3$ | = 5.2% |
| Telecommunications (including teleprocessing) | $DP_4$ | = 15.8% |

the result per cost share is:

| | |
|---|---|
| Computation | $108,485 |
| Storage | 39,534 |
| Input/Output | 9,743 |
| Telecommunications | 29,604 |

Since CPU time is assumed to be the accounting factor for computing performance, the resulting hourly rate (in round figures) is

$$P_{cpu} = 549.00$$

For reasons of simplicity, storage performance can be added to channel utilization accounting, assuming that the storage media are more or less equally utilized and that the channel usage times are registered by the operating system.

If one further assumes that all channels attached to the storage units are utilized an average of 500 hours per month, the following rate results for channel utilization as representing data storage performance:

$$1 \text{ Channel utilization hour} = P_{kn} = \$82.29$$

Center for Data Processing
University of Tubingen
Brunnenstrasse 27
Tel. (07071) 29 6968

Fee Statement for Univac
and TR440

Date: 11/19/81

Institute for Biological Sciences    Auf der Morgenstelle 1

Cost Center No. 16210071

Month of September 1984

Cost Share in DM for

| User | Job Number | Computing Time | Channel Time | Lines | Cards | Terminal Time | Plotter | Total |
|---|---|---|---|---|---|---|---|---|
| Professor Engelman | BBENOTO1 | 34.53 | 23.93 | 39.75 | 0.00 | 0.00 | 231.99 | 330.20 |
| | | 34.53 | 23.93 | 39.75 | 0.00 | 0.00 | 231.99 | 330.20 |
| Reserved Disk Storage | | | | | | | | 3.27 |
| September Total | | | | | | | | 333.47 |

Month of October 1984

Cost Share in DM for

| User | Job Number | Computing Time | Channel Time | Lines | Cards | Terminal Time | Plotter | Total |
|---|---|---|---|---|---|---|---|---|
| Professor Engelman | BBENOTO1 | 12.39 | 14.03 | 43.15 | 0.00 | 0.00 | 157.56 | 227.13 |
| | | 12.39 | 14.03 | 43.15 | 0.00 | 0.00 | 157.56 | 227.13 |
| Reserved Disk Storage | | | | | | | | 1.73 |
| October Total | | | | | | | | 228.86 |

Total Cost: DM 562.33

The above sum has been charged to your cost center.
Please adjust your budget accordingly.

**Figure 9.6** Sample Invoice Produced Automatically and Based on a Performance Logging System

The price for input/output performance remains to be determined. If the I/O devices are to be considered separately, their costs have to be split up. At an average of 20 million lines per month, the price per 100 lines is:

$$P_{PL} = \$.05$$

This price includes punched card read-in in cases where they are still used in significant numbers. The devices for them should have already been written off.

Calculations for this simplified procedure should be handled by the following formula:

$$K = t_{CPU} \times P_{CPU} + t_{kn} \times P_{kn} + N_{pr} \times P_{pr}100$$

where t = time in hours
where $N_{pr}$ = number of lines printed per program

Figure 9.6 is an example of an automatically produced account at the Center for Data Processing at the University of Tübingen. The fomula used differs only insofar as the I/O units are considered separately and punched cards are included. Today various types of standard systems are used.

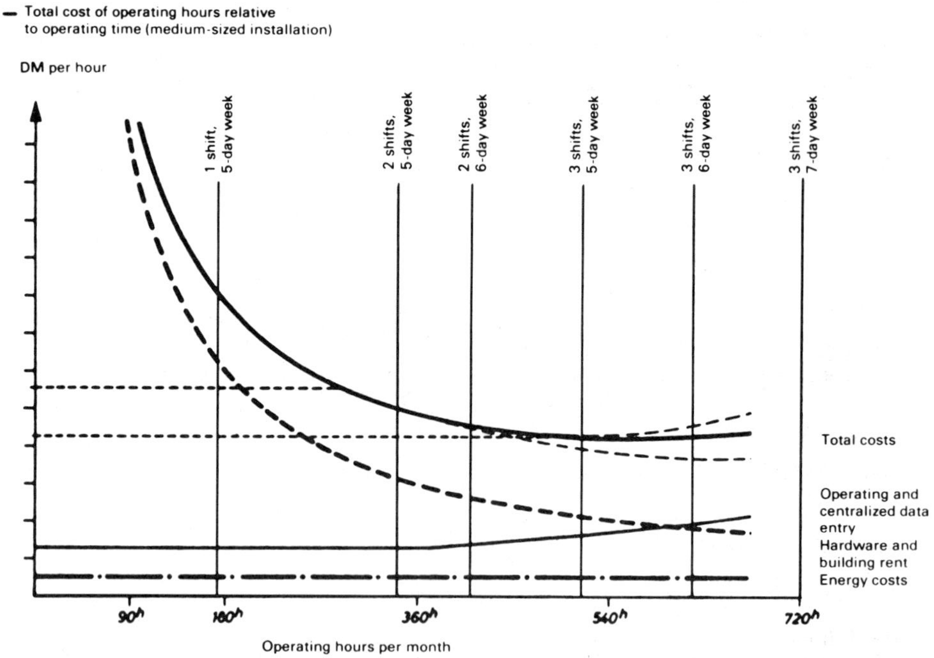


**Figure 9.7** Total Cost of Operating Hours Relative to Operating Time in a Medium-Sized EDP Installation

Figure 9.7 represents an overview of the overall operating costs relative to total operating time in a medium-sized EDP installation. The data flow in this type of accounting system is of special significance. Figure 9.8 represents such a data flow. Essential steps such as data security, compression, correction, and billing are clearly indicated.

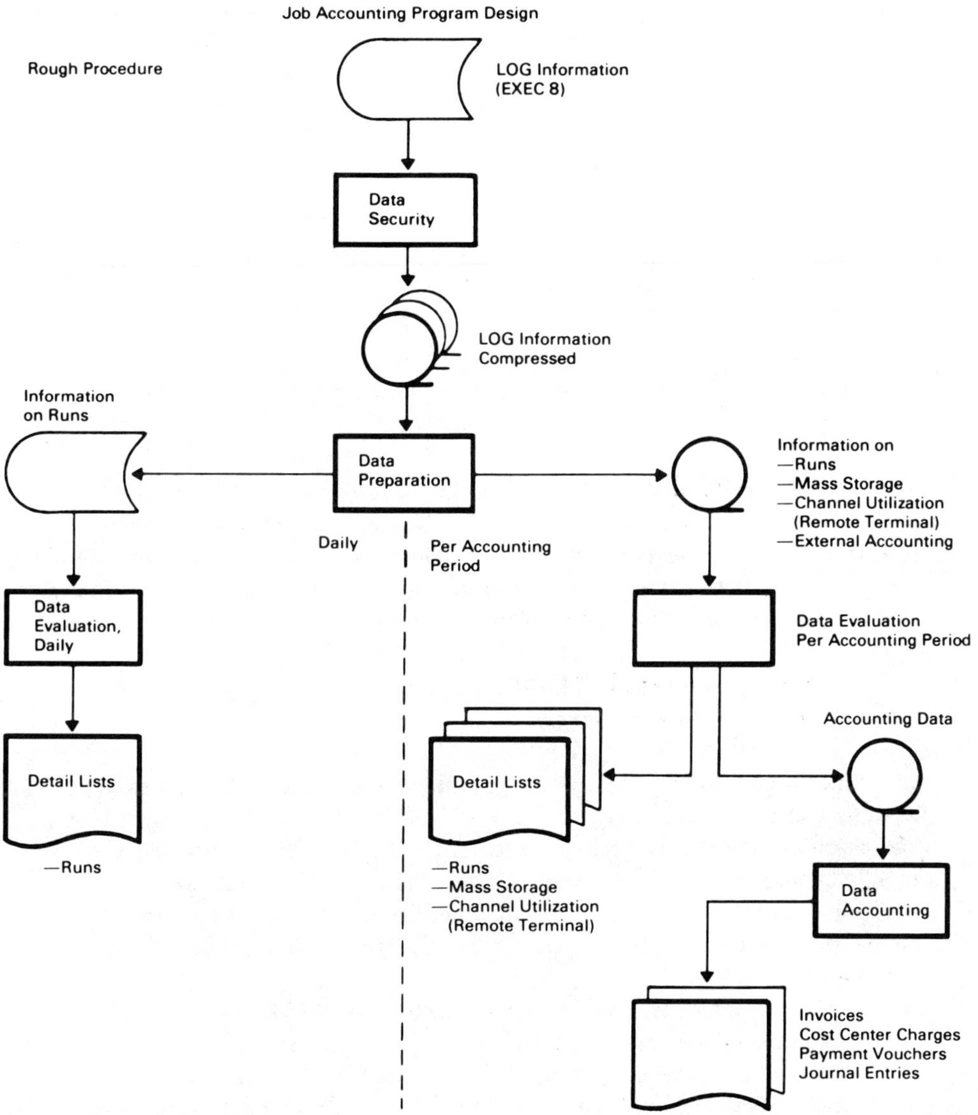


**Figure 9.8** Data Flow in an Accounting System

# TEN

# COMPUTER CENTER HANDBOOK

The extensive reflections presented thus far have demonstrated that this cost-intensive resource requires a detailed apparatus of operating instructions and regulations in order to run economically and be functionally efficient. Many computer centers have therefore developed organizational handbooks which are often part of the overall handbook of the enterprise.

> ***An organizational handbook is defined as a structured set of applicable and valid operational rules and regulations.***

Since organizational handbooks are widely used outside of computer centers as well, it suffices to emphasize only the general characteristics here. Instructions, and especially their organized presentation, are of particular importance in as rapidly changing a field as data processing. The handling of EDP tasks requires uniform managerial direction. If this direction is made known to all employees in all its details and justifications it can serve as a motivating factor in the realization of computer center goals.

Since the practical development of such a handbook is associated with considerable personnel expenditures, only larger computer centers have carried out this task to its logical conclusion, primarily because their size and complexity demanded it. Only an overview of this type makes it possible to recognize the internal logic of the body of rules and to present it as a consistent product. In enterprises with centralized systems analysis/programming, the organizational handbook of the computer center represents, therefore, only a portion of the handbook for the entire EDP operation.

This points out an essential feature in the organizational and external form of the book: it must be structured in such a way that sections of it can be made available for daily use at each appropriate work station. The term "handbook" does not necessarily mean that it must exist in bound form. A breakdown into separate parts is often more useful. This facilitates its use at the work station without the necessity of having the entire book at hand. On the other hand, this method requires constant updating and distribution services and provisions for this must be included at the initial planning stage.

When developing a computer center handbook the following requirements must be met:

Clear structure

Clear typographical presentation

Uniform terminology

Avoidance of repetitions and overlaps

Published by a central office

Ongoing updating and supplementation

Clearly determined user circle

Fulfills the requirements of a reference work

The following is a practical suggestion for developing a clearly structured handbook, as structure is the single most predominant point.

## 10.1 Structure

The first page of the handbook and of each of the separately used parts should list the following emergency procedures:

Important telephone numbers

What to do in case of fire

- Emergency system shutdown
- Call fire department (phone number)
- Shut down air conditioning and other devices
- Use only approved fire extinguishers

What to do in case of air-conditioning problems

- Prepare for system shutdown
- Shut down the system if the disturbance lasts over 10 minutes
- Shut down the air conditioning if the maximum temperature or humidity values have been exceeded
- Notify emergency services (phone number)

What to do in case of flood

- Shut down the system
- Notify emergency services
- Shut down the air conditioning

What to do in case of an accident

- Emergency system shutdown in case of an electrical accident
- Notify medical emergency service (phone number)
- Give first aid

### 10.1.1 Content of General Section

Organizational structure of the computer center and its position in the enterprise (with flowchart)

Personnel directory with telephone numbers

Staff organization

Physical layout

House rules (all employees receive a separate copy at the time of hiring, as well as all guests staying for any length of time)

Energy supply plan

Working hours and hours set aside for consultation

Job descriptions with clear delineation of responsibilities

Job and task distribution (specific allocation of tasks)

Guidelines for external communications (signatures, orders, etc.)

Filing system

Training (for apprentices, operators, etc.)

Forms (samples of forms used in the computer center)

Documentation guidelines

Data security regulations

## 10.1.2 Content of Specific Sections

System configuration

Work procedures (handling instructions for materials and devices)

Console operation instructions—operating instructions for normal and exceptional situations, error report listing, start-up and shut-down procedures—that can also be posted separately at the console

Job card and control card system

Subprogram library listing

Documentation instructions (for program descriptions)

Data reception control instructions

Data entry guidelines

Guidelines for operations scheduling (rules for priority assignments, philosophy of machine utilization)

Guidelines for coordination and output control

Guidelines for data security

Shipping and mailing guidelines (a shipping log)

Machine time logging system

Guidelines for systems, software, and air-conditioning maintenance (including maintenance times)

Archive guidelines (storage regulations, description of filing system, etc.)

Library of technical literature

System identification (numerical systems)

Evaluation procedures (sample form to determine cost-effectiveness)

## 10.1.3 General Usage Regulations

Description of tasks assumed by the computer center

Guarantees and liabilities associated with tasks (for example in reruns)

Safety and security measures for the users

Restrictions imposed on the user circle

Job accounting and fees

General contractual conditions (for outside jobs)

### 10.1.3 Supplement

It goes without saying that this structure is subject to individual adaptations. Each organization consists of human beings who determine its form. The computer center, in addition, has machines which, on account of their often pronounced individuality, are perceived as human partners.

# BIBLIOGRAPHY

**Chapter 1.** Types of Computer Centers and Their Tasks

Schaeffer, H. *Data Center Operations: A Guide to Effective Planning, Processing and Performance*. Englewood Cliffs, NJ: Prentice-Hall, 1981.

Vince, N., Ed. "Computer Operations," *Infotech State of the Art Report*, Series 10, No. 4. Berkshire, England: Pergamon, 1982.

Austin, J. E. "Planning Computer Services for a Complex Environment." *Proceedings AFIPS 1971, Fall Joint Computer Conference*, pp. 541–547.

Freeman, D. N. and Ragland, J. R. "Response-Efficiency Trade-off in a Multiple University System," *Datamation*, March 1970, pp. 112–113. (1.9)

Gonter, R. H. "Characteristics of Jobs Processed in a University Computer Center," *Proceedings ECODU Meeting*, March 1971. (1.13)

Ralston, A. "University EDP: Get It All Together," *Datamation*, 17, 5, pp. 24–26. (1.37)

Thwaites, B. "The Role of Computers in British Universities," *IUCC Newsletter*, Vol. 3.1, 1974, p. 7. (1.50.)

**Chapter 2.** Organizational Structure

Eisenhut, Peter S. "Data Processing User Service Management," *The Economics of Information Processing*, Vol. 2, Robert Goldberg and Harold Lorin (Eds). New York: Wiley, 1982.

NOTE: Numbers in parenthesis following reference refers to citation number in German 2nd edition. The German edition contains an extensive bibliography of German references.

Frank, Michael R. *The Effective EDP Manager*. New York: American Management Association, 1981.

Albrecht, L. K. *Organization and Management of Information Processing Systems*. New York: Macmillan, 1973. (2.1)

Haupt, D. "The Direction of Data Processing During the Last 20 Years," *ECODU-31 Proceedings*, Helsinki, 1981, pp. 2-1–2-3. (2.16)

IBM: *Managing the Data Processing Organization*, 1st ed. Lindingo, Form GE 19-5208-0, Oct. 1976. (2.24)

IBM: *Organizing the Data Processing Installation*. Form GC 20-1622, Oct. 1971. (2.25)

Nolan, R.L. "Managing the Computer Resource: A Stage Hypothesis," *Comm. of the ACM*, 16 J. 1973 H. 7, pp. 399–405. (2.42)

Nunn, J. L. "Closing the Gap Between EDP and the User," *Journal of Systems Management*, 22, 11, Nov. 1971, pp. 22–25. (2.43)

Withington, F. G. *The Organization of the Data Processing Function*. New York: Wiley, 1972. (2.61)

## **Chapter 3.** Operational Organization

Cordata, J. W. *Managing DP Hardware*. Englewood Cliffs, NJ: Prentice-Hall, 1983.

Fuori, W., et al. *Introduction to Computer Operations*, 2nd ed. Englewood Cliffs, NJ: Prentice-Hall, 1981.

Kelvin-Kelley, W. "Console Operations Management," *The Economics of Information Processing*, Vol. 2, R. Goldberg and H. Lorin (Eds.). New York: Wiley, 1982.

Knight, A. "The Space Manager," *Infotech State of the Art Report*, Series 10, No. 4. Berkshire, England: Pergamon, 1982.

Langworth, G. *Management Handbook of Computer Operations*. Manchester, England: National Computing Centre, 1983.

AFIPS: *Security Checklist for Computer Center Self-Audits*. Arlington AFIPS, 1979. (3.2)

Albrecht, L. K. *Organization and Management of Information Processing Systems*. New York: Macmillan, 1973. (3.5)

Egger, J. "Managing Multiple Computer Installations; Criteria," *SEAS—Proceedings; Spring Technical Meeting*, Bari, 1981, pp. 127–137. (3.35)

IBM: *Disk Pack and Cartridge Handling Procedures*. Form GA 26-5756. (3.72)

IBM: *Management Planning Guide for a Manual of Data Processing Standards*. IBM Form GC 20-1670-2, February 1971. (3.74)

IBM: *Problem and Change Management in Data Processing*. Form GE 19-5201, August 1976. (3.75)

Persson, L. "Designing for Minimum Downtime," *Datamation*, November 1974, p. 51. (3.133)

Rubin, M. L. *Data Processing Administration: Handbook of Data Processing Management*, Vol. 6. New York: Van Nostrand Reinhold, 1971, pp. 387–497. (3.144)

Guido, A. A. *The Operatorless DP-Center*. Proc. SEAS Spring Meeting 1982, p. 131.

## Chapter 4. Data Protection and Data Security in the Computer Center

Ellison, J. R. "Operations Security," *Infotech State of the Art Report*, pp. 133–146, Bergshire, 1982.

Hamilton, P. *Computer Security*. New York: Van Nostrand Reinhold, 1979.

Pritchard, J. A. T. *Security in On-Line Systems*. Manchester, England: National Computing Centre, 1979.

Squires, T. *Computer Security: The Personnel Aspect*. Manchester, England: National Computing Centr , 1980.

Beardsley, C. W. "Is Your Computer Insecure?" *IEEE Spektrum*, Vol. 9, No. 1, 1972, p. 67. (4.6)

Wong, U. K. "Telecommunications—Operations Strategy for Security and Backup," *Infotech State of the Art Report*, Vol. 10, No. 6. Pergamon, 1982, p. 277.

Chandy, K. M., and Ramamoorthy, C. V. "Rollback and Recovery Strategies for Computer Programs," *IEEE Trans. on Comp.*, 1972, No. 6, pp. 546–556. (4.12)

Chastain, D. R. "Security vs. Performance," *Datamation*, November 1973, p. 110. (4.13)

Jacobsen, R. V. "Planning for Backup Facilities," *Computer Service*, May 1974. (4.35)

Van Tassel, D. *Computer Security Management*. Englewood Cliffs, NJ: Prentice-Hall, 1972. (4.73)

## Chapter 5. Computer Center Personnel

Brandon, D. H. *Data Processing Organization and Manpower Planning*. New York: Van Nostrand Reinhold, 1974.

Hansen, P. *Job Description in Data Processing*. Manchester, England: National Computing Centre, 1977.

Avery, R. D. and Hoyle, J. C. "Evaluating Computing Personnel," *Datamation*, July 1973, pp. 69–73. (5.1)

Couger, J. D. *Motivating and Managing Computer Personnel*. New York: Wiley, 1980. (5.8)

Ewers, J. "Taking Management's Measure," *Datamation*, May 1980, pp. 184–190. (5.14)

IBM: *Interactive Instructional System/Virtual Storage*. IBM Form GT 12-2803, November 1980. (5.33)

Leeson, M. *Computer Operation, Procedures and Management*. Stuttgart: SRA-Verlag, 1978. (5.48)

Lyon, J. K. *The Database Administrator*. New York: Wiley, 1976. (5.54)

Rubin, M. L. *Data Processing Administration, Handbook of Data Processing Management*, Vol. 6, pp. 37–142. New York: Van Nostrand, Reinhold, 1971. (5.68)

Chandor, A. *Choosing and Keeping Computer Staff*. London: Allen and Unwin, 1979.

## Chapter 6. Aspects of Communication

Ditri, A., et al. "Managing and Reporting on EDP Functions," *Managing the EDP Function*. New York: McGraw-Hill, 1971. (6.3)

"A Policy of Documentation," *IUCC-Newsletter*. Vol. 3, 1, 1974, pp. 13–15. (6.10)

## Chapter 7. Planning and Control

Bytheway, A. J. "Capacity Management Tools for Operations," *Infotech State of the Art Report*, 10, 6. Pergamon 1982, p. 82.

Axelrod, C. W. *Computer Productivity, A Planning Guide for Cost Effective Management*. New York: Wiley, 1982.

Walker, G. S. *Control of Data Processing Production*. Manchester, England: National Computing Centre, 1980.

Cordata, J. W. *Managing DP Hardware*. Englewood Cliffs, NJ: Prentice-Hall, 1983.

Boles, S. J. "User Behavior on an Interactive Computer System," *IBM Systems Journal*, 14, 1, 1974, p. 2 (7.9)

Chester, K. W. "Computer Resource Allocation," *Datamation*, September, 1974, p. 107. (7.20)

Ganning, R. G. "The Internal Auditor and the Computer," *EDP Analyzer*, Vol. 13, 3, March 1975. (7.37)

IBM: *Problem and Change Management in Data Processing*. IBM Form GE 19-5201-0, August 1976. (7.66)

IBM: *Tuning Handbook*, MST/MVT, Form C12-1044. (7.67)

IBM: *Management Control for Data Processing*. April 1976, IBM Form GF 20-0006-1. (7.72)

Thomas, A. J., and Douglas, I. J. *Audit of Computer Systems*. NCC Mandarter 1981.

Mair, W. C., et al. *Computer Control and Audit*, 2nd ed. Minneapolis: Institute of Internal Auditors, Touche Ross & Co., 1976. (7.105)

Schubring, D. *Operations Statistics and User Accounting*. Proc. ECODU 34, 1982, pp. 1–16.

## Chapter 8. Planning and Implementing a Computer Center

Waring, L. P. *Electrical Power Supply to Computer Installations*, Manchester, England: National Computing Centre, 1981.

Papenfusz, S. M. "Energy Conservation for Decision Makers," *Das Rechenzentrum*, 1980, pp. 144–151. (8.22)

Rubin, L. M. *Data Processing Administration: Handbook of Data Processing Management*, Vol. 6, pp. 333–369 (Physical Installation Planning). New York: Van Nostrand Reinhold, 1971. (8.29)

Cassel, W. R. *Human Factors Considerations in Control Center Design*. Proc. VIM3J, 1982, pp. 2–56.

## Chapter 9. Budgeting for the Computer Center

Cordada, J. W. *EDP Cost and Charges: Finance, Budgets and Cost Control in Data Processing*. Englewood Cliffs, NJ: Prentice-Hall, 1980.

Axelrod, C. W. *Computer Productivity, A Planning Guide for Cost Effective Management*. New York: Wiley, 1982.

Goldberg, R., and Lorin, H. (Eds.). *The Economics of Information Processing*. Vols. 1 & 2. New York: Wiley, 1981.

Schaeffer, H. *Data Center Operations: A Guide to Effective Planning, Processing, and Performance*. Englewood Cliffs, NJ: Prentice-Hall, 1981.

Durant, R. "Cost Analysis of Data Processing Centers," *Economics of Informatics*, A. B. Frielink, ed. North-Holland Publ. 1975, pp. 100–112. (9.15)

Gladney, H. M., Johnson, D. L., and Stone, R. L., "Computer Installation Accounting," *IBM Systems Journal*, 14,4, 1975, pp. 314–339. (9.24)

Golin, S. J. "Resource Pricing in a Multiprogramming Environment," *Installations Management Review*, 3, 1, 1974, pp. 3–11. (9.25)

Hamilton, K. L. *The Pricing of Computer Services, A Bibliography*, National Technical Information Services, January 1978, AD/A-048 782. (9.34)

IBM: *Planning Guide for Job Accounting*, Form Nr. GC 24-5079-1. (9.45)

IBM: *System Management Facilities*. Form Nr. GC 28-6712-4. (9.46)

Rettus, R. C., and Smith, R. A., "Accounting Control of Data Processing," *IBM Systems Journal*, 11, 1, 1972, pp.74–92. (9.85)

Rubin, M. L. *Data Processing Administration: Handbook of Data Processing Management*, Vol. 6, pp. 143–180 (Data Processing Budget and Cost Control). New York: Van Nostrand Reinhold, 1971. (9.88)

Conte, S. D., and Rhoads, B. "Operating Budgets for Computer Centers," *Encyclopedia of Computer Science and Technology* (Ed. J. Belzer and A. Holzman), Vol. 11. New York: Dekker, 1978, p. 354.

NOTE: Numbers in parenthesis following reference refers to citation number in German 2nd edition. The German edition contains an extensive bibliography of German references.

# INDEX

Italic numbers refer to illustrations.